COLLECT
BRITISH
STAMPS

A STANLEY GIBBONS CHECKLIST OF
THE STAMPS OF GREAT BRITAIN

D1078532

2006 (57th) Edition

STANLEY GIBBONS LTD
By Appointment to H.M. the Queen
Stanley Gibbons Ltd, London Philatelists.

London and Ringwood

COLLECT BRITISH STAMPS

The 2006 edition

From the famous Penny Black of 1840 to the absorbing issues of today, the stamps of Great Britain are highly popular with collectors. *Collect British Stamps* has been our message since very early days – but particularly since the First Edition of this checklist in September 1967. This 57th edition includes all the recent issues. Prices have been carefully revised to reflect today's market. Total sales of *Collect British Stamps* are now over 3·8 million copies.

Collect British Stamps appears in the autumn of each year. A more detailed Great Britain catalogue, the *Concise,* is published each spring. The *Great Britain Concise* incorporates many additional listings covering watermark varieties, phosphor omitted errors, missing colour errors, stamp booklets and special commemorative First Day Cover postmarks. It is ideally suited for the collector who wishes to discover more about GB stamps.

Listings in this edition of *Collect British Stamps* include all 2005 issues which have appeared up to the publication date.

Scope. *Collect British Stamps* comprises:

- All stamps with different watermark (*wmk*) or perforation (*perf*).
- Visible plate numbers on the Victorian issues.
- Graphite-lined and phosphor issues, including variations in the numbers of phosphor bands.
- First Day Covers for Definitives from 1936, Regionals and all Special Issues.
- Presentation, Gift and Souvenir Packs.
- Post Office Yearbooks.
- Regional issues and War Occupation stamps of Guernsey and Jersey.
- Postage Due and Official Stamps.
- Post Office Picture Cards (PHQ cards).
- Commemorative gutter pairs and 'Traffic Light' gutter pairs listed as mint sets.
- Royal Mail Postage Labels priced as sets and on P.O. First Day Cover.

Stamps of the independent postal administrations of Guernsey, Isle of Man and Jersey are contained in *Collect Channel Islands and Isle of Man Stamps.*

Layout. Stamps are set out chronologically by date of issue. In the catalogue lists the first numeral is the Stanley Gibbons catalogue number; the black (boldface) numeral alongside is the type number referring to the respective illustration. A blank in this column implies that the number immediately above is repeated. The denomination and colour of the stamp are then shown. Before February 1971 British currency was:

£1 = 20s   One pound = twenty shillings *and*
1s = 12d   One shilling = twelve pence.

Upon decimalisation this became:

£1 = 100p   One pound = one hundred (new) pence.

The catalogue list then shows two price columns. The left-hand is for unused stamps and the right-hand for used. Corresponding small boxes are provided in which collectors may wish to check off the items in their collection.

Our method of indicating prices is:
Numerals for pence, e.g. 10 denotes 10p (10 pence). Numerals for pounds and pence, e.g. 4·25 denotes £4·25 (4 pounds and 25 pence). For £100 and above, prices are in whole pounds and so include the £ sign and omit the zeros for pence.

Colour illustrations. The colour illustrations of stamps are intended as a guide only; they may differ in shade from the originals.

Size of illustrations. To comply with Post Office regulations stamp illustrations are three-quarters linear side. Separate illustrations of surcharges, overprints and watermarks are actual size.

Prices. Prices quoted in this catalogue are our selling prices at the time the book went to press. They are for stamps in fine condition; in issues where condition varies we may ask more for the superb and less for the sub-standard. The unused prices for stamps of Queen Victoria to King George V are for lightly hinged examples. Unused prices for King Edward VIII to Queen Elizabeth II are for unmounted mint (though when not available unmounted, mounted stamps are often supplied at a lower price). Prices for used stamps refer to fine postally used copies. All prices are subject to change without prior notice and we give no guarantee to supply all stamps priced, since it is not possible to keep every catalogued item in stock. Individual low value stamps sold at 399, Strand are liable to an additional handling charge. Commemorative issues may only be available in complete sets.

In the price columns:

† = Does not exist.

(—) or blank = Exists, or may exist, but price cannot be quoted.

* = Not normally issued (the so-called 'Abnormals' of 1862–80).

Perforations. The 'perforation' is the number of holes in a length of 2 cm, as measured by the Gibbons *Instanta* gauge. The stamp is viewed against a dark background with the transparent gauge put on top of it. Perforations are quoted to the nearest half. Stamps without perforation are termed 'imperforate'.

From 1992 certain stamps occur with a large elliptical (oval) hole inserted in each line of vertical perforations. The £10 definitive, No. 1658, is unique in having two such holes in the horizontal perforations.

Elliptical perforations

Se-tenant combinations. *Se-tenant* means 'joined together'. Some sets include stamps of different design arranged *se-tenant* as blocks or strips and these are often collected unsevered as issued. Where such combinations exist the stamps are priced both mint and used, as singles or complete sets. The set price for mint refers to the unsevered combination plus singles of any other values in the set. The used set price is for single stamps of all values.

First day covers. Prices for first day covers are for complete sets used on plain covers (Nos. 430/8, 453/60, 462/78b, 485/90, and 503/12) or on special covers (Nos. 461, 479/84, 491/502 and 513 onwards), the stamps of which are cancelled with ordinary operational postmarks (1924–1962) or by the *standard* 'First Day of Issue' postmarks (1963 onwards). The British Post Office did not provide 'First Day' treatment for every definitive issued after 1963. Where the stamps in a set were issued on different days, prices are for a cover from each day.

Presentation Packs. Special packs comprising slip-in cards with printed information inside a protective covering, were introduced for the 1964 Shakespeare issue. Collectors packs, containing commemoratives from the preceding twelve months, were issued from 1967. Some packs with text in German from 1968–69 exist as does a Japanese version of the pack for Nos. 916/17. Yearbooks, hardbound and illustrated in colour within a slip cover, joined the product range in 1984.

PHQ cards. Since 1973 the Post Office has produced a series of picture cards, which can be sent through the post as postcards. Each card shows an enlarged colour reproduction of a current British stamp, either of one or more values from a set or of all values. Cards are priced here in fine mint condition for sets complete as issued. The Post Office gives each card a 'PHQ' serial number, hence the term. The cards are usually on sale shortly before the date of issue of the stamps, but there is no officially designated 'first day'.

Used prices are for cards franked with the stamp depicted, on the obverse or reverse; the stamp being cancelled with an official postmark for first day of issue.

For 1973–76 issues cards with stamps on the obverse are worth about 25% more than the prices quoted.

Gutter pairs. Almost all modern Great Britain commemoratives are produced in sheets containing two panes of stamps separated by a blank horizontal or vertical margin known as a gutter. This feature first made its appearance on some supplies of the 1972 Royal Silver Wedding 3p, and marked the introduction of Harrison & Sons' new 'Jumelle' stamp-printing press. There are advantages for both the printer and the Post Office in such a lay-out which has now been used for almost all com-memorative issues since 1974.

The term 'gutter pair' is used for a pair of stamps separated by part of the blank gutter margin.

We do not list gutter pairs for self-adhesive stamps since, although the production format is the same, the stamps are separated by die-cutting.

Traffic light gutter pair

Gutter pair

Most printers include some form of colour check device on the sheet margins, in addition to the cylinder or plate numbers. Harrison & Sons used round 'dabs' or spots of colour, resembling traffic lights. For the period from the 1972 Royal Silver Wedding until the end of 1979 these colour dabs appeared in the gutter margin. Gutter pairs show-ing these 'traffic lights' are worth considerably more than the normal version.

From the 2004 Entente Cordiale set, Walsall reintroduced traffic lights in the gutters of certain sets. Where these extend over more than one sec-tion of gutter margin on any stamp they are priced as blocks rather than pairs.

Catalogue numbers used. This checklist uses the same catalogue numbers as other current Stanley Gibbons catalogues.

Latest issue date for stamps recorded in this edi-tion is 1 November 2005.

STANLEY GIBBONS LTD

Head Office: 399 Strand, London WC2R OLX.
Auction Room and Specialist Stamp Departments– Open Monday–Friday 9.30 a.m. to 5 p.m.
Shop – Open Monday to Friday 9 a.m. to 5.30 p.m. and Saturday 9.30 a.m. to 5.30 p.m.
Telephone 0207-836 8444 for all departments
E-mail: enquiries@stanleygibbons.co.uk
Website: www.stanleygibbons.com

Stanley Gibbons Publications:
Parkside, Christchurch Road, Ringwood, Hants BH24 3SH. Telephone: 01425 472363
Publications Mail Order, FREEPHONE: 0800 611622
E-mail: info@stanleygibbons.co.uk

ISBN: 0-85259-611-1
© Stanley Gibbons Ltd 2005

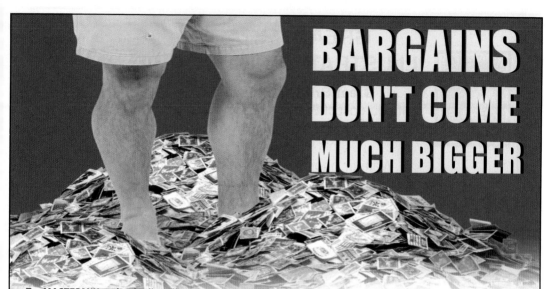

BARGAINS DON'T COME MUCH BIGGER

Try MASTERMIX and quite literally, you get bargains by the bag load, thousands of unsorted stamps. What an opportunity to experience the thrill of that elusive find, spread them out, see what you can find.

Just one perf type? Just one shade? Just one watermark variety? Just one of thousands?

PLUS- Free
Penny Blacks!

Every Mastermix purchase of £6 and over, earns you 100 Masterpoints or more. When you have 2,000 you can claim your free, genuine 1840 Penny Black, or one of many other gifts. When you have another 2,000, you can claim another one. It's easy - and it costs you nothing whatsoever.

FREE HOME TRIAL FOR 15 DAYS

Send only £6 now and we'll mail your Mastermix selection within 24 hours. If you're not delighted, return in the pre-paid envelope for a full refund. If you wish to keep some stamps, your prepayment covers the first 600 stamps.

P O Box 31 Lingfield Surrey RH7 6FD UK
Tel: +44 (0) 1342 834671
Fax : +44 (0) 1342 833892

**see us online at
www.apexstamps.com**

AMAZING VALUE
and there's more...

So convinced are we, you will be delighted with Mastermix value, that we will send you a free u/m set of the scarce 1962 Genghis Khan set of Mongolia, SG 291/4, cat £35, on dealers' lists for as much as **TWICE** the cost of your Mastermix..

Or keep the complete sending for just £4.00 more.

* Average count for complete selection 2000 - 3000

JUST SEND £6 NOW

YES - Please send me a trial selection of your world mixture. I enclose a remittance of £6.00*, or please charge my credit card as shown below. I may return my mixture in good order within 15 days of receipt for a full refund. Please also enclose my free u/m Genghis Khan set cat £35 which I may keep whether or not I make further purchases

Name _____

Address _____

_____

e-mail: _____

Credit Card No. _____

Expiry Date. _____

CBS'06   * £8.50 outside UK&CI.

1837 (20 June)–1901 (22 Jan.)

IDENTIFICATION. In this checklist Victorian stamps are classified firstly according to which printing method was used –line-engraving, embossing or surface-printing.

Corner letters. Numerous stamps also have letters in all four, or just the lower corners. These were an anti-forgery device and the letters differ from stamp to stamp. If present in all four corners the upper pair are the reverse of the lower. Note the importance of these corner letters in the way the checklist is arranged.

Watermarks. Further classification depends on watermarks: these are illustrated in normal position, with stamps priced accordingly.

1854–57 (i) *Wmk Small Crown Type* **2** *Perf* 16

17	**1b**	1d red-brown	£250	18·00	□	□
19	**3**	2d blue	£2500	85·00	□	□

(ii) *Wmk Small Crown Type* **2** *Perf* 14

24	**1b**	1d red-brown	£400	45·00	□	□
23	**3**	2d blue	£4500	£180	□	□

(iii) *Wmk Large Crown Type* **4** *Perf* 16

26	**1b**	1d red	£700	80·00	□	□
27	**3**	2d blue	£6000	£325	□	□

(iv) *Wmk Large Crown Type* **4** *Perf* 14

40	**1b**	1d red	40·00	9·00	□	□
34	**3**	2d blue	£1750	50·00	□	□

7

1 Line-engraved Issues

1   1a   1b   5   8   6

3 White lines added above and below head

2 Small Crown watermark

4 Large Crown watermark

9 Watermark extending over three stamps

Letters in lower corners

1840 *Wmk Small Crown Type* **2** *Imperforate*

Cat No.	Type		Unused	Used		
2	**1**	1d black	£5500	£250	□	□
5	**1a**	2d blue	£14000	£600	□	□

1841

8	**1b**	1d red-brown	£300	15·00	□	□
14	**3**	2d blue	£2700	75·00	□	□

Letters in all four corners

Plate numbers. Stamps included a 'plate number' in their design and this affects valuation. The cheapest plates are priced here; see complete list of plate numbers overleaf.

1858–70 (i) *Wmk Type* **9** *Perf* 14

48	**7**	½d red	90·00	15·00	□	□

(ii) *Wmk Large Crown Type* **4** *Perf* 14

43	**5**	1d red	15·00	2·00	□	□
52	**8**	1½d red	£400	50·00	□	□
45	**6**	2d blue	£300	10·00	□	□

Positions of Plate Numbers

Shows Plate 9 ($\frac{1}{2}$d) Shows Plate 170 (1d, 2d) Shows Plate 3 (1$\frac{1}{2}$d)

HALFPENNY VALUE (S.G. 48)

Plate	Un.	Used	Plate	Un.	Used
1	£200	70·00 □ □	11	£100	15·00 □ □
3	£150	35·00 □ □	12	£100	15·00 □ □
4	£130	25·00 □ □	13	£100	15·00 □ □
5	90·00	15·00 □ □	14	£100	15·00 □ □
6	£100	15·00 □ □	15	£150	35·00 □ □
8	£250	95·00 □ □	19	£175	50·00 □ □
9	£4000	£700 □ □	20	£210	70·00 □ □
10	£110	15·00 □ □			

Plates 2, 7, 16, 17 and 18 were not completed, while Plates 21 and 22 though made were not used. Plate 9 was a reserve plate, not greatly used.

PENNY VALUE (S.G. 43)

Plate	Un.	Used	Plate	Un.	Used	Plate	Un.	Used	Plate	Un.	Used	Plate	Un.	Used
71	35·00	3·00 □ □	112	70·00	2·25 □ □	154	50·00	2·00 □ □	190	50·00	6·00 □ □			
72	40·00	4·00 □ □	113	50·00	12·00 □ □	155	50·00	2·25 □ □	191	30·00	7·00 □ □			
73	40·00	3·00 □ □	114	£250	12·00 □ □	156	45·00	2·00 □ □	192	50·00	2·00 □ □			
74	40·00	2·00 □ □	115	90·00	2·25 □ □	157	50·00	2·00 □ □	193	30·00	2·00 □ □			
76	35·00	2·00 □ □	116	75·00	9·00 □ □	158	30·00	2·00 □ □	194	50·00	8·00 □ □			
77	(—)	£120000 □ □	117	45·00	2·00 □ □	159	30·00	2·00 □ □	195	50·00	8·00 □ □			
78	90·00	2·00 □ □	118	50·00	2·00 □ □	160	30·00	2·00 □ □	196	50·00	5·00 □ □			
79	30·00	2·00 □ □	119	45·00	2·00 □ □	161	60·00	7·00 □ □	197	55·00	9·00 □ □			
80	45·00	2·00 □ □	120	15·00	2·00 □ □	162	50·00	7·00 □ □	198	40·00	6·00 □ □			
81	45·00	2·20 □ □	121	40·00	9·50 □ □	163	50·00	3·00 □ □	199	55·00	6·00 □ □			
82	90·00	4·00 □ □	122	15·00	2·00 □ □	164	50·00	3·00 □ □	200	60·00	2·00 □ □			
83	£110	7·00 □ □	123	40·00	2·00 □ □	165	45·00	2·00 □ □	201	30·00	5·00 □ □			
84	60·00	2·25 □ □	124	28·00	2·00 □ □	166	45·00	6·00 □ □	202	60·00	8·00 □ □			
85	40·00	2·25 □ □	125	40·00	2·00 □ □	167	45·00	2·00 □ □	203	30·00	16·00 □ □			
86	50·00	4·00 □ □	127	55·00	2·25 □ □	168	50·00	8·00 □ □	204	55·00	2·25 □ □			
87	30·00	2·00 □ □	129	40·00	8·00 □ □	169	60·00	7·00 □ □	205	55·00	3·00 □ □			
88	£130	8·00 □ □	130	55·00	2·25 □ □	170	35·00	2·00 □ □	206	55·00	9·00 □ □			
89	40·00	2·00 □ □	131	65·00	16·00 □ □	171	15·00	2·00 □ □	207	60·00	9·00 □ □			
90	40·00	2·00 □ □	132	£130	22·00 □ □	172	30·00	2·00 □ □	208	55·00	16·00 □ □			
91	55·00	6·00 □ □	133	£110	9·00 □ □	173	70·00	9·00 □ □	209	50·00	9·00 □ □			
92	35·00	2·00 □ □	134	15·00	2·00 □ □	174	30·00	2·00 □ □	210	65·00	12·00 □ □			
93	50·00	2·00 □ □	135	95·00	26·00 □ □	175	60·00	3·50 □ □	211	70·00	20·00 □ □			
94	45·00	5·00 □ □	136	90·00	20·00 □ □	176	60·00	2·25 □ □	212	60·00	11·00 □ □			
95	40·00	2·00 □ □	137	28·00	2·25 □ □	177	40·00	2·00 □ □	213	60·00	11·00 □ □			
96	45·00	2·00 □ □	138	18·00	2·00 □ □	178	60·00	3·50 □ □	214	65·00	18·00 □ □			
97	40·00	3·50 □ □	139	60·00	16·00 □ □	179	50·00	2·25 □ □	215	65·00	18·00 □ □			
98	50·00	6·00 □ □	140	18·00	2·00 □ □	180	60·00	5·00 □ □	216	70·00	18·00 □ □			
99	55·00	5·00 □ □	141	£110	9·00 □ □	181	45·00	2·00 □ □	217	70·00	7·00 □ □			
100	60·00	2·25 □ □	142	70·00	24·00 □ □	182	90·00	5·00 □ □	218	65·00	8·00 □ □			
101	60·00	9·00 □ □	143	60·00	15·00 □ □	183	55·00	3·00 □ □	219	90·00	70·00 □ □			
102	45·00	2·00 □ □	144	95·00	20·00 □ □	184	30·00	2·25 □ □	220	40·00	7·00 □ □			
103	50·00	3·50 □ □	145	30·00	2·25 □ □	185	50·00	3·00 □ □	221	70·00	16·00 □ □			
104	75·00	5·00 □ □	146	40·00	6·00 □ □	186	65·00	2·25 □ □	222	80·00	40·00 □ □			
105	90·00	7·00 □ □	147	50·00	3·00 □ □	187	50·00	2·00 □ □	223	90·00	60·00 □ □			
106	55·00	2·00 □ □	148	40·00	3·00 □ □	188	70·00	10·00 □ □	224	£100	50·00 □ □			
107	60·00	7·00 □ □	149	40·00	6·00 □ □	189	£110	9·00 □ □	225	£2000	£650 □ □			
108	80·00	2·25 □ □	150	15·00	2·00 □ □									
109	85·00	3·50 □ □	151	60·00	9·00 □ □									
110	60·00	9·00 □ □	152	60·00	5·50 □ □									
111	50·00	2·25 □ □	153	£100	9·00 □ □									

Plates 69, 70, 75, 77, 126 and 128 were prepared but rejected. No stamps therefore exist, except for a very few from Plate 77 which somehow reached the public. Plate 177 stamps, by accident or design, are sometimes passed off as the rare Plate 77.

THREE-HALFPENNY VALUE (S.G. 52)

Plate	Un.	Used	Plate	Un.	Used
(1)	£500	65·00 □ □	3	£400	50·00 □ □

Plate 1 did *not* have the plate number in the design. Plate 2 was not completed and no stamps exist.

TWOPENNY VALUE (S.G. 45)

Plate	Un.	Used	Plate	Un.	Used
7	£1100	45·00 □ □	13	£325	20·00 □ □
8	£1000	32·00 □ □	14	£425	25·00 □ □
9	£300	10·00 □ □	15	£400	25·00 □ □
12	£1650	£120 □ □			

Plates 10 and 11 were prepared but rejected.

2 Embossed Issues

Prices are for stamps cut square and with average to fine embossing. Stamps with exceptionally clear embossing are worth more.

12

11

10

13

1847–54 *Wmk* **13** *(6d), no wmk (others) Imperforate*

59	12	6d lilac	£6000	£750	□	□
57	11	10d brown	£5000	£1000	□	□
54	10	1s green	£7500	£700	□	□

3 Surface-printed Issues

IDENTIFICATION. Check first whether the design includes corner letters or not, as mentioned for 'Line-engraved Issues'. The checklist is divided up according to whether any letters are small or large, also whether they are white (uncoloured) or printed in the colour of the stamp. Further identification then depends on watermark.

PERFORATION. Except for Nos. 126/9 all the following issues of Queen Victoria are perf 14.

14

15 Small Garter

16 Medium Garter

17 Large Garter

18

19

20 Emblems

No corner letters

1855–57 (*i*) *Wmk Small Garter Type* **15**

62	14	4d red	£4500	£350	□	□

(*ii*) *Wmk Medium Garter Type* **16**

64	14	4d red	£4000	£325	□	□

(*iii*) *Wmk Large Garter Type* **17**

66a	14	4d red	£1000	90·00	□	□

(*iv*) *Wmk Emblems Type* **20**

70	18	6d lilac	£800	85·00	□	□
72	19	1s green	£1100	£250	□	□

Plate numbers. Stamps Nos. 90/163 should be checked for the 'plate numbers' indicated, as this affects valuation (the cheapest plates are priced here). The mark '*Pl.*' shows that several numbers exist, priced in separate list overleaf.

Plate numbers are the small numerals appearing in duplicate in some part of the frame design or adjacent to the lower corner letters (in the 5s value a single numeral above the lower inscription).

21

22

23

24

25

Small white corner letters

1862–64 *Wmk Emblems Type* **20**, *except 4d (Large Garter Type* **17**)

76	21	3d red	£1400	£225	□	□
80	22	4d red	£1000	80·00	□	□
84	23	6d lilac	£1250	80·00	□	□
87	24	9d bistre	£2500	£300	□	□
90	25	1s green *Pl.*	£1500	£150	□	□

26 **27** **28** (hyphen in SIX-PENCE) **32** **33** Spray of Rose **34**

29 **30** **31**

Large white corner letters

1865–67 *Wmk Emblems Type* **20** *except 4d (Large Garter Type* **17***)*

92	**26**	3d red (Plate 4)	£1200	£150	☐ ☐
94	**27**	4d vermilion *Pl.*	£425	50·00	☐ ☐
97	**28**	6d lilac *Pl.*	£650	75·00	☐ ☐
98	**29**	9d straw *Pl.*	£2000	£450	☐ ☐
99	**30**	10d brown (Plate 1) . . .	† £25000		☐
101	**31**	1s green (Plate 4)	£1300	£150	☐ ☐

1867–80 *Wmk Spray of Rose Type* **33**

103	**26**	3d red *Pl.*	£400	50·00	☐ ☐
105	**28**	6d lilac (with hyphen) (Plate 6)	£1000	75·00	☐ ☐
109		6d mauve (without hyphen) *Pl.*	£450	75·00	☐ ☐
110	**29**	9d straw (Plate 4)	£1500	£250	☐ ☐
112	**30**	10d brown *Pl.*	£2100	£275	☐ ☐
117	**31**	1s green *Pl.*	£550	32·00	☐ ☐
119	**32**	2s blue *Pl.*	£2200	£140	☐ ☐
121		2s brown (Plate 1) . . .	£14000	£2500	☐ ☐

1872–73 *Wmk Spray of Rose Type* **33**

122*b*	**34**	6d brown *Pl.*	£500	45·00	☐ ☐
125		6d grey (Plate 12)	£1250	£200	☐ ☐

PLATE NUMBERS
on stamps of 1862–83

Cat No.		Plate No.	Un.	Used	

Small White Corner Letters (1862–64)

| 90 | 1s green | 2 | £1500 | £150 | ☐ ☐ |
| | | 3 | £18500 | | ☐ ☐ |

Plate 2 is actually numbered as '1' and Plate 3 as '2' on the stamps.

Large White Corner Letters (1865–83)

103	3d red	4	£750	£170	☐ ☐
		5	£400	50·00	☐ ☐
		6	£425	50·00	☐ ☐
		7	£500	55·00	☐ ☐
		8	£475	50·00	☐ ☐
		9	£475	55·00	☐ ☐
		10	£600	£100	☐ ☐
94	4d verm	7	£525	90·00	☐ ☐
		8	£475	55·00	☐ ☐
		9	£475	55·00	☐ ☐
		10	£525	£100	☐ ☐
		11	£475	55·00	☐ ☐
		12	£450	50·00	☐ ☐
		13	£475	50·00	☐ ☐
		14	£525	80·00	☐ ☐
97	6d lilac	5	£650	75·00	☐ ☐
		6	£2000	£140	☐ ☐
109	6d mauve	8	£450	90·00	☐ ☐
		9	£450	75·00	☐ ☐
		10	*	£19000	☐ ☐
122*b*	6d brown	11	£550	75·00	☐ ☐
123	6d buff	12	£1800	£250	☐ ☐
98	9d straw	4	£2000	£450	☐ ☐
		5	£14000		☐ ☐
112	10d brown	1	£1850	£275	☐ ☐
		2	£19000	£7000	☐ ☐
117	1s green	4	£750	50·00	☐ ☐
		5	£625	35·00	☐ ☐
		6	£950	35·00	☐ ☐
		7	£900	60·00	☐ ☐
119	2s blue	1	£1800	£125	☐ ☐
		3	*	£6000	☐ ☐
126	5s red	1	£4500	£550	☐ ☐
		2	£7000	£850	☐ ☐

Large Coloured Corner Letters (1873–83)

139	2½d mauve	1	£450	75·00	☐ ☐
		2	£450	75·00	☐ ☐
		3	£700	£110	☐ ☐
141	2½d mauve	3	£850	90·00	☐ ☐
		4	£380	45·00	☐ ☐
		5	£380	45·00	☐ ☐
		6	£380	45·00	☐ ☐
		7	£380	45·00	☐ ☐
		8	£380	45·00	☐ ☐
		9	£380	45·00	☐ ☐
		10	£420	60·00	☐ ☐
		11	£380	45·00	☐ ☐
		12	£380	45·00	☐ ☐
		13	£380	45·00	☐ ☐
		14	£380	45·00	☐ ☐
		15	£380	45·00	☐ ☐
		16	£380	45·00	☐ ☐
		17	£1100	£220	☐ ☐
142	2½d blue	17	£350	50·00	☐ ☐
		18	£375	35·00	☐ ☐
		19	£350	30·00	☐ ☐
		20	£350	35·00	☐ ☐
157	2½d blue	21	£375	30·00	☐ ☐
		22	£325	30·00	☐ ☐
		23	£325	25·00	☐ ☐
143	3d red	11	£325	40·00	☐ ☐
		12	£380	40·00	☐ ☐
		14	£400	40·00	☐ ☐
		15	£325	40·00	☐ ☐
		16	£325	40·00	☐ ☐
		17	£380	40·00	☐ ☐
		18	£380	40·00	☐ ☐
		19	£325	40·00	☐ ☐
		20	£450	75·00	☐ ☐
158	3d red	20	£500	£120	☐ ☐
		21	£375	70·00	☐ ☐
152	4d verm	15	£1600	£400	☐ ☐
		16	*	£20000	☐ ☐
153	4d green	15	£900	£250	☐ ☐
		16	£800	£225	☐ ☐
		17	*	£13500	☐ ☐
160	4d brown	17	£325	55·00	☐ ☐
		18	£325	55·00	☐ ☐
147	6d grey	13	£375	55·00	☐ ☐
		14	£375	55·00	☐ ☐
		15	£375	55·00	☐ ☐
		16	£375	55·00	☐ ☐
		17	£600	£125	☐ ☐
161	6d grey	17	£375	60·00	☐ ☐
		18	£325	60·00	☐ ☐
150	1s green	8	£550	95·00	☐ ☐
		9	£550	95·00	☐ ☐
		10	£550	£120	☐ ☐
		11	£550	£100	☐ ☐
		12	£475	80·00	☐ ☐
		13	£475	80·00	☐ ☐
		14	*	£20000	☐ ☐
163	1s brown	13	£550	£120	☐ ☐
		14	£425	£120	☐ ☐

35　　　　　　　　**36**

37

38

39　Maltese Cross　　　　**40**　Large Anchor

1867–83 (*i*) *Wmk Maltese Cross Type* **39** *Perf* 15½ × 15

126	**35**	5s red *Pl.*	£4500	£550	☐	☐
128	**36**	10s grey (Plate 1)	£35000	£2200	☐	☐
129	**37**	£1 brown (Plate 1)	£45000	£3250	☐	☐

(*ii*) *Wmk Large Anchor Type* **40** *Perf* 14

134	**35**	5s red (Plate 4)	£12000	£2500	☐	☐
135	**36**	10s grey (Plate 1)	£55000	£3000	☐	☐
132	**37**	£1 brown (Plate 1) . .	£70000	£7500	☐	☐
137	**38**	£5 orange (Plate 1) . . .	£8000	£3800	☐	☐

  (image 43)

41　　　　　**42**　　　　　**43**

44　　　　　**45**　　　　　**46**

47　Small Anchor　　　　**48**　Orb

Large coloured corner letters

1873–80 (*i*) *Wmk Small Anchor Type* **47**

139	**41**	2½d mauve *Pl.*	£450	75·00	☐	☐

(*ii*) *Wmk Orb Type* **48**

141	**41**	2½d mauve *Pl.*	£380	45·00	☐	☐
142		2½d blue *Pl.*	£350	50·00	☐	☐

(*iii*) *Wmk Spray of Rose Type* **33**

143	**42**	3d red *Pl.*	£325	40·00	☐	☐
145	**43**	6d pale buff (Plate 13) .	* £13000		☐	☐
147		6d grey *Pl.*	£375	55·00	☐	☐
150	**44**	1s green *Pl.*	£475	80·00	☐	☐
151		1s brown (Plate 13) . . .	£3000	£550	☐	☐

(*iv*) *Wmk Large Garter Type* **17**

152	**45**	4d vermilion *Pl.*	£1600	£400	☐	☐
153		4d green *Pl.*	£800	£225	☐	☐
154		4d brown (Plate 17) . . .	£1400	£400	☐	☐
156	**46**	8d orange (Plate 1) . . .	£1000	£275	☐	☐

49　Imperial Crown　　**(50)**　Surcharges in red　**(51)**

1880–83 *Wmk Imperial Crown Type* **49**

157	**41**	2½d blue *Pl.*	£325	25·00	☐	☐
158	**42**	3d red *Pl.*	£375	70·00	☐	☐
159		3d on 3d lilac (surch Type **50**)	£425	£125	☐	☐
160	**45**	4d brown *Pl.*	£325	55·00	☐	☐
161	**43**	6d grey *Pl.*	£325	60·00	☐	☐
162		6d on 6d lilac (surch Type **51**)	£475	£125	☐	☐
163	**44**	1s brown *Pl.*	£425	£120	☐	☐

52　　　　　　**53**　　　　　　**54**

55　　　　　　**56**

1880–81 *Wmk Imperial Crown Type* **49**

164	**52**	½d green	40·00	10·00	☐	☐
166	**53**	1d brown	20·00	10·00	☐	☐
167	**54**	1½d brown	£150	40·00	☐	☐
168	**55**	2d red	£225	80·00	☐	☐
169	**56**	5d indigo	£575	£100	☐	☐

Die I

Die II

57　　　　　　Die I　　　　　　Die II

1881 *Wmk Imperial Crown Type* **49**

(a) 14 *dots in each corner, Die I*

171	**57**	1d lilac	£190	28·00	☐	☐

(b) 16 *dots in each corner, Die II*

174	**57**	1d mauve	2·50	1·50	☐	☐

58　　　　　　**59**

60

Coloured letters in the corners

1883–84 *Wmk Anchor Type* **40**

178	**58**	2s 6d lilac	£400	£140	☐	☐
181	**59**	5s red	£700	£200	☐	☐
183	**60**	10s blue	£1500	£475	☐	☐

61

1884 *Wmk* 3 *Imperial Crowns Type* **49**

185	**61**	£1 brown	£20000	£2000	☐	☐

1888 *Wmk* 3 *Orbs Type* **48**

186	**61**	£1 brown	£45000	£3250	☐	☐

1891 *Wmk* 3 *Imperial Crowns Type* **49**

212	**61**	£1 green	£3000	£650	☐	☐

62　　　　　　**63**　　　　　　**64**

65　　　　　　**66**

1883–84 *Wmk Imperial Crown Type* **49** (*sideways on horiz designs*)

187	**52**	½d blue	20·00	7·00	☐	☐
188	**62**	1½d lilac	90·00	35·00	☐	☐
189	**63**	2d lilac	£150	65·00	☐	☐
190	**64**	2½d lilac	70·00	12·00	☐	☐
191	**65**	3d lilac	£180	85·00	☐	☐
192	**66**	4d dull green	£400	£175	☐	☐
193	**62**	5d dull green	£400	£175	☐	☐
194	**63**	6d dull green	£425	£200	☐	☐
195	**64**	9d dull green	£800	£375	☐	☐
196	**65**	1s dull green	£850	£200	☐	☐

The above prices are for stamps in the true dull green colour. Stamps which have been soaked, causing the colour to run are virtually worthless.

71   72   73

74   75   76

77   78   79

80   81   82

'Jubilee' issue

1887–1900 *The bicoloured stamps have the value tablets, or the frames including the value tablets, in the second colour. Wmk Imperial Crown Type* **49**

197e	**71**	½d vermilion	. . . . . .	1·50	1·00	☐	☐
213		½d green*	. . . .	1·75	2·00	☐	☐
198	**72**	1½d purple and green	. .	15·00	7·00	☐	☐
200	**73**	2d green and red	. . .	28·00	12·00	☐	☐
201	**74**	2½d purple on blue	. . . .	22·00	3·00	☐	☐
203	**75**	3d purple on yellow	. .	22·00	3·25	☐	☐
205	**76**	4d green and brown	. .	30·00	13·00	☐	☐
206	**77**	4½d green and red	. . . .	10·00	40·00	☐	☐
207a	**78**	5d purple and blue	. . . .	35·00	11·00	☐	☐
208	**79**	6d purple on red	. . . .	30·00	10·00	☐	☐
209	**80**	9d purple and blue	. . .	60·00	40·00	☐	☐
210	**81**	10d purple and red	. . . .	45·00	38·00	☐	☐
211	**82**	1s green	. . . .	£200	60·00	☐	☐
214		1s green and red	. . . .	50·00	£125	☐	☐
	Set of 14	. . . .		£500	£325	☐	☐

*The ½d No. 213 in blue is a colour changeling.

KING EDWARD VII

1901 (22 Jan.)–1910 (6 May)

83   84   85

86   87   88

89   90   91

92   93

94   95   96

97

1902–13 *Wmks Imperial Crown Type* **49** (½*d to* 1*s*), *Anchor Type* **40** (2*s* 6*d to* 10*s*), *Three Crowns Type* **49** (£1) (*a*) *Perf* 14

215	83	½d blue-green	2·00	1·50	□	□
217		½d yellow-green	2·00	1·50	□	□
219		1d red	2·00	1·50	□	□
221	84	1½d purple and green . .	35·00	18·00	□	□
291	85	2d green and red	25·00	20·00	□	□
231	86	2½d blue	20·00	10·00	□	□
234	87	3d purple on yellow . .	35·00	15·00	□	□
238	88	4d green and brown . .	40·00	18·00	□	□
240		4d orange	20·00	15·00	□	□
294	89	5d purple and blue . . .	30·00	20·00	□	□
297	83	6d purple	30·00	20·00	□	□
249	90	7d grey	10·00	18·00	□	□
307	91	9d purple and blue . . .	60·00	60·00	□	□
311	92	10d purple and red	70·00	60·00	□	□
314	93	1s green and red	55·00	35·00	□	□
260	94	2s 6d purple	£220	£120	□	□
318	95	5s red	£350	£175	□	□
265	96	10s blue	£650	£450	□	□
320	97	£1 green	£1500	£700	□	□
		Set of 15 (*to* 1*s*)	£400	£275	□	□

(*b*) *Perf* 15 × 14

279	83	½d green	40·00	45·00	□	□
281		1d red	15·00	15·00	□	□
283	86	2½d blue	22·00	15·00	□	□
285	87	3d purple on yellow . .	45·00	15·00	□	□
286	88	4d orange	30·00	15·00	□	□
		Set of 5	£130	90·00	□	□

KING GEORGE V

1910 (6 May)–1936 (20 Jan.)

PERFORATION. All the following issues are Perf 15 × 14 except vertical commemorative stamps which are 14 × 15, unless otherwise stated.

98 (Hair dark)   99 (Lion unshaded)   100

1911–12 *Wmk Imperial Crown Type* **49**

322	98	½d green	4·00	4·00	□	□
327	99	1d red	4·50	2·50	□	□

1912 *Wmk Royal Cypher* ('*Simple*') *Type* **100**

335	98	½d green	40·00	40·00	□	□
336	99	1d red	30·00	30·00	□	□

101 (Hair light)   102 (Lion shaded)   103

1912 *Wmk Imperial Crown Type* **49**

339	101	½d green	8·00	4·00	□	□
341	102	1d red	5·00	2·00	□	□

1912 *Wmk Royal Cypher* ('*Simple*') *Type* **100**

344	101	½d green	7·00	3·00	□	□
345	102	1d red	8·00	3·00	□	□

1912 *Wmk Royal Cypher* ('*Multiple*') *Type* **103**

346	101	½d green	12·00	8·00	□	□
350	102	1d red	18·00	10·00	□	□

104   105   106

107 **108**

1912–24 *Wmk Royal Cypher Type* **100**

351	**105**	½d green	1·00	1·00 □ □
357	**104**	1d red	1·00	1·00 □ □
362	**105**	1½d brown	4·00	1·50 □ □
368	**106**	2d orange	4·00	3·00 □ □
371	**104**	2½d blue	12·00	4·00 □ □
375	**106**	3d violet	5·00	3·00 □ □
379		4d grey-green	15·00	2·00 □ □
381	**107**	5d brown	15·00	5·00 □ □
385		6d purple	15·00	7·00 □ □
		a. Perf 14	90·00	£110 □ □
387		7d olive-green	20·00	10·00 □ □
390		8d black on yellow . . .	32·00	11·00 □ □
392	**108**	9d black	15·00	6·00 □ □
393*a*		9d olive-green	£100	30·00 □ □
394		10d blue	22·00	20·00 □ □
395		1s brown	20·00	4·00 □ □
	Set of 15	. . . .	£250	95·00 □ □

1913 *Wmk Royal Cypher* ('*Multiple*') *Type* **103**

397	**105**	½d green	£150	£180 □ □
398	**104**	1d red	£225	£225 □ □

See also Nos. 418/29.

109

110

T 109. *Background around portrait consists of horizontal lines*
1913–18 *Wmk Single Cypher Type* **110** *Perf* 11 × 12

413*a*	**109**	2s 6d brown	£100	65·00 □ □
416		5s red	£250	£110 □ □
417		10s blue	£375	£160 □ □
403		£1 green	£1800	£1000 □ □
	Set of 4	. . . .	£2250	£1200 □ □

See also Nos. 450/2.

111

1924–26 *Wmk Block Cypher Type* **111**

418	**105**	½d green	1·00	1·00 □ □
419	**104**	1d red	1·00	1·00 □ □
420	**105**	1½d brown	1·00	1·00 □ □
421	**106**	2d orange	2·50	2·50 □ □
422	**104**	2½d blue	5·00	3·00 □ □
423	**106**	3d violet	10·00	2·50 □ □
424		4d grey-green	12·00	2·50 □ □
425	**107**	5d brown	20·00	3·00 □ □
426*a*		6d purple	3·00	1·50 □ □
427	**108**	9d olive-green	12·00	3·50 □ □
428		10d blue	40·00	40·00 □ □
429		1s brown	22·00	3·00 □ □
	Set of 12	. . . .	£110	60·00 □ □

112 **112a**

British Empire Exhibition
1924–25 *Wmk* **111** *Perf* 14 (*a*) 23.4.24. *Dated '*1924'

430	**112**	1d red	10·00	11·00 □ □
431	**112a**	1½d brown	15·00	15·00 □ □
	First Day Cover			£400 □

(*b*) 9.5.25. *Dated '*1925'

432	**112**	1d red	15·00	30·00 □ □
433	**112a**	1½d brown	40·00	70·00 □ □
	First Day Cover	. . . .		£1500 □

113 **114** **115**

116 St George and the Dragon

117

Ninth Universal Postal Union Congress
1929 (10 MAY) (a) *Wmk* **111**

434	**113**	½d green	. . . .	2·25	2·25 ☐	☐
435	**114**	1d red	. . . .	2·25	2·25 ☐	☐
436		1½d brown	. . . .	2·25	1·75 ☐	☐
437	**115**	2½d blue	. . . .	10·00	10·00 ☐	☐

(b) *Wmk* **117** *Perf* 12

438	**116**	£1 black	. . . .	£750	£600 ☐	☐
434/7 *Set of 4*			. . . .	15·00	14·50 ☐	☐
434/7 *First Day Cover (4 vals.)*			. . . . .	£550		☐
434/8 *First Day Cover (5 vals.)*			. . . . .	£7500		☐

118   **119**   **120**

121   **122**

1934–36 *Wmk* **111**

439	**118**	½d green	. . . .	50	50 ☐	☐
440	**119**	1d red	. . . .	50	50 ☐	☐
441	**118**	1½d brown	. . . .	50	50 ☐	☐
442	**120**	2d orange	. . . .	75	75 ☐	☐
443	**119**	2½d blue	. . . .	1·50	1·25 ☐	☐
444	**120**	3d violet	. . . .	1·50	1·25 ☐	☐
445		4d grey-green	. . . . . .	2·00	1·25 ☐	☐
446	**121**	5d brown	. . . .	6·50	2·75 ☐	☐
447	**122**	9d olive-green	. . . . .	12·00	2·25 ☐	☐
448		10d blue	. . . .	15·00	10·00 ☐	☐
449		1s brown	. . . .	15·00	1·25 ☐	☐
	Set of 11		. . . .	50·00	20·00 ☐	☐

T 109 (re-engraved). Background around portrait consists of horizontal and diagonal lines
1934 *Wmk* **110** *Perf* 11 × 12

450	**109**	2s 6d brown	. . . .	70·00	40·00 ☐	☐
451		5s red	. . . .	£160	85·00 ☐	☐
452		10s blue	. . . .	£340	80·00 ☐	☐
	Set of 3		. . . .	£525	£190 ☐	☐

123   **123a**

123b   **123c**

Silver Jubilee
1935 (7 MAY) *Wmk* **111**

453	**123**	½d green	. . . .	1·00	1·00 ☐	☐
454	**123a**	1d red	. . . .	1·50	2·00 ☐	☐
455	**123b**	1½d brown	. . . .	1·00	1·00 ☐	☐
456	**123c**	2½d blue	. . . .	5·00	6·00 ☐	☐
	Set of 4		. . . .	8·00	9·25 ☐	☐
	First Day Cover		. . . .		£600	☐

KING EDWARD VIII

1936 (20 Jan.–10 Dec.)

124

125

1936 *Wmk* **125**

457	**124**	½d green	30	30 □ □
458		1d red	60	50 □ □
459		1½d brown	30	30 □ □
460		2½d blue	30	85 □ □
	Set of 4	. . . .	1·25	1·75 □ □

First Day Covers

1 Sept. 1936	Nos. 457, 459/60	£150 □
14 Sept. 1936	No. 458	£170 □·

Collectors are reminded that for issues from 1936 to date, prices in the unused column are for unmounted mint.

KING GEORGE VI

1936 (11 Dec.)–1952 (6 Feb.)

126 King George VI
and Queen Elizabeth

127

Coronation

1937 (13 MAY) *Wmk* **127**

461	**126**	1½d brown	30	30 □ □
		First Day Cover		35·00 □

128

129

130

King George VI and National Emblems

1937–47 *Wmk* **127**

462	**128**	½d green	30	25 □ □
463		1d scarlet	30	25 □ □
464		1½d brown	30	25 □ □
465		2d orange	1·20	50 □ □
466		2½d blue	40	25 □ □
467		3d violet	5·00	1·00 □ □
468	**129**	4d green	60	75 □ □
469		5d brown	3·50	85 □ □
470		6d purple	1·50	60 □ □
471	**130**	7d green	5·00	60 □ □
472		8d red	7·50	80 □ □
473		9d deep green	6·50	80 □ □
474		10d blue	7·00	80 □ □
474*a*		11d plum	3·00	2·75 □ □
475		1s brown	9·00	75 □ □
	Set of 15	. . . .	45·00	10·00 □ □

First Day Covers

10 May 1937	Nos. 462/3, 466	45·00 □
30 July 1937	No. 464	45·00 □
31 Jan. 1938	Nos. 465, 467	95·00 □
21 Nov. 1938	Nos. 468/9	60·00 □
30 Jan. 1939	No. 470	55·00 □
27 Feb. 1939	Nos. 471/2	80·00 □
1 May 1939	Nos. 473/4, 475	£450 □
29 Dec. 1947	No. 474*a*	50·00 □

For later printings of the lower values in apparently lighter shades and different colours, see Nos. 485/90 and 503/8.

130a King George VI   **131**

132   **132a**

133

1939–48 *Wmk* **133** *Perf* 14

476	**130a**	2s 6d brown	. . . .	35·00	6·00	☐ ☐
476a		2s 6d green	. . . .	11·00	1·50	☐ ☐
477	**131**	5s red	. . . .	20·00	2·00	☐ ☐
478	**132**	10s dark blue	. . . . . .	£225	20·00	☐ ☐
478a		10s bright blue	. . . . .	20·00	5·00	☐ ☐
478b	**132a**	£1 brown	. . . .	20·00	26·00	☐ ☐
	Set of 6	. . . .		£300	55·00	☐ ☐

First Day Covers

21 Aug. 1939	No. 477	. . . .	£750 ☐
4 Sept. 1939	No. 476	. . . .	£1500 ☐
30 Oct. 1939	No. 478	. . . .	£2750 ☐
9 Mar. 1942	No. 476a	. . . .	£1500 ☐
30 Nov. 1942	No. 478a	. . . .	£3250 ☐
1 Oct. 1948	No. 478b	. . . .	£275 ☐

134   Queen Victoria and King George VI

Centenary of First Adhesive Postage Stamps

1940 (6 MAY) *Wmk* **127** *Perf* 14½ × 14

479	**134**	½d green	. . . .	30	75	☐ ☐
480		1d red	. . . .	1·00	75	☐ ☐
481		1½d brown	. . . .	50	1·50	☐ ☐
482		2d orange	. . . .	1·00	75	☐ ☐
483		2½d blue	. . . .	2·25	50	☐ ☐
484		3d violet	. . . .	3·00	3·50	☐ ☐
	Set of 6	. . . .		8·75	5·25	☐ ☐
	First Day Cover	. . . .			55·00	☐

Head as Nos. 462–7, but with lighter background

1941–42 *Wmk* **127**

485	**128**	½d pale green	. . . . . .	30	30	☐ ☐
486		1d pale red	. . . .	30	30	☐ ☐
487		1½d pale brown	. . . . . .	60	80	☐ ☐
488		2d pale orange	. . . . .	50	50	☐ ☐
489		2½d light blue	. . . . . .	30	30	☐ ☐
490		3d pale violet	. . . . . .	2·50	1·00	☐ ☐
	Set of 6	. . . .		3·50	2·75	☐ ☐

First Day Covers

21 July 1941	No. 489	. . . .	45·00 ☐
11 Aug. 1941	No. 486	. . . .	22·00 ☐
1 Sept. 1941	No. 485	. . . .	22·00 ☐
6 Oct. 1941	No. 488	. . . .	60·00 ☐
3 Nov. 1941	No. 490	. . . .	£110 ☐
28 Sept. 1942	No. 487	. . . .	55·00 ☐

135   Symbols of Peace and   **136**   Symbols of Peace and
       Reconstruction   Reconstruction

Victory

1946 (11 JUNE) *Wmk* **127**

491	**135**	2½d blue	. . . .	20	20	☐ ☐
492	**136**	3d violet	. . . .	20	50	☐ ☐
	First Day Cover	. . . .			65·00	☐

137   King George VI   **138**   King George VI
       and Queen Elizabeth   and Queen Elizabeth

Royal Silver Wedding

1948 (26 APR.) *Wmk* **127**

493	**137**	2½d blue	. . . .	35	20	☐ ☐
494	**138**	£1 blue	. . . .	40·00	40·00	☐ ☐
	First Day Cover	. . . .			£425	☐

1948 (10 MAY)

Stamps of 1d and 2½d showing seaweed-gathering were on sale at eight Head Post Offices elsewhere in Great Britain, but were primarily for use in the Channel Islands and are listed there (see after Regional Issues).

139 Globe and Laurel Wreath

140 Speed

141 Olympic Symbol

142 Winged Victory

Olympic Games

1948 (29 JULY) *Wmk* **127**

495	**139**	2½d blue	35	10	□	□
496	**140**	3d violet	35	50	□	□
497	**141**	6d purple	70	40	□	□
498	**142**	1s brown	1·50	1·50	□	□
		Set of 4	2·25	2·00	□	□
		First Day Cover		45·00		□

143 Two Hemispheres

144 U.P.U. Monument, Berne

145 Goddess Concordia, Globe and Points of Compass

146 Posthorn and Globe

75th Anniversary of Universal Postal Union

1949 (10 OCT.) *Wmk* **127**

499	**143**	2½d blue	25	10	□	□
500	**144**	3d violet	25	50	□	□
501	**145**	6d purple	50	75	□	□
502	**146**	1s brown	1·00	1·25	□	□
		Set of 4	1·50	2·50	□	□
		First Day Cover		80·00		□

4d as No. 468 and others as Nos. 485/9, but colours changed

1950–51 *Wmk* **127**

503	**128**	½d pale orange	30	30	□	□
504		1d light blue	30	30	□	□
505		1½d pale green	65	60	□	□
506		2d pale brown	75	40	□	□
507		2½d pale red	60	40	□	□
508	**129**	4d light blue	2·00	1·75	□	□
		Set of 6	4·00	3·25	□	□

First Day Covers

2 Oct. 1950	No. 508	£120	□
3 May 1951	Nos. 503/7	55·00	□

147 HMS *Victory*

148 White Cliffs of Dover

149 St George and the Dragon

150 Royal Coat of Arms

1951 (3 MAY) *Wmk* **133** *Perf* 11 × 12

509	**147**	2s 6d green	2·00	1·00	□	□
510	**148**	5s red	40·00	1·00	□	□
511	**149**	10s blue	10·00	7·50	□	□
512	**150**	£1 brown	48·00	18·00	□	□
		Set of 4	95·00	25·00	□	□
		First Day Cover		£925		□

151 Commerce and Prosperity

152 Festival Symbol

Festival of Britain

1951 (3 MAY) *Wmk* **127**

513	**151**	2½d red	20	15	□	□
514	**152**	4d blue	30	35	□	□
		Set of 2	40	40	□	□
		First Day Cover		38·00		□

QUEEN ELIZABETH II
6 February, 1952

153 Tudor Crown   **154**

155   **156**   **157**

158   **159**   **160**

1952–54 *Wmk* **153**

515	**154**	½d orange	10	15	□	□
516		1d blue	20	20	□	□
517		1½d green	10	20	□	□
518		2d brown	20	20	□	□
519	**155**	2½d red	15	15	□	□
520		3d lilac	75	55	□	□
521	**156**	4d blue	3·25	1·25	□	□
		4½d (*See Nos.* 577, 594, 609 *and* 616*b*)				
522	**157**	5d brown	75	3·50	□	□
523		6d purple	4·00	1·00	□	□
524		7d green	9·50	5·50	□	□
525	**158**	8d magenta	75	85	□	□
526		9d bronze-green	23·00	4·75	□	□
527		10d blue	18·00	4·75	□	□
528		11d plum	35·00	15·00	□	□
529	**159**	1s bistre	80	50	□	□
530	**160**	1s 3d green	4·50	3·25	□	□
531	**159**	1s 6d indigo	14·00	3·75	□	□
		Set of 17	£100	40·00	□	□

First Day Covers

5 Dec. 1952	Nos. 517, 519	25·00	□
6 July 1953	Nos. 522, 525, 529	50·00	□
31 Aug. 1953	Nos. 515/16, 518	50·00	□
2 Nov. 1953	Nos. 521, 530/1	£170	□
18 Jan. 1954	Nos. 520, 523/4	£110	□
8 Feb. 1954	Nos. 526/8	£225	□

See also Nos. 540/56, 561/6, 570/94 and 599/618*a* and for stamps as Types **154/60** with face values in decimal currency see Nos. 2031/3, 2258/9, **MS**2326, **MS**2367 and 2378/9.

161   **162**

163   **164**

Coronation

1953 (3 JUNE) *Wmk* **153**

532	**161**	2½d red	20	25	□	□
533	**162**	4d blue	1·10	1·90	□	□
534	**163**	1s 3d green	5·00	3·00	□	□
535	**164**	1s 6d blue	10·00	4·75	□	□
		Set of 4	16·00	9·00	□	□
		First Day Cover		75·00		□

For £1 values as Type **163** see Nos. **MS**2147 and 2380.

165   St Edward's Crown

166   Carrickfergus Castle   **167**   Caernarvon Castle

168   Edinburgh Castle   **169**   Windsor Castle

1955 (1–23 SEPT.) *Wmk* **165** *Perf* 11 × 12

536	**166**	2s 6d brown	9·00	2·00	□	□
537	**167**	5s red	35·00	4·00	□	□

538	168	10s blue	85·00	14·00	☐	☐
539	169	£1 black	£130	35·00	☐	☐
		Set of 4	£225	50·00	☐	☐
		First Day Cover (Nos. 538/9)				
		(1 Sept.)		£800		☐
		First Day Cover (Nos. 536/7)				
		(23 Sept.)		£600		☐

See also Nos. 595a/8a and 759/62.

1955–58 Wmk **165**

540	154	½d orange	15	15	☐	☐
541		1d blue	30	15	☐	☐
542		1½d green	25	30	☐	☐
543		2d red-brown	25	35	☐	☐
543b		2d light red-brown . . .	20	20	☐	☐
544	155	2½d red	20	25	☐	☐
545		3d lilac	25	25	☐	☐
546	156	4d blue	1·25	45	☐	☐
547	157	5d brown	6·00	6·00	☐	☐
548		6d purple	4·50	1·25	☐	☐
549		7d green	50·00	10·00	☐	☐
550	158	8d magenta	7·00	1·25	☐	☐
551		9d bronze-green	20·00	2·75	☐	☐
552		10d blue	20·00	2·75	☐	☐
553		11d plum	50	1·10	☐	☐
554	159	1s bistre	22·00	65	☐	☐
555	160	1s 3d green	30·00	1·60	☐	☐
556	159	1s 6d indigo	23·00	1·60	☐	☐
		Set of 18	£160	27·00	☐	☐

170 Scout Badge and 'Rolling Hitch'

171 'Scouts coming to Britain'

172 Globe within a Compass

173

World Scout Jubilee Jamboree
1957 (1 Aug.) Wmk **165**

557	170	2½d red	50	50	☐	☐
558	171	4d blue	75	1·50	☐	☐
559	172	1s 3d green	4·50	4·50	☐	☐
		Set of 3	5·00	5·75	☐	☐
		First Day Cover		25·00		☐

46th Inter Parliamentary Union Conference
1957 (12 Sept.) Wmk **165**

560	173	4d blue	1·00	1·00	☐	☐
		First Day Cover		£140		☐

Graphite-lined and Phosphor Issues

These are used in connection with automatic sorting machinery, originally experimentally at Southampton but now also operating elsewhere. In such areas these stamps were the normal issue, but from mid 1967 all low-value stamps bear phosphor markings.

The graphite lines were printed in black on the back, beneath the gum; two lines per stamp except for the 2d (see below).

174   **175**   (2d only)
(Stamps viewed from back)

In November 1959, phosphor bands, printed on the front, replaced the graphite. They are wider than the graphite, not easy to see, but show as broad vertical bands at certain angles to the light.

Values representing the rate for printed papers (and second class mail from 1968) have one band and others have two, three or four bands according to size and format. From 1972 onwards some commemorative stamps were printed with 'all-over' phosphor.

In the small stamps the bands are on each side with the single band at left (except where otherwise stated). In the large-size commemorative stamps the single band may be at left, centre or right varying in different issues. The bands are vertical on both horizontal and vertical designs except where otherwise stated.

See also notes on page 37.

Graphite-lined issue
1957 (19 Nov.) Two graphite lines on the back, except 2d value, which has one line. Wmk **165**

561	154	½d orange	25	25	☐	☐
562		1d blue	40	40	☐	☐
563		1½d green	1·20	1·40	☐	☐
564		2d light red-brown . . .	1·60	2·25	☐	☐
565	155	2½d red	8·50	7·00	☐	☐
566		3d lilac	80	50	☐	☐
		Set of 6	12·00	10·50	☐	☐
		First Day Cover		85·00		☐

See also Nos. 587/94.

176 Welsh Dragon

177 Flag and Games Emblem

178 Welsh Dragon

Sixth British Empire and Commonwealth Games, Cardiff
1958 (18 July) *Wmk* **165**

567	**176**	3d lilac	20	20	☐	☐
568	**177**	6d mauve	40	45	☐	☐
569	**178**	1s 3d green	2·25	2·40	☐	☐
	Set of 3	. . . .	2·50	2·75	☐	☐
	First Day Cover			75·00		☐

179 Multiple Crowns

WATERMARK. All the following issues to No. 755 are Watermark **179** (sideways on the vertical commemorative stamps) unless otherwise stated.

1958–65 *Wmk* **179**

570	**154**	½d orange	10	10	☐	☐
571		1d blue	10	10	☐	☐
572		1½d green	10	15	☐	☐
573		2d light red-brown . . .	10	10	☐	☐
574	**155**	2½d red	10	20	☐	☐
575		3d lilac	10	20	☐	☐
576*a*	**156**	4d blue	15	15	☐	☐
577		4½d brown	10	25	☐	☐
578	**157**	5d brown	30	40	☐	☐
579		6d purple	30	25	☐	☐
580		7d green	50	45	☐	☐
581	**158**	8d magenta	60	40	☐	☐
582		9d bronze-green	60	40	☐	☐
583		10d blue	1·00	50	☐	☐
584	**159**	1s bistre	45	30	☐	☐
585	**160**	1s 3d green	45	30	☐	☐
586	**159**	1s 6d indigo	5·00	60	☐	☐
	Set of 17	. . . .	8·00	4·25	☐	☐
	First Day Cover (No. 577)					
	(9 Feb. 1959)			£250		☐

For full information on all future British issues, collectors should write to Royal Mail, Freepost EH3647, 21 South Gyle Crescent, Edinburgh EH12 9PE.

Graphite-lined issue
1958–59 *Two graphite lines on the back, except* 2d *value, which has one line. Wmk* **179**

587	**154**	½d orange	3·25	4·00	☐	☐
588		1d blue	1·50	1·50	☐	☐
589		1½d green	60·00	48·00	☐	☐
590		2d light red-brown . . .	9·00	3·50	☐	☐
591	**155**	2½d red	10·00	10·00	☐	☐
592		3d lilac	50	65	☐	☐
593	**156**	4d blue	5·50	5·00	☐	☐
594		4½d brown	6·50	5·00	☐	☐
	Set of 8	. . . .	85·00	70·00	☐	☐

The prices quoted for Nos. 587 and 589 are for examples with inverted watermark. Stamps with upright watermark are priced at: ½d £9 *mint, £9 used and* 1½d £90 *mint, £80 used.*

1959–63 *Wmk* **179** *Perf* 11 × 12

595*a*	**166**	2s 6d brown	35	40	☐	☐
596*a*	**167**	5s red	1·20	50	☐	☐
597*a*	**168**	10s blue	4·50	4·50	☐	☐
598*a*	**169**	£1 black	11·00	8·00	☐	☐
	Set of 4	. . . .	15·00	11·00	☐	☐

Phosphor-Graphite issue
1959 (18 Nov.) *Two phosphor bands on front and two graphite lines on back, except* 2d *value, which has one band on front and one line on back* (a) *Wmk* **165**

599	**154**	½d orange	4·00	3·75	☐	☐
600		1d blue	11·00	11·00	☐	☐
601		1½d green	4·00	4·00	☐	☐

		(b) *Wmk* **179**				
605	**154**	2d light red-brown				
		(1 band)	5·00	4·25	☐	☐
606	**155**	2½d red	22·00	18·00	☐	☐
607		3d lilac	10·00	8·00	☐	☐
608	**156**	4d blue	20·00	16·00	☐	☐
609		4½d brown	30·00	20·00	☐	☐
	Set of 8	. . . .	85·00	70·00	☐	☐

Phosphor issue
1960–67 *Two phosphor bands on front, except where otherwise stated. Wmk* **179**

610	**154**	½d orange	10	15	☐	☐
611		1d blue	10	10	☐	☐
612		1½d green	15	15	☐	☐
613		2d light red-brown				
		(1 band)	16·00	18·00	☐	☐
613*a*		2d light red-brown				
		(2 bands)	10	15	☐	☐
614	**155**	2½d red (2 bands)	20	30	☐	☐
614*a*		2½d red (1 band)	60	75	☐	☐
615		3d lilac (2 bands)	60	55	☐	☐
615*c*		3d lilac (1 side band) . .	60	55	☐	☐
615*e*		3d lilac (1 centre band) .	40	45	☐	☐
616*a*	**156**	4d blue	25	25	☐	☐
616*b*		4½d brown	25	30	☐	☐

616c	**157**	5d brown	25	35	☐	☐
617		6d purple	30	30	☐	☐
617a		7d green	55	50	☐	☐
617b	**158**	8d magenta	40	45	☐	☐
617c		9d bronze-green	60	55	☐	☐
617d		10d blue	70	60	☐	☐
617e	**159**	1s bistre	40	35	☐	☐
618	**160**	1s 3d green	1·90	2·50	☐	☐
618a	**159**	1s 6d indigo	2·00	2·00	☐	☐
		Set of 17 (*one of each value*) . .	7·50	8·00	☐	☐

No. 615c exists with the phosphor band at the left or right of the stamp.

180 Postboy of 1660

181 Posthorn of 1660

Tercentenary of Establishment of 'General Letter Office'
1960 (7 JULY)

619	**180**	3d lilac	50	50	☐	☐
620	**181**	1s 3d green	3·75	4·25	☐	☐
		Set of 2	3·75	4·25	☐	☐
		First Day Cover	55·00		☐	

182 Conference Emblem

First Anniversary of European Postal and Telecommunications Conference
1960 (19 SEPT.)

621	**182**	6d green and purple . .	1·50	50	☐	☐
622		1s 6d brown and blue . . .	8·50	5·00	☐	☐
		Set of 2	9·75	5·50	☐	☐
		First Day Cover	55·00		☐	

183 Thrift Plant

184 'Growth of Savings'

185 Thrift Plant

Centenary of Post Office Savings Bank
1961 (28 AUG.)

623A	**183**	2½d black and red	25	25	☐	☐
624A	**184**	3d orange-brown and violet	20	20	☐	☐
625A	**185**	1s 6d red and blue	2·50	2·25	☐	☐
		Set of 3	2·75	2·50	☐	☐
		First Day Cover		65·00		☐

186 C.E.P.T. Emblem

187 Doves and Emblem

188 Doves and Emblem

European Postal and Telecommunications (C.E.P.T.) Conference, Torquay
1961 (18 SEPT.)

626	**186**	2d orange, pink and brown	15	20	☐	☐
627	**187**	4d buff, mauve and ultramarine	15	25	☐	☐
628	**188**	10d turquoise, green and blue	15	80	☐	☐
		Set of 3	40	1·10	☐	☐
		First Day Cover		6·00		☐

189 Hammer Beam Roof, Westminster Hall

190 Palace of Westminster

Seventh Commonwealth Parliamentary Conference

1961 (25 SEPT.)

629	**189**	6d purple and gold . . .	25	25 □	□
630	**190**	1s 3d green and blue . . .	2·50	2·75 □	□
		Set of 2	2·75	3·00 □	□
		First Day Cover		30·00	□

191 'Units of Productivity'

192 'National Productivity'

193 'Unified Productivity'

National Productivity Year

1962 (14 NOV.) *Wmk* **179** (*inverted on 2½d and 3d*)

631	**191**	2½d green and red	20	20 □	□
		p. Phosphor	60	50 □	□
632	**192**	3d blue and violet	25	25 □	□
		p. Phosphor	1·50	80 □	□
633	**193**	1s 3d red, blue and green .	1·50	2·00 □	□
		p. Phosphor	35·00	22·00 □	□
		Set of 3 (Ordinary)	1·75	1·90 □	□
		Set of 3 (Phosphor)	30·00	22·00 □	□
		First Day Cover (Ordinary)		48·00	□
		First Day Cover (Phosphor) . . .		£150	□

194 Campaign Emblem and Family

195 Children of Three Races

Freedom from Hunger

1963 (21 MAR.) *Wmk* **179** (*inverted*)

634	**194**	2½d crimson and pink . .	25	10 □	□
		p. Phosphor	3·00	1·25 □	□
635	**195**	1s 3d brown and yellow . .	1·75	1·90 □	□
		p. Phosphor	30·00	23·00 □	□
		Set of 2 (Ordinary)	1·75	2·00 □	□
		Set of 2 (Phosphor)	30·00	24·00 □	□
		First Day Cover (Ordinary)		32·00	□
		First Day Cover (Phosphor) . . .		52·00	□

196 'Paris Conference'

Paris Postal Conference Centenary

1963 (7 MAY) *Wmk* **179** (*inverted*)

636	**196**	6d green and mauve . .	30	50 □	□
		p. Phosphor	6·00	7·00 □	□
		First Day Cover (Ordinary)		16·00	□
		First Day Cover (Phosphor) . . .		37·00	□

197 Posy of Flowers

198 Woodland Life

National Nature Week

1963 (16 MAY)

637	**197**	3d multicoloured	15	15 □	□
		p. Phosphor	55	60 □	□
638	**198**	4½d multicoloured	25	35 □	□
		p. Phosphor	2·75	3·00 □	□
		Set of 2 (Ordinary)	30	50 □	□
		Set of 2 (Phosphor)	3·25	3·50 □	□
		First Day Cover (Ordinary)		22·00	□
		First Day Cover (Phosphor) . . .		40·00	□

199 Rescue at Sea

200 19th-century Lifeboat

201 Lifeboatmen

Ninth International Lifeboat Conference, Edinburgh

1963 (31 MAY)

639	**199**	2½d blue, black and red .	25	25 □	□
		p. Phosphor	50	60 □	□
640	**200**	4d multicoloured	50	50 □	□
		p. Phosphor	50	60 □	□

641	**201**	1s 6d sepia, yellow and				
		blue	3·00	3·25	☐	☐
		p. Phosphor	48·00	28·00	☐	☐
		Set of 3 (*Ordinary*)	3·25	3·50	☐	☐
		Set of 3 (*Phosphor*)	48·00	28·00	☐	☐
		First Day Cover (*Ordinary*)		35·00		☐
		First Day Cover (*Phosphor*) . . .		55·00		☐

202 Red Cross

203

204

Red Cross Centenary Congress
1963 (15 Aug.)

642	**202**	3d red and lilac	25	25	☐	☐
		p. Phosphor	1·10	1·00	☐	☐
643	**203**	1s 3d red, blue and grey . .	3·00	3·00	☐	☐
		p. Phosphor	35·00	27·00	☐	☐
644	**204**	1s 6d red, blue and bistre .	3·00	3·00	☐	☐
		p. Phosphor	35·00	27·00	☐	☐
		Set of 3 (*Ordinary*)	5·00	5·75	☐	☐
		Set of 3 (*Phosphor*)	65·00	55·00	☐	☐
		First Day Cover (*Ordinary*)		40·00		☐
		First Day Cover (*Phosphor*) . . .		90·00		☐

205 'Commonwealth Cable'

Opening of COMPAC (Trans-Pacific Telephone Cable)
1963 (3 Dec.)

645	**205**	1s 6d blue and black	2·75	2·50	☐	☐
		p. Phosphor	16·00	15·50	☐	☐
		First Day Cover (*Ordinary*)		28·00		☐
		First Day Cover (*Phosphor*) . . .		40·00		☐

206 Puck and Bottom
(*A Midsummer
Night's Dream*)

207 Feste (*Twelfth Night*)

208 Balcony Scene
(*Romeo and Juliet*)

209 'Eve of Agincourt'
(*Henry V*)

210 Hamlet contemplating
Yorick's skull (*Hamlet*)
and Queen Elizabeth II

Shakespeare Festival
1964 (23 Apr.) Perf 11 × 12 (*2s 6d*) or 15 × 14 (*others*)

646	**206**	3d bistre, black and				
		violet-blue	15	15	☐	☐
		p. Phosphor	25	30	☐	☐
647	**207**	6d multicoloured	30	30	☐	☐
		p. Phosphor	75	1·00	☐	☐
648	**208**	1s 3d multicoloured	75	1·00	☐	☐
		p. Phosphor	4·00	6·50	☐	☐
649	**209**	1s 6d multicoloured	1·00	85	☐	☐
		p. Phosphor	8·00	8·00	☐	☐
650	**210**	2s 6d deep slate-purple . .	2·75	2·75	☐	☐
		Set of 5 (*Ordinary*)	4·50	4·50	☐	☐
		Set of 4 (*Phosphor*)	12·00	14·00	☐	☐
		First Day Cover (*Ordinary*)		12·00		☐
		First Day Cover (*Phosphor*) . . .		17·00		☐
		Presentation Pack (*Ordinary*) . .	22·00			☐

PRESENTATION PACKS were first introduced by the G.P.O. for the Shakespeare Festival issue. The packs include one set of stamps and details of the designs, the designer and the stamp printer. They were issued for almost all later definitive and special issues.

211 Flats near Richmond Park
('Urban Development')

212 Shipbuilding Yards, Belfast
('Industrial Activity')

213 Beddgelert Forest Park,
Snowdonia ('Forestry')

214 Nuclear Reactor, Dounreay
('Technological Development')

20th International Geographical Congress, London

1964 (1 July)

651	**211**	2½d multicoloured	10	10 ☐ ☐
		p. Phosphor	40	50 ☐ ☐
652	**212**	4d multicoloured	30	30 ☐ ☐
		p. Phosphor	1·25	1·25 ☐ ☐
653	**213**	8d multicoloured	75	85 ☐ ☐
		p. Phosphor	2·50	2·75 ☐ ☐
654	**214**	1s 6d multicoloured	3·50	3·50 ☐ ☐
		p. Phosphor	28·00	22·00 ☐ ☐
		Set of 4 (Ordinary)	4·50	4·50 ☐ ☐
		Set of 4 (Phosphor)	30·00	24·00 ☐ ☐
		First Day Cover (Ordinary)		22·00 ☐
		First Day Cover (Phosphor) . . .		40·00 ☐
		Presentation Pack (Ordinary) . . £160		☐

215 Spring Gentian

216 Dog Rose

217 Honeysuckle

218 Fringed Water Lily

Tenth International Botanical Congress, Edinburgh

1964 (5 Aug.)

655	**215**	3d violet, blue and green	25	25 ☐ ☐
		p. Phosphor	40	40 ☐ ☐
656	**216**	6d multicoloured	50	50 ☐ ☐
		p. Phosphor	2·50	2·75 ☐ ☐
657	**217**	9d multicoloured	1·75	2·25 ☐ ☐
		p. Phosphor	4·50	4·00 ☐ ☐
658	**218**	1s 3d multicoloured	2·50	2·50 ☐ ☐
		p. Phosphor	25·00	20·00 ☐ ☐
		Set of 4 (Ordinary)	4·50	4·50 ☐ ☐
		Set of 4 (Phosphor)	30·00	24·00 ☐ ☐
		First Day Cover (Ordinary)		24·00 ☐
		First Day Cover (Phosphor) . . .		40·00 ☐
		Presentation Pack (Ordinary) . . £160		☐

219 Forth Road Bridge

220 Forth Road and Railway Bridges

Opening of Forth Road Bridge

1964 (4 Sept.)

659	**219**	3d black, blue and violet	10	10 ☐ ☐
		p. Phosphor	1·00	1·50 ☐ ☐
660	**220**	6d blackish lilac, blue and red	40	40 ☐ ☐
		p. Phosphor	4·50	4·75 ☐ ☐
		Set of 2 (Ordinary)	50	50 ☐ ☐
		Set of 2 (Phosphor)	5·00	5·75 ☐ ☐
		First Day Cover (Ordinary)		7·00 ☐
		First Day Cover (Phosphor) . . .		18·00 ☐
		Presentation Pack (Ordinary) . . £380		☐

221 Sir Winston Churchill   **221a** Sir Winston Churchill

Churchill Commemoration

1965 (8 July)

661	**221**	4d black and drab	10	10 ☐ ☐
		p. Phosphor	25	25 ☐ ☐
662	**221a**	1s 3d black and grey	30	40 ☐ ☐
		p. Phosphor	2·50	3·00 ☐ ☐
		Set of 2 (Ordinary)	40	50 ☐ ☐
		Set of 2 (Phosphor)	2·75	3·25 ☐ ☐
		First Day Cover (Ordinary)		7·00 ☐
		First Day Cover (Phosphor) . . .		9·00 ☐
		Presentation Pack (Ordinary) . . 65·00		☐

222 Simon de Montfort's Seal

223 Parliament Buildings
(after engraving by Hollar, 1647)

700th Anniversary of Simon de Montfort's Parliament

1965 (19 July)

663	**222**	6d green	20	20 ☐ ☐
		p. Phosphor	60	1·00 ☐ ☐
664	**223**	2s 6d black, grey and drab	80	1·50 ☐ ☐
		Set of 2 (Ordinary)	1·00	1·25 ☐ ☐
		First Day Cover (Ordinary)		15·00 ☐
		First Day Cover (Phosphor) . . .		26·00 ☐
		Presentation Pack (Ordinary) . . 65·00		☐

224 Bandsmen and Banner   225 Three Salvationists

Salvation Army Centenary
1965 (9 Aug.)

665	224	3d multicoloured	25	25	☐	☐
		p. Phosphor	25	40	☐	☐
666	225	1s 6d multicoloured	1·00	1·50	☐	☐
		p. Phosphor	2·50	2·75	☐	☐
		Set of 2 (Ordinary)	1·00	1·50	☐	☐
		Set of 2 (Phosphor)	2·50	3·00	☐	☐
		First Day Cover (Ordinary)		23·00		☐
		First Day Cover (Phosphor) . . .		33·00		☐

226 Lister's Carbolic Spray   227 Lister and Chemical Symbols

Centenary of Joseph Lister's Discovery of Antiseptic Surgery
1965 (1 Sept.)

667	226	4d indigo, chestnut and grey	25	15	☐	☐
		p. Phosphor	25	25	☐	☐
668	227	1s black, purple and blue	1·00	1·10	☐	☐
		p. Phosphor	2·00	2·50	☐	☐
		Set of 2 (Ordinary)	1·00	1·25	☐	☐
		Set of 2 (Phosphor)	2·25	2·50	☐	☐
		First Day Cover (Ordinary)		12·00		☐
		First Day Cover (Phosphor) . . .		15·00		☐

228 Trinidad Carnival Dancers   229 Canadian Folk Dancers

Commonwealth Arts Festival
1965 (1 Sept.)

669	228	6d black and orange . .	20	20	☐	☐
		p. Phosphor	30	50	☐	☐
670	229	1s 6d black and violet . . .	80	1·10	☐	☐
		p. Phosphor	2·50	3·50	☐	☐
		Set of 2 (Ordinary)	1·00	1·25	☐	☐
		Set of 2 (Phosphor)	2·75	3·50	☐	☐
		First Day Cover (Ordinary)		16·50		☐
		First Day Cover (Phosphor) . . .		22·00		☐

230 Flight of Supermarine Spitfires   231 Pilot in Hawker Hurricane Mk I

232 Wing-tips of Supermarine Spitfire and Messerschmitt Bf 109   233 Supermarine Spitfires attacking Heinkel HE 111H Bomber

234 Supermarine Spitfire attacking Junkers Ju 87B 'Stuka' Dive-bomber   235 Hawker Hurricanes Mk I over Wreck of Dornier Do-17Z Bomber

The above were issued together *se-tenant* in blocks of six (3 × 2) within the sheet.

236 Anti-aircraft Artillery in Action   237 Air Battle over St Paul's Cathedral

25th Anniversary of Battle of Britain
1965 (13 Sept.)

671	230	4d olive and black	1·00	1·00	☐	☐
		a. Block of 6. Nos. 671/6	6·00	10·00	☐	☐
		p. Phosphor	1·25	1·50	☐	☐
		pa. Block of 6. Nos. 671p/6p	10·00	15·00	☐	☐
672	231	4d olive, blackish olive and black	1·00	1·00	☐	☐
		p. Phosphor	1·25	1·50	☐	☐
673	232	4d multicoloured	1·00	1·00	☐	☐
		p. Phosphor	1·25	1·50	☐	☐
674	233	4d olive and black	1·00	1·00	☐	☐
		p. Phosphor	1·25	1·50	☐	☐
675	234	4d olive and black	1·00	1·00	☐	☐
		p. Phosphor	1·25	1·50	☐	☐

676	**235**	4d multicoloured	1·00	1·00	☐	☐
		p. Phosphor	1·25	1·50	☐	☐
677	**236**	9d violet, orange and purple	1·75	2·00	☐	☐
		p. Phosphor	1·75	2·50	☐	☐
678	**237**	1s 3d multicoloured	1·75	2·00	☐	☐
		p. Phosphor	1·75	2·50	☐	☐
		Set of 8 (Ordinary)	8·50	8·50	☐	☐
		Set of 8 (Phosphor)	10·00	12·50	☐	☐
		First Day Cover (Ordinary)		25·00	☐	
		First Day Cover (Phosphor) . . .		28·00	☐	
		Presentation Pack (Ordinary) . .	65·00		☐	

242 Telecommunications Network 243 Radio Waves and Switchboard

238 Tower and Georgian Buildings   239 Tower and Nash Terrace, Regent's Park

Opening of Post Office Tower
1965 (8 Oct.)

679	**238**	3d yellow, blue and green	10	15	☐	☐
		p. Phosphor	15	15	☐	☐
680	**239**	1s 3d green and blue . . .	30	45	☐	☐
		p. Phosphor	30	50	☐	☐
		Set of 2 (Ordinary)	40	60	☐	☐
		Set of 2 (Phosphor)	45	65	☐	☐
		First Day Cover (Ordinary)		6·50		☐
		First Day Cover (Phosphor) . . .		7·00		☐
		Presentation Pack (Ordinary) . .	6·00			☐
		Presentation Pack (Phosphor) . .	6·00			☐

240 U.N. Emblem   241 I.C.Y. Emblem

20th Anniversary of UNO and International Co-operation Year
1965 (25 Oct.)

681	**240**	3d black, orange and blue	25	20	☐	☐
		p. Phosphor	25	30	☐	☐
682	**241**	1s 6d black, purple and blue	1·00	80	☐	☐
		p. Phosphor	2·75	3·00	☐	☐
		Set of 2 (Ordinary)	1·00	1·00	☐	☐
		Set of 2 (Phosphor)	2·50	3·25	☐	☐
		First Day Cover (Ordinary)		12·00		☐
		First Day Cover (Phosphor) . . .		14·00		☐

I.T.U. Centenary
1965 (15 Nov.)

683	**242**	9d multicoloured	50	40	☐	☐
		p. Phosphor	1·00	75	☐	☐
684	**243**	1s 6d multicoloured	1·50	1·25	☐	☐
		p. Phosphor	4·25	5·25	☐	☐
		Set of 2 (Ordinary)	1·50	1·60	☐	☐
		Set of 2 (Phosphor)	4·25	6·00	☐	☐
		First Day Cover (Ordinary)		17·00		☐
		First Day Cover (Phosphor) . . .		20·00		☐

244 Robert Burns (after Skirving chalk drawing)   245 Robert Burns (after Nasmyth portrait)

Burns Commemoration
1966 (25 Jan.)

685	**244**	4d black, indigo and blue	15	15	☐	☐
		p. Phosphor	25	50	☐	☐
686	**245**	1s 3d black, blue and orange	40	70	☐	☐
		p. Phosphor	2·25	2·25	☐	☐
		Set of 2 (Ordinary)	55	85	☐	☐
		Set of 2 (Phosphor)	2·50	2·25	☐	☐
		First Day Cover (Ordinary)		4·00		☐
		First Day Cover (Phosphor) . . .		6·00		☐
		Presentation Pack (Ordinary) . .	55·00			☐

246 Westminster Abbey   247 Fan Vaulting, Henry VII Chapel

900th Anniversary of Westminster Abbey
1966 (28 Feb.) Perf 15 × 14 (3d) or 11 × 12 (2s 6d)

687	**246**	3d black, brown and blue	15	20	☐	☐
		p. Phosphor	20	25	☐	☐

688	247	2s 6d black	55	80 ☐	☐
		Set of 2	70	1·00 ☐	☐
		First Day Cover (Ordinary)		6·00	☐
		First Day Cover (Phosphor) . . .		14·00	☐
		Presentation Pack (Ordinary) . .	45·00		☐

248 View near Hassocks, Sussex

249 Antrim, Northern Ireland

250 Harlech Castle, Wales

251 Cairngorm Mountains, Scotland

Landscapes
1966 (2 MAY)

689	248	4d black, yellow-green and blue	10	15 ☐	☐
		p. Phosphor	10	15 ☐	☐
690	249	6d black, green and blue	15	20 ☐	☐
		p. Phosphor	15	20 ☐	☐
691	250	1s 3d black, yellow and blue	25	35 ☐	☐
		p. Phosphor	25	35 ☐	☐
692	251	1s 6d black, orange and blue	40	35 ☐	☐
		p. Phosphor	40	40 ☐	☐
		Set of 4 (Ordinary)	80	95 ☐	☐
		Set of 4 (Phosphor)	80	1·00 ☐	☐
		First Day Cover (Ordinary)		7·00	☐
		First Day Cover (Phosphor) . . .		8·50	☐

252 Players with Ball

253 Goalmouth Mêlée

254 Goalkeeper saving Goal

World Cup Football Championship
1966 (1 JUNE)

693	252	4d multicoloured	10	25 ☐	☐
		p. Phosphor	10	25 ☐	☐
694	253	6d multicoloured	15	25 ☐	☐
		p. Phosphor	15	25 ☐	☐
695	254	1s 3d multicoloured	50	1·00 ☐	☐
		p. Phosphor	50	1·00 ☐	☐
		Set of 3 (Ordinary)	70	1·00 ☐	☐
		Set of 3 (Phosphor)	50	1·00 ☐	☐
		First Day Cover (Ordinary)		20·00	☐
		First Day Cover (Phosphor) . . .		22·00	☐
		Presentation Pack (Ordinary) . .	15·00		☐

255 Black-headed Gull

256 Blue Tit

257 European Robin

258 Blackbird

The above were issued *se-tenant* in blocks of four within the sheet.

British Birds
1966 (8 AUG.)

696	255	4d multicoloured	20	20 ☐	☐
		a. Block of 4. Nos. 696/9	1·00	2·00 ☐	☐
		p. Phosphor	20	20 ☐	☐
		pa. Block of 4. Nos. 696p/9p	75	2·00 ☐	☐
697	256	4d multicoloured	20	20 ☐	☐
		p. Phosphor	20	20 ☐	☐
698	257	4d multicoloured	20	20 ☐	☐
		p. Phosphor	20	20 ☐	☐
699	258	4d multicoloured	20	20 ☐	☐
		p. Phosphor	20	20 ☐	☐
		Set of 4 (Ordinary)	1·00	1·00 ☐	☐
		Set of 4 (Phosphor)	75	1·00 ☐	☐
		First Day Cover (Ordinary)		8·00	☐
		First Day Cover (Phosphor) . . .		8·00	☐
		Presentation Pack (Ordinary) . .	10·00		☐

259 Cup Winners

England's World Cup Football Victory
1966 (18 AUG.)

700	**259**	4d multicoloured	30	30	☐	☐
		First Day Cover		13·00		☐

260 Jodrell Bank Radio Telescope

261 British Motor-cars

262 SR N6 Hovercraft

263 Windscale Reactor

British Technology
1966 (19 SEPT.)

701	**260**	4d black and lemon . . .	15	10	☐	☐
		p. Phosphor	10	10	☐	☐
702	**261**	6d red, blue and orange	25	20	☐	☐
		p. Phosphor	15	25	☐	☐
703	**262**	1s 3d multicoloured	50	40	☐	☐
		p. Phosphor	35	40	☐	☐
704	**263**	1s 6d multicoloured	50	60	☐	☐
		p. Phosphor	50	60	☐	☐
		Set of 4 (Ordinary)	1·00	1·10	☐	☐
		Set of 4 (Phosphor)	1·00	1·10	☐	☐
		First Day Cover (Ordinary)		6·00		☐
		First Day Cover (Phosphor) . . .		6·00		☐
		Presentation Pack (Ordinary) . .	9·00		☐	

264

265

266

267

268

269

The above show battle scenes, they were issued together *se-tenant* in horizontal strips of six within the sheet.

270 Norman Ship

271 Norman Horsemen attacking Harold's Troops

900th Anniversary of Battle of Hastings
1966 (14 OCT.) *Designs show scenes from Bayeux Tapestry* Wmk **179** (*sideways on* 1s 3d)

705	**264**	4d multicoloured	10	30	☐	☐
		a. Strip of 6. Nos. 705/10	1·90	6·00	☐	☐
		p. Phosphor	10	30	☐	☐
		pa. Strip of 6. Nos.				
		705p/10p	1·90	6·00	☐	☐
706	**265**	4d multicoloured	10	30	☐	☐
		p. Phosphor	10	30	☐	☐
707	**266**	4d multicoloured	10	30	☐	☐
		p. Phosphor	10	30	☐	☐
708	**267**	4d multicoloured	10	30	☐	☐
		p. Phosphor	10	30	☐	☐
709	**268**	4d multicoloured	10	30	☐	☐
		p. Phosphor	10	30	☐	☐
710	**269**	4d multicoloured	10	30	☐	☐
		p. Phosphor	10	30	☐	☐

711	**270**	6d multicoloured	10	30	□	□
		p. Phosphor	10	30	□	□
712	**271**	1s 3d multicoloured	20	75	□	□
		p. Phosphor	20	75	□	□
		Set of 8 *(Ordinary)*	2·00	2·25	□	□
		Set of 8 *(Phosphor)*	2·00	2·25	□	□
		First Day Cover (Ordinary)		8·00		□
		First Day Cover (Phosphor)		9·00		□
		Presentation Pack (Ordinary) ..	9·00			□

272 King of the Orient

273 Snowman

Christmas

1966 (1 DEC.) *Wmk* **179** *(upright on* 1s 6d*)*

713	**272**	3d multicoloured	10	25	□	□
		p. Phosphor	10	25	□	□
714	**273**	1s 6d multicoloured	30	50	□	□
		p. Phosphor	30	50	□	□
		Set of 2 *(Ordinary)*	40	40	□	□
		Set of 2 *(Phosphor)*	40	45	□	□
		First Day Cover (Ordinary)		2·50		□
		First Day Cover (Phosphor) ...		2·00		□
		Presentation Pack (Ordinary) ..	12·00			□

274 Sea Freight

275 Air Freight

European Free Trade Association (EFTA)

1967 (20 FEB.)

715	**274**	9d multicoloured	25	20	□	□
		p. Phosphor	25	20	□	□
716	**275**	1s 6d multicoloured	50	45	□	□
		p. Phosphor	25	40	□	□
		Set of 2 *(Ordinary)*	50	65	□	□
		Set of 2 *(Phosphor)*	50	60	□	□
		First Day Cover (Ordinary)		3·00		□
		First Day Cover (Phosphor) ...		3·00		□
		Presentation Pack (Ordinary) ..	3·50			□

276 Hawthorn and Bramble

277 Larger Bindweed and Viper's Bugloss

278 Ox-eye Daisy, Coltsfoot and Buttercup

279 Bluebell, Red Campion and Wood Anemone

The above sheet were issued together *se-tenant* in blocks of four within the sheet.

280 Dog Violet

281 Primroses

British Wild Flowers

1967 (24 APR.)

717	**276**	4d multicoloured	20	20	□	□
		a. Block of 4. Nos. 717/20	80	3·00	□	□
		p. Phosphor	10	15	□	□
		pa Block of 4. Nos. 717p/20p	50	2·75	□	□
718	**277**	4d multicoloured	20	20	□	□
		p. Phosphor	10	15	□	□
719	**278**	4d multicoloured	20	20	□	□
		p. Phosphor	10	15	□	□
720	**279**	4d multicoloured	20	20	□	□
		p. Phosphor	10	15	□	□
721	**280**	9d multicoloured	20	25	□	□
		p. Phosphor	15	25	□	□
722	**281**	1s 9d multicoloured	25	35	□	□
		p. Phosphor	20	30	□	□
		Set of 6 *(Ordinary)*	1·00	1·25	□	□
		Set of 6 *(Phosphor)*	75	1·00	□	□
		First Day Cover (Ordinary)		5·00		□
		First Day Cover (Phosphor) ...		6·00		□
		Presentation Pack (Ordinary) ..	5·25			□
		Presentation Pack (Phosphor) ..	5·25			□

282 (value at left)

282a (value at right)

I   II

Two *types* of the 2d.

I. Value spaced away from left side of stamp.

II. Value close to left side from new multi-positive. This results in the portrait appearing in the centre, thus conforming with the other values.

1967–69 *Two phosphor bands, except where otherwise stated. No wmk.*

723	282	½d orange-brown	10	20	☐	☐
724		1d olive (2 bands)	10	10	☐	☐
725		1d olive (1 centre band)	30	35	☐	☐
726		2d lake-brown (Type I) (2 bands)	10	15	☐	☐
727		2d lake-brown (Type II) (2 bands)	15	20	☐	☐
728		2d lake-brown (Type II) (1 centre band)	70	90	☐	☐
729		3d violet (1 centre band)	15	10	☐	☐
730		3d violet (2 bands) . . .	30	35	☐	☐
731		4d sepia (2 bands) . . .	10	10	☐	☐
732		4d olive-brown (1 centre band)	10	10	☐	☐
733		4d vermilion (1 centre band)	10	10	☐	☐
734		4d vermilion (1 side band)	1·50	1·90	☐	☐
735		5d blue	10	10	☐	☐
736		6d purple	20	25	☐	☐
737	282a	7d emerald	40	35	☐	☐
738		8d vermilion	20	45	☐	☐
739		8d turquoise-blue	50	60	☐	☐
740		9d green	40	25	☐	☐
741	282	10d drab	50	50	☐	☐
742		1s violet	45	25	☐	☐
743		1s 6d blue and deep blue .	50	50	☐	☐
		c. Phosphorised paper .	80	80	☐	☐
744		1s 9d orange and black . .	50	45	☐	☐
		Set of 16 (one of each value and colour)	4·00	4·00	☐	☐
		Presentation Pack (one of each value)	7·00		☐	
		Presentation Pack (German) . . .	90·00		☐	

First Day Covers

5 June 1967	Nos. 731, 742, 744	3·00 ☐
8 Aug. 1967	Nos. 729, 740, 743	3·00 ☐
5 Feb. 1968	Nos. 723/4, 726, 736	3·00 ☐
1 July 1968	Nos. 735, 737/8, 741	3·00 ☐

No. 734 exists with phosphor band at the left or right.

283 'Master Lambton' (Sir Thomas Lawrence)

284 'Mares and Foals in a Landscape' (George Stubbs)

285 'Children Coming Out of School' (L. S. Lowry)

British Paintings

1967 (10 JULY) *Two phosphor bands. No wmk*

748	283	4d multicoloured	10	10	☐	☐
749	284	9d multicoloured	15	15	☐	☐
750	285	1s 6d multicoloured	25	35	☐	☐
		Set of 3	30	50	☐	☐
		First Day Cover	3·00			☐
		Presentation Pack	5·50			☐

286 *Gipsy Moth IV*

Sir Francis Chichester's World Voyage

1967 (24 JULY) *Three phosphor bands. No wmk*

751	286	1s 9d multicoloured	20	20	☐	☐
		First Day Cover	1·25			☐

287 Radar Screen

288 *Penicillium notatum*

289 Vickers VC-10 Jet Engines

290 Television Equipment

British Discovery and Invention

1967 (19 Sept.) *Two phosphor bands (except 4d. three bands).* *Wmk* **179** (*sideways on* 1s 9d)

752	287	4d yellow, black and vermilion	10	10	☐	☐
753	288	1s multicoloured	10	20	☐	☐
754	289	1s 6d multicoloured	20	25	☐	☐
755	290	1s 9d multicoloured	20	30	☐	☐
		Set of 4	50	75	☐	☐
		First Day Cover		2·50		☐
		Presentation Pack	4·00			☐

NO WATERMARK. All the following issues are on unwatermarked paper unless otherwise stated.

291 'The Adoration of the Shepherds' (School of Seville)

292 'Madonna and Child' (Murillo)

293 'The Adoration of the Shepherds' (Louis Le Nain)

Christmas

1967 *Two phosphor bands (except 3d, one phosphor band)*

756	291	3d multicoloured (27 Nov.)	10	15	☐	☐
757	292	4d multicoloured (18 Oct.)	10	15	☐	☐
758	293	1s 6d multicoloured (27 Nov.)	15	50	☐	☐
		Set of 3	30	50	☐	☐
		First Day Covers (2)		1·50		☐

Gift Pack 1967

1967 (27 Nov.) *Comprises Nos. 715p/22p and 748/58*

GP758c	Gift Pack	3·00	☐

1967–68 *No wmk. Perf* 11 × 12

759	166	2s 6d brown	30	45	☐	☐
760	167	5s red	70	75	☐	☐
761	168	10s blue	4·75	6·25	☐	☐
762	169	£1 black	4·50	6·00	☐	☐
		Set of 4	9·25	12·00	☐	☐

294 Tarr Steps, Exmoor

295 Aberfeldy Bridge

296 Menai Bridge

297 M4 Viaduct

British Bridges

1968 (29 Apr.) *Two phosphor bands*

763	294	4d multicoloured	10	10	☐	☐
764	295	9d multicoloured	10	15	☐	☐
765	296	1s 6d multicoloured	15	25	☐	☐
766	297	1s 9d multicoloured	20	30	☐	☐
		Set of 4	50	70	☐	☐
		First Day Cover		1·50		☐
		Presentation Pack	3·00			☐

298 'TUC' and Trades Unionists

299 Mrs Emmeline Pankhurst (statue)

300 Sopwith Camel and English Electric Lightning Fighters

301 Captain Cook's *Endeavour* and Signature

27

British Anniversaries. Events described on stamps

1968 (29 MAY) *Two phosphor bands*

767	298	4d multicoloured	10	10	□	□
768	299	9d violet, grey and black	10	15	□	□
769	300	1s multicoloured	15	15	□	□
770	301	1s 9d ochre and brown . .	35	35	□	□
		Set of 4	50	50	□	□
		First Day Cover		4·00		□
		Presentation Pack	3·00		□	

302 'Queen Elizabeth I'
(Unknown Artist)

303 'Pinkie' (Lawrence)

304 'Ruins of St Mary
Le Port' (Piper)

305 'The Hay Wain'
(Constable)

British Paintings

1968 (12 AUG.) *Two phosphor bands*

771	302	4d multicoloured	10	10	□	□
772	303	1s multicoloured	10	20	□	□
773	304	1s 6d multicoloured	20	25	□	□
774	305	1s 9d multicoloured	25	40	□	□
		Set of 4	50	85	□	□
		First Day Cover		2·00		□
		Presentation Pack	2·00		□	
		Presentation Pack (German) . . .	12·00		□	

Gift Pack 1968

1968 (16 SEPT.) *Comprises Nos. 763/74*

GP774c	Gift Pack	6·00	□
GP774d	Gift Pack (German)	28·00	□

Collectors Pack 1968

1968 (16 SEPT.) *Comprises Nos. 752/8 and 763/74*

CP774e	Collectors Pack	7·00	□

306 Girl and Boy
with Rocking Horse

307 Girl with Doll's
House

308 Boy with Train
Set

Christmas

1968 (25 NOV.) *Two phosphor bands (except 4d, one centre phosphor band)*

775	306	4d multicoloured	10	15	□	□
776	307	9d multicoloured	15	25	□	□
777	308	1s 6d multicoloured	15	50	□	□
		Set of 3	30	50	□	□
		First Day Cover		1·20		□
		Presentation Pack	5·00		□	
		Presentation Pack (German) . . .	14·00		□	

RMS Queen Elizabeth 2

309 Queen Elizabeth 2

310 Elizabethan Galleon

311 East Indiaman

312 Cutty Sark

SS Great Britain

313 Great Britain

RMS Mauretania

314 Mauretania I

The 9d and 1s values were arranged in horizontal strips of three and pairs respectively throughout the sheet.

British Ships
1969 (15 JAN.) *One horiz phosphor band (5d), two phosphor bands (9d) or two vert phosphor bands at right (1s)*

778	**309**	5d multicoloured	10	15	□	□
779	**310**	9d multicoloured	10	25	□	□
		a. Strip of 3. Nos. 779/81	1·50	3·00	□	□
780	**311**	9d multicoloured	10	25	□	□
781	**312**	9d multicoloured	10	25	□	□
782	**313**	1s multicoloured	40	35	□	□
		a. Pair. Nos. 782/3 . . .	1·25	2·50	□	□
783	**314**	1s multicoloured	40	35	□	□
	Set of 6	1·50	1·40	□	□
	First Day Cover		6·00		□
	Presentation Pack	4·00		□	
	Presentation Pack (German) . . .	40·00		□	

315 Concorde in Flight

316 Plan and Elevation Views

317 Concorde's Nose and Tail

First Flight of Concorde
1969 (3 MAR.) *Two phosphor bands*

784	**315**	4d multicoloured	25	25	□	□
785	**316**	9d multicoloured	55	75	□	□

786	**317**	1s 6d deep blue, grey and light blue	75	1·00	□	□
	Set of 3	1·00	1·50	□	□
	First Day Cover		4·00		□
	Presentation Pack	12·00		□	
	Presentation Pack (German) . . .	40·00		□	

318 (See also Type **357**)

1969 (5 MAR.) *P* 12

787	**318**	2s 6d brown	35	30	□	□
788		5s lake	1·75	60	□	□
789		10s ultramarine	6·00	7·00	□	□
790		£1 black	3·25	1·50	□	□
	Set of 4	10·00	8·50	□	□
	First Day Cover		9·50		□
	Presentation Pack	16·00		□	
	Presentation Pack (German) . . .	60·00		□	

319 Page from the *Daily Mail*, and Vickers FB-27 Vimy Aircraft

320 Europa and C.E.P.T. Emblems

321 I.L.O. Emblem

322 Flags of N.A.T.O. Countries

323 Vickers FB-27 Vimy Aircraft and Globe showing Flight

Anniversaries. Events described on stamps
1969 (2 APR.) *Two phosphor bands*

791	**319**	5d multicoloured	10	15	□	□
792	**320**	9d multicoloured	15	25	□	□

793	321	1s claret, red and blue .	15	25	□	□
794	322	1s 6d multicoloured	15	30	□	□
795	323	1s 9d olive, yellow and				
		turquoise-green . . .	20	40	□	□
		Set of 5	50	1·00	□	□
		First Day Cover		3·00		□
		Presentation Pack	3·50		□	
		Presentation Pack (German) . . .	55·00		□	

330 The King's Gate, Caernarvon Castle   331 The Eagle Tower, Caernarvon Castle

324 Durham Cathedral   325 York Minster

332 Queen Eleanor's Gate, Caernarvon Castle   333 Celtic Cross, Margam Abbey

The 5d values were printed *se-tenant* in strips of three throughout the sheet

326 St Giles' Cathedral, Edinburgh   327 Canterbury Cathedral

The above were issued together *se-tenant* in blocks of four within the sheet.

334 Prince Charles

328 St Paul's Cathedral   329 Liverpool Metropolitan Cathedral

British Architecture (Cathedrals)

1969 (28 MAY) Two phosphor bands

796	324	5d multicoloured	10	20	□	□
		a. Block of 4. Nos. 796/9	1·10	2·50	□	□
797	325	5d multicoloured	10	20	□	□
798	326	5d multicoloured	10	20	□	□
799	327	5d multicoloured	10	20	□	□
800	328	9d multicoloured	25	50	□	□
801	329	1s 6d multicoloured	25	50	□	□
		Set of 6	1·10	1·30	□	□
		First Day Cover		3·00		□
		Presentation Pack	3·25		□	
		Presentation Pack (German) . . .	30·00		□	

Investiture of H.R.H. The Prince of Wales

1969 (1 JULY) Two phosphor bands

802	330	5d multicoloured	10	15	□	□
		a. Strip of 3. Nos. 802/4	30	1·50	□	□
803	331	5d multicoloured	10	15	□	□
804	332	5d multicoloured	10	15	□	□
805	333	9d multicoloured	15	30	□	□
806	334	1s black and gold	15	30	□	□
		Set of 5	50	1·00	□	□
		First Day Cover		1·50		□
		Presentation Pack	2·50		□	
		Presentation Pack (German) . . .	28·00		□	

335 Mahatma Gandhi

Gandhi Centenary Year

1969 (13 Aug.) *Two phosphor bands*

807	**335**	1s 6d multicoloured	. . . .	30	30 ☐	☐
		First Day Cover	. . . .		1·00	☐

Collectors Pack 1969

1969 (15 Sept.) *Comprises Nos. 775/86 and 791/807*

CP807b	Collectors Pack	. . . .	25·00	☐

336 National Giro

337 Telecommunications — International Subscriber Dialling

338 Telecommunications — Pulse Code Modulation

339 Postal Mechanisation — Automatic Sorting

British Post Office Technology

1969 (1 Oct.) *Two phosphor bands. Perf* $13\frac{1}{2} \times 14$

808	**336**	5d multicoloured	. . . .	10	10 ☐	☐
809	**337**	9d green, blue and black		15	20 ☐	☐
810	**338**	1s green, lavender and black	. . . .	15	20 ☐	☐
811	**339**	1s 6d multicoloured	. . . .	15	35 ☐	☐
		Set of 4	. . . .	50	75 ☐	☐
		First Day Cover	. . . .		1·50	☐
		Presentation Pack	. . . .	2·75		☐

340 Herald Angel

341 The Three Shepherds

342 The Three Kings

Christmas

1969 (26 Nov.) *Two phosphor bands (5d, 1s 6d) or one centre band (4d)*

812	**340**	4d multicoloured	. . . .	10	10 ☐	☐
813	**341**	5d multicoloured	. . . .	15	15 ☐	☐
814	**342**	1s 6d multicoloured	. . . .	20	20 ☐	☐
		Set of 3	. . . .	30	30 ☐	☐
		First Day Cover	. . . .		1·00	☐
		Presentation Pack	. . . .	2·50		☐

343 Fife Harling

344 Cotswold Limestone

345 Welsh Stucco

346 Ulster Thatch

British Rural Architecture

1970 (11 Feb.) *Two phosphor bands*

815	**343**	5d multicoloured	. . . .	10	10 ☐	☐
816	**344**	9d multicoloured	. . . .	10	25 ☐	☐
817	**345**	1s multicoloured	. . . .	15	25 ☐	☐
818	**346**	1s 6d multicoloured	. . . .	20	40 ☐	☐
		Set of 4	. . . .	50	75 ☐	☐
		First Day Cover	. . . .		1·50	☐
		Presentation Pack	. . . .	3·25		☐

347 Signing the Declaration of Arbroath

348 Florence Nightingale attending Patients

349 Signing of International Co-operative Alliance

350 Pilgrims and *Mayflower*

351 Sir William Herschel, Francis Baily, Sir John Herschel and Telescope

Anniversaries. Events described on stamps
1970 (1 APR.) *Two phosphor bands*

819	347	5d multicoloured	. . . .	10	10	☐	☐
820	348	9d multicoloured	. . . .	15	15	☐	☐
821	349	1s multicoloured	. . . .	20	25	☐	☐
822	350	1s 6d multicoloured	. . . .	20	30	☐	☐
823	351	1s 9d multicoloured	. . . .	25	30	☐	☐
		Set of 5	. . . .	75	1·00	☐	☐
		First Day Cover	. . . .		2·00		☐
		Presentation Pack	. . . .	3·00			☐

352 'Mr Pickwick and Sam' (*Pickwick Papers*)

353 'Mr and Mrs Micawber' (*David Copperfield*)

354 'David Copperfield and Betsy Trotwood' (*David Copperfield*)

355 'Oliver asking for more' (*Oliver Twist*)

356 'Grasmere' (from engraving by J. Farrington, R.A.)

The 5d values were issued together *se-tenant* in blocks of four within the sheet.

Literary Anniversaries. Events described on stamps
1970 (3 JUNE) *Two phosphor bands*

824	352	5d multicoloured	. . . .	10	25	☐	☐
		a. Block of 4. Nos. 824/7		75	2·00	☐	☐
825	353	5d multicoloured	. . . .	10	25	☐	☐

826	354	5d multicoloured	. . . .	10	25	☐	☐
827	355	5d multicoloured	. . . .	10	25	☐	☐
828	356	1s 6d multicoloured	. . . .	25	50	☐	☐
		Set of 5	. . . .	1·00	1·50	☐	☐
		First Day Cover	. . . .		2·00		☐
		Presentation Pack	. . . .	3·00			☐

356a

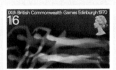

357 (Value redrawn)

Decimal Currency
1970 (17 JUNE)–**72** *10p and some printings of the 50p were issued on phosphor paper. Perf 12*

829	356a	10p cerise	. . . .	50	75	☐	☐
830		20p olive-green	. . . . . .	60	25	☐	☐
831		50p ultramarine	. . . . .	1·25	40	☐	☐
831*b*	357	£1 black (6 Dec. 1972)	.	3·50	80	☐	☐
		Set of 4	. . . .	5·25	2·00	☐	☐
		First Day Cover (*Nos. 829/31*)	. .		2·75		☐
		First Day Cover (*No. 831b*)	. . . .		3·00		☐
		Presentation Pack (*P.O. Pack No.* 18)					
		(*Nos. 829/31*)	. . . .	9·00			☐
		Presentation Pack (*P.O. Pack No.* 38)					
		(*Nos. 830/1, 790 or 831b*)	. . .	10·00			☐

358 Runners

359 Swimmers

360 Cyclists

Ninth British Commonwealth Games, Edinburgh
1970 (15 JULY) *Two phosphor bands. Perf 13½ × 14*

832	358	5d pink, emerald, greenish yellow and yellow-green	25	25	☐	☐
833	359	1s 6d greenish blue, lilac, brown and Prussian blue	50	50	☐	☐

834	360	1s 9d yellow-orange, lilac, salmon and red-brown	....	50	50 ☐ ☐
		Set of 3	....	75	75 ☐ ☐
		First Day Cover	....		1·20 ☐
		Presentation Pack	....	3·00	☐

Collectors Pack 1970

1970 (14 SEPT.) *Comprises Nos. 808/28 and 832/4*

| CP834a | Collectors Pack | .... | 25·00 | ☐ |

| 361 | 1d Black (1840) | 362 | 1s Green (1847) | 363 | 4d Carmine (1855) |

'Philympia 70' Stamp Exhibition

1970 (18 SEPT.) *Two phosphor bands. Perf* 14 × 14½

835	361	5d multicoloured	....	25	10 ☐ ☐
836	362	9d multicoloured	....	25	30 ☐ ☐
837	363	1s 6d multicoloured	....	25	45 ☐ ☐
		Set of 3	....	50	75 ☐ ☐
		First Day Cover	....		1·50 ☐
		Presentation Pack	....	2·75	☐

| 364 | Shepherds and Apparition of the Angel | 365 | Mary, Joseph and Christ in the Manger |

| 366 | The Wise Men bearing Gifts |

Christmas

1970 (25 NOV.) *Two phosphor bands* (5d, 1s 6d) *or one centre phosphor band* (4d)

838	364	4d multicoloured	....	15	10 ☐ ☐
839	365	5d multicoloured	....	15	15 ☐ ☐
840	366	1s 6d multicoloured	....	25	30 ☐ ☐
		Set of 3	....	50	50 ☐ ☐
		First Day Cover	....		1·50 ☐
		Presentation Pack	....	2·75	☐

PRINTING PROCESSES

There is a basic distinction between stamps printed by photogravure and those printed by lithography. Sorting the two is not as difficult as it sounds and with a little experience it should become easy to tell which method of production was employed for a particular stamp.

The tiny dots of the printing screen give uneven edges to the values on photogravure stamps (right). Litho values have clean, clear outlines (left).

All you need is a reasonably good glass giving a magnification of ×4 or more (×10 is even better!).

The image on a photogravure stamp is created from a pattern or 'screen', of minute dots which is not evident when looking at the stamp without a glass but show up quite clearly under magnification, especially in the Queen's face and around the margin of the stamp design where it meets the white background of the paper. Now look at the value; here also, what looks to the naked eye like a straight line is in fact made up of rows of tiny little dots.

'Screens' of dots are also used in the production of litho printed stamps but they are only required where the printer is attempting to produce shades and tints as is necessary in the Queen's head portion of the stamp. Where solid colour is used, as in the background of the majority of values, there is no need to resort to a screen of dots and the background is printed as a solid mass of colour. If you look at the margins or the values of stamps produced in this way you will not see any evidence of dots—just a clear clean break between the inked portion of the stamp and the uninked white of the paper.

367

367a

Decimal Currency
1971–96. *Type* **367**

(*a*) *Printed in photogravure by Harrison and Sons (except for some ptgs of Nos. X879 and X913 which were produced by Enschedé) with phosphor bands. Perf* 15 × 14

X841	½p turquoise-blue (2 bands)	10	10 □ □
X842	½p turquoise-blue (1 side band)	55·00	25·00 □ □
X843	½p turquoise-blue (1 centre band)	40	25 □ □
X844	1p crimson (2 bands) . . .	10	15 □ □
X845	1p crimson (1 centre band)	25	20 □ □
X846	1p crimson ('all-over' phosphor)	15	25 □ □
X847	1p crimson (1 side band) .	1·00	1·25 □ □
X848	1½p black (2 bands)	15	25 □ □
X849	2p myrtle-green (face value as in T **367**) (2 bands) .	15	20 □ □
X850	2p myrtle-green (face value as in T **367**) ('all-over' phosphor)	25	30 □ □
X851	2½p magenta (1 centre band)	20	15 □ □
X852	2½p magenta (1 side band) .	1·50	1·75 □ □
X853	2½p magenta (2 bands) . . .	25	50 □ □
X854	2½p rose-red (2 bands) . . .	40	60 □ □
X855	3p ultramarine (2 bands) .	20	25 □ □
X856	3p ultramarine (1 centre band)	15	20 □ □
X857	3p bright magenta (Type I) (2 bands)	35	35 □ □
X858	3½p olive-grey (2 bands) . .	25	30 □ □
X859	3½p olive-grey (1 centre band)	30	35 □ □
X860	3½p purple-brown (1 centre band)	1·25	1·25 □ □
X861	4p ochre-brown (2 bands)	20	25 □ □
X862	4p greenish blue (2 bands)	1·75	2·00 □ □
X863	4p greenish blue (1 centre band)	1·50	1·90 □ □
X864	4p greenish blue (1 side band)	1·75	1·75 □ □
X865	4½p grey-blue (2 bands) . .	25	30 □ □
X866	5p pale violet (2 bands) . .	20	20 □ □
X867	5p claret (1 centre band) .	2·00	2·25 □ □
X868	5½p violet (2 bands)	25	30 □ □
X869	5½p violet (1 centre band) .	25	30 □ □
X870	6p light emerald (2 bands)	25	20 □ □
X871	6½p greenish blue (2 bands)	30	35 □ □
X872	6½p greenish blue (1 centre band)	25	20 □ □
X873Ea	6½p greenish blue (1 side band)	55	55 □ □
X874	7p purple-brown (2 bands)	30	35 □ □
X875	7p purple-brown (1 centre band)	25	30 □ □
X876Ea	7p purple-brown (1 side band)	45	50 □ □
X877	7½p chestnut (2 bands) . . .	25	35 □ □
X878	8p rosine (2 bands)	25	30 □ □
X879	8p rosine (1 centre band) .	25	30 □ □
X880	8p rosine (1 side band) . .	60	75 □ □
X881	8½p yellowish green (2 bands)	30	25 □ □
X882	9p yellow-orange and black (2 bands)	45	55 □ □
X883	9p deep violet (2 bands) .	35	25 □ □
X884	9½p purple (2 bands)	35	45 □ □
X885	10p orange-brown and chestnut (2 bands) . . .	35	30 □ □
X886	10p orange-brown (Type I) (2 bands)	35	25 □ □
	b. Type II	22·00	22·00 □ □
X887	10p orange-brown (Type I) ('all-over' phosphor) . . .	35	45 □ □
X888	10p orange-brown (Type I) (1 centre band)	35	25 □ □
X889	10p orange-brown (Type I) (1 side band)	70	80 □ □
X890	10½p yellow (2 bands)	40	45 □ □
X891	10½p blue (2 bands)	45	50 □ □
X892	11p brown-red (2 bands) . .	40	30 □ □
X893	11½p drab (1 centre band) . .	40	35 □ □
X894	11½p drab (1 side band) . . .	55	70 □ □
X895	12p yellowish green (2 bands)	45	45 □ □
X896	12p bright emerald (1 centre band)	45	45 □ □
X897	12p bright emerald (1 side band)	80	85 □ □
X898	12½p light emerald (1 centre band)	45	40 □ □
X899	12½p light emerald (1 side band)	70	75 □ □
X900	13p pale chestnut (1 centre band)	40	40 □ □
X901	13p pale chestnut (1 side band)	50	60 □ □
X902	14p grey-blue (2 bands) . .	75	80 □ □
X903	14p deep blue (1 centre band)	40	50 □ □
X904	14p deep blue (1 side band)	4·00	4·00 □ □
X905	15p bright blue (1 centre band)	65	65 □ □
X906Ea	15p bright blue (1 side band)	3·00	3·00 □ □
X907	15½p pale violet (2 bands) . .	60	65 □ □
X908	16p olive-drab (2 bands) . .	1·25	1·40 □ □
X909	17p grey-blue (2 bands) . .	60	60 □ □
X910	17p deep blue (1 centre band)	80	85 □ □
X911Ea	17p deep blue (1 side band)	1·25	1·25 □ □
X912	18p deep olive-grey (2 bands	70	80 □ □

X913	18p bright green (1 centre band)	60	50	□	□
X914	19p bright orange-red (2 bands)	1·50	1·50	□	□
X915	20p dull purple (2 bands)	1·20	90	□	□
X916	20p brownish black (2 bands)	1·50	1·60	□	□
X917	22p bright orange-red (2 bands)	1·50	1·25	□	□
X917a	25p rose-red (2 bands)	7·00	7·00	□	□
X918	26p rosine (Type I) (2 bands)	7·00	7·50	□	□
X919	31p purple (2 bands)	15·00	15·00	□	□
X920	34p ochre-brown (2 bands)	7·00	7·50	□	□
X921	50p ochre-brown (2 bands)	2·00	75	□	□
X922	50p ochre (2 bands)	4·50	4·50	□	□

(b) *Printed in photogravure by Harrison and Sons on phosphorised paper. Perf* 15 × 14

X924	½p turquoise-blue	10	15	□	□
X925	1p crimson	10	15	□	□
X926	2p myrtle-green (face value as in T **367**)	15	20	□	□
X927	2p deep green (smaller value as in T **367a**)	15	20	□	□
X928	2p myrtle-green (smaller value as in T **367a**)	3·25	3·25	□	□
X929	2½p rose-red	15	20	□	□
X930	3p bright magenta (Type I)	20	25	□	□
	c. Type II	90	70	□	□
X931	3½p purple-brown	50	60	□	□
X932	4p greenish blue	25	40	□	□
X933	4p new blue	20	25	□	□
X934	5p pale violet	30	35	□	□
X935	5p dull red-brown	25	30	□	□
X936	6p yellow-olive	30	30	□	□
X937	7p brownish red	1·10	1·25	□	□
X938	8½p yellowish green	40	50	□	□
X939	10p orange-brown (Type I)	35	35	□	□
X940	10p dull orange (Type II)	40	35	□	□
X941	11p brown-red	70	80	□	□
X942	11½p ochre-brown	55	55	□	□
X943	12p yellowish green	45	45	□	□
X944	13p olive-grey	45	50	□	□
X945	13½p purple-brown	60	60	□	□
X946	14p grey-blue	50	50	□	□
X947	15p ultramarine	60	60	□	□
X948	15½p pale violet	60	50	□	□
X949	16p olive-drab	55	55	□	□
X950	16½p pale chestnut	80	75	□	□
X951	17p light emerald	60	60	□	□
X952	17p grey-blue	60	60	□	□
X953	17½p pale chestnut	70	75	□	□
X954	18p deep violet	70	70	□	□
X955	18p deep olive-grey	75	60	□	□
X956	19p bright orange-red	80	60	□	□
X957	19½p olive-grey	2·00	2·00	□	□
X958	20p dull purple	1·00	75	□	□
X959	20p turquoise-green	75	70	□	□
X960	20p brownish black	1·00	1·00	□	□

X961	20½p ultramarine	1·25	1·25	□	□
X962	22p blue	90	75	□	□
X963	22p yellow-green	90	80	□	□
X964	22p bright orange-red	90	80	□	□
X965	23p brown-red	1·25	1·00	□	□
X966	23p bright green	1·10	1·10	□	□
X967	24p violet	1·40	1·50	□	□
X968	24p Indian red	2·00	1·60	□	□
X969	24p chestnut	80	80	□	□
X970	25p purple	1·00	1·00	□	□
X971	26p rosine (Type I)	1·10	60	□	□
	b. Type II	3·50	4·00	□	□
X972	26p drab	1·50	1·25	□	□
X973	27p chestnut	1·25	1·25	□	□
X974	27p violet	1·50	1·25	□	□
X975	28p deep violet	1·25	1·25	□	□
X976	28p ochre	1·40	1·25	□	□
X977	28p deep bluish grey	1·40	1·25	□	□
X978	29p ochre-brown	1·75	1·75	□	□
X979	29p deep mauve	1·75	1·75	□	□
X980	30p deep olive-grey	1·25	1·25	□	□
X981	31p purple	1·25	1·25	□	□
X982	31p ultramarine	1·60	1·50	□	□
X983	32p greenish blue	1·90	1·75	□	□
X984	33p light emerald	1·75	1·60	□	□
X985	34p ochre-brown	1·75	1·75	□	□
X986	34p deep bluish grey	2·00	1·90	□	□
X987	34p deep mauve	1·75	1·75	□	□
X988	35p sepia	1·60	1·60	□	□
X989	35p yellow	1·75	1·60	□	□
X990	37p rosine	2·00	1·75	□	□
X991	39p bright mauve	1·75	1·75	□	□

(c) *Printed in photogravure by Harrison and Sons on ordinary paper. Perf* 15 × 14

X992	50p ochre-brown	1·75	70	□	□
X993	75p grey-black (smaller values as T **367a**)	3·25	1·50	□	□

(d) *Printed in photogravure by Harrison and Sons on ordinary paper or phosphorised paper. Perf* 15 × 14

X994	50p ochre	2·00	70	□	□

(e) *Printed in lithography by John Waddington. Perf* 14

X996	4p greenish blue (2 bands)	25	35	□	□
X997	4p greenish blue (phosphorised paper)	45	40	□	□
X998	20p dull purple (2 bands)	1·25	1·20	□	□
X999	20p dull purple (phosphorised paper)	1·75	1·20	□	□

(f) *Printed in lithography by Questa. Perf* 14 (*Nos* X1000, X1003/4 *and* X1023) *or* 15 × 14 (*others*)

X1000	2p emerald-green (face value as in T **367**) (phosphorised paper)	20	25	□	□
	a. Perf 15 × 14	35	35	□	□
X1001	2p bright green and deep green (smaller value as				

	in T **367a**) (phosphorised paper)	75	70	□	□
X1002	4p greenish blue (phosphorised paper) .	70	75	□	□
X1003	5p light violet (phosphorised paper) .	40	40	□	□
X1004	5p claret (phosphorised paper)	50	50	□	□
	a. Perf 15 × 14	65	60	□	□
X1005	13p pale chestnut (1 centre band)	70	75	□	□
X1006	13p pale chestnut (1 side band)	75	75	□	□
X1007	14p deep blue (1 centre band)	2·00	2·00	□	□
X1008	17p deep blue (1 centre band)	80	80	□	□
X1009	18p deep olive-grey (phosphorised paper) .	90	95	□	□
X1010	18p deep olive-grey (2 bands)	7·50	7·50	□	□
X1011	18p bright green (1 centre band)	75	75	□	□
X1012	18p bright green (1 side band)	1·25	1·40	□	□
X1013	19p bright orange-red (phosphorised paper) .	2·20	2·00	□	□
X1014	20p dull purple (phosphorised paper) .	1·40	1·40	□	□
X1015	22p yellow-green (2 bands)	9·00	9·00	□	□
X1016	22p bright orange-red (phosphorised paper) .	1·00	90	□	□
X1017	24p chestnut (phosphorised paper)	90	1·10	□	□
X1018	24p chestnut (2 bands) . . .	1·40	1·40	□	□
X1019	33p light emerald (phosphorised paper) .	2·50	2·50	□	□
X1020	33p light emerald (2 bands)	1·50	1·50	□	□
X1021	34p bistre-brown (2 bands)	7·50	7·50	□	□
X1022	39p bright mauve (2 bands)	1·50	1·60	□	□
X1023	75p black (face value as T **367**) (ordinary paper)	3·00	1·50	□	□
	a. Perf 15 × 14	3·50	2·25	□	□
X1024	75p brownish grey and black (smaller value as T **367a**) (ordinary paper)	9·00	8·50	□	□

(g) Printed in lithography by Walsall. Perf 14

X1050	2p deep green (phosphorised paper) .	1·10	1·10	□	□
X1051	14p deep blue (1 side band)	4·50	4·50	□	□
X1052	19p bright orange-red (2 bands)	3·00	3·00	□	□
X1053	24p chestnut (phosphorised paper)	1·10	1·25	□	□
X1054	29p deep mauve (2 bands) .	3·00	3·00	□	□
X1055	29p deep mauve (phosphorised paper) .	4·50	4·50	□	□
X1056	31p ultramarine (phosphorised paper) .	1·40	1·40	□	□
X1057	33p light emerald (phosphorised paper) .	1·25	1·25	□	□
X1058	39p bright mauve (phosphorised paper) .	1·60	1·60	□	□

Presentation Pack (P.O. Pack No. 26) (*contains* ½p (X841), 1p (X844), 1½p (X848), 2p (X849), 2½p (X851), 3p (X855), 3½p (X858), 4p (X861), 5p (X866), 6p (X870), 7½p (X877), 9p (X882)) . . . . 5·00 □

Presentation Pack ('Scandinavia 71') (*contents as above*) . . . . 30·00 □

Presentation Pack (P.O. Pack No. 37) (*contains* ½p (X841), 1p (X844), 1½p (X848), 2p (X849), 2½p (X851), 3p (X855 *or* X856), 3½p (X858 *or* X859), 4p (X861), 4½p (X865), 5p (X866), 5½p (X868 *or* X869), 6p (X870), 7½p (X877), 8p (X878), 9p (X882), 10p (X885)) . . . . 8·00 □
  Later issues of this pack included the 6½p (X871) or the 6½p (X872) and 7p (X874).

Presentation Pack (P.O. Pack No. 90) (*contains* ½p (X841), 1p (X844), 1½p (X848), 2p (X849), 2½p (X851), 3p (X856), 5p (X866), 6½p (X872), 7p (X874 *or* X875), 7½p (X877), 8p (X878), 8½p (X881), 9p (X883), 9½p (X884), 10p (X886), 10½p (X890), 11p (X892), 20p (X915), 50p (X921)) . . . 5·00 □

Presentation Pack (P.O. Pack No. 129a) (*contains* 2½p (X929), 3p (X930), 4p (X996), 10½p (X891), 11½p (X893), 11½p (X942), 12p (X943), 13p (X944), 13½p (X945), 14p (X946), 15p (X947), 15½p (X948), 17p (X951), 17½p (X953), 18p (X954), 22p (X962), 25p (X970), 75p (X1023) . . . . 20·00 □

Presentation Pack (P.O. Pack No. 1) (*contains* ½p (X924), 1p (X925), 2p (X1000), 3p (X930), 3½p (X931), 4p (X997), 5p (X1004), 10p (X888), 12½p (X898), 16p (X949), 16½p (X950), 17p (X952), 20p (X999), 20½p (X961), 23p (X965), 26p (X971), 28p (X975), 31p (X981), 50p (X992), 75p (X1023)) . . 40·00 □

Presentation Pack (P.O. Pack No. 5) (*contains* ½p (X924), 1p (X925), 2p (X1000a), 3p (X930), 4p (X997), 5p (X1004a), 10p (X939), 13p (X900), 16p (X949), 17p (X952), 18p (X955),

20p (X999), 22p (X963), 24p (X967),
26p (X971), 28p (X975), 31p (X981),
34p (X985), 50p (X992), 75p (X1023a))   34·00   ☐

Presentation Pack (P.O. Pack No. 9)
(*contains* 1p (X925), 2p (X1000a), 3p
(X930), 4p (X997), 5p (X1004a), 7p
(X937), 10p (X939), 12p (X896), 13p
(X900), 17p (X952), 18p (X955), 20p
(X999), 22p (X963), 24p (X967), 26p
(X971), 28p (X975), 31p (X981), 34p
(X985), 50p (X992), 75p (X1023a))   34·00   ☐

Presentation Pack (P.O. Pack No. 15)
(*contains* 14p (X903), 19p (X956),
20p (X959), 23p (X966), 27p (X973),
28p (X976), 32p (X983), 35p (X988))   12·00   ☐

Presentation Pack (P.O. Pack No. 19)
(*contains* 15p (X905), 20p (X960),
24p (X968), 29p (X979), 30p (X980),
34p (X986), 37p (X990)) . . . . . .   10·00   ☐

Presentation Pack (P.O. Pack No. 22)
(*contains* 10p (X940), 17p (X910),
22p (X964), 26p (X972), 27p (X974),
31p (X982), 33p (X984)) . . . . . .   9·00   ☐

Presentation Pack (P.O. Pack No. 24)
(*contains* 1p (X925), 2p (X927), 3p
(X930), 4p (X933), 5p (X935), 10p
(X940), 17p (X910), 20p (X959), 22p
(X964), 26p (X972), 27p (X974), 30p
(X980), 31p (X982), 32p (X983), 33p
(X984), 37p (X990), 50p (X994), 75p
(X993)) . . . .   25·00   ☐

Presentation Pack (P.O. Pack No. 25)
(*contains* 6p (X936), 18p (X913), 24p
(X969), 28p (X977), 34p (X987), 35p
(X989), 39p (X991)) . . . .   9·00   ☐

First Day Covers

15 Feb. 1971	½p, 1p, 1½p, 2p, 2½p, 3p, 3½p, 4p, 5p, 6p, 7½p, 9p (*Nos.* X841, X844, X848/9, X851, X855, X858, X861, X866, X870, X877, X882) (*Covers carry* 'POSTING DELAYED BY THE POST OFFICE STRIKE 1971' *cachet*)	2·50	☐
11 Aug. 1971	10p (*No.* X885)	1·50	☐
24 Oct. 1973	4½p, 5½p, 8p (*Nos.* X865, X868, X878)	1·50	☐
4 Sept. 1974	6½p (*No.* X871)	1·50	☐
15 Jan. 1975	7p (*No.* X874)	1·00	☐
24 Sept. 1975	8½p (*No.* X881)	1·50	☐
25 Feb. 1976	9p, 9½p, 10p, 10½p, 11p, 20p (*Nos.* X883/4, X886, X890, X892, X915)	3·50	☐

2 Feb. 1977	50p (*No.* X921)	1·75	☐
26 April 1978	10½p (*No.* X891)	1·20	☐
15 Aug. 1979	11½p, 13p, 15p (*Nos.* X942, X944, X947)	1·75	☐
30 Jan. 1980	4p, 12p, 13½p, 17p, 17½p, 75p (*Nos.* X996, X943, X945, X951, X953, X1023)	3·25	☐
22 Oct. 1980	3p, 22p (*Nos.* X930, X962) . . .	1·50	☐
14 Jan. 1981	2½p, 11½p, 14p, 15½p, 18p, 25p (*Nos.* X929, X893, X946, X948, X954, X970)	2·00	☐
27 Jan. 1982	5p, 12½p, 16½p, 19½p, 26p, 29p (*Nos.* X1004, X898, X950, X957, X971, X978)	3·50	☐
30 Mar. 1983	3½p, 16p, 17p, 20½p, 23p, 28p, 31p (*Nos.* X931, X949, X952, X961, X965, X975, X981)	5·00	☐
28 Aug. 1984	13p, 18p, 22p, 24p, 34p (*Nos.* X900, X955, X963, X967, X985) .	3·00	☐
29 Oct. 1985	7p, 12p (*Nos.* X937, X896) . . .	3·00	☐
23 Aug. 1988	14p, 19p, 20p, 23p, 27p, 28p, 32p, 35p (*Nos.* X903, X956, X959, X966, X973, X976, X983, X988) .	6·00	☐
26 Sept. 1989	15p, 20p, 24p, 29p, 30p, 34p, 37p (*Nos.* X905, X960, X968, X979/80, X986, X990)	5·00	☐
4 Sept. 1990	10p, 17p, 22p, 26p, 27p, 31p, 33p (*Nos.* X940, X910, X964, X972, X974, X982, X984)	5·50	☐
10 Sept. 1991	6p, 18p, 24p, 28p, 34p, 35p, 39p (*Nos.* X936, X913, X969, X977, X987, X989, X991)	6·00	☐

For similar stamps, but with elliptical perforations see Nos. Y1667/1803 in 1993.

PHOSPHOR BANDS. See notes on page 15.
Phosphor bands are applied to the stamps, after the design has been printed, by a separate cylinder. On issues with 'all-over' phosphor the 'band' covers the entire stamp. Parts of the stamp covered by phosphor bands, or the entire surface for 'all-over' phosphor versions, appear matt.

Nos. X847, X852, X864, X873, X876, X880, X889, X894, X897, X899, X901, X906, X911, X1006 and X1012 exist with the phosphor band at the left or right of the stamp.

PHOSPHORISED PAPER. First introduced as an experiment for a limited printing of the 1s 6d value (No. 743c) in 1969, this paper has the phosphor, to activate the automatic sorting machinery, added to the paper coating before the stamps were printed. Issues on this paper have a completely shiny surface. Although not adopted after this first trial further experiments on the 8½p in 1976 led to this paper being used for new printings of current values.

368 'A Mountain Road'
(T. P. Flanagan)

369 'Deer's Meadow'
(Tom Carr)

370 'Slieve na brock'
(Colin Middleton)

'Ulster '71' Paintings

1971 (16 JUNE) *Two phosphor bands*

881	**368**	3p multicoloured	. . . .	25	25	☐	☐
882	**369**	7½p multicoloured	. . . .	50	50	☐	☐
883	**370**	9p multicoloured	. . . .	50	50	☐	☐
		Set of 3	. . . .	1·00	1·00	☐	☐
		First Day Cover	. . . .		1·75	☐	
		Presentation Pack	. . . .	6·00		☐	

371 John Keats
(150th Death Anniv)

372 Thomas Gray
(Death Bicentenary)

373 Sir Walter Scott (Birth
Bicentenary)

Literary Anniversaries. Events described above

1971 (28 JULY) *Two phosphor bands*

884	**371**	3p black, gold and blue	. .	25	10	☐	☐
885	**372**	5p black, gold and olive	.	45	50	☐	☐
886	**373**	7½p black, gold and brown		45	50	☐	☐
		Set of 3	. . . .	1·00	1·10	☐	☐
		First Day Cover	. . . .		2·00	☐	
		Presentation Pack	. . . .	5·50		☐	

374 Servicemen and Nurse
of 1921

375 Roman Centurion

376 Rugby Football, 1871

British Anniversaries. Events described on stamps

1971 (25 AUG.) *Two phosphor bands*

887	**374**	3p multicoloured	. . . .	25	25	☐	☐
888	**375**	7½p multicoloured	. . . .	50	50	☐	☐
889	**376**	9p multicoloured	. . . .	50	50	☐	☐
		Set of 3	. . . .	1·00	1·00	☐	☐
		First Day Cover	. . . .		2·50	☐	
		Presentation Pack	. . . .	5·50		☐	

377 Physical Sciences
Building, University
College of Wales,
Aberystwyth

378 Faraday Building,
Southampton
University

379 Engineering Department,
Leicester University

380 Hexagon Restaurant,
Essex University

British Architecture (Modern University Buildings)

1971 (22 SEPT.) *Two phosphor bands*

890	**377**	3p multicoloured	. . . .	10	10	☐	☐
891	**378**	5p multicoloured	. . . .	25	20	☐	☐

892	379	7½p ochre, black and purple-brown	45	55	□	□
893	380	9p multicoloured	75	80	□	□
		Set of 4	1·25	1·50	□	□
		First Day Cover		2·00		□
		Presentation Pack		6·50		□

Collectors Pack 1971

1971 (29 Sept.) *Comprises Nos. 835/40 and 881/93*

CP893a	Collectors Pack	50·00		□

381   Dream of the Wise Men   382   Adoration of the Magi

383   Ride of the Magi

Christmas

1971 (13 Oct.) *Two phosphor bands (3p, 7½p) or one centre phosphor band (2½p)*

894	381	2½p multicoloured	10	10	□	□
895	382	3p multicoloured	10	10	□	□
896	383	7½p multicoloured	55	75	□	□
		Set of 3	50	75	□	□
		First Day Cover		2·00		□
		Presentation Pack	4·50		□

384   Sir James Clark Ross   385   Sir Martin Frobisher

386   Henry Hudson   387   Capt. Robert F. Scott

British Polar Explorers

1972 (16 Feb.) *Two phosphor bands*

897	384	3p multicoloured	10	10	□	□
898	385	5p multicoloured	15	15	□	□
899	386	7½p multicoloured	45	50	□	□
900	387	9p multicoloured	70	85	□	□
		Set of 4	1·25	1·50	□	□
		First Day Cover		2·50		□
		Presentation Pack	5·25		□

388   Statuette of Tutankhamun   389   19th-century Coastguard

390   Ralph Vaughan Williams and Score

Anniversaries. Events described on stamps

1972 (26 Apr.) *Two phosphor bands*

901	388	3p multicoloured	25	25	□	□
902	389	7½p multicoloured	50	50	□	□
903	390	9p multicoloured	50	50	□	□
		Set of 3	1·00	1·00	□	□
		First Day Cover		2·25		□
		Presentation Pack	4·25		□

For full information on all future British issues, collectors should write to Royal Mail, Freepost EH3647, 21 South Gyle Crescent, Edinburgh EH12 9PE.

391 St Andrew's, Greensted- juxta- Ongar, Essex

392 All Saints, Earls Barton, Northants

393 St Andrew's, Letheringsett, Norfolk

394 St Andrew's, Helpringham, Lincs

395 St Mary the Virgin, Huish Episcopi, Somerset

British Architecture (Village Churches)
1972 (21 JUNE) Two phosphor bands

904	391	3p multicoloured	. . . . .	10	10 □	□
905	392	4p multicoloured	. . . . .	10	20 □	□
906	393	5p multicoloured	. . . . .	15	20 □	□
907	394	7½p multicoloured	. . . . .	50	75 □	□
908	395	9p multicoloured	. . . . .	50	80 □	□
		Set of 5	. . . . .	1·25	1·90 □	□
		First Day Cover	. . . .		2·75	□
		Presentation Pack	. . . .	10·00		□

'Belgica '72' Souvenir Pack
1972 (24 JUNE) Comprises Nos. 894/6 and 904/8

CP908b	Souvenir Pack	. . . . 10·00	□

396 Microphones, 1924–69

397 Horn Loudspeaker

398 TV Camera, 1972

399 Oscillator and Spark Transmitter, 1897

Broadcasting Anniversaries. Events described on stamps
1972 (13 SEPT.) Two phosphor bands

909	396	3p multicoloured	. . . . .	10	10 □	□
910	397	5p multicoloured	. . . . .	10	20 □	□
911	398	7½p multicoloured	. . . . .	45	50 □	□
912	399	9p multicoloured	. . . . .	50	50 □	□
		Set of 4	. . . .	1·00	1·25 □	□
		First Day Cover	. . . .		2·75	□
		Presentation Pack	. . . .	4·25		□

400 Angel holding Trumpet

401 Angel playing Lute

402 Angel playing Harp

Christmas

1972 (18 Oct.) *Two phosphor bands (3p, 7½p) or one centre phosphor band (2½p)*

913	**400**	2½p multicoloured	10	10	☐	☐
914	**401**	3p multicoloured	10	10	☐	☐
915	**402**	7½p multicoloured	50	45	☐	☐
		Set of 3	60	45	☐	☐
		First Day Cover		1·50		☐
		Presentation Pack	4·00			☐

403   Queen Elizabeth II
and Prince Philip

404   Europe

Royal Silver Wedding

1972 (20 Nov.) *3p 'all-over' phosphor, 20p without phosphor*

916	**403**	3p brownish black, deep blue and silver	25	25	☐	☐
917		20p brownish black, reddish purple and silver	1·00	1·00	☐	☐
		Set of 2	1·00	1·00	☐	☐
		First Day Cover		1·50		☐
		Presentation Pack	4·00			☐
		Presentation Pack (Japanese) . .	9·50			☐
		Souvenir Book	4·00			☐
		Gutter Pair (3p)	80			☐
		Traffic Light Gutter Pair (3p) . . .	20·00			☐

Collectors Pack 1972

1972 (20 Nov.) *Comprises Nos. 897/918*

CP918a	Collectors Pack	27·00		☐

Nos. 920/1 were issued horizontally *se-tenant* throughout the sheet.

Britain's Entry into European Communities

1973 (3 Jan.) *Two phosphor bands*

919	**404**	3p multicoloured	25	25	☐	☐
920		5p multicoloured (blue jigsaw)	25	50	☐	☐
		a. Pair. Nos. 920/1	1·00	1·50	☐	☐
921		5p multicoloured (green jigsaw)	25	50	☐	☐
		Set of 3	1·00	1·00	☐	☐
		First Day Cover		2·00		☐
		Presentation Pack	3·00			☐

Oak: Quercus robur

405   Oak Tree

British Trees (1st Issue)

1973 (28 Feb.) *Two phosphor bands*

922	**405**	9p multicoloured	35	40	☐	☐
		First Day Cover		1·75		☐
		Presentation Pack	2·75			☐

See also No. 949.

406   David Livingstone

407   H. M. Stanley

The above were issued horizontally *se-tenant* throughout the sheet.

408   Sir Francis Drake

409   Sir Walter Raleigh

410   Charles Sturt

British Explorers

1973 (18 Apr.) *'All-over' phosphor*

923	**406**	3p multicoloured	40	25	☐	☐
		a. Pair. Nos. 923/4	80	1·00	☐	☐

924	**407**	3p multicoloured	. . . .	40	25 ☐ ☐
925	**408**	5p multicoloured	. . . .	40	50 ☐ ☐
926	**409**	7½p multicoloured	. . . .	40	50 ☐ ☐
927	**410**	9p multicoloured	. . . .	40	75 ☐ ☐
		Set of 5	. . . .	1·50	1·75 ☐ ☐
		First Day Cover	. . . .		2·50 ☐
		Presentation Pack	. . . .	4·50	☐

411   **412**

413

County Cricket 1873–1973

1973 (16 MAY) *Designs show sketches of W. G. Grace by Harry Furniss. Queen's head in gold. 'All-over' phosphor*

928	**411**	3p black and brown	. . . .	25	25 ☐ ☐
929	**412**	7½p black and green	. . . .	75	75 ☐ ☐
930	**413**	9p black and blue	. . . .	1·25	1·00 ☐ ☐
		Set of 3	. . . .	1·75	1·50 ☐ ☐
		First Day Cover	. . . .		3·00 ☐
		Presentation Pack	. . . .	4·50	☐
		Souvenir Book	. . . .	7·00	☐
		PHQ Card (No. 928)	. . . . . .	70·00	£275 ☐ ☐

The PHQ Card did not become available until mid-July. The used price quoted is for an example used in July or August 1973.

414   'Self-portrait' (Sir   **415**   'Self-portrait' (Sir
      Joshua Reynolds)   Henry Raeburn)

416   'Nelly O'Brien' (Sir   **417**   'Rev R. Walker
      Joshua Reynolds)   (The Skater)'
                                     (Sir Henry
                                     Raeburn)

Artistic Anniversaries. Events described on stamps

1973 (4 JULY) *'All-over' phosphor*

931	**414**	3p multicoloured	. . . . .	10	10 ☐ ☐
932	**415**	5p multicoloured	. . . . .	30	30 ☐ ☐
933	**416**	7½p multicoloured	. . . . .	30	30 ☐ ☐
934	**417**	9p multicoloured	. . . . .	60	60 ☐ ☐
		Set of 4	. . . .	1·20	1·20 ☐ ☐
		First Day Cover	. . . .		2·00 ☐
		Presentation Pack	. . . .	3·25	☐

418   Court Masque Costumes   **419**   St Paul's Church,
                                            Covent Garden

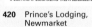

420   Prince's Lodging,   **421**   Court Masque Stage
      Newmarket   Scene

The 3p and 5p values were printed horizontally *se-tenant* within the sheet.

400th Anniversary of the Birth of Inigo Jones (architect and designer)

1973 (15 AUG.) *'All-over' phosphor*

935	**418**	3p deep mauve, black and gold	. . . .	10	25 ☐ ☐
		a. Pair. Nos. 935/6	. . . .	30	50 ☐ ☐
936	**419**	3p deep brown, black and gold	. . . .	10	25 ☐ ☐

937	420	5p blue, black and gold . .	35	50 ☐ ☐
		a. Pair. Nos. 937/8	1·00	1·25 ☐ ☐
938	421	5p grey-olive, black and gold	35	50 ☐ ☐
		Set of 4	1·25	1·25 ☐ ☐
		First Day Cover		2·00 ☐
		Presentation Pack	3·50	☐
		PHQ Card (No. 936)	£200	£200 ☐ ☐

422 Palace of Westminster seen from Whitehall

423 Palace of Westminster seen from Millbank

19th Commonwealth Parliamentary Conference
1973 (12 Sept.) *'All-over' phosphor*

939	422	8p black, grey and pale buff	45	50 ☐ ☐
940	423	10p gold and black	45	40 ☐ ☐
		Set of 2	75	75 ☐ ☐
		First Day Cover		1·50 ☐
		Presentation Pack	3·00	☐
		Souvenir Book	7·00	☐
		PHQ Card (No. 939)	40·00	£150 ☐ ☐

424 Princess Anne and Captain Mark Phillips

Royal Wedding
1973 (14 Nov.) *'All-over' phosphor*

941	424	3½p violet and silver	25	25 ☐ ☐
942		20p brown and silver . . .	1·00	75 ☐ ☐
		Set of 2	1·00	75 ☐ ☐
		First Day Cover		1·50 ☐
		Presentation Pack	2·75	☐
		PHQ Card (No. 941)	9·00	50·00 ☐ ☐
		Set of 2 Gutter Pairs	2·75	☐
		Set of 2 Traffic Light Gutter Pairs	£110	☐

425 **426**

427

428

429

430 'Good King Wenceslas, the Page and Peasant'

The 3p values depict the carol 'Good King Wenceslas' and were printed horizontally *se-tenant* within the sheet.

Christmas
1973 (28 Nov.) *One phosphor band (3p) or 'all-over' phosphor (3½p)*

943	425	3p multicoloured	20	25 ☐ ☐
		a. Strip of 5. Nos. 943/7 .	2·25	3·50 ☐ ☐
944	426	3p multicoloured	20	25 ☐ ☐
945	427	3p multicoloured	20	25 ☐ ☐
946	428	3p multicoloured	20	25 ☐ ☐
947	429	3p multicoloured	20	25 ☐ ☐
948	430	3½p multicoloured	20	25 ☐ ☐
		Set of 6	2·25	2·50 ☐ ☐
		First Day Cover		2·50 ☐
		Presentation Pack	4·00	☐

Collectors Pack 1973
1973 (28 Nov.) *Comprises Nos. 919/48*

| CP948k | Collectors Pack . . . . | 27·00 | ☐ |

431 Horse Chestnut

British Trees (2nd issue)
1974 (27 Feb.) *'All-over' phosphor*

949	431	10p multicoloured	40	35 ☐ ☐
		First Day Cover		1·25 ☐
		Presentation Pack	2·50	☐
		PHQ Card	£140	£150 ☐ ☐
		Gutter Pair	2·00	☐
		Traffic Light Gutter Pair	65·00	☐

432 First Motor Fire-engine, 1904

433 Prize-winning Fire-engine, 1863

434 First Steam Fire-engine, 1830

435 Fire-engine, 1766

Bicentenary of the Fire Prevention (Metropolis) Act

1974 (24 APR.) *'All-over' phosphor*

950	432	3½p multicoloured	25	10	☐	☐
951	433	5½p multicoloured	25	30	☐	☐
952	434	8p multicoloured	50	50	☐	☐
953	435	10p multicoloured	50	50	☐	☐
		Set of 4	1·25	1·25	☐	☐
		First Day Cover		3·00	☐	
		Presentation Pack	2·75		☐	
		PHQ Card (No. 950)	£140	£150	☐	☐
		Set of 4 Gutter Pairs	4·00		☐	
		Set of 4 Traffic Light Gutter Pairs	65·00		☐	

436 P & O Packet *Peninsular*, 1888

437 Farman H.F. III Biplane, 1911

438 Airmail-blue Van and Postbox, 1930

439 Imperial Airways Short S.21 Flying Boat *Maia*, 1937

Centenary of Universal Postal Union

1974 (12 JUNE) *'All-over' phosphor*

954	436	3½p multicoloured	25	10	☐	☐
955	437	5½p multicoloured	25	30	☐	☐
956	438	8p multicoloured	25	35	☐	☐
957	439	10p multicoloured	50	40	☐	☐
		Set of 4	1·00	1·00	☐	☐
		First Day Cover		2·00		☐
		Presentation Pack	2·75		☐	
		Set of 4 Gutter Pairs	3·00		☐	
		Set of 4 Traffic Light Gutter Pairs	45·00		☐	

440 Robert the Bruce

441 Owain Glyndŵr

442 Henry V

443 The Black Prince

Medieval Warriors

1974 (10 JULY) *'All-over' phosphor*

958	440	4½p multicoloured	25	10	☐	☐
959	441	5½p multicoloured	25	35	☐	☐
960	442	8p multicoloured	50	50	☐	☐
961	443	10p multicoloured	50	50	☐	☐
		Set of 4	1·25	1·25	☐	☐
		First Day Cover		3·00		☐
		Presentation Pack	4·00		☐	
		PHQ Cards (set of 4)	28·00	55·00	☐	☐
		Set of 4 Gutter Pairs	4·00		☐	
		Set of 4 Traffic Light Gutter Pairs	70·00		☐	

444 Churchill in Royal Yacht Squadron Uniform

445 Prime Minister, 1940

446 Secretary for War and Air, 1919

447 War Correspondent, South Africa, 1899

Birth Centenary of Sir Winston Churchill

1974 (9 Oct.) *Queen's head and inscription in silver. 'All-over' phosphor*

962	444	4½p green and blue	20	15	□	□
963	445	5½p grey and black	35	35	□	□
964	446	8p rose and lake	60	50	□	□
965	447	10p stone and brown . . .	60	50	□	□
		Set of 4	1·60	1·50	□	□
		First Day Cover		2·00		□
		Presentation Pack	2·50		□	
		Souvenir Book	3·00		□	
		PHQ Card (No. 963)	6·00	32·00	□	□
		Set of 4 Gutter Pairs	4·00		□	
		Set of 4 Traffic Light Gutter Pairs	34·00		□	

448 Adoration of the Magi (York Minster, *c* 1355)

449 The Nativity (St Helen's Church, Norwich, *c* 1480)

450 Virgin and Child (Ottery St Mary Church, *c* 1350)

451 Virgin and Child (Worcester Cathedral, *c* 1224)

Christmas

1974 (27 Nov.) *Designs show church roof bosses. One phosphor band (3½p) or 'all-over' phosphor (others)*

966	448	3½p multicoloured	10	10	□	□
967	449	4½p multicoloured	10	10	□	□

968	450	8p multicoloured	25	50	□	□
969	451	10p multicoloured	50	50	□	□
		Set of 4	1·00	1·00	□	□
		First Day Cover		2·00		□
		Presentation Pack	2·25		□	
		Set of 4 Gutter Pairs	3·50		□	
		Set of 4 Traffic Light Gutter Pairs	36·00		□	

Collectors Pack 1974

1974 (27 Nov.) *Comprises Nos. 949/69*

CP969*a*	Collectors Pack	13·00		□

452 Invalid in Wheelchair

Health and Handicap Funds

1975 (22 Jan.) *'All-over' phosphor*

970	452	4½p + 1½p azure and blue . .	25	25	□	□
		First Day Cover		1·00		□
		Gutter Pair	50		□	
		Traffic Light Gutter Pair	2·25		□	

453 'Peace – Burial at Sea'

454 'Snowstorm – Steamer off a Harbour's Mouth'

455 'The Arsenal, Venice'

456 'St Laurent'

Birth Bicentenary of J. M. W. Turner (painter)

1975 (19 Feb.) *'All-over' phosphor*

971	453	4½p multicoloured	25	25	□	□
972	454	5½p multicoloured	25	25	□	□

973	**455**	8p multicoloured	25	50	☐	☐
974	**456**	10p multicoloured	50	50	☐	☐
		Set of 4	1·00	1·00	☐	☐
		First Day Cover		1·50		☐
		Presentation Pack	2·00		☐	
		PHQ Card (No. 972)	42·00	34·00	☐	☐
		Set of 4 Gutter Pairs	2·25		☐	
		Set of 4 Traffic Light Gutter Pairs	11·50		☐	

462 Sailing Dinghies   **463** Racing Keel Boats

457 Charlotte Square,   **458** The Rows,
Edinburgh   Chester

464 Cruising Yachts   **465** Multihulls

The above were printed horizontally *se-tenant* throughout the sheet.

Sailing
1975 (11 JUNE) *'All-over' phosphor*

980	**462**	7p multicoloured	25	20	☐	☐
981	**463**	8p multicoloured	35	40	☐	☐
982	**464**	10p multicoloured	35	45	☐	☐
983	**465**	12p multicoloured	50	50	☐	☐
		Set of 4	1·25	1·25	☐	☐
		First Day Cover		2·00		☐
		Presentation Pack	2·50		☐	
		PHQ Card (No. 981)	5·75	30·00	☐	☐
		Set of 4 Gutter Pairs	2·50		☐	
		Set of 4 Traffic Light Gutter Pairs	25·00		☐	

459 Royal Observatory,   **460** St George's Chapel,
Greenwich   Windsor

466 Stephenson's   **467** *Abbotsford,*
Locomotion, 1825   1876

461 National Theatre, London

European Architectural Heritage Year
1975 (23 APR.) *'All-over' phosphor*

975	**457**	7p multicoloured	25	25	☐	☐
		a. Pair. Nos. 975/6	90	1·00	☐	☐
976	**458**	7p multicoloured	25	25	☐	☐
977	**459**	8p multicoloured	40	30	☐	☐
978	**460**	10p multicoloured	40	30	☐	☐
979	**461**	12p multicoloured	40	35	☐	☐
		Set of 5	1·50	1·25	☐	☐
		First Day Cover		2·50		☐
		Presentation Pack	2·50		☐	
		PHQ Cards (Nos. 975/7)	11·00	40·00	☐	☐
		Set of 5 Gutter Pairs	5·50		☐	
		Set of 5 Traffic Light Gutter Pairs	22·00		☐	

468 *Caerphilly Castle, 1923*   **469** High Speed Train, 1975

150th Anniversary of Public Railways
1975 (13 AUG.) *'All-over' phosphor*

984	**466**	7p multicoloured	25	25	☐	☐
985	**467**	8p multicoloured	50	50	☐	☐

986	**468**	10p multicoloured	50	50	☐	☐
987	**469**	12p multicoloured	40	50	☐	☐
		Set of 4	1·50	1·50	☐	☐
		First Day Cover		2·50		☐
		Presentation Pack	2·50		☐	
		Souvenir Book	4·00		☐	
		PHQ Cards (set of 4)	70·00	72·00	☐	☐
		Set of 4 Gutter Pairs	3·00		☐	
		Set of 4 Traffic Light Gutter Pairs	14·00		☐	

470 Palace of Westminster

62nd Inter-Parliamentary Union Conference

1975 (3 Sept.) *'All-over' phosphor*

988	**470**	12p multicoloured	50	40	☐	☐
		First Day Cover		80		☐
		Presentation Pack	1·25		☐	
		Gutter Pair	1·00		☐	
		Traffic Light Gutter Pair	4·50		☐	

471 Emma and Mr Woodhouse (*Emma*)

472 Catherine Morland (*Northanger Abbey*)

473 Mr Darcy (*Pride and Prejudice*)

474 Mary and Henry Crawford (*Mansfield Park*)

Birth Bicentenary of Jane Austen (novelist)

1975 (22 Oct.) *'All-over' phosphor*

989	**471**	8½p multicoloured	25	20	☐	☐
990	**472**	10p multicoloured	45	45	☐	☐

991	**473**	11p multicoloured	45	45	☐	☐
992	**474**	13p multicoloured	50	50	☐	☐
		Set of 4	1·50	1·25	☐	☐
		First Day Cover		2·50		☐
		Presentation Pack	2·50		☐	
		PHQ Cards (set of 4)	24·00	42·00	☐	☐
		Set of 4 Gutter Pairs	2·50		☐	
		Set of 4 Traffic Light Gutter Pairs	11·00		☐	

475 Angels with Harp and Lute

476 Angel with Mandolin

477 Angel with Horn

478 Angel with Trumpet

Christmas

1975 (26 Nov.) *One phosphor band (6½p). phosphor-inked (8½p)* (*background*) *or 'all-over' phosphor (others)*

993	**475**	6½p multicoloured	25	25	☐	☐
994	**476**	8½p multicoloured	25	40	☐	☐
995	**477**	11p multicoloured	50	45	☐	☐
996	**478**	13p multicoloured	50	45	☐	☐
		Set of 4	1·25	1·25	☐	☐
		First Day Cover		1·50		☐
		Presentation Pack	2·50		☐	
		Set of 4 Gutter Pairs	2·75		☐	
		Set of 4 Traffic Light Gutter Pairs	11·00		☐	

Collectors Pack 1975

1975 (26 Nov.) *Comprises Nos. 970/96*

CP996a	Collectors Pack	9·00		☐

479 Housewife

480 Policeman

481 District Nurse   **482** Industrialist

487 Benjamin Franklin (bust by Jean-Jacques Caffieri)

Telephone Centenary
1976 (10 MAR.) *'All-over' phosphor*

997	**479**	8½p multicoloured	25	20	☐	☐
998	**480**	10p multicoloured	40	40	☐	☐
999	**481**	11p multicoloured	50	50	☐	☐
1000	**482**	13p multicoloured	60	60	☐	☐
		Set of 4	1·50	1·50	☐	☐
		First Day Cover		1·50		☐
		Presentation Pack	2·50		☐	
		Set of 4 Gutter Pairs	2·75		☐	
		Set of 4 Traffic Light Gutter Pairs	11·00		☐	

Bicentenary of American Revolution
1976 (2 JUNE) *'All-over' phosphor*

1005	**487**	11p multicoloured	50	50	☐	☐
		First Day Cover		1·50		☐
		Presentation Pack	1·25		☐	
		PHQ Card	4·25	20·00	☐	☐
		Gutter Pair	75		☐	
		Traffic Light Gutter Pair	4·00		☐	

483 Hewing Coal (Thomas Hepburn)   **484** Machinery (Robert Owen)

488 'Elizabeth of Glamis'   **489** 'Grandpa Dickson'

485 Chimney Cleaning (Lord Shaftesbury)   **486** Hands clutching Prison Bars (Elizabeth Fry)

Social Reformers
1976 (28 APR.) *'All-over' phosphor*

1001	**483**	8½p multicoloured	25	20	☐	☐
1002	**484**	10p multicoloured	40	40	☐	☐
1003	**485**	11p black, slate-grey and drab	50	50	☐	☐
1004	**486**	13p slate-grey, black and green	60	60	☐	☐
		Set of 4	1·50	1·50	☐	☐
		First Day Cover		1·50		☐
		Presentation Pack	2·50		☐	
		PHQ Card (No. 1001)	6·00	20·00	☐	☐
		Set of 4 Gutter Pairs	2·75		☐	
		Set of 4 Traffic Light Gutter Pairs	11·00		☐	

490 'Rosa Mundi'   **491** 'Sweet Briar'

Centenary of Royal National Rose Society
1976 (30 JUNE) *'All-over' phosphor*

1006	**488**	8½p multicoloured	15	10	☐	☐
1007	**489**	10p multicoloured	40	40	☐	☐
1008	**490**	11p multicoloured	50	50	☐	☐
1009	**491**	13p multicoloured	65	65	☐	☐
		Set of 4	1·50	1·50	☐	☐
		First Day Cover		1·50		☐
		Presentation Pack	2·50		☐	
		PHQ Cards (set of 4)	28·00	35·00	☐	☐
		Set of 4 Gutter Pairs	3·00		☐	
		Set of 4 Traffic Light Gutter Pairs	14·00		☐	

492 Archdruid

493 Morris Dancing

494 Scots Piper

495 Welsh Harpist

British Cultural Traditions

1976 (4 AUG.) *'All-over' phosphor*

1010	**492**	8½p multicoloured	25	20	□	□
1011	**493**	10p multicoloured	40	40	□	□
1012	**494**	11p multicoloured	45	45	□	□
1013	**495**	13p multicoloured	60	60	□	□
		Set of 4	1·50	1·50	□	□
		First Day Cover		2·00		□
		Presentation Pack	2·50			□
		PHQ Cards (set of 4)	18·00	28·00	□	□
		Set of 4 Gutter Pairs	3·00			□
		Set of 4 Traffic Light Gutter Pairs	13·00			□

496 The Canterbury Tales

497 The Tretyse of Love

For full information on all future British issues, collectors should write to Royal Mail, Freepost EH3647, 21 South Gyle Crescent, Edinburgh EH12 9PE.

498 Game and Playe of Chesse

499 Early Printing Press

500th Anniversary of British Printing

1976 (29 SEPT.) *'All-over' phosphor*

1014	**496**	8½p black, blue and gold .	25	20	□	□
1015	**497**	10p black, olive-green and gold	40	40	□	□
1016	**498**	11p black, grey and gold .	45	45	□	□
1017	**499**	13p brown, ochre and gold .	60	60	□	□
		Set of 4	1·50	1·50	□	□
		First Day Cover		1·75		□
		Presentation Pack	2·50			□
		PHQ Cards (set of 4)	10·00	28·00	□	□
		Set of 4 Gutter Pairs	3·00			□
		Set of 4 Traffic Light Gutter Pairs	8·00			□

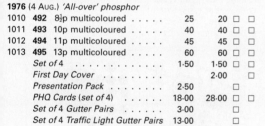

500 Virgin and Child

501 Angel with Crown

502 Angel appearing to Shepherds

503 The Three Kings

Christmas

1976 (24 NOV.) *Designs show English medieval embroidery. One phosphor band (6½p) or 'all-over' phosphor (others)*

1018	**500**	6½p multicoloured	25	25	□	□
1019	**501**	8½p multicoloured	35	25	□	□
1020	**502**	11p multicoloured	40	45	□	□

1021	**503**	13p multicoloured	45	50 ☐	☐
		Set of 4	1·25	1·25 ☐	☐
		First Day Cover		1·50	☐
		Presentation Pack	2·50		☐
		PHQ Cards (set of 4)	4·50	26·00 ☐	☐
		Set of 4 Gutter Pairs	2·75		☐
		Set of 4 Traffic Light Gutter Pairs	8·00		☐

Collectors Pack 1976
1976 (24 Nov.) Comprises Nos. 997/1021

CP1021a	Collectors Pack	13·50		☐

8½p

504 Lawn Tennis

10p

505 Table Tennis

11p

506 Squash

13p

507 Badminton

Racket Sports
1977 (12 Jan.) Phosphorised paper

1022	**504**	8½p multicoloured	25	20 ☐	☐
1023	**505**	10p multicoloured	40	40 ☐	☐
1024	**506**	11p multicoloured	45	40 ☐	☐
1025	**507**	13p multicoloured	45	50 ☐	☐
		Set of 4	1·25	1·25 ☐	☐
		First Day Cover		2·00	☐
		Presentation Pack	2·25		☐
		PHQ Cards (set of 4)	8·00	24·00 ☐	☐
		Set of 4 Gutter Pairs	3·00		☐
		Set of 4 Traffic Light Gutter Pairs	7·00		☐

£1

508

1977 (2 Feb.)–**87** Type **508** Ordinary paper

1026	£1 green and olive	3·00	25 ☐	☐
1026b	£1·30 drab and deep greenish blue	5·50	6·00 ☐	☐
1026c	£1·33 pale mauve and grey-black	7·50	7·00 ☐	☐
1026d	£1·41 drab and deep greenish blue	8·50	8·50 ☐	☐
1026e	£1·50 pale mauve and grey-black	6·00	5·00 ☐	☐
1026f	£1·60 drab and deep greenish blue	6·50	7·00 ☐	☐
1027	£2 green and brown	9·00	50 ☐	☐
1028	£5 pink and blue	22·00	3·00 ☐	☐
	Set of 8	60·00	32·00 ☐	☐
	Presentation Pack (P.O. Pack No. 91 (small size)) (Nos. 1026/8))	48·00		☐
	Presentation Pack (P.O. Pack No.13 (large size)) (Nos. 1026, 1027/8)	£160		☐
	Presentation Pack (P.O. Pack No. 14) (No. 1026f)	12·00		☐
	Set of 8 Gutter Pairs	£150		☐
	Set of 8 Traffic Light Gutter Pairs	£180		☐

First Day Covers

2 Feb. 1977	Nos. 1026, 1027/8	8·00	☐
3 Aug. 1983	No. 1026b	6·50	☐
28 Aug. 1984	No. 1026c	8·00	☐
17 Sept. 1985	No. 1026d	8·50	☐
2 Sept. 1986	No. 1026e	5·50	☐
15 Sept. 1987	No. 1026f	8·00	☐

8½p

509 Steroids — Conformational Analysis

10p

510 Vitamin C — Synthesis

11p

511 Starch — Chromatography

13p

512 Salt — Crystallography

Centenary of Royal Institute of Chemistry
1977 (2 Mar.) 'All-over' phosphor

1029	**509**	8½p multicoloured	25	20 ☐	☐
1030	**510**	10p multicoloured	45	45 ☐	☐
1031	**511**	11p multicoloured	45	45 ☐	☐

1032	**512**	13p multicoloured	45	45 ☐	☐
		Set of 4	1·25	1·25 ☐	☐
		First Day Cover		1·50	☐
		Presentation Pack	2·25	☐	
		PHQ Cards (set of 4)	8·00	18·00 ☐	☐
		Set of 4 Gutter Pairs	3·00	☐	
		Set of 4 Traffic Light Gutter Pairs	7·00	☐	

513

Silver Jubilee

1977 (11 May–15 June) *'All-over' phosphor*

1033	**513**	8½p multicoloured	25	25 ☐	☐
1034		9p multicoloured (15 June)	25	25 ☐	☐
1035		10p multicoloured	25	25 ☐	☐
1036		11p multicoloured	50	50 ☐	☐
1037		13p multicoloured	50	50 ☐	☐
		Set of 5	1·50	1·25 ☐	☐
		First Day Covers (2)		2·00	☐
		Presentation Pack (ex 9p)	2·00	☐	
		Souvenir Book (ex 9p)	3·00	☐	
		PHQ Cards (set of 5)	14·00	20·00 ☐	☐
		Set of 5 Gutter Pairs	3·50	☐	
		Set of 5 Traffic Light Gutter Pairs	7·00	☐	

517 'Gathering of Nations'

Commonwealth Heads of Government Meeting, London

1977 (8 June) *'All-over' phosphor*

1038	**517**	13p black, deep green, rose			
		and silver	50	50 ☐	☐
		First Day Cover		1·50	☐
		Presentation Pack	1·50	☐	
		PHQ Card	3·00	6·00 ☐	☐
		Gutter Pair	1·00	☐	
		Traffic Light Gutter Pair	2·00	☐	

518 Hedgehog   **519** Brown Hare

520 Red Squirrel   **521** Otter

522 Badger

T **518/22** were printed together, *se-tenant*, throughout the sheet.

British Wildlife

1977 (5 Oct.) *'All-over' phosphor*

1039	**518**	9p multicoloured	40	40 ☐	☐
		a. Strip of 5. Nos.			
		1039/43	1·40	2·10 ☐	☐
1040	**519**	9p multicoloured	25	40 ☐	☐
1041	**520**	9p multicoloured	25	40 ☐	☐
1042	**521**	9p multicoloured	25	40 ☐	☐
1043	**522**	9p multicoloured	25	40 ☐	☐
		Set of 5	1·50	1·75 ☐	☐
		First Day Cover		3·00	☐
		Presentation Pack	2·50	☐	
		PHQ Cards (set of 5)	3·00	7·00 ☐	☐
		Gutter Strip of 10	2·50	☐	
		Traffic Light Gutter Strip of 10 .	5·00	☐	

523 'Three French Hens, Two Turtle Doves and a Partridge in a Pear Tree'

524 'Six Geese a laying, Five Gold Rings, Four Colly Birds'

525 'Eight Maids a-milking, Seven Swans a-swimming'

526 'Ten Pipers piping, Nine Drummers drumming'

527 'Twelve Lords a-leaping, Eleven Ladies dancing'

528 'A Partridge in a Pear Tree'

T 523/8 depict the carol 'The Twelve Days of Christmas'.
T 523/7 were printed horizontally *se-tenant* throughout the sheet.

Christmas

1977 (23 Nov.) *One centre phosphor band* (7p) *or 'all-over' phosphor* (9p)

1044	**523**	7p multicoloured	20	15	□	□
		a. Strip of 5. Nos. 1044/8	1·50	2·00	□	□
1045	**524**	7p multicoloured	20	15	□	□
1046	**525**	7p multicoloured	20	15	□	□
1047	**526**	7p multicoloured	20	15	□	□
1048	**527**	7p multicoloured	20	15	□	□
1049	**528**	9p multicoloured	35	20	□	□
		Set of 6	1·25	90	□	□
		First Day Cover		2·00		□
		Presentation Pack	2·25			□
		PHQ Cards (set of 6)	3·00	6·00	□	□
		Set of 6 Gutter Pairs	3·00			□
		Set of 6 Traffic Light Gutter Pairs	5·00			□

Collectors Pack 1977

1977 (23 Nov.) *Comprises Nos. 1022/5, 1029/49*

CP1049b	Collectors Pack	9·50		□

529 Oil — North Sea Production Platform

530 Coal — Modern Pithead

531 Natural Gas — Flame Rising from Sea

532 Electricity — Nuclear Power Station and Uranium Atom

Energy Resources

1978 (25 Jan.) *'All-over' phosphor*

1050	**529**	9p multicoloured	25	25	□	□
1051	**530**	10½p multicoloured	25	25	□	□
1052	**531**	11p multicoloured	50	50	□	□
1053	**532**	13p multicoloured	50	50	□	□
		Set of 4	1·25	1·25	□	□
		First Day Cover		1·50		□
		Presentation Pack	2·00			□
		PHQ Cards (set of 4)	3·00	6·00	□	□
		Set of 4 Gutter Pairs	2·75			□
		Set of 4 Traffic Light Gutter Pairs	4·50			□

533 Tower of London

534 Holyroodhouse

535 Caernarvon Castle

536 Hampton Court Palace

British Architecture (Historic Buildings)

1978 (1 Mar.) *'All-over' phosphor*

1054	533	9p multicoloured	25	20	□	□
1055	534	10½p multicoloured	25	40	□	□
1056	535	11p multicoloured	60	40	□	□
1057	536	13p multicoloured	60	40	□	□
		Set of 4	1·50	1·25	□	□
		First Day Cover		1·50		□
		Presentation Pack	2·00		□	
		PHQ Cards (set of 4)	3·00	6·00	□	□
		Set of 4 Gutter Pairs	3·00		□	
		Set of 4 Traffic Light Gutter Pairs	4·50		□	
MS1058		121 × 90 mm. Nos. 1054/7 . .	1·25	1·75	□	□
		First Day Cover		2·00		□

No. **MS**1058 was sold at 53½p, the premium being used for the London 1980 Stamp Exhibition.

537 State Coach

538 St Edward's Crown

539 The Sovereign's Orb

540 Imperial State Crown

25th Anniversary of Coronation

1978 (31 May) *'All-over' phosphor*

1059	537	9p gold and blue	35	25	□	□
1060	538	10½p gold and red	45	45	□	□
1061	539	11p gold and green	45	45	□	□
1062	540	13p gold and violet	50	50	□	□
		Set of 4	1·50	1·50	□	□
		First Day Cover		1·50		□
		Presentation Pack	2·00		□	
		Souvenir Book	3·00		□	
		PHQ Cards (set of 4)	3·00	6·00	□	□
		Set of 4 Gutter Pairs	3·00		□	
		Set of 4 Traffic Light Gutter Pairs	4·25		□	

541 Shire Horse

542 Shetland Pony

543 Welsh Pony

544 Thoroughbred

Horses

1978 (5 July) *'All-over' phosphor*

1063	541	9p multicoloured	20	10	□	□
1064	542	10½p multicoloured	35	40	□	□
1065	543	11p multicoloured	35	45	□	□
1066	544	13p multicoloured	45	50	□	□
		Set of 4	1·25	1·25	□	□
		First Day Cover		1·50		□
		Presentation Pack	1·75		□	
		PHQ Cards (set of 4)	2·25	5·75	□	□
		Set of 4 Gutter Pairs	3·00		□	
		Set of 4 Traffic Light Gutter Pairs	4·50		□	

545 Penny-farthing and 1884 Safety Bicycle

546 1920 Touring Bicycles

547 Modern Small-wheel Bicycles

548 1978 Road-racers

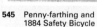

Centenaries of Cyclists Touring Club and British Cycling Federation

1978 (2 Aug.) *'All-over' phosphor*

1067	**545**	9p multicoloured	25	20	☐	☐
1068	**546**	10½p multicoloured	35	40	☐	☐
1069	**547**	11p multicoloured	40	40	☐	☐
1070	**548**	13p multicoloured	50	50	☐	☐
		Set of 4	1·25	1·25	☐	☐
		First Day Cover		1·50		☐
		Presentation Pack	1·75		☐	
		PHQ Cards (set of 4)	2·25	5·00	☐	☐
		Set of 4 Gutter Pairs	2·75		☐	
		Set of 4 Traffic Light Gutter Pairs	4·50		☐	

549 Singing Carols round the Christmas Tree

550 The Waits

551 18th-Century Carol Singers

552 'The Boar's Head Carol'

Christmas

1978 (22 Nov.) *One centre phosphor band (7p) or 'all-over' phosphor (others)*

1071	**549**	7p multicoloured	25	25	☐	☐
1072	**550**	9p multicoloured	25	25	☐	☐
1073	**551**	11p multicoloured	50	50	☐	☐
1074	**552**	13p multicoloured	50	50	☐	☐
		Set of 4	1·25	1·25	☐	☐
		First Day Cover		1·50		☐
		Presentation Pack	1·75		☐	
		PHQ Cards (set of 4)	2·25	5·00	☐	☐
		Set of 4 Gutter Pairs	2·50		☐	
		Set of 4 Traffic Light Gutter Pairs	4·25		☐	

Collectors Pack 1978

1978 (22 Nov.) *Comprises Nos. 1050/7, 1059/74*

CP1074a	*Collectors Pack*	9·25		☐

553 Old English Sheepdog

554 Welsh Springer Spaniel

555 West Highland Terrier

556 Irish Setter

Dogs

1979 (7 Feb.) *'All-over' phosphor*

1075	**553**	9p multicoloured	25	20	☐	☐
1076	**554**	10½p multicoloured	40	40	☐	☐
1077	**555**	11p multicoloured	40	40	☐	☐
1078	**556**	13p multicoloured	40	50	☐	☐
		Set of 4	1·25	1·25	☐	☐
		First Day Cover		1·50		☐
		Presentation Pack	1·75		☐	
		PHQ Cards (set of 4)	2·50	5·00	☐	☐
		Set of 4 Gutter Pairs	7·50		☐	
		Set of 4 Traffic Light Gutter Pairs	4·25		☐	

557 Primrose

558 Daffodil

559 Bluebell

560 Snowdrop

Spring Wild Flowers

1979 (21 Mar.) *'All-over' phosphor*

1079	**557**	9p multicoloured	25	20	☐	☐
1080	**558**	10½p multicoloured	25	45	☐	☐
1081	**559**	11p multicoloured	50	45	☐	☐
1082	**560**	13p multicoloured	50	40	☐	☐
		Set of 4	1·25	1·25	☐	☐
		First Day Cover		1·50		☐
		Presentation Pack	1·75		☐	
		PHQ Cards (set of 4)	2·50	4·50	☐	☐
		Set of 4 Gutter Pairs	2·50		☐	
		Set of 4 Traffic Light Gutter Pairs	4·25		☐	

561

562

563

564

T **561/4** show hands placing the flags of the member nations into ballot boxes.

First Direct Elections to European Assembly

1979 (9 May) *Phosphorised paper*

1083	**561**	9p multicoloured	25	20	☐	☐
1084	**562**	10½p multicoloured	35	35	☐	☐
1085	**563**	11p multicoloured	40	40	☐	☐
1086	**564**	13p multicoloured	45	40	☐	☐
		Set of 4	1·25	1·25	☐	☐
		First Day Cover		1·50		☐
		Presentation Pack	1·75		☐	
		PHQ Cards (set of 4)	2·25	4·50	☐	☐
		Set of 4 Gutter Pairs	2·50		☐	
		Set of 4 Traffic Light Gutter Pairs	4·25		☐	

565 'Saddling "Mahmoud" for the Derby, 1936' (Sir Alfred Munnings)

566 'The Liverpool Great National Steeple Chase, 1839' (aquatint by F. C. Turner)

567 'The First Spring Meeting, Newmarket, 1793' (J. N. Sartorius)

568 'Racing at Dorsett Ferry, Windsor, 1684' (Francis Barlow)

Horseracing Paintings and Bicentenary of The Derby (9p)

1979 (6 June) *'All-over' phosphor*

1087	**565**	9p multicoloured	25	25	☐	☐
1088	**566**	10½p multicoloured	25	25	☐	☐
1089	**567**	11p multicoloured	50	50	☐	☐
1090	**568**	13p multicoloured	50	50	☐	☐
		Set of 4	1·25	1·25	☐	☐
		First Day Cover		1·50		☐
		Presentation Pack	1·75		☐	
		PHQ Cards (set of 4)	2·25	4·50	☐	☐
		Set of 4 Gutter Pairs	2·50		☐	
		Set of 4 Traffic Light Gutter Pairs	4·25		☐	

569 The Tale of Peter Rabbit (Beatrix Potter)

570 The Wind in the Willows (Kenneth Grahame)

571 Winnie-the-Pooh (A. A. Milne)

572 Alice's Adventures in in Wonderland (Lewis Carroll)

T **569/72** depict original illustrations from the four books.

International Year of the Child
1979 (11 JULY) *'All-over' phosphor*

1091	**569**	9p multicoloured	30	25 ☐	☐
1092	**570**	10½p multicoloured	35	35 ☐	☐
1093	**571**	11p multicoloured	40	40 ☐	☐
1094	**572**	13p multicoloured	60	60 ☐	☐
		Set of 4	1·50	1·50 ☐	☐
		First Day Cover		1·50	☐
		Presentation Pack	2·00		☐
		PHQ Cards (set of 4)	2·50	4·50 ☐	☐
		Set of 4 Gutter Pairs	3·00		☐
		Set of 4 Traffic Light Gutter Pairs	4·25		☐

573 Sir Rowland Hill, 1795–1879

574 General Post, *c* 1839

575 London Post, *c* 1839

576 Uniform Postage, 1840

Death Centenary of Sir Rowland Hill (postal reformer)
1979 (22 AUG.–24 OCT.) *'All-over' phosphor*

1095	**573**	10p multicoloured	25	20 ☐	☐
1096	**574**	11½p multicoloured	25	35 ☐	☐
1097	**575**	13p multicoloured	50	45 ☐	☐
1098	**576**	15p multicoloured	75	50 ☐	☐
		Set of 4	1·50	1·50 ☐	☐
		First Day Cover		1·50	☐
		Presentation Pack	1·50		☐
		PHQ Cards (set of 4)	2·25	4·25 ☐	☐
		Set of 4 Gutter Pairs	3·00		☐
		Set of 4 Traffic Light Gutter Pairs	4·25		☐
MS1099	89 × 121 mm. Nos. 1095/8 . .		1·25	1·50 ☐	☐
		First Day Cover (24 Oct.)		1·50	☐

No. **MS**1099 was sold at 59½p, the premium being used for the London 1980 Stamp Exhibition.

577 Policeman on the Beat

578 Policeman directing Traffic

579 Mounted Policewoman

580 River Patrol Boat

150th Anniversary of Metropolitan Police
1979 (26 SEPT.) *Phosphorised paper*

1100	**577**	10p multicoloured	30	20 ☐	☐
1101	**578**	11½p multicoloured	35	35 ☐	☐
1102	**579**	13p multicoloured	40	55 ☐	☐
1103	**580**	15p multicoloured	60	55 ☐	☐
		Set of 4	1·50	1·50 ☐	☐
		First Day Cover		1·50	☐
		Presentation Pack	1·75		☐
		PHQ Cards (set of 4)	2·25	4·25 ☐	☐
		Set of 4 Gutter Pairs	3·00		☐
		Set of 4 Traffic Light Gutter Pairs	4·25		☐

581 The Three Kings

582 Angel appearing to the Shepherds

583 The Nativity

584 Mary and Joseph travelling to Bethlehem

585 The Annunciation

Christmas

1979 (21 Nov.) *One centre phosphor band (8p) or phosphorised paper (others)*

1104	581	8p multicoloured	25	20	☐	☐
1105	582	10p multicoloured	25	25	☐	☐
1106	583	11½p multicoloured	25	35	☐	☐
1107	584	13p multicoloured	50	50	☐	☐
1108	585	15p multicoloured	50	50	☐	☐
		Set of 5	1·50	1·50	☐	☐
		First Day Cover		1·50		☐
		Presentation Pack	2·00		☐	
		PHQ Cards (set of 5)	2·50	4·25	☐	☐
		Set of 5 Gutter Pairs	3·50		☐	
		Set of 5 Traffic Light Gutter Pairs	4·50		☐	

Collectors Pack 1979

1979 (21 Nov.) *Comprises Nos. 1075/98, 1100/8*

CP1108a	Collectors Pack	12·00	☐

586 Common Kingfisher

587 Dipper

588 Moorhen

589 Yellow Wagtails

Centenary of Wild Bird Protection Act

1980 (16 Jan.) *Phosphorised paper*

1109	586	10p multicoloured	20	10	☐	☐
1110	587	11½p multicoloured	40	35	☐	☐

1111	588	13p multicoloured	50	55	☐	☐
1112	589	15p multicoloured	50	55	☐	☐
		Set of 4	1·50	1·50	☐	☐
		First Day Cover		1·50		☐
		Presentation Pack	1·50		☐	
		PHQ Cards (set of 4)	2·25	4·50	☐	☐
		Set of 4 Gutter Pairs	3·50		☐	

590 *Rocket* approaching Moorish Arch, Liverpool

591 First and Second Class Carriages passing through Olive Mount Cutting

592 Third Class Carriage and Sheep Truck crossing Chat Moss

593 Horsebox and Carriage Truck near Bridgewater Canal

594 Goods Truck and Mail-coach at Manchester

T **590**/4 were printed together, *se-tenant,* in horizontal strips of 5 throughout the sheet.

150th Anniversary of Liverpool and Manchester Railway

1980 (12 Mar.) *Phosphorised paper*

1113	590	12p multicoloured	40	40	☐	☐
		a. Strip of 5. Nos. 1113/17	1·75	1·75	☐	☐
1114	591	12p multicoloured	40	40	☐	☐
1115	592	12p multicoloured	40	40	☐	☐
1116	593	12p multicoloured	40	40	☐	☐
1117	594	12p multicoloured	40	40	☐	☐
		Set of 5	1·75	1·50	☐	☐
		First Day Cover		1·75		☐
		Presentation Pack	2·00		☐	
		PHQ Cards (set of 5)	4·25	4·50	☐	☐
		Gutter block of 10	3·75		☐	

595 Montage of London Buildings

'London 1980' International Stamp Exhibition

1980 (9 APR.–7 MAY) *Phosphorised paper. Perf 14½ × 14*

1118	**595**	50p agate	1·50	1·50	☐	☐
		First Day Cover		1·50		☐
		Presentation Pack	1·75		☐	
		PHQ Card	2·25	3·00	☐	☐
		Gutter Pair	3·25		☐	
MS1119		90 × 123 mm. No. 1118 . . .	1·50	1·75	☐	☐
		First Day Cover (7 May)		2·00		☐

No. **MS**1119 was sold at 75p, the premium being used for the exhibition.

10½P Buckingham Palace

12P The Albert Memorial

596 Buckingham Palace   597 The Albert Memorial

13½P Royal Opera House

15P Hampton Court

598 Royal Opera House   599 Hampton Court

17½P Kensington Palace

600 Kensington Palace

London Landmarks

1980 (7 MAY) *Phosphorised paper*

1120	**596**	10½p multicoloured	25	10	☐	☐
1121	**597**	12p multicoloured	25	15	☐	☐
1122	**598**	13½p multicoloured	40	50	☐	☐
1123	**599**	15p multicoloured	50	75	☐	☐
1124	**600**	17½p multicoloured	75	75	☐	☐
		Set of 5	2·00	2·00	☐	☐
		First Day Cover		2·00		
		Presentation Pack	2·00		☐	
		PHQ Cards (*set of 5*)	2·25	3·00	☐	☐
		Set of 5 Gutter Pairs	4·25		☐	

12P

13½P

601 Charlotte Brontë (*Jane Eyre*)   602 George Eliot (*The Mill on the Floss*)

15P

17½P

603 Emily Brontë (*Wuthering Heights*)   604 Mrs Gaskell (*North and South*)

T **601/4** show authoresses and scenes from their novels. T **601/2** also include the 'Europa' C.E.P.T. emblem.

Famous Authoresses

1980 (9 JULY) *Phosphorised paper*

1125	**601**	12p multicoloured	35	20	☐	☐
1126	**602**	13½p multicoloured	40	45	☐	☐
1127	**603**	15p multicoloured	50	45	☐	☐
1128	**604**	17½p multicoloured	50	50	☐	☐
		Set of 4	1·50	1·50	☐	☐
		First Day Cover		1·50		☐
		Presentation Pack	2·00		☐	
		PHQ Cards (*set of 4*)	2·50	3·00	☐	☐
		Set of 4 Gutter Pairs	3·75		☐	

605 Queen Elizabeth the Queen Mother

80th Birthday of Queen Elizabeth the Queen Mother
1980 (4 Aug.) *Phosphorised paper*

1129	**605**	12p multicoloured	75	75	☐	☐
		First Day Cover		1·50		☐
		PHQ Card	2·25	1·75	☐	☐
		Gutter Pair	1·50		☐

606 Sir Henry Wood

607 Sir Thomas Beecham

608 Sir Malcolm Sargent

609 Sir John Barbirolli

British Conductors
1980 (10 Sept.) *Phosphorised paper*

1130	**606**	12p multicoloured	30	10	☐	☐
1131	**607**	13½p multicoloured	45	40	☐	☐
1132	**608**	15p multicoloured	50	55	☐	☐
1133	**609**	17½p multicoloured	50	55	☐	☐
		Set of 4	1·50	1·50	☐	☐
		First Day Cover		1·75		☐
		Presentation Pack	2·00		☐
		PHQ Cards (set of 4)	2·25	3·75	☐	☐
		Set of 4 Gutter Pairs	3·75		☐

For full information on all future British issues, collectors should write to Royal Mail, Freepost EH3647, 21 South Gyle Crescent, Edinburgh EH12 9PE.

610 Running

611 Rugby

612 Boxing

613 Cricket

Sports Centenaries
1980 (10 Oct.) *Phosphorised paper. Perf* 14 × 14½

1134	**610**	12p multicoloured	25	20	☐	☐
1135	**611**	13½p multicoloured	50	50	☐	☐
1136	**612**	15p multicoloured	50	45	☐	☐
1137	**613**	17½p multicoloured	50	50	☐	☐
		Set of 4	1·50	1·50	☐	☐
		First Day Cover		1·75		☐
		Presentation Pack	2·00		☐
		PHQ Cards (set of 4)	2·25	3·75	☐	☐
		Set of 4 Gutter Pairs	3·75		☐

Centenaries:—12p Amateur Athletics Association; 13½p Welsh Rugby Union; 15p Amateur Boxing Association; 17½p First England v Australia Test Match.

614 Christmas Tree

615 Candles

616 Apples and Mistletoe

617 Crown, Chains and Bell

618 Holly

Christmas

1980 (19 Nov.) *One centre phosphor band* (10p) *or phosphorised paper* (*others*)

1138	**614**	10p multicoloured	20	10 □ □
1139	**615**	12p multicoloured	20	20 □ □
1140	**616**	13½p multicoloured	40	40 □ □
1141	**617**	15p multicoloured	55	50 □ □
1142	**618**	17½p multicoloured	55	50 □ □
		Set of 5	1·75	1·50 □ □
		First Day Cover		1·75 □
		Presentation Pack	2·00	□
		PHQ Cards (*set of 5*)	2·25	4·00 □ □
		Set of 5 Gutter Pairs	4·50	□

Collectors Pack 1980

1980 (19 Nov.) *Comprises Nos. 1109/18, 1120/42*

CP1142*a* *Collectors Pack* . . . . 15·00 □

619 St Valentine's Day   620 Morris Dancers

621 Lammastide   622 Medieval Mummers

T **619/20** also include the 'Europa' C.E.P.T. emblem.

Folklore

1981 (6 Feb.) *Phosphorised paper*

1143	**619**	14p multicoloured	25	25 □ □
1144	**620**	18p multicoloured	50	50 □ □
1145	**621**	22p multicoloured	75	80 □ □
1146	**622**	25p multicoloured	1·00	1·10 □ □
		Set of 4	2·25	2·50 □ □
		First Day Cover		2·00 □
		Presentation Pack	2·25	□
		PHQ Cards (*set of 4*)	2·25	3·25 □ □
		Set of 4 Gutter Pairs	5·25	□

623 Blind Man with Guide Dog   624 Hands spelling 'Deaf' in Sign Language

625 Disabled Man in Wheelchair   626 Disabled Artist painting with Foot

International Year of the Disabled

1981 (25 Mar.) *Phosphorised paper*

1147	**623**	14p multicoloured	50	25 □ □
1148	**624**	18p multicoloured	50	50 □ □
1149	**625**	22p multicoloured	75	85 □ □
1150	**626**	25p multicoloured	1·00	1·00 □ □
		Set of 4	2·25	2·50 □ □
		First Day Cover		2·00 □
		Presentation Pack	2·25	□
		PHQ Cards (*set of 4*)	2·25	3·25 □ □
		Set of 4 Gutter Pairs	4·25	□

627 *Aglais urticae*   628 *Maculinea arion*

629 *Inachis io*   630 *Carterocephalus palaemon*

Butterflies

1981 (13 MAY) *Phosphorised paper*

1151	**627**	14p multicoloured	25	20	☐	☐
1152	**628**	18p multicoloured	75	70	☐	☐
1153	**629**	22p multicoloured	70	85	☐	☐
1154	**630**	25p multicoloured	75	85	☐	☐
		Set of 4	2·25	2·50	☐	☐
		First Day Cover		2·00		☐
		Presentation Pack	2·25		☐	
		PHQ Cards (set of 4)	2·25	6·00	☐	☐
		Set of 4 Gutter Pairs	4·75		☐	

631 Glenfinnan, Scotland

632 Derwentwater, England

633 Stackpole Head, Wales

634 Giant's Causeway, N. Ireland

635 St Kilda, Scotland

50th Anniversary of National Trust for Scotland (British landscapes)

1981 (24 JUNE) *Phosphorised paper*

1155	**631**	14p multicoloured	15	25	☐	☐
1156	**632**	18p multicoloured	45	50	☐	☐
1157	**633**	20p multicoloured	70	75	☐	☐
1158	**634**	22p multicoloured	75	1·00	☐	☐
1159	**635**	25p multicoloured	90	1·25	☐	☐
		Set of 5	2·50	3·25	☐	☐
		First Day Cover		2·25		☐
		Presentation Pack	3·00		☐	
		PHQ Cards (set of 5)	2·50	5·00	☐	☐
		Set of 5 Gutter Pairs	6·00		☐	

636 Prince Charles and Lady Diana Spencer

Royal Wedding

1981 (22 JULY) *Phosphorised paper*

1160	**636**	14p multicoloured	65	25	☐	☐
1161		25p multicoloured	1·25	1·50	☐	☐
		Set of 2	1·90	1·50	☐	☐
		First Day Cover		2·75		☐
		Presentation Pack	3·00		☐	
		Souvenir Book	3·00		☐	
		PHQ Cards (set of 2)	2·50	5·00	☐	☐
		Set of 2 Gutter Pairs	4·00		☐	

637 'Expeditions'

638 'Skills'

639 'Service'

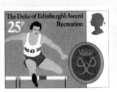

640 'Recreation'

25th Anniversary of Duke of Edinburgh's Award Scheme

1981 (12 AUG.) *Phosphorised paper. Perf 14*

1162	**637**	14p multicoloured	25	20	☐	☐
1163	**638**	18p multicoloured	45	50	☐	☐
1164	**639**	22p multicoloured	70	70	☐	☐
1165	**640**	25p multicoloured	80	80	☐	☐
		Set of 4	2·00	2·00	☐	☐
		First Day Cover		2·00		☐
		Presentation Pack	2·50		☐	
		PHQ Cards (set of 4)	4·25	4·50	☐	☐
		Set of 4 Gutter Pairs	5·00		☐	

641 Cockle-dredging from Linsey II

642 Hauling Trawl Net

643 Lobster Potting

644 Hoisting Seine Net

Fishing Industry

1981 (23 SEPT.) *Phosphorised paper*

1166	**641**	14p multicoloured	. . . . .	25	25	□	□
1167	**642**	18p multicoloured	. . . . .	50	50	□	□
1168	**643**	22p multicoloured	. . . . .	85	85	□	□
1169	**644**	25p multicoloured	. . . . .	85	85	□	□
		Set of 4	. . . .	2·25	2·50	□	□
		First Day Cover	. . . .		2·00		□
		Presentation Pack	. . . .	2·50			□
		PHQ Cards (set of 4)	. . . . . .	2·25	4·50	□	□
		Set of 4 Gutter Pairs	. . . . . .	5·00			□

Nos. 1166/9 were issued on the occasion of the centenary of Royal National Mission to Deep Sea Fishermen.

Samantha Brown, age 5

Tracy Jenkins, age 14

645 Father Christmas

646 Jesus Christ

Lucinda Blackmore, age 6

Stephen Moore, age 16

647 Flying Angel

648 Joseph and Mary arriving at Bethlehem

Sophie Sharp, age 8

649 Three Kings approaching Bethlehem

Christmas. Children's Pictures

1981 (18 Nov.) *One phosphor band (11½p) or phosphorised paper (others)*

1170	**645**	11½p multicoloured	. . . . .	25	20	□	□
1171	**646**	14p multicoloured	. . . . .	35	20	□	□
1172	**647**	18p multicoloured	. . . . .	50	60	□	□
1173	**648**	22p multicoloured	. . . . .	75	75	□	□
1174	**649**	25p multicoloured	. . . . .	85	85	□	□
		Set of 5	. . . .	2·50	2·50	□	□
		First Day Cover	. . . .		2·00		□
		Presentation Pack	. . . .	3·00			□
		PHQ Cards (set of 5)	. . . . . .	2·25	5·50	□	□
		Set of 5 Gutter Pairs	. . . . . .	5·50			□

Collectors Pack 1981

1981 (18 Nov.) *Comprises Nos. 1143/74*

CP1174a Collectors Pack . . . . 17·50 □

650 Charles Darwin and Giant Tortoises

651 Darwin and Marine Iguanas

652 Darwin, Cactus Ground Finch and Large Ground Finch

653 Darwin and Prehistoric Skulls

Death Centenary of Charles Darwin

1982 (10 FEB.) *Phosphorised paper*

1175	**650**	15½p multicoloured	. . . . .	50	20	□	□
1176	**651**	19½p multicoloured	. . . . .	50	60	□	□
1177	**652**	26p multicoloured	. . . . .	75	85	□	□
1178	**653**	29p multicoloured	. . . . .	75	90	□	□
		Set of 4	. . . .	2·25	2·50	□	□
		First Day Cover	. . . .		2·25		□
		Presentation Pack	. . . .	3·00			□
		PHQ Cards (set of 4)	. . . . . .	2·50	6·00	□	□
		Set of 4 Gutter Pairs	. . . . . .	5·25			□

654 Boys' Brigade

655 Girls' Brigade

656 Boy Scout Movement

657 Girl Guide Movement

Youth Organizations

1982 (24 Mar.) *Phosphorised paper*

1179	**654**	15½p multicoloured	25		15	☐	☐
1180	**655**	19½p multicoloured	50		55	☐	☐
1181	**656**	26p multicoloured	85		85	☐	☐
1182	**657**	29p multicoloured	1·00		1·10	☐	☐
		Set of 4	2·50		2·50	☐	☐
		First Day Cover			2·25		☐
		Presentation Pack	3·00				☐
		PHQ Cards (set of 4)	2·50		6·00	☐	☐
		Set of 4 Gutter Pairs	5·50				☐

Nos. 1179/82 were issued on the occasion of the 75th anniversary of the Boy Scout Movement, the 125th birth anniversary of Lord Baden-Powell and the centenary of the Boys' Brigade (1983).

658 Ballerina

659 Harlequin

660 Hamlet

661 Opera Singer

Europa. British Theatre

1982 (28 Apr.) *Phosphorised paper*

1183	**658**	15½p multicoloured	25		15	☐	☐
1184	**659**	19½p multicoloured	50		50	☐	☐
1185	**660**	26p multicoloured	1·00		1·00	☐	☐
1186	**661**	29p multicoloured	1·00		1·00	☐	☐
		Set of 4	2·50		2·50	☐	☐
		First Day Cover			2·25		☐
		Presentation Pack	3·00				☐
		PHQ Cards (set of 4)	2·50		6·00	☐	☐
		Set of 4 Gutter Pairs	8·00				☐

662 Henry VIII and Mary Rose

663 Admiral Blake and Triumph

664 Lord Nelson and HMS *Victory*

665 Lord Fisher and HMS *Dreadnought*

666 Viscount Cunningham and HMS *Warspite*

Maritime Heritage

1982 (16 JUNE) *Phosphorised paper*

1187	**662**	15½p multicoloured	35	25	☐	☐
1188	**663**	19½p multicoloured	50	50	☐	☐
1189	**664**	24p multicoloured	75	85	☐	☐
1190	**665**	26p multicoloured	75	85	☐	☐
1191	**666**	29p multicoloured	1·00	1·00	☐	☐
		Set of 5	3·00	3·50	☐	☐
		First Day Cover		2·50		☐
		Presentation Pack	3·50		☐	
		PHQ Cards (set of 5)	2·50	6·00	☐	☐
		Set of 5 *Gutter Pairs*	7·00		☐	

667 'Strawberry Thief'
(William Morris)

668 Untitled
(Steiner and Co)

669 'Cherry Orchard'
(Paul Nash)

670 'Chevron'
(Andrew Foster)

British Textiles

1982 (23 JULY) *Phosphorised paper*

1192	**667**	15½p multicoloured	25	25	☐	☐
1193	**668**	19½p multicoloured	75	75	☐	☐
1194	**669**	26p multicoloured	75	1·00	☐	☐
1195	**670**	29p multicoloured	1·00	1·25	☐	☐
		Set of 4	2·50	2·75	☐	☐
		First Day Cover		2·50		☐
		Presentation Pack	2·75		☐	
		PHQ Cards (set of 4)	2·50	6·00	☐	☐
		Set of 4 *Gutter Pairs*	5·50		☐	

Nos 1192/5 were issued on the occasion of the 250th birth anniversary of Sir Richard Arkwright (inventor of spinning machine).

For full information on all future British issues, collectors should write to Royal Mail, Freepost EH3647, 21 South Gyle Crescent, Edinburgh EH12 9PE.

671 Development of Communications

672 Modern Technological Aids

Information Technology

1982 (8 SEPT.) *Phosphorised paper. Perf* 14 × 15

1196	**671**	15½p multicoloured	75	25	☐	☐
1197	**672**	26p multicoloured	50	1·00	☐	☐
		Set of 2	1·25	1·25	☐	☐
		First Day Cover		1·75		☐
		Presentation Pack	1·50		☐	
		PHQ Cards (set of 2)	2·00	5·25	☐	☐
		Set of 2 *Gutter Pairs*	2·75		☐	

673 Austin 'Seven' and
'Metro'

674 Ford 'Model T' and
'Escort'

675 Jaguar 'SS1' and 'XJ6'

676 Rolls-Royce 'Silver
Ghost' and 'Silver Spirit'

British Motor Industry

1982 (13 OCT.) *Phosphorised paper. Perf* 14½ × 14

1198	**673**	15½p multicoloured	50	25	☐	☐
1199	**674**	19½p multicoloured	75	75	☐	☐
1200	**675**	26p multicoloured	75	75	☐	☐
1201	**676**	29p multicoloured	1·00	1·00	☐	☐
		Set of 4	2·50	2·50	☐	☐
		First Day Cover		2·50		☐
		Presentation Pack	3·00		☐	
		PHQ Cards (set of 4)	2·50	6·00	☐	☐
		Set of 4 *Gutter Pairs*	6·25		☐	

677 'While Shepherds Watched'

678 'The Holly and the Ivy'

679 'I Saw Three Ships'

680 'We Three Kings'

681 'Good King Wenceslas'

Christmas. Carols

1982 (17 Nov.) *One phosphor band (12½p) or phosphorised paper (others).*

1202	**677**	12½p multicoloured	. . . . .	25	20 □	□
1203	**678**	15½p multicoloured	. . . . .	50	20 □	□
1204	**679**	19½p multicoloured	. . . . .	65	75 □	□
1205	**680**	26p multicoloured	. . . . .	75	80 □	□
1206	**681**	29p multicoloured	. . . . .	1·00	90 □	□
		Set of 5	. . . .	3·00	2·50 □	□
		First Day Cover	. . . .		2·50	□
		Presentation Pack	. . . .	3·25		□
		PHQ Cards (set of 5)	. . . . .	2·50	6·00 □	□
		Set of 5 Gutter Pairs	. . . . . .	5·25		□

Collectors Pack 1982

1982 (17 Nov.) *Comprises Nos.* 1175/1206
CP1206a   Collectors Pack   . . . .   26·00   □

682 Atlantic Salmon   **683** Northern Pike

684 Brown Trout   **685** Eurasian Perch

British River Fishes

1983 (26 Jan.) *Phosphorised paper*

1207	**682**	15½p multicoloured	. . . . .	30	10 □	□
1208	**683**	19½p multicoloured	. . . . .	60	60 □	□
1209	**684**	26p multicoloured	. . . . .	75	85 □	□
1210	**685**	29p multicoloured	. . . . .	1·00	1·10 □	□
		Set of 4	. . . .	2·50	2·50 □	□
		First Day Cover	. . . .		2·50	□
		Presentation Pack	. . . .	2·75		□
		PHQ Cards (set of 4)	. . . . .	3·00	7·00 □	□
		Set of 4 Gutter Pairs	. . . . . .	5·00		□

686 Tropical Island   **687** Desert

688 Temperate Farmland   **689** Mountain Range

Commonwealth Day. Geographical Regions

1983 (9 Mar.) *Phosphorised paper*

1211	**686**	15½p multicoloured	. . . . .	40	25 □	□
1212	**687**	19½p multicoloured	. . . . .	75	75 □	□
1213	**688**	26p multicoloured	. . . . .	75	75 □	□
1214	**689**	29p multicoloured	. . . . .	1·00	1·00 □	□
		Set of 4	. . . .	2·50	2·50 □	□
		First Day Cover	. . . .		2·50	□
		Presentation Pack	. . . .	3·00		□
		PHQ Cards (set of 4)	. . . . .	2·50	6·50 □	□
		Set of 4 Gutter Pairs	. . . . . .	6·00		□

690 Humber Bridge

691 Thames Flood Barrier

692 *Iolair* (oilfield emergency support vessel)

697 Paratroopers, The Parachute Regiment (1983)

British Army Uniforms
1983 (6 JULY) *Phosphorised paper*

1218	**693** 16p multicoloured	50	10	□	□
1219	**694** 20½p multicoloured	50	60	□	□
1220	**695** 26p multicoloured	75	90	□	□
1221	**696** 28p multicoloured	75	90	□	□
1222	**697** 31p multicoloured	75	85	□	□
	Set of 5	3·00	3·25	□	□
	First Day Cover		3·00	□	
	Presentation Pack	3·50		□	
	PHQ Cards (set of 5)	3·50	6·50	□	□
	Set of 5 Gutter Pairs	7·50		□	

Nos. 1218/22 were issued on the occasion of the 350th anniversary of The Royal Scots, the senior line regiment of the British Army.

Europa. Engineering Achievements
1983 (25 MAY) *Phosphorised paper*

1215	**690** 16p multicoloured	50	25	□	□
1216	**691** 20½p multicoloured	1·00	1·00	□	□
1217	**692** 28p multicoloured	1·00	1·00	□	□
	Set of 3	2·25	2·00	□	□
	First Day Cover		2·25	□	
	Presentation Pack	2·50		□	
	PHQ Cards (set of 3)	2·50	5·75	□	□
	Set of 3 Gutter Pairs	7·00		□	

693 Musketeer and Pikeman, The Royal Scots (1633)

694 Fusilier and Ensign, The Royal Welch Fusiliers (mid-18th century)

698 20th-Century Garden, Sissinghurst

699 19th-Century Garden, Biddulph Grange

695 Riflemen, 95th Rifles (The Royal Green Jackets) (1805)

696 Sergeant (khaki service uniform) and Guardsman full dress), The Irish Guards (1900).

700 18th-Century Garden, Blenheim

701 17th-Century Garden, Pitmedden

British Gardens

1983 (24 Aug.) *Phosphorised paper. Perf* 14

1223	**698**	16p multicoloured	50	10	☐	☐
1224	**699**	20½p multicoloured	50	55	☐	☐
1225	**700**	28p multicoloured	75	90	☐	☐
1226	**701**	31p multicoloured	1·00	90	☐	☐
		Set of 4	2·50	2·25	☐	☐
		First Day Cover		2·25		☐
		Presentation Pack	3·00		☐	
		PHQ Cards (*set of 4*)	3·00	6·25	☐	☐
		Set of 4 Gutter Pairs	6·00		☐	

702   Merry-go-round

703   Big Wheel, Helter-skelter
        and Performing Animals

704   Side-shows

705   Early Produce Fair

British Fairs

1983 (5 Oct.) *Phosphorised paper*

1227	**702**	16p multicoloured	35	25	☐	☐
1228	**703**	20½p multicoloured	75	75	☐	☐
1229	**704**	28p multicoloured	75	1·00	☐	☐
1230	**705**	31p multicoloured	1·00	1·00	☐	☐
		Set of 4	2·50	2·75	☐	☐
		First Day Cover		2·50		☐
		Presentation Pack	3·00		☐	
		PHQ Cards (*set of 4*)	3·00	6·25	☐	☐
		Set of 4 Gutter Pairs	6·00		☐	

Nos. 1227/30 were issued to mark the 850th anniversary of St Bartholomew's Fair, Smithfield, London.

706   'Christmas Post'
        (pillar-box)

707   'The Three Kings'
        (chimney-pots)

708   'World at Peace'
        (Dove and Blackbird)

709   'Light of Christmas'
        (street lamp)

710   'Christmas Dove'
        (hedge sculpture)

Christmas

1983 (16 Nov.) *One phosphor band* (12½p) *or phosphorised paper* (*others*)

1231	**706**	12½p multicoloured	25	25	☐	☐
1232	**707**	16p multicoloured	50	25	☐	☐
1233	**708**	20½p multicoloured	75	1·00	☐	☐
1234	**709**	28p multicoloured	75	1·00	☐	☐
1235	**710**	31p multicoloured	1·25	1·25	☐	☐
		Set of 5	3·25	3·25	☐	☐
		First Day Cover		2·75		☐
		Presentation Pack	3·50		☐	
		PHQ Cards (*set of 5*)	3·00	6·25	☐	☐
		Set of 5 Gutter Pairs	6·50		☐	

Collectors Pack 1983

1983 (16 Nov.) *Comprises Nos.* 1207/35

CP1235*a*	Collectors Pack	32·00		☐

711   Arms of the
        College of Arms

712   Arms of King Richard III
        (founder)

713   Arms of the
        Earl Marshal of England

714   Arms of the
        City of London

500th Anniversary of College of Arms

1984 (17 JAN.) *Phosphorised paper. Perf 14½*

1236	**711**	16p multicoloured	50	15	☐	☐
1237	**712**	20½p multicoloured	50	65	☐	☐
1238	**713**	28p multicoloured	1·00	1·10	☐	☐
1239	**714**	31p multicoloured	1·25	1·25	☐	☐
		Set of 4	3·00	3·00	☐	☐
		First Day Cover		2·75		☐
		Presentation Pack	3·25		☐	
		PHQ Cards (set of 4)	3·00	6·50	☐	☐
		Set of 4 Gutter Pairs	6·25		☐	

715 Highland Cow

716 Chillingham Wild Bull

717 Hereford Bull

718 Welsh Black Bull

719 Irish Moiled Cow

British Cattle

1984 (6 MAR.) *Phosphorised paper*

1240	**715**	16p multicoloured	35	15	☐	☐
1241	**716**	20½p multicoloured	55	60	☐	☐
1242	**717**	26p multicoloured	75	75	☐	☐
1243	**718**	28p multicoloured	75	85	☐	☐
1244	**719**	31p multicoloured	1·00	90	☐	☐
		Set of 5	3·00	3·00	☐	☐
		First Day Cover		3·00		☐
		Presentation Pack	4·00		☐	
		PHQ Cards (set of 5)	3·00	6·50	☐	☐
		Set of 5 Gutter Pairs	7·25		☐	

Nos. 1240/4 marked the centenary of the Highland Cattle Society and the bicentenary of the Royal Highland and Agricultural Society of Scotland.

720 Festival Hall, Liverpool

721 Milburngate Shopping Centre, Durham

722 Bush House, Bristol

723 Commercial Street Housing Scheme, Perth

Urban Renewal

1984 (10 APR.) *Phosphorised paper*

1245	**720**	16p multicoloured	30	10	☐	☐
1246	**721**	20½p multicoloured	50	60	☐	☐
1247	**722**	28p multicoloured	1·00	1·00	☐	☐
1248	**723**	31p multicoloured	1·00	1·00	☐	☐
		Set of 4	2·50	2·50	☐	☐
		First Day Cover		2·50		☐
		Presentation Pack	3·00		☐	
		PHQ Cards (set of 4)	3·00	6·25	☐	☐
		Set of 4 Gutter Pairs	6·50		☐	

Nos. 1245/8 marked the opening of the International Gardens Festival, Liverpool, and the 150th anniversaries of the Royal Institute of British Architects and the Chartered Institute of Building.

724 C.E.P.T. 25th Anniversary Logo

725 Abduction of Europa

Nos. 1249/50 and 1251/2 were each printed together, *se-tenant*, in horizontal pairs throughout the sheets.

For full information on all future British issues, collectors should write to Royal Mail, Freepost EH3647, 21 South Gyle Crescent, Edinburgh EH12 9PE.

Europa. 25th Anniversary of C.E.P.T. and 2nd European Parliamentary Elections

1984 (15 MAY) *Phosphorised paper*

1249	**724**	16p greenish slate, deep blue and gold	50	25	☐	☐
		a. Horiz pair. Nos. 1249/50	1·50	1·25	☐	☐
1250	**725**	16p greenish slate, deep blue, black and gold .	50	25	☐	☐
1251	**724**	20½p Venetian red, deep magenta and gold . .	1·25	1·25	☐	☐
		a. Horiz pair. Nos. 1251/2	2·50	2·50	☐	☐
1252	**725**	20½p Venetian red, deep magenta, black and gold	1·25	1·25	☐	☐
		Set of 4	3·00	2·75	☐	☐
		First Day Cover		3·50		☐
		Presentation Pack	4·00		☐	
		PHQ Cards (set of 4)	3·00	6·25	☐	☐
		Set of 2 Gutter Blocks of 4 . . .	8·00		☐	

726 Lancaster House

London Economic Summit Conference

1984 (5 JUNE) *Phosphorised paper*

1253	**726**	31p multicoloured	1·25	1·25	☐	☐
		First Day Cover		2·25		☐
		PHQ Card	1·00	3·50	☐	☐
		Gutter Pair	2·50		☐	

727 View of Earth from 'Apollo 11'

728 Navigational Chart of English Channel

729 Greenwich Observatory

730 Sir George Airey's Transit Telescope

Centenary of Greenwich Meridian

1984 (26 JUNE) *Phosphorised paper. Perf* 14 × 14½

1254	**727**	16p multicoloured	50	25	☐	☐
1255	**728**	20½p multicoloured	75	75	☐	☐
1256	**729**	28p multicoloured	1·00	75	☐	☐
1257	**730**	31p multicoloured	1·00	1·00	☐	☐
		Set of 4	3·00	2·50	☐	☐
		First Day Cover		2·50		☐
		Presentation Pack	3·50		☐	
		PHQ Cards (set of 4)	3·00	6·25	☐	☐
		Set of 4 Gutter Pairs	6·50		☐	

731 Bath Mail Coach, 1784

732 Attack on Exeter Mail, 1816

733 Norwich Mail in Thunderstorm, 1827

734 Holyhead and Liverpool Mails leaving London, 1828

735 Edinburgh Mail Snowbound, 1831

T **731/5** were printed together, *se-tenant*, in horizontal strips of 5 throughout the sheet.

Bicentenary of First Mail Coach Run, Bath and Bristol to London

1984 (31 July) *Phosphorised paper*

1258	**731**	16p multicoloured	40	35	☐	☐
		a. Horiz strip of 5. Nos.				
		1258/62	2·50	2·75	☐	☐
1259	**732**	16p multicoloured	40	35	☐	☐
1260	**733**	16p multicoloured	40	35	☐	☐
1261	**734**	16p multicoloured	40	35	☐	☐
1262	**735**	16p multicoloured	40	35	☐	☐
		Set of 5	2·50	1·60	☐	☐
		First Day Cover		3·00		☐
		Presentation Pack	3·00		☐	
		Souvenir Book	7·50		☐	
		PHQ Cards (set of 5)	3·00	6·50	☐	☐
		Gutter Block of 10	6·50		☐	

736 Nigerian Clinic

737 Violinist and Acropolis, Athens

738 Building Project, Sri Lanka

739 British Council Library

50th Anniversary of The British Council

1984 (25 Sept.) *Phosphorised paper*

1263	**736**	17p multicoloured	50	25	☐	☐
1264	**737**	22p multicoloured	85	1·00	☐	☐
1265	**738**	31p multicoloured	85	1·00	☐	☐
1266	**739**	34p multicoloured	1·00	1·00	☐	☐
		Set of 4	3·00	3·00	☐	☐
		First Day Cover		3·00		☐
		Presentation Pack	3·25		☐	
		PHQ Cards (set of 4)	3·00	6·25	☐	☐
		Set of 4 Gutter Pairs	6·50		☐	

For full information on all future British issues, collectors should write to Royal Mail, Freepost EH3647, 21 South Gyle Crescent, Edinburgh EH12 9PE.

740 The Holy Family

741 Arrival in Bethlehem

742 Shepherd and Lamb

743 Virgin and Child

744 Offering of Frankincense

Christmas

1984 (20 Nov.) *One phosphor band (13p) or phosphorised paper (others)*

1267	**740**	13p multicoloured	25	25	☐	☐
1268	**741**	17p multicoloured	50	50	☐	☐
1269	**742**	22p multicoloured	75	75	☐	☐
1270	**743**	31p multicoloured	1·00	1·00	☐	☐
1271	**744**	34p multicoloured	1·00	1·00	☐	☐
		Set of 5	3·25	3·25	☐	☐
		First Day Cover		3·00		☐
		Presentation Pack	3·75		☐	
		PHQ Cards (set of 5)	3·00	6·25	☐	☐
		Set of 5 Gutter Pairs	7·00		☐	

Collectors Pack 1984

1984 (20 Nov.) *Comprises Nos. 1236/71*

CP1271a	Collectors Pack	37·00		☐

Post Office Yearbook

1984 *Comprises Nos. 1236/71 in hardbound book with slip case*

YB1271a	Yearbook	90·00		☐

745 'Flying Scotsman'   **746** 'Golden Arrow'

747 'Cheltenham Flyer'   **748** 'Royal Scot'

749 'Cornish Riviera'

Famous Trains

1985 (22 JAN.) *Phosphorised paper*

1272	745	17p multicoloured	75	25	☐	☐
1273	746	22p multicoloured	75	1·00	☐	☐
1274	747	29p multicoloured	1·00	1·25	☐	☐
1275	748	31p multicoloured	1·25	1·50	☐	☐
1276	749	34p multicoloured	1·50	1·50	☐	☐
		Set of 5	5·00	5·00	☐	☐
		First Day Cover		3·25		☐
		Presentation Pack	6·00			☐
		PHQ Cards (set of 5)	6·00	15·00	☐	☐
		Set of 5 Gutter Pairs	11·00			☐

Nos. 1272/6 were issued on the occasion of the 150th anniversary of the Great Western Railway Company.

750 *Bombus terrestris* (bee)   **751** *Coccinella septempunctata* (ladybird)

752 *Decticus verrucivorus* (bush-cricket)   **753** *Lucanus cervus* (stag beetle)

754 *Anax imperator* (dragonfly)

Insects

1985 (12 MAR.) *Phosphorised paper*

1277	750	17p multicoloured	40	10	☐	☐
1278	751	22p multicoloured	60	55	☐	☐
1279	752	29p multicoloured	85	90	☐	☐
1280	753	31p multicoloured	1·00	1·00	☐	☐
1281	754	34p multicoloured	1·00	90	☐	☐
		Set of 5	3·25	3·25	☐	☐
		First Day Cover		3·50		☐
		Presentation Pack	4·50			☐
		PHQ Cards (set of 5)	3·00	7·50	☐	☐
		Set of 5 Gutter Pairs	8·75			☐

Nos. 1277/81 were issued on the occasion of the centenaries of the Royal Entomological Society of London's Royal Charter and of the Selborne Society.

755 'Water Music', by Handel   **756** 'The Planets', by Holst

THIRTY·ONE·PENCE

THE·FIRST·CUCKOO
Frederick Delius

THIRTY·FOUR·PENCE

SEA·PICTURES
Edward Elgar

757 'The First Cuckoo', by Delius

758 'Sea Pictures', by Elgar

Europa. European Music Year
1985 (14 May) *Phosphorised paper. Perf 14½*

1282	755	17p multicoloured	55	10	☐	☐
1283	756	22p multicoloured	75	90	☐	☐
1284	757	31p multicoloured	1·50	1·25	☐	☐
1285	758	34p multicoloured	1·50	1·25	☐	☐
		Set of 4	4·00	3·25	☐	☐
		First Day Cover		4·00		☐
		Presentation Pack	4·75			☐
		PHQ Cards (set of 4)	3·00	7·00	☐	☐
		Set of 4 Gutter Pairs	10·00			☐

Nos. 1282/5 were issued on the occasion of the 300th birth anniversary of Handel.

759 R.N.L.I. Lifeboat and Signal Flags

760 Beachy Head Lighthouse and Chart

761 'Marecs A' Communications Satelite and Dish Aerials

762 Buoys

Safety at Sea
1985 (18 June) *Phosphorised paper. Perf 14*

1286	759	17p multicoloured	40	25	☐	☐
1287	760	22p multicoloured	60	75	☐	☐
1288	761	31p multicoloured	90	1·00	☐	☐
1289	762	34p multicoloured	1·00	1·25	☐	☐
		Set of 4	2·75	3·00	☐	☐
		First Day Cover		3·00		☐
		Presentation Pack	3·75			☐
		PHQ Cards (set of 4)	3·00	7·00	☐	☐
		Set of 4 Gutter Pairs	7·00			☐

Nos. 1286/9 were issued to mark the bicentenary of the unimmersible lifeboat and the 50th anniversary of Radar.

763 Datapost Motorcyclist, City of London

764 Rural Postbus

765 Parcel Delivery in Winter

766 Town Letter Delivery

350 Years of Royal Mail Public Postal Service
1985 (30 July) *Phosphorised paper*

1290	763	17p multicoloured	50	10	☐	☐
1291	764	22p multicoloured	75	70	☐	☐
1292	765	31p multicoloured	1·00	1·00	☐	☐
1293	766	34p multicoloured	1·00	1·00	☐	☐
		Set of 4	2·75	2·50	☐	☐
		First Day Cover		3·25		☐
		Presentation Pack	3·75			☐
		PHQ Cards (set of 4)	3·00	7·00	☐	☐
		Set of 4 Gutter Pairs	7·00			☐

767 King Arthur and Merlin

768 The Lady of the Lake

769 Queen Guinevere and
Sir Lancelot

770 Sir Galahad

Arthurian Legends

1985 (3 SEPT.) *Phosphorised paper*

1294	**767**	17p multicoloured	50	25	□	□
1295	**768**	22p multicoloured	75	75	□	□
1296	**769**	31p multicoloured	1·25	1·25	□	□
1297	**770**	34p multicoloured	1·25	1·25	□	□
		Set of 4	3·50	3·00	□	□
		First Day Cover		2·50		□
		Presentation Pack	3·50		□	
		PHQ *Cards* (*set of 4*)	3·00	7·00	□	□
		Set of 4 Gutter Pairs	7·00		□	

Nos. 1294/7 were issued to mark the 500th anniversary of the
printing of Sir Thomas Malory's *Morte d'Arthur.*

771 Peter Sellers
(from photo by
Bill Brandt)

772 David Niven
(from photo by
Cornell Lucas)

773 Charlie Chaplin
(from photo by
Lord Snowdon)

774 Vivien Leigh
(from photo by
Angus McBean)

775 Alfred Hitchcock (from
photo by Howard Coster)

British Film Year

1985 (8 OCT.) *Phosphorised paper. Perf* 14½

1298	**771**	17p multicoloured	45	25	□	□
1299	**772**	22p multicoloured	60	75	□	□
1300	**773**	29p multicoloured	1·00	1·25	□	□
1301	**774**	31p multicoloured	1·10	1·50	□	□
1302	**775**	34p multicoloured	1·40	1·50	□	□
		Set of 5	4·00	4·50	□	□
		First Day Cover		5·00		□
		Presentation Pack	5·50		□	
		Souvenir Book	11·50		□	
		PHQ *Cards* (*set of* 5)	3·00	8·50	□	□
		Set of 5 *Gutter Pairs*	10·50		□	

776 Principal Boy

777 Genie

778 Dame

779 Good Fairy

780 Pantomime Cat

Christmas. Pantomime Characters

1985 (19 NOV.) *One phosphor band* (12p) *or phosphorised
paper* (*others*)

1303	**776**	12p multicoloured	50	15	□	□
1304	**777**	17p multicoloured	50	25	□	□
1305	**778**	22p multicoloured	75	1·10	□	□
1306	**779**	31p multicoloured	1·25	1·35	□	□
1307	**780**	34p multicoloured	1·25	1·35	□	□
		Set of 5	4·00	4·00	□	□
		First Day Cover		4·50		□
		Presentation Pack	4·25		□	
		PHQ *Cards* (*Set of* 5)	3·00	7·00	□	□
		Set of 5 *Gutter Pairs*	8·00		□	

Collectors Pack 1985

1985 (19 Nov.) *Comprises Nos.* 1272/1307
CP1307*a* Collectors Pack . . . . 35·00 □

Post Office Yearbook

1985 *Comprises Nos.* 1272/1307 *in hardbound book with slip case*
YB1307*a* Yearbook . . . . 80·00 □

17 PENCE · INDUSTRY YEAR 1986

781 Light Bulb and North Sea Oil Drilling Rig (Energy)

22 PENCE · INDUSTRY YEAR 1986

782 Thermometer and Pharmaceutical Laboratory (Health)

31 PENCE · INDUSTRY YEAR 1986

783 Garden Hoe and Steel Works (Steel)

34 PENCE · INDUSTRY YEAR 1986

784 Loaf of Bread and and Cornfield (Agriculture)

Industry Year

1986 (14 Jan.) *Phosphorised paper. Perf* 14½ × 14

1308	**781**	17p multicoloured	75	25	□	□
1309	**782**	22p multicoloured	50	75	□	□
1310	**783**	31p multicoloured	1·25	1·35	□	□
1311	**784**	34p multicoloured	1·25	1·35	□	□
		Set of 4	3·50	3·50	□	□
		First Day Cover		3·00	□	
		Presentation Pack	3·75		□	
		PHQ Cards (set of 4)	3·50	6·50	□	□
		Set of 4 Gutter Pairs	7·00		□	

785 Dr Edmond Halley as Comet

786 *Giotto* Spacecraft approaching Comet

787 'Twice in a Lifetime'

788 Comet orbiting Sun and Planets

Appearance of Halley's Comet

1986 (18 Feb.) *Phosphorised paper*

1312	**785**	17p multicoloured	50	25	□	□
1313	**786**	22p multicoloured	75	75	□	□
1314	**787**	31p multicoloured	1·25	1·25	□	□
1315	**788**	34p multicoloured	1·25	1·35	□	□
		Set of 4	3·50	3·50	□	□
		First Day Cover		3·50	□	
		Presentation Pack	3·75		□	
		PHQ Cards (set of 4)	4·00	6·50	□	□
		Set of 4 Gutter Pairs	7·00		□	

HER MAJESTY THE QUEEN

Sixtieth Birthday 17p

789 Queen Elizabeth II in 1928, 1942 and 1952

HER MAJESTY THE QUEEN

Sixtieth Birthday 17p

790 Queen Elizabeth II in 1958, 1973 and 1982

Nos. 1316/17 and 1318/19 were each printed together, *se-tenant*, in horizontal pairs throughout the sheets.

60th Birthday of Queen Elizabeth II

1986 (21 Apr.) *Phosphorised paper*

1316	**789**	17p multicoloured	60	50	□	□
		a. Horiz pair. Nos. 1316/17	1·50	1·50	□	□
1317	**790**	17p multicoloured	60	50	□	□
1318	**789**	34p multicoloured	1·40	1·75	□	□
		a. Horiz pair. Nos. 1318/19	3·00	4·00	□	□
1319	**790**	34p multicoloured	1·40	1·75	□	□
		Set of 4	4·50	4·00	□	□
		First Day Cover		4·00	□	
		Presentation Pack	5·50		□	
		Souvenir Book	8·50		□	
		PHQ Cards (set of 4)	5·00	6·50	□	□
		Set of 2 Gutter Blocks of 4 . . .	11·00		□	

For full information on all future British issues, collectors should write to Royal Mail, Freepost EH3647, 21 South Gyle Crescent, Edinburgh EH12 9PE.

791 Barn Owl

792 Pine Marten

793 Wild Cat

794 Natterjack Toad

Europa. Nature Conservation. Endangered Species

1986 (20 MAY) *Phosphorised paper. Perf 14½ × 14*

1320	791	17p multicoloured	40	10	☐	☐
1321	792	22p multicoloured	80	1·00	☐	☐
1322	793	31p multicoloured	1·25	1·25	☐	☐
1323	794	34p multicoloured	1·40	1·40	☐	☐
		Set of 4	3·50	3·50	☐	☐
		First Day Cover		4·00		☐
		Presentation Pack	4·00		☐	
		PHQ Cards (set of 4)	3·50	6·50	☐	☐
		Set of 4 Gutter Pairs	10·00		☐	

795 Peasants Working in Fields

796 Freemen working at Town Trades

797 Knight and Retainers

798 Lord at Banquet

900th Anniversary of Domesday Book

1986 (17 JUNE) *Phosphorised paper*

1324	795	17p multicoloured	40	10	☐	☐
1325	796	22p multicoloured	85	85	☐	☐
1326	797	31p multicoloured	1·25	1·40	☐	☐
1327	798	34p multicoloured	1·25	1·40	☐	☐
		Set of 4	3·50	3·50	☐	☐
		First Day Cover		4·00		☐
		Presentation Pack	4·00		☐	
		PHQ Cards (set of 4)	3·50	6·50	☐	☐
		Set of 4 Gutter Pairs	7·00		☐	

799 Athletics   800 Rowing

801 Weightlifting   802 Rifle-shooting

803 Hockey

Thirteenth Commonwealth Games, Edinburgh (Nos. 1328/31) and World Men's Hockey Cup, London (No. 1332)

1986 (15 JULY) *Phosphorised paper*

1328	799	17p multicoloured	40	25	☐	☐
1329	800	22p multicoloured	55	75	☐	☐
1330	801	29p multicoloured	75	1·00	☐	☐
1331	802	31p multicoloured	1·00	1·25	☐	☐
1332	803	34p multicoloured	1·25	1·25	☐	☐
		Set of 5	2·50	2·50	☐	☐
		First Day Cover		2·50		☐
		Presentation Pack	2·75		☐	
		PHQ Cards (set of 5)	4·00	7·50	☐	☐
		Set of 5 Gutter Pairs	8·75		☐	

No. 1332 also marked the centenary of the Hockey Association.

804 Prince Andrew and Miss Sarah Ferguson **805**

Royal Wedding
1986 (22 July) *One side band* (12p) *or phosphorised paper* (17p)

1333	804	12p multicoloured	50	30	☐	☐
1334	805	17p multicoloured	1·00	1·25	☐	☐
		Set of 2	1·50	1·50	☐	☐
		First Day Cover		2·00		☐
		Presentation Pack	1·75		☐	
		PHQ Cards (*set of* 2)	2·25	5·00	☐	☐
		Set of 2 *Gutter Pairs*	3·00		☐	

806 Stylised Cross on Ballot Paper

32nd Commonwealth Parliamentary Conference, London
1986 (19 Aug.) *Phosphorised paper. Perf* 14 × 14½

1335	806	34p multicoloured	1·25	1·25	☐	☐
		First Day Cover		1·75		☐
		PHQ Card	1·00	3·00	☐	☐
		Gutter Pair	2·75		☐	

807 Lord Dowding and Hawker Hurricane Mk. I

808 Lord Tedder and Hawker Typhoon 1B

809 Lord Trenchard and De Havilland D.H.9A

810 Sir Arthur Harris and Avro Type 683 Lancaster

811 Lord Portal and De Havilland D.H.98 Mosquito

History of the Royal Air Force
1986 (16th Sept.) *Phosphorised paper. Perf* 14½ × 14

1336	807	17p multicoloured	50	10	☐	☐
1337	808	22p multicoloured	75	95	☐	☐
1338	809	29p multicoloured	1·00	1·25	☐	☐
1339	810	31p multicoloured	1·50	1·75	☐	☐
1340	811	34p multicoloured	1·75	1·85	☐	☐
		Set of 5	5·00	5·50	☐	☐
		First Day Cover		5·50		☐
		Presentation Pack	5·50		☐	
		PHQ Cards (*set of* 5)	4·50	10·00	☐	☐
		Set of 5 *Gutter Pairs*	12·00		☐	

Nos. 1336/40 were issued to celebrate the 50th anniversary of the first R.A.F. Commands.

812 The Glastonbury Thorn

813 The Tanad Valley Plygain

814 The Hebrides Tribute

815 The Dewsbury Church Knell

816   The Hereford Boy Bishop

Christmas. Folk Customs

1986 (18 Nov.–2 Dec.) *One phosphor band* (12p, 13p) *or phosphorised paper* (*others*)

1341	812	12p multicoloured (2 Dec.)	50	50	□	□
1342		13p multicoloured	25	15	□	□
1343	813	18p multicoloured	50	15	□	□
1344	814	22p multicoloured	1·00	1·00	□	□
1345	815	31p multicoloured	1·25	1·00	□	□
1346	816	34p multicoloured	1·25	1·10	□	□
		Set of 6	3·75	3·50	□	□
		First Day Covers (2)		3·75		□
		Presentation Pack (Nos. 1342/6)	3·75		□	
		PHQ Cards (set of 5) (Nos. 1342/6)	3·50	7·00	□	□
		Set of 6 Gutter Pairs	9·00		□	

Collectors Pack 1986

1986 (18 Nov.) *Comprises Nos. 1308/40, 1342/6*

CP1346a	Collectors Pack	37·00		□

Post Office Yearbook

1986 *Comprises Nos. 1308/40, 1342/6 in hardbound book with slip case*

YB1346a	Yearbook	70·00		□

817   North American
        Blanket Flower

818   Globe Thistle

819   Echeveria

820   Autumn Crocus

Flower Photographs by Alfred Lammer

1987 (20 Jan.) *Phosphorised paper. Perf* 14½ × 14

1347	817	18p multicoloured	40	10	□	□
1348	818	22p multicoloured	70	85	□	□
1349	819	31p multicoloured	1·10	1·25	□	□
1350	820	34p multicoloured	1·10	1·25	□	□
		Set of 4	3·25	3·25	□	□
		First Day Cover		3·50		□
		Presentation Pack	4·00		□	
		PHQ Cards (set of 4)	3·00	7·00	□	□
		Set of 4 Gutter Pairs	7·50		□	

821   The Principia   822   Motion of Bodies
        Mathematica   in Ellipses

823   Optick Treatise   824   The System of the World

300th Anniversary of The Principia Mathematica by Sir Isaac Newton

1987 (24 Mar.) *Phosphorised paper*

1351	821	18p multicoloured	50	15	□	□
1352	822	22p multicoloured	75	75	□	□
1353	823	31p multicoloured	1·25	1·50	□	□
1354	824	34p multicoloured	1·25	1·25	□	□
		Set of 4	3·50	3·25	□	□
		First Day Cover		3·75		□
		Presentation Pack	4·00		□	
		PHQ Cards (set of 4)	3·00	6·50	□	□
		Set of 4 Gutter Pairs	8·00		□	

For full information on all future British issues, collectors should write to Royal Mail, Freepost EH3647, 21 South Gyle Crescent, Edinburgh EH12 9PE.

825 Willis Faber and Dumas Building, Ipswich   **826** Pompidou Centre, Paris

827 Staatsgalerie, Stuttgart   **828** European Investment Bank, Luxembourg

Europa. British Architects in Europe

1987 (12 May) *Phosphorised paper*

1355	**825**	18p multicoloured	50	15	☐	☐
1356	**826**	22p multicoloured	75	75	☐	☐
1357	**827**	31p multicoloured	1·25	1·25	☐	☐
1358	**828**	34p multicoloured	1·25	1·25	☐	☐
		Set of 4	3·50	3·25	☐	☐
		First Day Cover		3·75		☐
		Presentation Pack	4·00			☐
		PHQ Cards (set of 4)	3·00	6·50	☐	☐
		Set of 4 Gutter Pairs	9·50			☐

829 Brigade Members with Ashford Litter, 1887   **830** Bandaging Blitz Victim, 1940

831 Volunteer with fainting Girl, 1965   **832** Transport of Transplant Organ by Air Wing, 1987

Centenary of St John Ambulance Brigade

1987 (16 June) *Phosphorised paper. Perf* 14 × 14½

1359	**829**	18p multicoloured	40	25	☐	☐
1360	**830**	22p multicoloured	60	75	☐	☐
1361	**831**	31p multicoloured	1·25	1·25	☐	☐
1362	**832**	34p multicoloured	1·25	1·25	☐	☐
		Set of 4	3·25	3·25	☐	☐
		First Day Cover		3·75		☐
		Presentation Pack	4·00			☐
		PHQ Cards (set of 4)	3·00	6·50	☐	☐
		Set of 4 Gutter Pairs	7·50			☐

833 Arms of the Lord Lyon King of Arms   **834** Scottish Heraldic Banner of Prince Charles

835 Arms of Royal Scottish Academy of Painting, Sculpture and Architecture   **836** Arms of Royal Society of Edinburgh

300th Anniversary of Revival of Order of the Thistle

1987 (21 July) *Phosphorised paper. Perf* 14½

1363	**833**	18p multicoloured	50	10	☐	☐
1364	**834**	22p multicoloured	75	90	☐	☐
1365	**835**	31p multicoloured	1·40	1·40	☐	☐
1366	**836**	34p multicoloured	1·50	1·40	☐	☐
		Set of 4	3·75	3·50	☐	☐
		First Day Cover		3·75		☐
		Presentation Pack	4·00			☐
		PHQ Cards (set of 4)	3·00	6·50	☐	☐
		Set of 4 Gutter Pairs	8·00			☐

For full information on all future British issues, collectors should write to Royal Mail, Freepost EH3647, 21 South Gyle Crescent, Edinburgh EH12 9PE.

837 Crystal Palace, 'Monarch of the Glen' (Landseer) and Grace Darling

838 Great Eastern, Beeton's Book of Household Management and Prince Albert

839 Albert Memorial, Ballot Box and Disraeli

840 Diamond Jubilee Emblem, Morse Key and Newspaper Placard for Relief of Mafeking

150th Anniversary of Queen Victoria's Accession

1987 (8 SEPT.) *Phosphorised paper*

1367	**837**	18p multicoloured	50	10	□	□
1368	**838**	22p multicoloured	80	75	□	□
1369	**839**	31p multicoloured	1·50	1·50	□	□
1370	**840**	34p multicoloured	1·60	1·60	□	□
		Set of 4	4·00	3·50	□	□
		First Day Cover		3·75		□
		Presentation Pack	4·25		□	
		PHQ Cards (set of 4)	3·00	6·50	□	□
		Set of 4 Gutter Pairs	9·00		□	

841 Pot by Bernard Leach

842 Pot by Elizabeth Fritsch

843 Pot by Lucie Rie

844 Pot by Hans Coper

Studio Pottery

1987 (13 OCT.) *Phosphorised paper. Perf* 14$\frac{1}{2}$ × 14

1371	**841**	18p multicoloured	50	25	□	□
1372	**842**	26p multicoloured	70	75	□	□
1373	**843**	31p multicoloured	1·25	1·25	□	□
1374	**844**	34p multicoloured	1·40	1·50	□	□
		Set of 4	3·50	3·50	□	□
		First Day Cover		3·75		□
		Presentation Pack	3·50		□	
		PHQ Cards (set of 4)	3·00	6·50	□	□
		Set of 4 Gutter Pairs	8·50		□	

Nos. 1371/4 also mark the birth centenary of Bernard Leach, the potter.

845 Decorating the Christmas Tree

846 Waiting for Father Christmas

847 Sleeping Child and Father Christmas in Sleigh

848 Child reading

849 Child playing Flute and Snowman

Christmas

1987 (17 NOV.) *One phosphor band* (13p) *or phosphorised paper* (*others*)

1375	**845**	13p multicoloured	30	10	□	□
1376	**846**	18p multicoloured	40	20	□	□
1377	**847**	26p multicoloured	80	1·00	□	□
1378	**848**	31p multicoloured	1·10	1·25	□	□
1379	**849**	34p multicoloured	1·25	1·50	□	□
		Set of 5	3·50	3·75	□	□
		First Day Cover		3·75		□
		Presentation Pack	3·50		□	
		PHQ Cards (set of 5)	3·00	6·50	□	□
		Set of 5 Gutter Pairs	8·50		□	

Collectors Pack 1987

1987 (17 Nov.) *Comprises Nos.* 1347/79

CP1379*a* Collectors Pack . . . . 37·00 ☐

Post Office Yearbook

1987 *Comprises Nos.* 1347/79 *in hardbound book with slip case*

YB1379*a* Yearbook . . . . 35·00 ☐

850 Short-spined Seascorpion ('Bull-rout') (Jonathan Couch)

851 Yellow Waterlily (Major Joshua Swatkin)

852 Whistling ('Bewick's') Swan (Edward Lear)

853 *Morchella esculenta* (James Sowerby)

Bicentenary of Linnean Society. Archive Illustrations

1988 (19 Jan.) *Phosphorised paper*

1380	850	18p multicoloured	55	10	☐	☐
1381	851	26p multicoloured	85	1·00	☐	☐
1382	852	31p multicoloured	1·10	1·25	☐	☐
1383	853	34p multicoloured	1·25	1·40	☐	☐
		Set of 4	3·25	3·25	☐	☐
		First Day Cover		3·75		☐
		Presentation Pack	4·00		☐	
		PHQ Cards (set of 4)	3·00	6·50	☐	☐
		Set of 4 Gutter Pairs	8·00		☐	

854 Revd William Morgan (Bible translator, 1588)

855 William Salesbury (New Testament translator, 1567)

856 Bishop Richard Davies (New Testament translator, 1567)

857 Bishop Richard Parry (editor of Revised Welsh Bible, 1620)

400th Anniversary of Welsh Bible

1988 (1 Mar.) *Phosphorised paper. Perf* $14\frac{1}{2} \times 14$

1384	854	18p multicoloured	40	10	☐	☐
1385	855	26p multicoloured	70	95	☐	☐
1386	856	31p multicoloured	1·25	1·25	☐	☐
1387	857	34p multicoloured	1·40	1·25	☐	☐
		Set of 4	3·25	3·25	☐	☐
		First Day Cover		3·75		☐
		Presentation Pack	4·00		☐	
		PHQ Cards (set of 4)	3·00	6·50	☐	☐
		Set of 4 Gutter Pairs	8·00		☐	

858 Gymnastics (Centenary of British Amateur Gymnastics Association)

859 Downhill Skiing (Ski Club of Great Britain)

860 Tennis (Centenary of Lawn Tennis Association)

861 Football (Centenary of Football League)

Sports Organizations

1988 (22 Mar.) *Phosphorised paper. Perf 14½*

1388	858	18p multicoloured	40	15 □ □
1389	859	26p multicoloured	70	80 □ □
1390	860	31p multicoloured	1·10	1·25 □ □
1391	861	34p multicoloured	1·25	1·25 □ □
		Set of 4	3·25	3·25 □ □
		First Day Cover		3·50 □
		Presentation Pack	4·00	□
		PHQ Cards (set of 4)	2·50	6·00 □ □
		Set of 4 Gutter Pairs	8·00	□

862 *Mallard* and Mailbags
on Pick-up Arms

863 Loading Transatlantic
Mail on Liner *Queen
Elizabeth*

864 Glasgow Tram No. 1173
and Pillar Box

865 Imperial Airways
Handley Page H.P.45
Horatius and Airmail Van

Europa. Transport and Mail Services in 1930's

1988 (10 May) *Phosphorised paper*

1392	862	18p multicoloured	50	15 □ □
1393	863	26p multicoloured	1·00	1·00 □ □
1394	864	31p multicoloured	1·10	1·25 □ □
1395	865	34p multicoloured	1·50	1·50 □ □
		Set of 4	3·50	3·50 □ □
		First Day Cover		3·75 □
		Presentation Pack	4·25	□
		PHQ Cards (set of 4)	2·25	6·00 □ □
		Set of 4 Gutter Pairs	11·00	□

866 Early Settler and
Sailing Clipper

867 Queen Elizabeth II
with British and
Australian Parliament
Buildings

868 W. G. Grace (cricketer)
and Tennis Racquet

869 Shakespeare,
John Lennon
(entertainer) and
Sydney Landmarks

Nos. 1396/7 and 1398/9 were each printed together, *se-tenant*, in horizontal pairs throughout the sheets, each pair showing a background design of the Australian flag.

Bicentenary of Australian Settlement

1988 (21 June) *Phosphorised paper. Perf 14½*

1396	866	18p multicoloured	60	50 □ □
		a. Horiz pair. Nos. 1396/7	1·25	1·50 □ □
1397	867	18p multicoloured	60	50 □ □
1398	868	34p multicoloured	1·25	1·25 □ □
		a. Horiz pair. Nos. 1398/9	2·25	2·75 □ □
1399	869	34p multicoloured	1·25	1·25 □ □
		Set of 4	3·50	3·25 □ □
		First Day Cover		3·25 □
		Presentation Pack	4·00	□
		Souvenir Book	15·00	□
		PHQ Cards (set of 4)	2·25	6·00 □ □
		Set of 2 Gutter Blocks of 4 . . .	8·25	□

Stamps in similar designs were also issued by Australia. These are included in the Souvenir Book.

870 Spanish Galeasse off
The Lizard

871 English Fleet leaving
Plymouth

872 Engagement off
Isle of Wight

873 Attack of English
Fire-ships, Calais

874 Armada in Storm, North Sea

Nos. 1400/4 were printed together, *se-tenant*, in horizontal strips of 5 throughout the sheet, forming a composite design.

400th Anniversary of Spanish Armada

1988 (19 July) *Phosphorised paper*

1400	870	18p multicoloured	70	65	☐	☐
		a. Horiz strip of 5. Nos. 1400/4	3·50	3·75	☐	☐
1401	871	18p multicoloured	70	65	☐	☐
1402	872	18p multicoloured	70	65	☐	☐
1403	873	18p multicoloured	70	65	☐	☐
1404	874	18p multicoloured	70	65	☐	☐
		Set of 5	3·00	3·00	☐	☐
		First Day Cover		3·50		☐
		Presentation Pack	3·75			☐
		PHQ Cards (set of 5)	2·75	7·00	☐	☐
		Gutter Block of 10	8·00			☐

875 'The Owl and the Pussy-cat'

876 'Edward Lear as a Bird' (self-portrait)

877 'Cat' (from alphabet book)

878 'There was a Young Lady whose Bonnet . . .' (limerick)

Death Centenary of Edward Lear (artist and author)

1988 (6–27 Sept.) *Phosphorised paper*

1405	875	19p black, pale cream and carmine	65	20	☐	☐
1406	876	27p black, pale cream and yellow	1·00	1·00	☐	☐
1407	877	32p black, pale cream and emerald	1·25	1·40	☐	☐
1408	878	35p black, pale cream and blue	1·40	1·40	☐	☐
		Set of 4	4·00	3·50	☐	☐
		First Day Cover		3·75		☐
		Presentation Pack	4·25			☐
		PHQ Cards (set of 4)	2·25	6·00	☐	☐
		Set of 4 Gutter Pairs	9·00			☐
MS1409		122 × 90 mm. Nos. 1405/8 . .	7·00	8·50	☐	☐
		First Day Cover (27 Sept.) . . .		8·50		☐

No. **MS**1409 was sold at £1·35, the premium being used for the 'Stamp World London 90' International Stamp Exhibition.

879 Carrickfergus Castle

880 Caernarvon Castle

881 Edinburgh Castle

882 Windsor Castle

1988 (18 Oct.) *Ordinary paper*

1410	879	£1 deep green	4·25	60	☐	☐
1411	880	£1·50 maroon	4·50	1·25	☐	☐
1412	881	£2 indigo	8·00	1·50	☐	☐
1413	882	£5 deep brown	21·00	5·50	☐	☐
		Set of 4	38·00	8·00	☐	☐
		First Day Cover		35·00		☐
		Presentation Pack	35·00			☐
		Set of 4 Gutter pairs	70·00			☐

For similar designs, but with silhouette of Queen's head see Nos. 1611/14 and 1993/6.

Minimum Price. The minimum price quoted is 10p. This represents a handling charge rather than a basis for valuing common stamps. Where the actual value of a stamp is less than 10p this may be apparent when set prices are shown, particularly for sets including a number of 10p stamps. It therefore follows that in valuing common stamps the 10p catalogue price should not be reckoned automatically since it covers a variation in real scarcity.

883 Journey to Bethlehem

884 Shepherds and Star

885 Three Wise Men

886 Nativity

887 The Annunciation

Christmas

1988 (15 Nov.) *One phosphor band (14p) or phosphorised paper (others)*

1414	**883**	14p multicoloured	45	25	□	□
1415	**884**	19p multicoloured	50	25	□	□
1416	**885**	27p multicoloured	90	1·00	□	□
1417	**886**	32p multicoloured	1·10	1·25	□	□
1418	**887**	35p multicoloured	1·40	1·25	□	□
		Set of 5	4·00	3·75	□	□
		First Day Cover		3·75	□	
		Presentation Pack	4·00		□	
		PHQ Cards (set of 5)	3·00	6·00	□	□
		Set of 5 Gutter Pairs	9·50		□	

Collectors Pack 1988

1988 (15 Nov.) *Comprises Nos. 1380/1408, 1414/18*
CP1418a   Collectors Pack . . . .   37·00   □

Post Office Yearbook

1988 *Comprises Nos. 1380/1404,* **MS**1409, *1414/18 in hardbound book with slip case*
YB1418a   Yearbook . . . .   35·00   □

888 Atlantic Puffin

889 Avocet

890 Oystercatcher

891 Northern Gannet

Centenary of Royal Society for the Protection of Birds

1989 (17 Jan.) *Phosphorised paper*

1419	**888**	19p multicoloured	25	20	□	□
1420	**889**	27p multicoloured	1·25	1·25	□	□
1421	**890**	32p multicoloured	1·25	1·25	□	□
1422	**891**	35p multicoloured	1·25	1·25	□	□
		Set of 4	3·50	3·50	□	□
		First Day Cover		4·00		□
		Presentation Pack	4·00		□	
		PHQ Cards (set of 4)	3·00	7·00	□	□
		Set of 4 Gutter Pairs	9·50		□	

892 Rose

893 Cupid

894 Yachts

895 Fruit

896 Teddy Bear

Nos. 1423/7 were printed together, *se-tenant*, in horizontal strips of five, two such strips forming the booklet pane with twelve half stamp-size labels.

Greetings Booklet Stamps

1989 (31 JAN.) *Phosphorised paper*

1423	892	19p multicoloured	3·50	3·00	☐ ☐
		a. Booklet pane. Nos.			
		1423/7 × 2	50·00		☐
		b. Horiz strip of 5. Nos.			
		1423/7	25·00	25·00	☐ ☐
1424	893	19p multicoloured	3·50	3·00	☐ ☐
1425	894	19p multicoloured	3·50	3·00	☐ ☐
1426	895	19p multicoloured	3·50	3·00	☐ ☐
1427	896	19p multicoloured	3·50	3·00	☐ ☐
		Set of 5	17·00	12·00	☐ ☐
		First Day Cover		25·00	☐

897 Fruit and Vegetables

898 Meat Products

899 Dairy Produce

900 Cereal Products

Food and Farming Year

1989 (7 MAR.) *Phosphorised paper. Perf* 14 × 14½

1428	897	19p multicoloured	45	15	☐ ☐
1429	898	27p multicoloured	90	85	☐ ☐
1430	899	32p multicoloured	1·25	1·40	☐ ☐
1431	900	35p multicoloured	1·40	1·50	☐ ☐
		Set of 4	3·50	3·50	☐ ☐
		First Day Cover		3·75	☐
		Presentation Pack	4·00		☐
		PHQ Cards (set of 4)	2·25	6·50	☐ ☐
		Set of 4 Gutter Pairs	8·50		☐

901 Mortar Board (150th Anniv of Public Education in England)

902 Cross on Ballot Paper (3rd Direct Elections to European Parliament)

903 Posthorn (26th Postal, Telegraph and Telephone International Congress, Brighton)

904 Globe (Inter-Parliamentary Union Centenary Conference, London)

Nos. 1432/3 and 1434/5 were each printed together, *se-tenant*, in horizontal pairs throughout the sheets.

Anniversaries

1989 (11 APR.) *Phosphorised paper. Perf* 14 × 14½

1432	901	19p multicoloured	1·00	50	☐ ☐
		a. Horiz pair. Nos. 1432/3	2·00	2·00	☐ ☐
1433	902	19p multicoloured	1·00	50	☐ ☐
1434	903	35p multicoloured	1·50	1·50	☐ ☐
		a. Horiz pair. Nos. 1434/5	3·00	4·00	☐ ☐
1435	904	35p multicoloured	1·50	1·50	☐ ☐
		Set of 4	3·50	3·50	☐ ☐
		First Day Cover		4·00	☐
		Presentation Pack	4·00		☐
		PHQ Cards (set of 4)	2·25	6·50	☐ ☐
		Set of 2 Gutter Strips of 4 . . .	9·00		☐

905 Toy Train and Airplane Airplane

906 Building Bricks

907 Dice and Board Games

908 Toy Robot, Boat and Doll's House

912a

Europa. Games and Toys

1989 (16 MAY) *Phosphorised paper*

1436	**905**	19p multicoloured	65	25	□	□
1437	**906**	27p multicoloured	95	1·00	□	□
1438	**907**	32p multicoloured	1·40	1·25	□	□
1439	**908**	35p multicoloured	1·50	1·25	□	□
		Set of 4	4·00	3·50	□	□
		First Day Cover		3·75		□
		Presentation Pack	4·25		□	
		PHQ Cards (set of 4)	2·25	6·50	□	□
		Set of 4 Gutter Pairs	10·50		□	

Industrial Archaeology

1989 (4–25 JULY) *Phosphorised paper*

1440	**909**	19p multicoloured	60	15	□	□
1441	**910**	27p multicoloured	1·00	1·10	□	□
1442	**911**	32p multicoloured	1·10	1·25	□	□
1443	**912**	35p multicoloured	1·25	1·50	□	□
		Set of 4	3·50	3·50	□	□
		First Day Cover		3·75		□
		Presentation Pack	4·00		□	
		PHQ Cards (set of 4)	2·25	6·50	□	□
		Set of 4 Gutter Pairs	8·50		□	
MS1444		122 × 90 mm. **912a** As Nos.				
		1440/3 but designs horizontal .	6·00	6·50	□	□
		First Day Cover (25 July)		6·50		□

No. **MS**1444 was sold at £1·40, the premium being used for the 'Stamp World London 90' International Stamp Exhibition.

909 Ironbridge, Shropshire

910 Tin Mine. St Agnes Head, Cornwall

913

914

Booklet Stamps

1989 (22 AUG.)–**92** (*a*) *Printed in photogravure by Harrison and Sons. Perf* 15 × 14

1445	**913**	(2nd) bright blue (1 centre band)	1·00	1·00	□	□
1446		(2nd) bright blue (1 side band) (20.3.90)	3·00	3·25	□	□
1447	**914**	(1st) black (phosphorised paper)	1·75	1·00	□	□
1448		(1st) brownish black (2 bands (20.3.90)	3·25	3·00	□	□

(*b*) *Printed in lithography by Walsall. Perf* 14

1449	**913**	(2nd) bright blue (1 centre band)	1·00	90	□	□
1450	**914**	(1st) black (2 bands)	2·50	2·40	□	□

911 Cotton Mills, New Lanark, Strathclyde

912 Pontcysylite Aqueduct, Clwyd

(c) Printed in lithography by Questa. Perf 15 × 14

1451	**913**	(2nd) bright blue (1 centre band) (19.9.89)	1·00	1·00 □ □
1451*a*		(2nd) bright blue (1 side band) (25.2.92)	3·00	3·00 □ □
1452	**914**	(1st) black (phosphorised paper) (19.9.89)	2·50	2·50 □ □
		First Day Cover (Nos. 1445, 1447)		5·00 □

For similar stamps showing changed colours see Nos. 1511/16, for those with elliptical perforations Nos. 1663*a*/6 and for self-adhesive versions Nos. 2039/40.

No. 1451*a* exists with the phosphor band at the left or right of the stamp.

915   Snowflake (×10)

916   *Calliphora erythrocephala* (fly) (×5)

917   Blood Cells (×500)

918   Microchip (×600)

150th Anniversary of Royal Microscopical Society
1989 (5 Sept.) *Phosphorised paper. Perf 14½ × 14*

1453	**915**	19p multicoloured	45	25 □ □
1454	**916**	27p multicoloured	95	1·00 □ □
1455	**917**	32p multicoloured	1·10	1·25 □ □
1456	**918**	35p multicoloured	1·25	1·25 □ □
		Set of 4	3·50	3·50 □ □
		First Day Cover		3·50 □
		Presentation Pack	4·00	□
		PHQ Cards (set of 4)	2·25	6·50 □ □
		Set of 4 Gutter Pairs	8·50	□

919   Royal Mail Coach

920   Escort of Blues and Royals

921   Lord Mayor's Coach

922   Coach Team passing St Paul's

923   Blues and Royals Drum Horse

Nos. 1457/61 were printed together, *se-tenant*, in horizontal strips of 5 throughout the sheet, forming a composite design.

Lord Mayor's Show, London
1989 (17 Oct.) *Phosphorised paper*

1457	**919**	20p multicoloured	70	40 □ □
		a. Horiz strip of 5. Nos. 1457/61	3·25	3·50 □ □
1458	**920**	20p multicoloured	70	40 □ □
1459	**921**	20p multicoloured	70	40 □ □
1460	**922**	20p multicoloured	70	40 □ □
1461	**923**	20p multicoloured	70	40 □ □
		Set of 5	2·75	2·00 □ □
		First Day Cover		2·75 □
		Presentation Pack	3·00	□
		PHQ Cards (set of 5)	3·00	6·50 □ □
		Gutter Strip of 10	8·00	□

Nos. 1457/61 commemorate the 800th anniversary of the installation of the first Lord Mayor of London.

924 14th-century Peasants from Stained-glass Window

925 Arches and Roundels, West Front

926 Octagon Tower

927 Arcade from West Transept

928 Triple Arch from West Front

Christmas. 800th Anniversary of Ely Cathedral

1989 (14 Nov.) *One phosphor band (Nos. 1462/3) or phosphorised paper (others)*

1462	924	15p gold, silver and blue .	40	15	□	□
1463	925	15p + 1p gold, silver and blue	50	40	□	□
1464	926	20p + 1p gold, silver and rosine	65	80	□	□
1465	927	34p + 1p gold, silver and emerald	1·25	1·75	□	□
1466	928	37p + 1p gold, silver and yellow-olive	1·40	1·90	□	□
		Set of 5	3·75	4·50	□	□
		First Day Cover		3·50		□
		Presentation Pack	4·50		□	
		PHQ Cards (set of 5)	3·00	6·00	□	□
		Set of 5 Gutter Pairs	9·00		□	

Collectors Pack 1989

1989 (14 Nov.) *Comprises Nos. 1419/22, 1428/43 and 1453/66*

CP1466a	Collectors Pack	38·00	□

Post Office Yearbook

1989 (14 Nov.) *Comprises Nos. 1419/22, 1428/44 and 1453/66 in hardback book with slip case*

YB1466a	Yearbook	42·00	□

929 Queen Victoria and Queen Elizabeth II

150th Anniversary of the Penny Black

1990 (10 Jan.–17 Apr.) (*a*) *Printed in photogravure by Harrison and Sons (Nos. 1468, 1470, 1472 from booklets only). Perf 15 × 14*

1467	929	15p bright blue (1 centre band)	80	80	□	□
1468		15p bright blue (1 side band) (30 Jan.)	3·75	3·75	□	□
1469		20p brownish black and cream (phosphorised paper)	1·00	1·00	□	□
1470		20p brownish black and . cream (2 bands) (30 Jan.)	2·75	2·75	□	□
1471		29p deep mauve (phosphorised paper)	1·75	1·75	□	□
1472		29p deep mauve (2 bands) (20 Mar.)	9·00	9·00	□	□
1473		34p deep bluish grey (phosphorised paper)	2·00	2·00	□	□
1474		37p rosine (phosphorised paper)	2·25	2·25	□	□
		Set of 5 (Nos. 1467, 1469, 1471, 1473/4)	7·00	7·00	□	□
		First Day Cover (Nos. 1467, 1469, 1471, 1473/4)		7·00		□
		Presentation Pack (Nos. 1467, 1469, 1471, 1473/4)	9·00		□	

(*b*) *Litho Walsall (booklets). Perf 14 (30 Jan.)*

1475	929	15p bright blue (1 centre band)	1·50	1·75	□	□
1476		20p brownish black and . cream (phosphorised paper)	1·60	1·75	□	□

(*c*) *Litho Questa (booklets). Perf 15 × 14 (17 Apr.)*

1477	929	15p bright blue (1 centre band)	2·25	2·25	□	□
1478		20p brownish black (phosphorised paper)	2·00	2·25	□	□

No. 1468 exists with the phosphor band at the left or right of the stamp.

For Type **929** redrawn with "1st" face value see No. 2133.

> **Minimum Price.** The minimum price quoted is 10p. This represents a handling charge rather than a basis for valuing common stamps. Where the actual value of a stamp is less than 10p this may be apparent when set prices are shown, particularly for sets including a number of 10p stamps. It therefore follows that in valuing common stamps the 10p catalogue price should not be reckoned automatically since it covers a variation in real scarcity.

1840·RSPCA·1990

930 Kitten

1840·RSPCA·1990

931 Rabbit

1840·RSPCA·1990

932 Duckling

1840·RSPCA·1990

933 Puppy

150th Anniversary of Royal Society for Prevention of Cruelty to Animals

1990 (23 Jan.) *Phosphorised paper. Perf* 14 × 14½

1479	**930**	20p multicoloured	75	50	☐	☐
1480	**931**	29p multicoloured	1·25	1·25	☐	☐
1481	**932**	34p multicoloured	1·25	1·50	☐	☐
1482	**933**	37p multicoloured	1·50	1·50	☐	☐
		Set of 4	4·25	4·25	☐	☐
		First Day Cover		3·50		☐
		Presentation Pack	4·50		☐	
		PHQ Cards (set of 4)	3·00	7·50	☐	☐
		Set of 4 Gutter Pairs	9·50		☐	

934 Teddy Bear

935 Dennis the Menace

936 Punch

937 Cheshire Cat

938 The Man in the Moon

939 The Laughing Policeman

940 Clown

941 Mona Lisa

942 Queen of Hearts

943 Stan Laurel (comedian)

T **934/43** were printed together, *se-tenant,* in booklet panes of 10.

Greetings Booklet Stamps. 'Smiles'

1990 (6 Feb.) *Two phosphor bands*

1483	**934**	20p multicoloured	3·50	2·50	☐	☐
		a. Booklet pane. Nos. 1483/92	30·00		☐	
1484	**935**	20p multicoloured	3·50	2·50	☐	☐
1485	**936**	20p multicoloured	3·50	2·50	☐	☐
1486	**937**	20p multicoloured	3·50	2·50	☐	☐
1487	**938**	20p multicoloured	3·50	2·50	☐	☐
1488	**939**	20p multicoloured	3·50	2·50	☐	☐
1489	**940**	20p multicoloured	3·50	2·50	☐	☐
1490	**941**	20p multicoloured	3·50	2·50	☐	☐
1491	**942**	20p multicoloured	3·50	2·50	☐	☐
1492	**943**	20p gold and grey-black .	3·50	2·50	☐	☐
		Set of 10	30·00	22·00	☐	☐
		First Day Cover		26·00		☐

For these designs with the face value expressed as '1st' see Nos. 1550/9.

For full information on all future British issues, collectors should write to Royal Mail, Freepost EH3647, 21 South Gyle Crescent, Edinburgh EH12 9PE.

944 Alexandra Palace ('Stamp World London 90' Exhibition)

945 Glasgow School of Art

946 British Philatelic Bureau, Edinburgh

947 Templeton Carpet Factory, Glasgow

Europa (*Nos. 1493 and 1495*) and 'Glasgow 1990 *European City of Culture*' (*Nos. 1494 and 1496*)

1990 (6 MAR.) *Phosphorised paper*

1493	944	20p multicoloured	50	25	☐	☐
1494	945	20p multicoloured	50	25	☐	☐
1495	946	29p multicoloured	1·25	1·75	☐	☐
1496	947	37p multicoloured	1·50	1·75	☐	☐
		Set of 4	3·50	3·50	☐	☐
		First Day Cover		3·50		☐
		Presentation Pack	4·25			☐
		PHQ Cards (set of 4)	3·00	6·00	☐	☐
		Set of 4 Gutter Pairs	10·00			☐

948 Export Achievement Award

949 Technological Achievement Award

Nos. 1497/8 and 1499/500 were each printed together, *se-tenant,* in horizontal pairs throughout the sheets.

25th Anniversary of Queen's Awards for Export and Technology

1990 (10 APR.) *Phosphorised paper. Perf* 14 × 14½

1497	948	20p multicoloured	70	50	☐	☐
		a. Horiz pair. Nos. 1497/8	1·40	1·60	☐	☐
1498	949	20p multicoloured	70	50	☐	☐
1499	948	37p multicoloured	1·25	1·50	☐	☐
		a. Horiz pair. Nos. 1499/1500	2·50	3·25	☐	☐
1500	949	37p multicoloured	1·25	1·50	☐	☐
		Set of 4	3·50	3·50	☐	☐
		First Day Cover		3·75		☐
		Presentation Pack	4·50			☐
		PHQ Cards (set of 4)	3·00	6·00	☐	☐
		Set of 2 Gutter Strips of 4 . . .	8·50			☐

949a

'Stamp World London 90' International Stamp Exhibition, London

1990 (3 MAY) *Sheet* 122 × 90 mm. *Phosphorised paper*

MS1501	949a	20p brownish black and cream	5·50	5·50	☐	☐
		First Day Cover		5·75		☐
		Souvenir Book (Nos. 1467, 1469, 1471, 1473/4 and MS1501 . .	20·00			☐

No. **MS**1501 was sold at £1, the premium being used for the exhibition.

950 Cycad and Sir Joseph Banks Building

951 Stone Pine and Princess of Wales Conservatory

KEW GARDENS 1840-1990   KEW GARDENS 1840-1990

952 Willow Tree and   953 Cedar Tree and Pagoda
     Palm House

150th Anniversary of Kew Gardens
1990 (5 June) *Phosphorised paper*

1502	**950**	20p multicoloured	55	15	☐	☐
1503	**951**	29p multicoloured	75	1·00	☐	☐
1504	**952**	34p multicoloured	1·25	1·60	☐	☐
1505	**953**	37p multicoloured	1·50	1·50	☐	☐
		Set of 4	3·50	3·75	☐	☐
		First Day Cover		3·75	☐	
		Presentation Pack	4·00		☐	
		PHQ Cards (set of 4)	3·00	6·00	☐	☐
		Set of 4 Gutter Pairs	9·00		☐	

954 Thomas Hardy and Clyffe Clump, Dorset

150th Birth Anniversary of Thomas Hardy (author)
1990 (10 July) *Phosphorised paper*

1506	**954**	20p multicoloured	80	75	☐	☐
		First Day Cover		1·50	☐	
		Presentation Pack	1·50		☐	
		PHQ Card	1·00	2·25	☐	☐
		Gutter Pair	1·75		☐	

955 Queen Elizabeth the   956 Queen Elizabeth
     Queen Mother

957 Elizabeth, Duchess   958 Lady Elizabeth
     of York   Bowes-Lyon

90th Birthday of Queen Elizabeth the Queen Mother
1990 (2 Aug.) *Phosphorised paper*

1507	**955**	20p multicoloured	95	25	☐	☐
1508	**956**	29p silver, indigo and grey-blue	1·40	1·50	☐	☐
1509	**957**	34p multicoloured	2·00	2·50	☐	☐
1510	**958**	37p silver, sepia and stone	2·25	2·50	☐	☐
		Set of 4	6·00	6·25	☐	☐
		First Day Cover		5·50	☐	
		Presentation Pack	7·00		☐	
		PHQ Cards (set of 4)	5·50	8·00	☐	☐
		Set of 4 Gutter Pairs	15·00		☐	

For these designs with Queen's head and frame in black see Nos. 2280/3.

Booklet Stamps
1990 (7 Aug.)–**92** *As Types* **913/14,** *but colours changed*

(*a*) *Photo Harrison. Perf* 15 × 14

1511	**913**	(2nd) deep blue (1 centre band)	1·50	1·50	☐	☐
1512	**914**	(1st) bright orange-red (phosphorised paper)	1·50	1·50	☐	☐

(*b*) *Litho Questa. Perf* 15 × 14

1513	**913**	(2nd) deep blue (1 centre band)	2·50	2·50	☐	☐
1514	**914**	(1st) bright orange-red (phosphorised paper)	1·00	1·00	☐	☐
1514a		(1st) bright orange-red (2 bands) (25.2.92) . . .	2·25	2·25	☐	☐

(*c*) *Litho Walsall. Perf* 14

1515	**913**	(2nd) deep blue (1 centre band)	1·00	1·00	☐	☐
1516	**914**	(1st) bright orange-red (phosphorised paper)	1·25	1·25	☐	☐
		c. Perf 13	2·75	3·00	☐	☐
		First Day Cover (*Nos.* 1515/16) .		5·00	☐	

For similar stamps with elliptical perforations see Nos. 1663*a*/6.

For full information on all future British issues, collectors should write to Royal Mail, Freepost EH3647, 21 South Gyle Crescent, Edinburgh EH12 9PE.

959 Victoria Cross

960 George Cross

961 Distinguished Service Cross and Distinguished Service Medal

962 Military Cross and Military Medal

963 Distinguished Flying Cross and Distinguished Flying Medal

Gallantry Awards

1990 (11 SEPT.) *Phosphorised paper*

1517	**959**	20p multicoloured	80	75	□	□
1518	**960**	20p multicoloured	80	75	□	□
1519	**961**	20p multicoloured	80	75	□	□
1520	**962**	20p multicoloured	80	75	□	□
1521	**963**	20p multicoloured	80	75	□	□
		Set of 5	3·75	3·50	□	□
		First Day Cover		3·75	□	
		Presentation Pack	4·00		□	
		PHQ Cards (*set of* 5)	3·00	8·00	□	□
		Set of 5 *Gutter Pairs*	9·25		□	

964 Armagh Observatory, Jodrell Bank Radio Telescope and La Palma Telescope

965 Newton's Moon and Tides Diagram with Early Telescopes

966 Greenwich Old Observatory and Early Astronomical Equipment

967 Stonehenge, Gyroscope and Navigating by Stars

Astronomy

1990 (16 OCT.) *Phosphorised paper. Perf* 14 × 14½

1522	**964**	22p multicoloured	65	15	□	□
1523	**965**	26p multicoloured	1·00	1·10	□	□
1524	**966**	31p multicoloured	1·25	1·40	□	□
1525	**967**	37p multicoloured	1·50	1·40	□	□
		Set of 4	3·75	3·75	□	□
		First Day Cover		4·00		□
		Presentation Pack	4·50		□	
		PHQ Cards (*set of* 4)	3·00	7·00	□	□
		Set of 4 *Gutter Pairs*	9·25		□	

Nos. 1522/5 commemorate the centenary of the British Astronomical Association and the bicentenary of the Armagh Observatory.

968 Building a Snowman

969 Fetching the Christmas Tree

970 Carol Singing

971 Tobogganing

972 Ice-skating

91

Christmas

1990 (13 Nov.) One phosphor band (17p) or phosphorised paper (others)

1526	**968**	17p multicoloured	. . . . .	50	15	☐	☐
1527	**969**	22p multicoloured	. . . . .	70	20	☐	☐
1528	**970**	26p multicoloured	. . . . .	70	1·10	☐	☐
1529	**971**	31p multicoloured	. . . . .	1·25	1·50	☐	☐
1530	**972**	37p multicoloured	. . . . .	1·25	1·50	☐	☐
		Set of 5	. . . .	4·00	4·00	☐	☐
		First Day Cover	. . . .		4·00		☐
		Presentation Pack	. . . .	4·50		☐	
		PHQ Cards (set of 5)	. . . . . .	3·00	7·00	☐	☐
		Set of 5 Gutter Pairs	. . . . . .	10·00		☐	

Collectors Pack 1990

1990 (13 Nov.) Comprises Nos. 1479/82, 1493/1510 and 1517/30

CP1530a	Collectors Pack	. . . . 40·00	☐

Post Office Yearbook

1990 Comprises Nos. 1479/82, 1493/1500, 1502/10 and 1517/30 in hardback book with slip case

YB1530a	Yearbook	. . . . 45·00	☐

973 'King Charles Spaniel'

974 'A Pointer'

975 'Two Hounds in a Landscape'

976 'A Rough Dog'

977 'Fino and Tiny'

Dogs. Paintings by George Stubbs

1991 (8 JAN.) Phosphorised paper. Perf 14 × 14½

1531	**973**	22p multicoloured	. . . . .	50	15	☐	☐
1532	**974**	26p multicoloured	. . . . .	75	1·25	☐	☐
1533	**975**	31p multicoloured	. . . . .	1·00	1·25	☐	☐
1534	**976**	33p multicoloured	. . . . .	1·25	1·25	☐	☐
1535	**977**	37p multicoloured	. . . . .	1·25	1·25	☐	☐
		Set of 5	. . . .	4·50	4·50	☐	☐
		First Day Cover	. . . .		5·00		☐
		Presentation Pack	. . . .	5·00		☐	
		PHQ Cards (set of 5)	. . . . . .	3·50	7·00	☐	☐
		Set of 5 Gutter Pairs	. . . . . .	11·00		☐	

978 Thrush's Nest

979 Shooting Star and Rainbow

980 Magpies and Charm Bracelet

981 Black Cat

982 Common Kingfisher with Key

983 Mallard and Frog

984 Four-leaf Clover in Boot and Match Box

985 Pot of Gold at End of Rainbow

986 Heart-shaped Butterflies

987 Wishing Well and Sixpence

T **978/87** were printed together, *se-tenant,* in booklet panes of 10 stamps and 12 half stamp-size labels, the backgrounds of the stamps forming a composite design.

Greetings Booklet Stamps. 'Good Luck'
1991 (5 Feb.) *Two phosphor bands*

1536	**978**	(1st) multicoloured	1·75	1·90	☐	☐
		a. Booklet pane. Nos.				
		1536/45	15·00		☐	
1537	**979**	(1st) multicoloured	1·75	1·90	☐	☐
1538	**980**	(1st) multicoloured	1·75	1·90	☐	☐
1539	**981**	(1st) multicoloured	1·75	1·90	☐	☐
1540	**982**	(1st) multicoloured	1·75	1·90	☐	☐
1541	**983**	(1st) multicoloured	1·75	1·90	☐	☐
1542	**984**	(1st) multicoloured	1·75	1·90	☐	☐
1543	**985**	(1st) multicoloured	1·75	1·90	☐	☐
1544	**986**	(1st) multicoloured	1·75	1·90	☐	☐
1545	**987**	(1st) multicoloured	1·75	1·90	☐	☐
		Set of 10	15·00	17·00	☐	☐
		First Day Cover		15·00		☐

988 Michael Faraday (inventor of electric motor) (Birth Bicentenary)

989 Charles Babbage (computer science pioneer) (Birth Bicentenary)

990 Radar Sweep of East Anglia (50th Anniv of Discovery by Sir Robert Watson-Watt)

991 Gloster Whittle E28/39 Aircraft over East Anglia (50th Anniv of First Flight of Sir Frank Whittle's Jet Engine)

Scientific Achievements
1991 (5 Mar.) *Phosphorised paper*

1546	**988**	22p multicoloured	60	50	☐	☐
1547	**989**	22p multicoloured	60	50	☐	☐
1548	**990**	31p multicoloured	1·20	1·50	☐	☐
1549	**991**	37p multicoloured	1·35	1·75	☐	☐
		Set of 4	3·50	4·00	☐	☐
		First Day Cover		3·75		☐
		Presentation Pack	4·25		☐	
		PHQ Cards (set of 4)	3·50	7·00	☐	☐
		Set of 4 *Gutter Pairs*	8·50		☐	

992 Teddy Bear

Nos. 1550/9 were originally printed together, *se-tenant,* in booklet panes of 10 stamps and 12 half stamp-size labels.

Greetings Booklet Stamps. 'Smiles'
1991 (26 Mar.) *As Nos. 1483/92, but inscribed '1st' as T* **992.** *Two phosphor bands. Perf* 15 × 14

1550	**992**	(1st) multicoloured	1·50	1·50	☐	☐
		a. Booklet pane. Nos.				
		1550/9	12·00		☐	
1551	**935**	(1st) multicoloured	1·50	1·50	☐	☐
1552	**936**	(1st) multicoloured	1·50	1·50	☐	☐
1553	**937**	(1st) multicoloured	1·50	1·50	☐	☐
1554	**938**	(1st) multicoloured	1·50	1·50	☐	☐
1555	**939**	(1st) multicoloured	1·50	1·50	☐	☐
1556	**940**	(1st) multicoloured	1·50	1·50	☐	☐
1557	**941**	(1st) multicoloured	1·50	1·50	☐	☐
1558	**942**	(1st) multicoloured	1·50	1·50	☐	☐
1559	**943**	(1st) multicoloured	1·50	1·50	☐	☐
		Set of 10	12·00	13·00	☐	☐
		First Day Cover		13·00		☐

The stamps were re-issued in sheets of 10 each with *se-tenant* label on 22 May 2000 in connection with 'customised' stamps available at 'Stamp Show 2000'. The labels show either a pattern of ribbons or a personal photograph.

A similar sheet, but in lithography instead of photogravure, and perforated 14½ × 14, appeared on 3 July 2001 with the labels showing either greetings or a personal photograph.

Three further sheets, also in lithography, appeared on 1 October 2002. One contained Nos. 1550/1 each ×10 with greetings labels. Both designs were also available in sheets of 20 with personal photographs.

993 Man looking at Space

994

995 Space looking at Man **996**

Nos. 1560/1 and 1562/3 were each printed together, *se-tenant*, in horizontal pairs throughout the sheets, each pair forming a composite design.

Europa. Europe in Space

1991 (23 Apr.) *Phosphorised paper*

1560	**993**	22p multicoloured	75	50	□	□
		a. Horiz pair. Nos. 1560/1	1·50	1·50	□	□
1561	**994**	22p multicoloured	75	50	□	□
1562	**995**	37p multicoloured	2·00	1·50	□	□
		a. Horiz pair. Nos. 1562/3	4·00	3·00	□	□
1563	**996**	37p multicoloured	2·00	1·50	□	□
		Set of 4	3·50	3·50	□	□
		First Day Cover		4·00		□
		Presentation Pack	5·00		□	
		PHQ Cards (set of 4)	3·00	7·00	□	□
		Set of 2 Gutter Strips of 4 . . .	12·00		□	

997 Fencing

998 Hurdling

999 Diving

1000 Rugby

World Student Games, Sheffield (Nos. 1564/6) and World Cup Rugby Championship, London (No. 1567)

1991 (11 June) *Phosphorised paper. Perf* 14½ × 14

1564	**997**	22p multicoloured	60	20	□	□
1565	**998**	26p multicoloured	1·00	1·00	□	□
1566	**999**	31p multicoloured	1·25	1·25	□	□
1567	**1000**	37p multicoloured	1·50	1·50	□	□
		Set of 4	3·50	3·50	□	□
		First Day Cover		4·00		□
		Presentation Pack	4·50		□	
		PHQ Cards (set of 4)	3·00	7·00	□	□
		Set of 4 Gutter Pairs	9·00		□	

1001 'Silver Jubilee' **1002** 'Mme Alfred Carrière'

1003 Rosa moyesii **1004** 'Harvest Fayre'

1005 'Mutabilis'

9th World Congress of Roses, Belfast

1991 (16 July) *Phosphorised paper. Perf* 14½ × 14

1568	**1001**	22p multicoloured	50	20	□	□
1569	**1002**	26p multicoloured	75	1·25	□	□
1570	**1003**	31p multicoloured	1·00	1·25	□	□
1571	**1004**	33p multicoloured	1·25	1·50	□	□
1572	**1005**	37p multicoloured	1·50	1·50	□	□
		Set of 5	4·50	5·00	□	□
		First Day Cover		5·00		□
		Presentation Pack	5·00		□	
		PHQ Cards (set of 5)	3·00	9·00	□	□
		Set of 5 Gutter Pairs	11·00		□	

1006 Iguanodon

1007 Stegosaurus

1013 Map of 1959

1014 Map of 1991

Bicentenary of Ordnance Survey. Maps of Hamstreet, Kent

1991 (17 Sept.) *Phosphorised paper. Perf* 14½ × 14

1578	**1011**	24p multicoloured	. . . .	60	20	☐	☐
1579	**1012**	28p multicoloured	. . . .	1·00	95	☐	☐
1580	**1013**	33p multicoloured	. . . .	1·25	1·40	☐	☐
1581	**1014**	39p multicoloured	. . . .	1·50	1·40	☐	☐
	Set of 4	. . . .		3·50	3·50	☐	☐
	First Day Cover	. . . .			4·25		☐
	Presentation Pack	. . . . . .		4·50			☐
	PHQ Cards (*set of 4*)	. . . . . .		3·00	7·00	☐	☐
	Set of 4 Gutter Pairs	. . . . . .		10·00			☐

1008 Tyrannosaurus

1009 Protoceratops

1015 Adoration of the Magi

1016 Mary and Baby Jesus in Stable

1010 Triceratops

150th Anniversary of Dinosaurs' Identification by Owen

1991 (20 Aug.) *Phosphorised paper. Perf* 14½ × 14

1573	**1006**	22p multicoloured	. . . .	60	20	☐	☐
1574	**1007**	26p multicoloured	. . . .	1·10	1·25	☐	☐
1575	**1008**	31p multicoloured	. . . .	1·25	1·25	☐	☐
1576	**1009**	33p multicoloured	. . . .	1·50	1·50	☐	☐
1577	**1010**	37p multicoloured	. . . .	1·60	1·50	☐	☐
	Set of 5	. . . .		5·75	5·00	☐	☐
	First Day Cover	. . . .			5·50		☐
	Presentation Pack	. . . .		6·00			☐
	PHQ Cards (*set of 5*)	. . . . . .		3·00	9·00	☐	☐
	Set of 5 Gutter Pairs	. . . . . .		12·00			☐

1017 Holy Family and Angel

1018 The Annunciation

1011 Map of 1816

1012 Map of 1906

1019 The Flight into Egypt

95

Christmas. Illuminated Manuscripts from the Bodleian Library, Oxford

1991 (12 Nov.) *One phosphor band* (18p) *or phosphorised paper* (*others*)

1582	**1015**	18p multicoloured	. . . .	75	10	☐	☐
1583	**1016**	24p multicoloured	. . . .	90	10	☐	☐
1584	**1017**	28p multicoloured	. . . .	95	1·25	☐	☐
1585	**1018**	33p multicoloured	. . . .	1·10	1·50	☐	☐
1586	**1019**	39p multicoloured	. . . .	1·25	1·75	☐	☐
		Set of 5	. . . .	4·50	4·50	☐	☐
		First Day Cover			4·50		☐
		Presentation Pack		4·50		☐	
		PHQ Cards (set of 5)		3·00	7·50	☐	☐
		Set of 5 *Gutter Pairs*		11·00		☐	

Collectors Pack 1991

1991 (12 Nov.) *Comprises Nos.* 1531/5, 1546/9 *and* 1560/86
CP1586*a*   *Collectors Pack* . . . . 40·00   ☐

Post Office Yearbook

1991 *Comprises Nos.* 1531/5, 1546/9 *and* 1560/86 *in hardback book with slip case*
YB1586*a*   *Yearbook* . . . . 45·00   ☐

1020   Fallow Deer in Scottish Forest

1021   Hare on North Yorkshire Moors

1022   Fox in the Fens

1023   Redwing and Home Counties Village

1024   Welsh Mountain Sheep in Snowdonia

The Four Seasons. Wintertime

1992 (14 Jan.) *One phosphor band* (18p) *or phosphorised paper* (*others*)

1587	**1020**	18p multicoloured	. . . .	55	25	☐	☐
1588	**1021**	24p multicoloured	. . . .	75	25	☐	☐
1589	**1022**	28p multicoloured	. . . .	1·00	1·25	☐	☐
1590	**1023**	33p multicoloured	. . . .	1·25	1·50	☐	☐
1591	**1024**	39p multicoloured	. . . .	1·40	1·75	☐	☐
		Set of 5	. . . .	4·50	4·50	☐	☐
		First Day Cover			4·50		☐
		Presentation Pack		4·50		☐	
		PHQ Cards (set of 5)		3·00	8·00	☐	☐
		Set of 5 *Gutter Pairs*		11·00		☐	

1025   Flower Spray

1026   Double Locket

1027   Key

1028   Model Car and Cigarette Cards

1029   Compass and Map

1030   Pocket Watch

1031   1854 1d. Red Stamp and Pen

1032   Pearl Necklace

1033 Marbles   **1034** Bucket, Spade and Starfish

1039 Queen Elizabeth and Commonwealth Emblem

T **1025/34** were printed together, *se-tenant*, in booklet panes of 10 stamps and 12 half stamp-size labels, the backgrounds of the stamps forming a composite design.

Nos. 1602/6 were printed together, *se-tenant*, in horizontal strips of 5 throughout the sheet.

Greetings Stamps. 'Memories'

1992 (28 JAN.) *Two phosphor bands*

1592	**1025**	(1st) multicoloured	1·50	1·50	☐	☐
		a. Booklet pane. Nos.				
		1592/1601	13·00		☐	
1593	**1026**	(1st) multicoloured	1·50	1·50	☐	☐
1594	**1027**	(1st) multicoloured	1·50	1·50	☐	☐
1595	**1028**	(1st) multicoloured	1·50	1·50	☐	☐
1596	**1029**	(1st) multicoloured	1·50	1·50	☐	☐
1597	**1030**	(1st) multicoloured	1·50	1·50	☐	☐
1598	**1031**	(1st) multicoloured	1·50	1·50	☐	☐
1599	**1032**	(1st) multicoloured	1·50	1·50	☐	☐
1600	**1033**	(1st) multicoloured	1·50	1·50	☐	☐
1601	**1034**	(1st) multicoloured	1·50	1·50	☐	☐
		Set of 10	13·00	13·00	☐	☐
		First Day Cover		13·00		☐
		Presentation Pack	17·00		☐	

40th Anniversary of Accession

1992 (6 FEB.) *Two phosphor bands. Perf* 14½ × 14

1602	**1035**	24p multicoloured	1·10	1·10	☐	☐
		a. Horiz strip of 5. Nos.				
		1602/6	6·00	7·00	☐	☐
1603	**1036**	24p multicoloured	1·10	1·10	☐	☐
1604	**1037**	24p multicoloured	1·10	1·10	☐	☐
1605	**1038**	24p multicoloured	1·10	1·10	☐	☐
1606	**1039**	24p multicoloured	1·10	1·10	☐	☐
		Set of 5	6·00	5·00	☐	☐
		First Day Cover		6·00		☐
		Presentation Pack	7·00		☐	
		PHQ Cards (set of 5)	3·00	7·50	☐	☐
		Gutter Block of 10	15·00		☐	

1035 Queen Elizabeth in Coronation Robes and Parliamentary Emblem   **1036** Queen Elizabeth in Garter Robes and Archiepiscopal Arms

1040 Tennyson in 1888 and 'The Beguiling of Merlin' (Sir Edward Burne-Jones)   **1041** Tennyson in 1856 and 'April Love' (Arthur Hughes)

1037 Queen Elizabeth with Baby Prince Andrew and Royal Arms   **1038** Queen Elizabeth at Trooping the Colour and Service Emblems

1042 Tennyson in 1864 and 'I am Sick of the Shadows' (John Waterhouse)   **1043** Tennyson as a Young Man and 'Mariana' (Dante Gabriel Rossetti)

Death Centenary of Alfred, Lord Tennyson (poet)

1992 (10 MAR.) *Phosphorised paper. Perf 14½ × 14*

1607	**1040**	24p multicoloured	60	20	☐	☐
1608	**1041**	28p multicoloured	85	85	☐	☐
1609	**1042**	33p multicoloured	1·40	1·60	☐	☐
1610	**1043**	39p multicoloured	1·50	1·60	☐	☐
		Set of 4	4·00	3·75	☐	☐
		First Day Cover		4·25	☐	
		Presentation Pack	4·50		☐	
		PHQ Cards (set of 4)	3·00	7·00	☐	☐
		Set of 4 Gutter Pairs	10·00		☐	

CARRICKFERGUS CASTLE   **1044**   Carrickfergus Castle

1992 (24 MAR.)–**95.** *Designs as Nos. 1410/13, but showing Queen's head in silhouette as T 1044. Perf 15 × 14 (with one elliptical hole on each vertical side)*

1611	**1044**	£1 bottle green and gold†	5·50	1·00	☐	☐
1612	**880**	£1·50 maroon and gold† . .	5·50	1·00	☐	☐
1613	**881**	£2 indigo and gold† . . .	7·50	1·00	☐	☐
1613a	**1044**	£3 reddish violet and gold†	18·50	3·00	☐	☐
1614	**882**	£5 deep brown and gold†	17·00	3·00	☐	☐
		Set of 5	48·00	8·00	☐	☐
		First Day Cover (Nos. 1611/13, 1614)		35·00	☐	
		First Day Cover (22 Aug. 1995) (No. 1613a)		10·00	☐	
		Presentation Pack (P.O. Pack No. 27) (Nos. 1611/13, 1614) . . .	38·00		☐	
		Presentation Pack (P.O. Pack No. 33) (No. 1613a)	30·00		☐	
		PHQ Cards (Nos. 1611/14) . . .	12·00		☐	
		PHQ Card (No. 1613a)	6·00	22·00	☐	☐
		Set of 5 Gutter Pairs	98·00		☐	

†The Queen's head on these stamps is printed in optically variable ink which changes colour from gold to green when viewed from different angles.

PHQ cards for Nos. 1611/13 and 1614 were not issued until 16 February 1993.

Nos. 1611/14 were printed by Harrison. For stamps with different lettering by Enschedé see Nos. 1993/6.

1045 British Olympic Association Logo (Olympic Games, Barcelona)

1046 British Paralympic Association Symbol (Paralympics '92, Barcelona)

1047 *Santa Maria* (500th Anniv of Discovery of America by Columbus)

1048 *Kaisei* (Japanese cadet brigantine) (Grand Regatta Columbus, 1992)

1049 British Pavilion, 'EXPO 92', Seville

Nos. 1615/16 were printed together, *se-tenant,* in horizontal pairs throughout the sheet.

Europa. International Events

1992 (7 APR.) *Phosphorised paper. Perf 14 × 14½*

1615	**1045**	24p multicoloured	1·00	75	☐	☐
		a. Horiz pair. Nos. 1615/16	2·25	1·75	☐	☐
1616	**1046**	24p multicoloured	1·00	75	☐	☐
1617	**1047**	24p multicoloured	1·00	75	☐	☐
1618	**1048**	39p multicoloured	1·40	1·50	☐	☐
1619	**1049**	39p multicoloured	1·40	1·50	☐	☐
		Set of 5	4·50	4·50	☐	☐
		First Day Cover		5·00	☐	
		Presentation Pack	5·25		☐	
		PHQ Cards (set of 5)	3·00	7·00	☐	☐
		Set of 3 Gutter Pairs and a Gutter Strip of 4	13·00		☐	

1050 Pikeman

1051 Drummer

1052 Musketeer

1053 Standard Bearer

350th Anniversary of the Civil War

1992 (16 JUNE) *Phosphorised paper. Perf* $14\frac{1}{2} \times 14$

1620	**1050**	24p multicoloured	60	20	☐	☐
1621	**1051**	28p multicoloured	85	85	☐	☐
1622	**1052**	33p multicoloured	1·40	1·50	☐	☐
1623	**1053**	39p multicoloured	1·50	1·75	☐	☐
	Set of 4		4·00	4·00	☐	☐
	First Day Cover			4·00		☐
	Presentation Pack		4·50			☐
	PHQ Cards (set of 4)		3·00	7·00	☐	☐
	Set of 4 Gutter Pairs		10·50			☐

1054 The Yeomen of the Guard

1055 The Gondoliers

1056 The Mikado

1057 The Pirates of Penzance

1058 *Iolanthe*

150th Birth Anniversary of Sir Arthur Sullivan (composer). Gilbert and Sullivan Operas

1992 (21 JULY) *One phosphor band* (18p) *or phosphorised paper* (*others*). *Perf* $14\frac{1}{2} \times 14$

1624	**1054**	18p multicoloured	50	20	☐	☐
1625	**1055**	24p multicoloured	80	20	☐	☐
1626	**1056**	28p multicoloured	95	1·00	☐	☐
1627	**1057**	33p multicoloured	1·50	1·60	☐	☐
1628	**1058**	39p multicoloured	1·60	1·60	☐	☐
	Set of 5		4·50	4·25	☐	☐
	First Day Cover			4·50		☐
	Presentation Pack		4·50			☐
	PHQ Cards (set of 5)		3·00	6·25	☐	☐
	Set of 5 Gutter Pairs		10·50			☐

1059 'Acid Rain Kills'

1060 'Ozone Layer'

1061 'Greenhouse Effect'

1062 'Bird of Hope'

Protection of the Environment. Children's Paintings

1992 (15 SEPT.) *Phosphorised paper. Perf* $14 \times 14\frac{1}{2}$

1629	**1059**	24p multicoloured	70	25	☐	☐
1630	**1060**	28p multicoloured	1·10	1·25	☐	☐
1631	**1061**	33p multicoloured	1·25	1·50	☐	☐
1632	**1062**	39p multicoloured	1·40	1·50	☐	☐
	Set of 4		4·00	3·75	☐	☐
	First Day Cover			4·00		☐
	Presentation Pack		4·50			☐
	PHQ Cards (set of 4)		3·00	6·25	☐	☐
	Set of 4 Gutter Pairs		10·00			☐

1063   European Star

Single European Market

1992 (13 Oct.) *Phosphorised paper*

1633	**1063**	24p multicoloured	1·00	1·00	□	□
		First Day Cover		1·50		□
		Presentation Pack	1·50		□	
		PHQ Card	1·50	4·00	□	□
		Gutter Pair	2·25		□	

1064 'Angel Gabriel',
St James's, Pangbourne

1065 'Madonna and Child',
St. Mary's, Bibury

1066 'King with Gold', Our Lady
and St Peter, Leatherhead

1067 'Shepherds', All Saints,
Porthcawl

1068 'Kings with Frankincense
and Myrrh', Our Lady and
St Peter, Leatherhead

Christmas. Stained Glass Windows

1992 (10 Nov.) *One phosphor band* (18p) *or phosphorised paper* (*others*)

1634	**1064**	18p multicoloured	50	15	□	□
1635	**1065**	24p multicoloured	75	15	□	□
1636	**1066**	28p multicoloured	1·00	1·10	□	□
1637	**1067**	33p multicoloured	1·25	1·50	□	□
1638	**1068**	39p multicoloured	1·25	1·50	□	□
		Set of 5	4·25	4·25	□	□
		First Day Cover		4·50		□
		Presentation Pack	4·50		□	
		PHQ Cards (set of 5)	3·00	7·50	□	□
		Set of 5 Gutter Pairs	10·00		□	

Collectors Pack 1992

1992 (10 Nov.) *Comprises Nos.* 1587/91, 1602/10 *and* 1615/38

CP1638a	Collectors Pack	45·00	□

Post Office Yearbook

1992 (11 Nov.) *Comprises Nos.* 1587/91, 1602/10 *and* 1615/38 *in hardback book with slip case*

YB1638a	Yearbook	55·00	□

1069 Mute Swan Cob
and St Catherine's,
Abbotsbury

1070 Cygnet and Decoy

1071 Swans and Cygnet

1072 Eggs in Nest and Tithe
Barn, Abbotsbury

1073 Young Swan and the Fleet

600th Anniversary of Abbotsbury Swannery

1993 (19 Jan.) *One phosphor band* (18p) *or phosphorised paper* (*others*)

1639	**1069**	18p multicoloured	1·25	25	□	□
1640	**1070**	24p multicoloured	1·10	25	□	□
1641	**1071**	28p multicoloured	1·40	2·25	□	□
1642	**1072**	33p multicoloured	1·75	2·50	□	□
1643	**1073**	39p multicoloured	1·90	2·50	□	□
		Set of 5	6·50	7·50	□	□
		First Day Cover		6·00		□
		Presentation Pack	7·00		□	
		PHQ Cards (set of 5)	4·25	8·50	□	□
		Set of 5 Gutter Pairs	15·00		□	

1074 Long John Silver and Parrot (*Treasure Island*)

1075 Tweedledum and Tweedledee (*Alice Through the Looking-Glass*)

1076 William (*William* books)

1077 Mole and Toad (*The Wind in the Willows*)

1078 Teacher and Wilfrid ('The Bash Street Kids')

1079 Peter Rabbit and Mrs Rabbit (*The Tale of Peter Rabbit*)

1080 Snowman (*The Snowman*) and Father Christmas (*Father Christmas*)

1081 The Big Friendly Giant and Sophie (*The BFG*)

1082 Bill Badger and Rupert Bear

1083 Aladdin and the Genie

T **1074/83** were printed together, *se-tenant,* in booklet panes of 10 stamps and 20 half stamp-size labels.

Greetings Stamps. 'Gift Giving'
1993 (2 FEB.) *Two phosphor bands. Perf 15 × 14 (with one elliptical hole on each vertical side)*

1644	**1074**	(1st) multicoloured	1·25	1·25	☐	☐
		a. Booklet pane. Nos. 1644/53	11·00	12·00	☐	☐
1645	**1075**	(1st) gold, cream and black	1·25	1·25	☐	☐
1646	**1076**	(1st) multicoloured	1·25	1·25	☐	☐
1647	**1077**	(1st) multicoloured	1·25	1·25	☐	☐
1648	**1078**	(1st) multicoloured	1·25	1·25	☐	☐
1649	**1079**	(1st) multicoloured	1·25	1·25	☐	☐
1650	**1080**	(1st) multicoloured	1·25	1·25	☐	☐
1651	**1081**	(1st) multicoloured	1·25	1·25	☐	☐
1652	**1082**	(1st) multicoloured	1·25	1·25	☐	☐
1653	**1083**	(1st) multicoloured	1·25	1·25	☐	☐
		Set of 10	11·00	11·00	☐	☐
		First Day Cover		12·00		☐
		Presentation Pack	16·00		☐	
		PHQ Cards (set of 10)	13·50	28·00	☐	☐

1084 Decorated Enamel Dial

1085 Escapement, Remontoire and Fusee

1086 Balance, Spring and Temperature Compensator

1087 Back of Movement

300th Birth Anniversary of John Harrison (inventor of the marine chronometer). Details of 'H4' Clock
1993 (16 FEB.) *Phosphorised paper. Perf 14½ × 14*

1654	**1084**	24p multicoloured	60	25	☐	☐
1655	**1085**	28p multicoloured	1·00	1·25	☐	☐
1656	**1086**	33p multicoloured	1·40	1·25	☐	☐
1657	**1087**	39p multicoloured	1·50	1·50	☐	☐
		Set of 4	4·00	4·00	☐	☐
		First Day Cover		4·00		☐
		Presentation Pack	4·25		☐	
		PHQ Cards (set of 4)	4·25	7·00	☐	☐
		Set of 4 Gutter Pairs	10·00		☐	

1088 Britannia

1993 (2 MAR.) *Granite paper. Perf* 14 × 14½ *(with two elliptical holes on each horizontal side)*

1658	**1088**	£10 multicoloured	30·00	12·00	□	□
		First Day Cover		25·00		□
		Presentation Pack	36·00		□	
		PHQ Card	5·00	35·00	□	□

1089 *Dendrobium hellwigianum*

1090 *Paphiopedilum Maudiae* 'Magnifcum'

1091 *Cymbidium lowianum*

1092 *Vanda Rothschildiana*

1093 *Dendrobium vexillarius var albiviride*

1093a

14th World Orchid Conference, Glasgow

1993 (16 MAR.) *One phosphor band (18p) or phosphorised paper (others)*

1659	**1089**	18p multicoloured	45	25	□	□
1660	**1090**	24p multicoloured	75	25	□	□
1661	**1091**	28p multicoloured	1·00	1·25	□	□
1662	**1092**	33p multicoloured	1·25	1·50	□	□
1663	**1093**	39p multicoloured	1·60	1·50	□	□
		Set of 5	4·50	4·50	□	□
		First Day Cover		4·50		□
		Presentation Pack	5·00		□	
		PHQ Cards (set of 5)	4·50	7·00	□	□
		Set of 5 Gutter Pairs	10·00		□	

Booklet Stamps

1993 (6 APR.)–**99** *As T* **913/14** *and* **1093a**, *but Perf* 14 *(No.* 1663b*) or* 15 × 14 *(others) (both with one elliptical hole on each vertical side)*

(*a*) *Photo*

Harrison (*No.* 1664)
Questa (*Nos.* 1663ab, 1664ab)
Walsall (*No.* 1663b)
Harrison (later *De La Rue*), Questa or Walsall (*No.* 1664a)
Harrison (later *De La Rue*), Enschedé, Questa or Walsall (*Nos.* 1663a, 1664b, 1664c)

1663a	**913**	(2nd) bright blue (1 centre band)	1·00	1·00	□	□
		ab. Perf 14	1·10	1·10	□	□
1663b		(2nd) bright blue (1 side band)	1·10	1·10	□	□
1664	**914**	(1st) bright orange-red (phosphorised paper)	1·50	1·25	□	□
1664a		(1st) bright orange-red (2 phosphor bands) . .	1·10	1·10	□	□
		ab. Perf 14	1·50	1·50	□	□
1664b		(1st) gold (2 phosphor bands)	1·00	1·00	□	□
1664c	**1093a**	(E) deep blue (2 phosphor bands) . .	1·25	1·25	□	□

(*b*) *Litho Questa or Walsall (No.* 1666 *also Enschedé)*

1665	**913**	(2nd) bright blue (1 centre band)	90	90	□	□
1666	**914**	(1st) bright orange-red (2 phosphor bands) . .	1·00	1·00	□	□

First Day Covers

21 Apr. 1997	(1st), 26p (Nos 1664b, Y1683b) .	£3·50	□
19 Jan. 1999	(E) (No 1664c)	£3·50	□

Nos. 1663a, 1664a, 1664c and 1665/6 also come from sheets.

No. 1663b exists with the phosphor band at the left or right of the stamp and was only issued in booklets.

No. 1664b was issued by Harrison in booklets and Walsall in sheets and booklets for the Queen's Golden Wedding on 21 April 1997. The gold colour was later adopted for the (1st) class rate, replacing bright orange-red.

For No. 1664b in presentation pack see Pack No. 38 listed below, No. Y1667 etc.

No. 1664c was valid for the basic European airmail rate, initially 30p.

For self-adhesive versions in these colours see Nos. 2039/40 and 2295/8.

1993–2005 *As Nos.* X841 *etc, but perf* 14 *(No.* Y1676*) or* 15 × 14 *(others) (both with one elliptical hole on each vertical side)*

(*a*) *Photo*

Enschedé:— 20p (Y1677), 29p, 35p (Y1688), 36p, 38p (Y1692), 41p (Y1696), 43p (Y1699)
Harrison:— 20p (Y1679), 25p (Y1681), 26p (Y1683b), 35p (Y1689), 41p (Y1697), 43p (Y1700)

Walsall:— 10p (Y1674a), 19p (Y1676), 38p (Y1693a), 43p (Y1700a)

Enschedé or Harrison (later De La Rue):— 4p, 5p, 6p, 10p (Y1674), 25p (Y1682), 31p, 39p (Y1694), £1

Enschedé, Harrison (later De La Rue) or Questa:— 1p, 2p

Enschedé, Harrison (later De La Rue) or Walsall:— 30p, 37p (Y1691), 42p, 50p, 63p

Harrison (later De La Rue) or Questa:— 19p (Y1675), 20p (Y1678), 26p (Y1683)

De La Rue or Walsall:— 38p (Y1693), 39p (Y1694b), 40p (Y1695), 64p, 65p, 68p

De La Rue:— 7p, 8p, 9p, 20p (Y1680), 33p, 34p, 35p (Y1689a), 37p (Y1691a), 40p (Y1695a), 41p (Y1698), 43p (Y1700b), 44p, 45p, 46p, £1·50, £2, £3, £5

Enschedé or De La Rue:— 35p (Y1689b), 47p

Y1667	**367**	1p crimson (2 bands) .	25	25	□	□
Y1668		2p deep green (2 bands)	25	25	□	□
Y1669		4p new blue (2 bands) .	25	25	□	□
Y1670		5p dull red-brown (2 bands)	25	25	□	□
Y1671		6p yellow-olive (2 bands)	25	30	□	□
Y1672		7p grey (2 bands)	35	35	□	□
Y1672a		7p bright magenta (2 bands)	25	25	□	□
Y1673		8p yellow (2 bands) . .	35	35	□	□
Y1673a		9p yellow-orange (2 bands)	15	20	□	□
Y1674		10p dull orange (2 bands)	35	35	□	□
		a. Perf 14	2·00	2·00	□	□
Y1675		19p bistre (1 centre band)	75	75	□	□
Y1676		19p bistre (1 side band) .	2·00	2·00	□	□
Y1677		20p turquoise-green (2 bands)	90	90	□	□
Y1678		20p bright green (1 centre band)	70	70	□	□
Y1679		20p bright green (1 side band)	1·50	1·50	□	□
Y1680		20p bright green (2 bands)	75	75	□	□
Y1681		25p rose-red (phosphorised paper)	1·10	1·10	□	□
Y1682		25p rose-red (2 bands) .	1·10	1·10	□	□
Y1683		26p red-brown (2 bands)	1·10	1·10	□	□
Y1683b		26p gold (2 bands)	1·10	1·10	□	□
Y1684		29p grey (2 bands)	1·25	1·25	□	□
Y1685		30p deep olive-grey (2 bands)	1·10	1·10	□	□
Y1686		31p deep mauve (2 bands)	1·20	1·20	□	□
Y1687		33p grey-green (2 bands)	1·50	1·50	□	□
Y1687a		34p yellow-olive (2 bands)	1·25	1·00	□	□
Y1688		35p yellow (2 bands) . .	1·50	1·50	□	□
Y1689		35p yellow (phosphorised paper)	7·50	7·50	□	□
Y1689a		35p sepia (2 bands) . . .	1·10	1·10	□	□
Y1689b		35p yellow-olive (1 centre band)	50	55	□	□
Y1690		36p bright ultramarine (2 bands)	1·50	1·50	□	□
Y1691		37p bright mauve (2 bands)	1·40	1·40	□	□
Y1691a		37p grey-black (2 bands)	1·40	1·40	□	□
Y1692		38p rosine (2 bands) . . .	1·50	1·50	□	□
Y1693		38p ultramarine (2 bands)	2·00	2·00	□	□
		a. Perf 14	7·50	7·50	□	□
Y1694		39p bright magenta (2 bands)	1·50	1·50	□	□
Y1694b		39p grey (2 bands)	1·20	1·20	□	□
Y1695		40p deep azure (2 bands)	1·40	1·40	□	□
Y1695a		40p turquoise-blue (2 bands)	1·30	1·30	□	□
Y1696		41p grey-brown (2 bands)	1·75	1·75	□	□
Y1697		41p drab (phosphorised paper)	7·50	7·50	□	□
Y1698		41p rosine (2 bands) . . .	1·40	1·40	□	□
Y1698a		42p deep olive-grey (2 bands)	1·40	1·40	□	□
Y1699		43p deep olive-brown (2 bands)	1·75	1·75	□	□
Y1700		43p sepia (2 bands) . . .	2·50	2·50	□	□
		a. Perf 14	2·50	2·50	□	□
Y1700b		43p emerald (2 bands) . .	1·40	1·40	□	□
Y1701		44p grey-brown (2 bands)	4·25	4·25	□	□
Y1702		45p bright mauve (2 bands)	1·50	1·50	□	□
Y1702a		46p yellow (2 bands) . .	70	75	□	□
Y1702b		47p turquoise-green (2 bands)	1·75	1·75	□	□
Y1703		50p ochre (2 bands) . . .	1·75	1·20	□	□
Y1704		63p light emerald (2 bands)	2·00	2·00	□	□
Y1705		64p turquoise-green (2 bands)	2·25	2·25	□	□
Y1706		65p greenish blue (2 bands)	2·10	2·10	□	□
Y1706a		68p grey-brown (2 bands)	2·10	2·10	□	□
Y1707		£1 bluish violet (2 bands)	3·25	3·00	□	□
Y1708		£1·50 brown-red (2 bands)	3·50	3·50	□	□
Y1709		£2 deep blue-green (2 bands)	5·00	5·00	□	□
Y1710		£3 deep mauve (2 bands)	7·50	5·00	□	□
Y1711		£5 azure (2 bands) . . .	12·00	6·00	□	□

(b) Litho Walsall (37p, 60p, 63p), Questa or Walsall (25p, 35p, 41p), Questa (others)

Y1743	**367**	1p lake (2 bands)	40	40	□	□
Y1748		6p yellow-olive (2 bands)	12·00	13·00	□	□
Y1749		10p dull orange (2 bands)	5·00	5·00	□	□
Y1750		19p bistre (1 side band) .	1·90	1·75	□	□
Y1751		20p bright yellow-green (1 centre band) . . .	2·25	2·25	□	□

103

Y1752	25p red (2 bands)	1·10	1·10 ☐ ☐	
Y1753	26p chestnut (2 bands) .	1·00	1·00 ☐ ☐	
Y1754	30p olive-grey (2 bands)	4·25	4·25 ☐ ☐	
Y1755	35p yellow (2 bands) ..	1·60	1·60 ☐ ☐	
Y1756	37p bright mauve (2 bands)	2·40	2·40 ☐ ☐	
Y1757	41p drab (2 bands) ...	1·75	1·75 ☐ ☐	
Y1758	60p dull blue-grey (2 bands)	2·50	2·50 ☐ ☐	
Y1759	63p light emerald (2 bands)	3·00	3·00 ☐ ☐	

(c) Recess Enschedé or De La Rue

Y1800	**367**	£1·50 red	4·25	2·00 ☐ ☐	
Y1801		£2 dull blue	6·00	2·25 ☐ ☐	
Y1802		£3 dull violet	9·00	3·00 ☐ ☐	
Y1803		£5 brown	15·00	5·00 ☐ ☐	

PHQ Card (No. Y1707) ..... 40 3·00 ☐ ☐

Presentation Pack (P.O. Pack No. 30) (contains 19p (Y1675), 25p (Y1681), 29p (Y1684), 36p (Y1690), 38p (Y1692), 41p (Y1696)) .. 7·00 ☐

Presentation Pack (P.O. Pack No. 34) (contains 1p (Y1667), 2p (Y1668), 4p (Y1669), 5p (Y1670), 6p (Y1671), 10p (Y1674), 19p (Y1675), 20p (Y1677), 25p (Y1682), 29p (Y1684), 30p (Y1685), 35p (Y1688), 36p (Y1690), 38p (Y1692), 41p (Y1696), 50p (Y1703), 60p (Y1758), £1 (Y1707)) ..... 30·00 ☐

Presentation Pack (P.O. Pack No. 35) (contains 20p (Y1678), 26p (Y1683), 31p (Y1686), 37p (Y1691), 39p (Y1694), 43p (Y1699), 63p (Y1704)) .... 9·50 ☐

Presentation Pack (P.O. Pack No. 38) (contains 1st (1664b), 26p (Y1683b)) .... 7·50 ☐

Presentation Pack (P.O. Pack No. 41) (contains 2nd (1663a), 1st (1664a), 1p (Y1667), 2p (Y1668), 4p (Y1669), 5p (Y1670), 6p (Y1671), 10p (Y1674), 20p (Y1678), 26p (Y1683), 30p (Y1685), 31p (Y1686), 37p (Y1691), 39p (Y1694), 43p (Y1700), 50p (Y1703), 63p (Y1704), £1 (Y1707)) .... 16·00 ☐

Presentation Pack (P.O. Pack No. 43 or 43A) *(contains* £1·50 (Y1800), £2 (Y1801), £3 (Y1802), £5 (Y1803)) .... 55·00 ☐

Presentation Pack (P.O. Pack No. 44) contains 7p (Y1672), 19p (Y1675), 38p (Y1693), 44p (Y1701), 64p (Y1705)) .... 11·00 ☐

Presentation Pack (P.O. Pack No. 49) (contains 8p (Y1673), 33p (Y1687), 40p (Y1695), 41p (Y1698), 45p (Y1702), 65p (Y1706)) .... 10·00 ☐

Presentation Pack (P.O. Pack No. 57) (contains 2nd (1663b), 1st (1664a), E (1664c), 1p (Y1667), 2p (Y1668), 4p (Y1669), 5p (Y1670), 8p (Y1673), 10p (Y1674), 20p (Y1680), 33p (Y1687), 40p (Y1695), 41p (Y1698), 45p (Y1702), 50p (Y1703), 65p (Y1706), £1 (Y1707)) .... 16·00 ☐

Presentation Pack (P.O. Pack No. 58) (contains 37p (Y1691a), 42p (Y1698a), 47p (Y1702a), 68p (Y1706a)) .... 7·50 ☐

Presentation Pack (P.O. Pack No. 62) (contains £1·50 (Y1708), £2 (Y1709), £3 (Y1710), £5 (Y1711)) .... 23·00 ☐

Presentation Pack (P.O. Pack No. 67) (contains 7p (No. Y1672a), 1st (1664b), 35p (Y1689b), 39p (Y1694b), 40p (Y1695a), 43p (Y1700b), Worldwide postcard (2359a)) .... 6·00 ☐

Presentation Pack (P.O. Pack No. 69) (contains 1p (Y1667), 2p (Y1668), 5p (Y1670), 9p (Y1673a), 10p (Y1674), 20p (Y1680), 35p (Y1689b), 40p (Y1695a), 42p (Y1698a), 46p (Y1702a), 47p (Y1702b), 50p (Y1703), 68p (Y1706a), £1 (Y1707), 2nd (2039), 1st (2295), Worldwide postcard (2357a), Europe (2358), Worldwide (2359) .... 11·50 ☐

For P.O. Pack No. 37 see below SG1977.

First Day Covers

26 Oct. 1993	19p, 25p, 29p, 36p, 38p, 41p (Nos. Y1675, Y1681, Y1684, Y1690, Y1692, Y1696)	6·00	☐
9 Aug. 1994	60p (No. Y1758)	4·00	☐
22 Aug. 1995	£1 (No. Y1707)	3·50	☐
25 June 1996	20p, 26p, 31p, 37p, 39p, 43p, 63p (Nos. Y1678, Y1683, Y1686, Y1691, Y1694, Y1699, Y1704)	8·00	☐
9 Mar. 1999	£1·50, £2, £3, £5 (Nos. Y1800/3)	27·00	☐
20 Apr. 1999	7p, 38p, 44p, 64p (Nos. Y1672, Y1693, Y1701, Y1705)	5·00	☐
25 Apr. 2000	8p, 33p, 40p, 41p, 45p, 65p (Nos. Y1673, Y1687, Y1695, Y1698, Y1702, Y1706)	5·00	☐

4 July 2002	37p, 42p, 47p, 68p, (Nos. Y1691a, Y1698a, Y1702a, Y1706a) . . .	4·00		□
6 May 2003	34p (No. Y1687a)	1·20		□
1 July 2003	£1·50, £2, £3, £5 (Nos. Y1708/11)	21·00		□
1 April 2004	7p, 35p, 39p, 40p, 43p, World-wide postcard (Nos. Y1672a, Y1689a, Y1694b, Y1695a, Y1700b, 2359a)	9·00		□
5 April 2005	9p, 35p, 46p (Nos. Y1673a, Y1689b, Y1702a)	2·20		□

Nos. Y1707 and Y1708/11 are printed in Iriodin ink which gives a shiny effect to the solid part of the background behind the Queen's head.

Nos. Y1689 and Y1697 were only issued in coils and Nos. Y1674a, Y1676, Y1679, Y1693a, Y1700a, Y1743 and Y1748/59 only in booklets.

No. Y1750 exists with the phosphor band at the left or right of the stamp, but Nos. Y1676 and Y1679 exist with band at right only.

> For self-adhesive versions of the 42p and 68p see Nos. 2297/8.

1094 'Family Group' (bronze sculpture) (Henry Moore)

1095 'Kew Gardens' (lithograph) (Edward Bawden)

1096 'St Francis and the Birds' (Stanley Spencer)

1097 'Still Life: Odyssey I' (Ben Nicholson)

Europa. Contemporary Art

1993 (11 MAY) Phosphorised paper. Perf 14 × 14½

1767	**1094**	24p multicoloured	60		20	□ □
1768	**1095**	28p multicoloured	90		1·00	□ □
1769	**1096**	33p multicoloured	1·25		1·40	□ □
1770	**1097**	39p multicoloured	1·40		1·50	□ □
		Set of 4	3·75		3·75	□ □
		First Day Cover			4·50	□
		Presentation Pack	4·50			□
		PHQ Cards (set of 4)	4·00		7·00	□ □
		Set of 4 Gutter Pairs	10·00			□

1098 Emperor Claudius (from gold coin)

1099 Emperor Hadrian (bronze head)

1100 Goddess Roma (from gemstone)

1101 Christ (Hinton St Mary mosaic)

Roman Britain

1993 (15 JUNE) Phosphorised paper with two phosphor bands. Perf 14 × 14½

1771	**1098**	24p multicoloured	60		20	□ □
1772	**1099**	28p multicoloured	90		1·00	□ □
1773	**1100**	33p multicoloured	1·25		1·40	□ □
1774	**1101**	39p multicoloured	1·40		1·50	□ □
		Set of 4	3·75		3·75	□ □
		First Day Cover			3·75	□
		Presentation Pack	4·50			□
		PHQ Cards (set of 4)	4·25		7·00	□ □
		Set of 4 Gutter Pairs	10·00			□

1102 Midland Maid and other Narrow Boats, Grand Junction Canal

1103 Yorkshire Maid and other Humber Keels, Stainforth and Keadby Canal

1104 Valley Princess and other Horse-drawn Barges, Brecknock and Abergavenny Canal

1105 Steam Barges including Pride of Scotland and and Fishing Boats, Crinan Canal

Inland Waterways

1993 (20 July) *Two phosphor bands. Perf* 14½ × 14

1775	**1102**	24p multicoloured	50	20	☐	☐
1776	**1103**	28p multicoloured	1·00	1·00	☐	☐
1777	**1104**	33p multicoloured	1·25	1·25	☐	☐
1778	**1105**	39p multicoloured	1·50	1·40	☐	☐
		Set of 4	3·75	3·50	☐	☐
		First Day Cover		3·75	☐	
		Presentation Pack	4·50		☐	
		PHQ Cards (set of 4)	4·25	7·00	☐	☐
		Set of 4 Gutter Pairs	9·00		☐	

Nos. 1775/8 commemorate the bicentenaries of the Acts of Parliament authorising the canals depicted.

1106 Horse Chestnut

1107 Blackberry

1108 Hazel

1109 Rowan

1110 Pear

The Four Seasons. Autumn. Fruits and Leaves

1993 (14 Sept.) *One phosphor band* (18p) *or phosphorised paper* (*others*)

1779	**1106**	18p multicoloured	50	20	☐	☐
1780	**1107**	24p multicoloured	75	20	☐	☐
1781	**1108**	28p multicoloured	1·10	1·25	☐	☐
1782	**1109**	33p multicoloured	1·40	1·50	☐	☐
1783	**1110**	39p multicoloured	1·50	1·50	☐	☐
		Set of 5	4·75	4·50	☐	☐
		First Day Cover		4·50	☐	
		Presentation Pack	4·75		☐	
		PHQ Cards (set of 5)	4·50	7·00	☐	☐
		Set of 5 Gutter Pairs	10·50		☐	

SHERLOCK HOLMES & DR WATSON
"THE REIGATE SQUIRE"

1111 The Reigate Squire

SHERLOCK HOLMES & SIR HENRY
"THE HOUND OF THE BASKERVILLES"

1112 The Hound of the Baskervilles

SHERLOCK HOLMES & LESTRADE
"THE SIX NAPOLEONS"

1113 The Six Napoleons

SHERLOCK HOLMES & MYCROFT
"THE GREEK INTERPRETER"

1114 The Greek Interpreter

SHERLOCK HOLMES & MORIARTY
"THE FINAL PROBLEM"

1115 The Final Problem

T **1111/15** were printed together, *se-tenant,* in horizontal strips of 5 throughout the sheet.

Sherlock Holmes. Centenary of the Publication of **The Final Problem**

1993 (12 Oct.) *Phosphorised paper. Perf* 14 × 14½

1784	**1111**	24p multicoloured	1·10	1·10	☐	☐
		a. Horiz strip of 5. Nos.				
		1784/8	5·00	5·25	☐	☐
1785	**1112**	24p multicoloured	1·10	1·10	☐	☐
1786	**1113**	24p multicoloured	1·10	1·10	☐	☐
1787	**1114**	24p multicoloured	1·10	1·10	☐	☐
1788	**1115**	24p multicoloured	1·10	1·10	☐	☐
		Set of 5	5·00	5·00	☐	☐
		First Day Cover		5·00	☐	
		Presentation Pack	5·00		☐	
		PHQ Cards (set of 5)	4·50	8·00	☐	☐
		Gutter Strip of 10	11·00		☐	

1116

Self-adhesive Booklet Stamp

1993 (19 Oct.) *Litho Walsall. Two phosphor bands. Die-cut perf 14 × 15 (with one elliptical hole on each vertical side)*

1789	**1116**	(1st) orange-red	. . . . .	1·25	1·40	□ □
		First Day Cover	. . . .		4·50	□
		Presentation Pack (*booklet pane*				
		of 20)	. . . .	20·00		□
		PHQ Card	. . . .	4·00	8·00	□ □

For similar 2nd and 1st designs printed in photogravure by Enschedé see Nos. 1976/7.

1117 Bob Cratchit and Tiny Tim

1118 Mr and Mrs Fezziwig

1119 Scrooge

1120 The Prize Turkey

1121 Mr Scrooge's Nephew

Christmas. 150th Anniversary of Publication of A Christmas Carol

1993 (9 Nov.) *One phosphor band* (19p) *or phosphorised paper (others)*

1790	**1117**	19p multicoloured	. . . .	60	15	□ □
1791	**1118**	25p multicoloured	. . . .	90	15	□ □
1792	**1119**	30p multicoloured	. . . .	1·25	1·50	□ □
1793	**1120**	35p multicoloured	. . . .	1·40	1·60	□ □
1794	**1121**	41p multicoloured	. . . .	1·40	1·60	□ □
		Set of 5	. . . .	4·50	4·50	□ □
		First Day Cover	. . . .		5·00	□
		Presentation Pack	. . . .	5·00		□
		PHQ Cards (*set of* 5)	. . . . . .	4·50	8·00	□ □
		Set of 5 Gutter Pairs	. . . . . .	11·00		□

Collectors Pack 1993

1993 (9 Nov.) *Comprises Nos.* 1639/43, 1654/7, 1659/63, 1767/88 *and* 1790/4

| CP1794a | Collectors Pack | . . . . . . | 45·00 | □ |

Post Office Yearbook

1993 (9 Nov.) *Comprises Nos.* 1639/43, 1654/7, 1659/63, 1767/88 *and* 1790/4 *in hardback book with slip case*

| YB1794a | Yearbook | . . . . | 65·00 | □ |

1122 Class 5 No. 44957 and Class B1 No. 61342 on West Highland Line

1123 Class A1 No. 60149 *Amadis* at Kings Cross

1124 Class 4 No. 43000 on Turntable at Blyth North

1125 Class 4 No. 42455 near Wigan Central

1126 Class Castle No. 7002 *Devizes Castle* on Bridge crossing Worcester and Birmingham Canal

Minimum Price. The minimum price quoted is 10p. This represents a handling charge rather than a basis for valuing common stamps. Where the actual value of a stamp is less than 10p this may be apparent when set prices are shown, particularly for sets including a number of 10p stamps. It therefore follows that in valuing common stamps the 10p catalogue price should not be reckoned automatically since it covers a variation in real scarcity.

The Age of Steam. Railway Photographs by Colin Gifford

1994 (18 Jan.) *One phosphor band* (19p) *or phosphorised paper with two bands* (others). *Perf* 14½

1795	**1122**	19p deep blue-green, grey-black and black	55	25	□	□
1796	**1123**	25p slate-lilac, grey-black and black	90	95	□	□
1797	**1124**	30p lake-brown, grey-black and black ...	1·40	1·40	□	□
1798	**1125**	35p deep claret, grey-black and black ...	1·50	1·60	□	□
1799	**1126**	41p indigo, grey-black and black	1·60	1·50	□	□
		Set of 5	5·50	5·00	□	□
		First Day Cover		5·50		□
		Presentation Pack	5·75			□
		PHQ Cards (set of 5)	5·75	11·00	□	□
		Set of 5 Gutter Pairs	12·00			□

1127 Dan Dare and the Mekon

1128 The Three Bears

1129 Rupert Bear

1130 Alice (*Alice in Wonderland*)

1131 Noggin and the Ice Dragon

1132 Peter Rabbit posting Letter

1133 Red Riding Hood and Wolf

1134 Orlando the Marmalade Cat

1135 Biggles

1136 Paddington Bear on Station

T **1127/36** were printed together, *se-tenant*, in booklet panes of 10 stamps and 20 half stamp-size labels.

Greeting Stamps. 'Messages'

1994 (1 Feb.) *Two phosphor bands. Perf* 15 × 14 (*with one elliptical hole on each vertical side*)

1800	**1127**	(1st) multicoloured	1·00	90	□	□
		a. Booklet pane. Nos. 1800/9	13·00	12·00	□	□
1801	**1128**	(1st) multicoloured	1·00	90	□	□
1802	**1129**	(1st) multicoloured	1·00	90	□	□
1803	**1130**	(1st) gold, bistre-yellow and black	1·00	90	□	□
1804	**1131**	(1st) multicoloured	1·00	90	□	□
1805	**1132**	(1st) multicoloured	1·00	90	□	□
1806	**1133**	(1st) multicoloured	1·00	90	□	□
1807	**1134**	(1st) multicoloured	1·00	90	□	□
1808	**1135**	(1st) multicoloured	1·00	90	□	□
1809	**1136**	(1st) multicoloured	1·00	90	□	□
		Set of 10	11·00	8·00	□	□
		First Day Cover		11·00		□
		Presentation Pack	18·00			□
		PHQ Cards (set of 10)	16·00	28·00	□	□

1137 Castell Y Waun (Chirk Castle), Clwyd, Wales

1138 Ben Arkle, Sutherland, Scotland

1139 Mourne Mountains, County Down, Northern Ireland

1140 Dersingham, Norfolk, England

Dolwyddelan, Gwynedd, Cymru /Wales

1141   Dolwyddelan, Gwynedd, Wales

25th Anniversary of Investiture of the Prince of Wales. Paintings by Prince Charles

1994 (1 MAR.) *One phosphor band* (19p) *or phosphorised paper* (*others*)

1810	**1137**	19p multicoloured	....	55		20 □	□
1811	**1138**	25p multicoloured	....	1·00		20 □	□
1812	**1139**	30p multicoloured	....	1·10		1·50 □	□
1813	**1140**	35p multicoloured	....	1·40		1·75 □	□
1814	**1141**	41p multicoloured	....	1·50		1·75 □	□
		Set of 5	....	5·00		5·00 □	□
		First Day Cover	....			5·00	□
		Presentation Pack	......	5·00			□
		PHQ Cards (set of 5)	.....	5·75		11·50 □	□
		Set of 5 Gutter Pairs	.....	11·00			□

1142   Bather at Blackpool

1143   'Where's my Little Lad?'

1144   'Wish You were Here!'

1145   Punch and Judy Show

1146   'The Tower Crane' Machine

Centenary of Picture Postcards

1994 (12 APR.) *One side band* (19p) *or two phosphor bands* (*others*). *Perf* 14 × 14½

1815	**1142**	19p multicoloured	60	20 □	□
1816	**1143**	25p multicoloured	90	20 □	□
1817	**1144**	30p multicoloured	1·10	1·50 □	□
1818	**1145**	35p multicoloured	1·40	1·75 □	□
1819	**1146**	41p multicoloured	1·50	1·75 □	□
		Set of 5	5·00	5·00 □	□
		First Day Cover		4·75	□
		Presentation Pack	5·00		□
		PHQ Cards (set of 5)	5·75	11·50 □	□
		Set of 5 Gutter Pairs	11·00		□

1147   British Lion and French Cockerel over Tunnel

1148   Symbolic Hands over Train

Nos. 1820/1 and 1822/3 were printed together, *se-tenant*, in horizontal pairs throughout the sheets.

Opening of Channel Tunnel

1994 (3 MAY) *Phosphorised paper. Perf* 14 × 14½

1820	**1147**	25p multicoloured	80	70 □	□
		a. Horiz pair. Nos. 1820/1	1·75	2·00 □	□
1821	**1148**	25p multicoloured	80	70 □	□
1822	**1147**	41p multicoloured	1·50	1·50 □	□
		a. Horiz pair. Nos. 1822/3	3·25	3·25 □	□
1823	**1148**	41p multicoloured	1·50	1·50 □	□
		Set of 4	4·50	4·50 □	□
		First Day Cover		4·50	□
		Presentation Pack	5·00		□
		Souvenir Book	47·00		□
		PHQ Cards (set of 4)	5·75	9·00 □	□

Stamps in similar designs were also issued by France and these are included in the Souvenir Book.

1149 Groundcrew replacing Smoke Canisters on Douglas Boston of 88 Sqn

1150 H.M.S. *Warspite* (battleship) shelling Enemy Positions

1154 The Old Course, St Andrews

1155 The 18th Hole, Muirfield

1151 Commandos landing on Gold Beach

1152 Infantry regrouping on Sword Beach

1156 The 15th Hole ('Luckyslap'), Carnoustie

1157 The 8th Hole ('The Postage Stamp'), Royal Troon

1153 Tank and Infantry advancing, Ouistreham

1158 The 9th Hole, Turnberry

Nos. 1824/8 were printed together, *se-tenant,* in horizontal strips of 5 throughout the sheet.

50th Anniversary of D-Day
1994 (6 JUNE) *Two phosphor bands. Perf* 14½ × 14

1824	**1149**	25p multicoloured	1·10	1·10	□	□
		a. Horiz strip of 5. Nos.				
		1824/8	5·00	5·50	□	□
1825	**1150**	25p multicoloured	1·10	1·10	□	□
1826	**1151**	25p multicoloured	1·10	1·10	□	□
1827	**1152**	25p multicoloured	1·10	1·10	□	□
1828	**1153**	25p multicoloured	1·10	1·10	□	□
		Set of 5	4·25	5·00	□	□
		First Day Cover		4·75		□
		Presentation Pack	5·50		□	
		PHQ Cards (*set of 5*)	5·00	9·00	□	□
		Gutter Block of 10	11·00		□	

Scottish Golf Courses
1994 (5 JULY) *One phosphor band* (19p) *or phosphorised paper* (*others*). *Perf* 14½ × 14

1829	**1154**	19p multicoloured	50	20	□	□
1830	**1155**	25p multicoloured	75	20	□	□
1831	**1156**	30p multicoloured	1·10	1·40	□	□
1832	**1157**	35p multicoloured	1·25	1·40	□	□
1833	**1158**	41p multicoloured	1·40	1·40	□	□
		Set of 5	4·50	4·25	□	□
		First Day Cover		4·75		□
		Presentation Pack	4·75		□	
		PHQ Cards (*set of 5*)	5·75	11·50	□	□
		Set of 5 Gutter Pairs	11·50		□	

Nos. 1829/33 commemorate the 250th anniversary of golf's first set of rules produced by the Honourable Company of Edinburgh Golfers.

1159 Royal Welsh Show, Llanelwedd

1160 All England Tennis Championships, Wimbledon

1161 Cowes Week

1162 Test Match, Lord's

1163 Braemar Gathering

The Four Seasons. Summertime. Events

1994 (2 AUG.) *One phosphor band* (19p) *or phosphorised paper* (*others*)

1834	**1159**	19p multicoloured	. . . .	50	20	☐ ☐
1835	**1160**	25p multicoloured	. . . .	75	20	☐ ☐
1836	**1161**	30p multicoloured	. . . .	1·10	1·25	☐ ☐
1837	**1162**	35p multicoloured	. . . .	1·25	1·60	☐ ☐
1838	**1163**	41p multicoloured	. . . .	1·40	1·60	☐ ☐
		Set of 5	. . . .	4·50	4·25	☐ ☐
		First Day Cover			4·50	☐
		Presentation Pack		4·50		☐
		PHQ *Cards* (*set of* 5)		5·75	11·50	☐ ☐
		Set of 5 *Gutter Pairs*		11·50		☐

1164 Ultrasonic Imaging

1165 Scanning Electron Microscopy

1166 Magnetic Resonance Imaging

1167 Computed Tomography

Europa. Medical Discoveries

1994 (27 SEPT.) *Phosphorised paper. Perf* 14 × 14½

1839	**1164**	25p multicoloured	. . . .	75	25	☐ ☐
1840	**1165**	30p multicoloured	. . . .	1·00	1·25	☐ ☐
1841	**1166**	35p multicoloured	. . . .	1·25	1·50	☐ ☐
1842	**1167**	41p multicoloured	. . . .	1·50	1·50	☐ ☐
		Set of 4	4·00	4·00	☐ ☐
		First Day Cover			4·75	☐
		Presentation Pack		4·75		☐
		PHQ *Cards* (*set of* 4)		5·75	10·00	☐ ☐
		Set of 4 *Gutter Pairs*		11·00		☐

1168 Virgin Mary and Joseph

1169 Three Wise Men

1170 Virgin and Child

1171 Shepherds

1172 Angels

Christmas. Children's Nativity Plays

1994 (1 Nov.) *One phosphor band* (19p) *or phosphorised paper (others)*

1843	**1168**	19p multicoloured	50	15 □ □
1844	**1169**	25p multicoloured	75	15 □ □
1845	**1170**	30p multicoloured	1·00	1·50 □ □
1846	**1171**	35p multicoloured	1·25	1·50 □ □
1847	**1172**	41p multicoloured	1·50	1·75 □ □
		Set of 5	4·50	4·75 □ □
		First Day Cover		4·75 □
		Presentation Pack	4·75	□
		PHQ Cards (set of 5)	5·75	11·50 □ □
		Set of 5 Gutter Pairs	10·50	□

Collectors Pack 1994

1994 (14 Nov.) *Comprises Nos. 1795/1847*
CP1847*a* Collectors Pack . . . . 55·00   □

Post Office Yearbook

1994 (14 Nov.) *Comprises Nos. 1795/9 and 1810/47 in hardback book with slip case*
YB1847*a* Yearbook . . . . 55·00   □

1173 Sophie (black cat)

1174 Puskas (Siamese) and Tigger (tabby)

1175 Chloe (ginger cat)

1176 Kikko (tortoiseshell) and Rosie (Abyssinian)

1177 Fred (black and white cat)

Cats

1995 (17 Jan.) *One phosphor band* (19p) *or two phosphor bands (others). Perf* 14½ × 14

1848	**1173**	19p multicoloured	75	20 □ □
1849	**1174**	25p multicoloured	75	25 □ □
1850	**1175**	30p multicoloured	1·00	1·50 □ □
1851	**1176**	35p multicoloured	1·25	1·50 □ □
1852	**1177**	41p multicoloured	1·50	1·50 □ □
		Set of 5	4·75	4·75 □ □
		First Day Cover		4·75 □
		Presentation Pack	5·50	□
		PHQ Cards (set of 5)	6·00	11·50 □ □
		Set of 5 Gutter Pairs	11·00	□

1178 Dandelions

1179 Sweet Chestnut Leaves

1180 Garlic Leaves

1181 Hazel Leaves

1182 Spring Grass

The Four Seasons. Springtime. Plant Sculptures by Andy Goldsworthy

1995 (14 Mar.) *One phosphor band* (19p) *or two phosphor bands (others)*

1853	**1178**	19p multicoloured	75	15 □ □
1854	**1179**	25p multicoloured	75	15 □ □
1855	**1180**	30p multicoloured	1·00	1·50 □ □
1856	**1181**	35p multicoloured	1·25	1·50 □ □
1857	**1182**	41p multicoloured	1·50	1·75 □ □
		Set of 5	4·75	4·75 □ □
		First Day Cover		4·75 □
		Presentation Pack	5·00	□
		PHQ Cards (set of 5)	6·00	11·50 □ □
		Set of 5 Gutter Pairs	11·50	□

1183 'La Danse a la Campagne' (Renoir)

1184 'Troilus and Criseyde' (Peter Brookes)

1185 'The Kiss' (Rodin)

1186 'Girls on the Town' (Beryl Cook)

1187 'Jazz' (Andrew Mockett)

1188 'Girls performing a Kathal Dance' (Aurangzeb period)

1189 'Alice Keppel with her Daughter' (Alice Hughes)

1190 'Children Playing' (L. S. Lowry)

1191 'Circus Clowns' (Emily Firmin and Justin Mitchell)

1192 Decoration from 'All the Love Poems of Shakespeare' (Eric Gill)

T **1183/92** were printed together, *se-tenant*, in booklet panes of 10 stamps and 20 half stamp-size labels.

Greetings Stamp. 'Greetings in Art'

1995 (21 MAR.) *Two phosphor bands. Perf* 14½ × 14 (*with one elliptical hole on each vertical side*)

1858	**1183**	(1st) multicoloured	1·00	80	□	□
		a. Booklet pane. Nos. 1858/67	11·50	11·00	□	□
1859	**1184**	(1st) multicoloured	1·00	80	□	□
1860	**1185**	(1st) multicoloured	1·00	80	□	□
1861	**1186**	(1st) multicoloured	1·00	80	□	□
1862	**1187**	(1st) multicoloured	1·00	80	□	□
1863	**1188**	(1st) multicoloured	1·00	80	□	□
1864	**1189**	(1st) purple-brown and silver	1·00	80	□	□
1865	**1190**	(1st) multicoloured	1·00	80	□	□
1866	**1191**	(1st) multicoloured	1·00	80	□	□
1867	**1192**	(1st) black, greenish yellow and silver ..	1·00	80	□	□
	Set of 10	....	11·00	7·25	□	□
	First Day Cover			11·50		□
	Presentation Pack		12·00		□	
	PHQ Cards (*set of* 10)		16·00	28·00	□	□

1193 Fireplace Decoration, Attingham Park, Shropshire

1194 Oak Seedling

1195 Carved Table Leg, Attingham Park

1196 St David's Head, Dyfed, Wales

1197 Elizabethan Window, Little Moreton Hall, Cheshire

Centenary of The National Trust

1995 (11 APR.) *One phosphor band (19p), two phosphor bands (25p, 35p) or phosphorised paper (30p, 41p)*

1868	**1193**	19p multicoloured	60	20	☐	☐
1869	**1194**	25p multicoloured	80	20	☐	☐
1870	**1195**	30p multicoloured	1·00	1·50	☐	☐
1871	**1196**	35p multicoloured	1·25	1·50	☐	☐
1872	**1197**	41p multicoloured	1·40	1·75	☐	☐
		Set of 5	4·50	4·75	☐	☐
		First Day Cover		4·75		☐
		Presentation Pack	4·75			☐
		PHQ Cards (set of 5)	6·00	11·50	☐	☐
		Set of 5 Gutter Pairs	11·00			☐

1198 British Troops and French Civilians celebrating

1199 Symbolic Hands and Red Cross

1200 St Paul's Cathedral and Searchlights

1201 Symbolic Hand releasing Peace Dove

1202 Symbolic Hands

For full information on all future British issues, collectors should write to Royal Mail, Freepost EH3647, 21 South Gyle Crescent, Edinburgh EH12 9PE.

Europa. Peace and Freedom

1995 (2 MAY) *One phosphor band (Nos. 1873/4) or two phosphor bands (others). Perf 14½ × 14*

1873	**1198**	19p silver, bistre-brown and grey-black . . .	70	40	☐	☐
1874	**1199**	19p multicoloured	70	40	☐	☐
1875	**1200**	25p silver, blue and grey-black	1·00	1·00	☐	☐
1876	**1201**	25p multicoloured	1·00	1·00	☐	☐
1877	**1202**	30p multicoloured	1·25	2·25	☐	☐
		Set of 5	4·25	4·25	☐	☐
		First Day Cover		4·75		☐
		Presentation Pack	5·00			☐
		PHQ Cards (set of 5)	6·00	11·50	☐	☐
		Set of 5 Gutter Pairs	10·50			☐

Nos. 1873 and 1875 commemorate the 50th anniversary of the end of the Second World War, No. 1874 the 125th anniversary of the British Red Cross Society and Nos. 1876/7 the 50th anniversary of the United Nations.

Nos. 1876/7 include the 'EUROPA' emblem.

For No. 1875 with the face value expressed as '1st' see No. **MS**2547.

1203 *The Time Machine*

1204 *The First Men in the Moon*

1205 *The War of the Worlds*

1206 *The Shape of Things to Come*

Science Fiction. Novels by H. G. Wells

1995 (6 JUNE) *Two phosphor bands. Perf 14½ × 14*

1878	**1203**	25p multicoloured	75	25	☐	☐
1879	**1204**	30p multicoloured	1·25	1·50	☐	☐
1880	**1205**	35p multicoloured	1·25	1·60	☐	☐
1881	**1206**	41p multicoloured	1·50	1·60	☐	☐
		Set of 4	4·25	4·50	☐	☐
		First Day Cover		4·75		☐
		Presentation Pack	5·00			☐
		PHQ Cards (set of 4)	5·00	10·00	☐	☐
		Set of 4 Gutter Pairs	10·00			☐

Nos. 1878/81 commemorate the centenary of publication of Wells's *The Time Machine*.

1207 The Swan, 1595

1208 The Rose, 1592

1212 Sir Rowland Hill and Uniform Penny Postage Petition

1213 Hill and Penny Black

1209 The Globe, 1599

1210 The Hope, 1613

1214 Guglielmo Marconi and Early Wireless

1215 Marconi and Sinking of *Titanic* (liner)

Pioneers of Communications

1995 (5 SEPT.) *One phosphor band* (19p) *or phosphorised paper* (*others*). *Perf* $14\frac{1}{2} \times 14$

1887	**1212**	19p silver, red and black	75	30 □ □
1888	**1213**	25p silver, brown and black	1·00	50 □ □
1889	**1214**	41p silver, grey-green and black	1·50	1·75 □ □
1890	**1215**	60p silver, deep ultramarine and black	1·75	2·25 □ □
		Set of 4	4·50	4·50 □ □
		First Day Cover		4·75 □
		Presentation Pack	5·00	□
		PHQ Cards (*set of 4*)	5·75	11·50 □ □
		Set of 4 Gutter Pairs	11·00	□

Nos. 1887/8 mark the birth bicentenary of Sir Rowland Hill and Nos. 1889/90 the centenary of the first radio transmissions.

1211 The Globe, 1614

T **1207/11** were printed together, *se-tenant*, in horizontal strips of 5 throughout the sheet, the backgrounds forming a composite design.

Reconstruction of Shakespeare's Globe Theatre

1995 (8 AUG.) *Two phosphor bands. Perf* $14\frac{1}{2}$

1882	**1207**	25p multicoloured	90	90 □ □
		a. Horiz strip of 5. Nos. 1882/6	4·50	4·75 □
1883	**1208**	25p multicoloured	90	90 □ □
1884	**1209**	25p multicoloured	90	90 □ □
1885	**1210**	25p multicoloured	90	90 □ □
1886	**1211**	25p multicoloured	90	90 □ □
		Set of 5	4·25	4·75 □
		First Day Cover		5·50 □
		Presentation Pack	5·00	□
		PHQ Cards (*set of 5*)	6·00	11·50 □ □
		Gutter Strip of 10	10·50	□

1216 Harold Wagstaff

1217 Gus Risman

1218 Jim Sullivan   **1219** Billy Batten

1220 Brian Bevan

Centenary of Rugby League

1995 (3 Oct.) *One phosphor band* (19p) *or two phosphor bands* (others). *Perf* 14 × 14½

1891	**1216**	19p multicoloured	. . . .	75	25	☐	☐
1892	**1217**	25p multicoloured	. . . .	75	30	☐	☐
1893	**1218**	30p multicoloured	. . . .	1·00	1·50	☐	☐
1894	**1219**	35p multicoloured	. . . .	1·00	1·60	☐	☐
1895	**1220**	41p multicoloured	. . . .	1·50	1·60	☐	☐
		Set of 5	. . . .	4·75	4·75	☐	☐
		First Day Cover	. . . .		4·75		☐
		Presentation Pack	. . . .	5·50		☐	
		PHQ Cards (set of 5)	. . . . .	6·00	11·50	☐	☐
		Set of 5 Gutter Pairs	. . . . . .	11·00		☐	

1221 European Robin in Mouth of Pillar Box

1222 European Robin on Railings and Holly

1223 European Robin on Snow-covered Milk Bottles

1224 European Robin on Road Sign

1225 European Robin on Door Knob and Christmas Wreath

Christmas. Christmas Robins

1995 (30 Oct.) *One phosphor band* (19p) *or two phosphor bands* (others)

1896	**1221**	19p multicoloured	. . . .	60	20	☐	☐
1897	**1222**	25p multicoloured	. . . .	85	30	☐	☐
1898	**1223**	30p multicoloured	. . . .	1·25	1·50	☐	☐
1899	**1224**	41p multicoloured	. . . .	1·60	1·75	☐	☐
1900	**1225**	60p multicoloured	. . . .	1·75	1·90	☐	☐
		Set of 5	. . . .	5·50	5·50	☐	☐
		First Day Cover	. . . .		5·25		☐
		Presentation Pack	. . . .	5·75		☐	
		PHQ Cards (set of 5)	. . . . .	6·00	11·50	☐	☐
		Set of 5 Gutter Pairs	. . . . .	12·00		☐	

The 19p value was re-issued on 3 October 2000 in sheets of 20 each with *se-tenant* label, in connection with 'customised' stamps available from the Philatelic Bureau. The labels show either Christmas greetings or a personal photograph.

Collectors Pack 1995

1995 (30 Oct.) *Comprises Nos. 1848/1900*
CP1900a   Collectors Pack   . . . .   55·00   ☐

Post Office Yearbook

1995 (30 Oct.) *Comprises Nos. 1848/57 and 1868/1900 in hardback book with slip case*
YB1900a   Yearbook   . . . .   55·00   ☐

1226 Opening Lines of 'To a Mouse' and Fieldmouse

1227 'O my Luve's like a red, red rose' and Wild Rose

1228 'Scots, wha hae wi Wallace bled' and Sir William Wallace

1229 'Auld Lang Syne' and Highland Dancers

Death Bicentenary of Robert Burns (Scottish poet)

1996 (25 Jan.) *One phosphor band (19p) or two phosphor bands (others). Perf 14½*

1901	**1226**	19p cream, bistre-brown and black	75	25	□	□
1902	**1227**	25p multicoloured	1·00	30	□	□
1903	**1228**	41p multicoloured	1·50	2·00	□	□
1904	**1229**	60p multicoloured	1·75	2·50	□	□
		Set of 4	4·50	4·50	□	□
		First Day Cover		4·75		□
		Presentation Pack	5·00			□
		PHQ Cards (set of 4)	6·00	11·50	□	□
		Set of 4 Gutter Pairs	10·50			□

1230 'MORE! LOVE'
(Mel Calman)

1231 'Sincerely'
(Charles Barsotti)

1232 'Do you have
something for the
HUMAN CONDITION?'
(Mel Calman)

1233 'MENTAL FLOSS
(Leo Cullum)

1234 '4.55 P.M.'
(Charles Barsotti)

1235 'Dear lottery prize winner
(Larry)

1236 'I'm writing to you
because...' (Mel Calman)

1237 'FETCH THIS, FETCH
THAT' (Charles Barsotti)

1238 'My day starts before
I'm ready for it' (Mel
Calman)

1239 'THE CHEQUE IN THE
POST' (Jack Ziegler)

T **1230/9** were printed together, *se-tenant*, in booklet panes of 10 stamps and 20 half stamp-size labels.

Greetings Stamps. Cartoons

1996 (26 Feb.–11 Nov.) *'All-over' phosphor. Perf 14½ × 14 (with one elliptical hole on each vertical side)*

1905	**1230**	(1st) black and bright mauve	80	75	□	□
		a. Booklet pane. Nos. 1905/14	10·00	11·00	□	□
		p. Two phosphor bands	1·25	1·25	□	□
		pa. Booklet pane. Nos. 1905p/14p (11 Nov.)	25·00	20·00	□	□
1906	**1231**	(1st) black and blue-green	80	75	□	□
		p. Two phosphor bands	1·25	1·25	□	□
1907	**1232**	(1st) black and new blue	80	75	□	□
		p. Two phosphor bands	1·25	1·25	□	□
1908	**1233**	(1st) black and bright violet	80	75	□	□
		p. Two phosphor bands	1·25	1·25	□	□
1909	**1234**	(1st) black and vermilion	80	75	□	□
		p. Two phosphor bands	1·25	1·25	□	□
1910	**1235**	(1st) black and new blue	80	75	□	□
		p. Two phosphor bands	1·25	1·25	□	□
1911	**1236**	(1st) black and vermilion	80	75	□	□
		p. Two phosphor bands	1·25	1·25	□	□
1912	**1237**	(1st) black and bright violet	80	75	□	□
		p. Two phosphor bands	1·25	1·25	□	□
1913	**1238**	(1st) black and blue-green	80	75	□	□
		p. Two phosphor bands	1·25	1·25	□	□
1914	**1239**	(1st) black and bright mauve	80	75	□	□
		p. Two phosphor bands	1·25	1·25	□	□
		Set of 10 (Nos. 1905/14)	9·00	6·75	□	□
		Set of 10 (Nos. 1905p/14p)	13·00	11·00	□	□
		First Day Cover (Nos. 1905/14)		11·00		□
		Presentation Pack (Nos. 1905/14)	16·00			□
		PHQ Cards (set of 10)	16·00	28·00	□	□

Nos. 1905/14 were re-issued on 18 December 2001 in sheets of 10, each stamp with a *se-tenant* label showing cartoon titles. They were again issued on 29 July 2003 in sheets of 20 containing two of each design, each stamp accompanied by a half stamp size label showing a crossword grid or personal photograph. Such sheets are perforated without elliptical holes.

For full information on all future British issues, collectors should write to Royal Mail, Freepost EH3647, 21 South Gyle Crescent, Edinburgh EH12 9PE.

1240 'Muscovy Duck'

1241 'Lapwing'

1247 Old Cinema Ticket

1248 Pathé News Still

1242 'White-fronted Goose'

1243 'Bittern'

1249 Cinema Sign, The Odeon, Manchester

1244 'Whooper Swan'

Centenary of Cinema

1996 (16 APR.) *One phosphor band (19p) or two phosphor bands (others). Perf 14 × 14½*

1920	**1245**	19p multicoloured	50		25	□ □
1921	**1246**	25p multicoloured	70		30	□ □
1922	**1247**	30p multicoloured	1·00		1·75	□ □
1923	**1248**	35p black, red and silver	1·25		2·00	□ □
1924	**1249**	41p multicoloured	1·50		2·25	□ □
		Set of 5	4·75		4·75	□ □
		First Day Cover			5·75	□
		Presentation Pack	5·50			□
		PHQ Cards (set of 5)	6·00		11·50	□ □
		Set of 5 *Gutter Pairs*	11·00			□

50th Anniversary of the Wildfowl and Wetlands Trust. Bird Paintings by C. F. Tunnicliffe

1996 (12 MAR.) *One phosphor band (19p) or phosphorised paper (others). Perf 14 × 14½*

1915	**1240**	19p multicoloured	70		25	□ □
1916	**1241**	25p multicoloured	90		30	□ □
1917	**1242**	30p multicoloured	1·00		1·25	□ □
1918	**1243**	35p multicoloured	1·10		1·50	□ □
1919	**1244**	41p multicoloured	1·50		1·60	□ □
		Set of 5	4·75		4·50	□ □
		First Day Cover			5·75	□
		Presentation Pack	5·00			□
		PHQ Cards (set of 5)	6·00		11·50	□ □
		Set of 5 *Gutter Pairs*	10·50			□

1250 Dixie Dean

1251 Bobby Moore

1245 The Odeon, Harrogate

1246 Laurence Olivier and Vivien Leigh in *Lady Hamilton* (film)

1252 Duncan Edwards

1253 Billy Wright

1254 Danny Blanchflower

European Football Championship

1996 (14 MAY) *One phosphor band (19p) or two phosphor bands (others). Perf 14½ × 14*

1925	**1250**	19p multicoloured	50	20 □ □
1926	**1251**	25p multicoloured	75	20 □ □
1927	**1252**	35p multicoloured	1·25	1·75 □ □
1928	**1253**	41p multicoloured	1·50	1·75 □ □
1929	**1254**	60p multicoloured	1·75	2·00 □ □
	Set of 5		5·50	5·75 □ □
	First Day Cover			5·75 □
	Presentation Pack		5·75	□
	PHQ Cards (set of 5)		6·00	11·50 □ □
	Set of 5 Gutter Pairs		12·00	□

1255 Athlete on Starting Blocks

1256 Throwing the Javelin

1257 Basketball

1258 Swimming

1259 Athlete celebrating and Olympic Rings

T **1255/9** were printed together, *se-tenant*, in horizontal strips of 5 throughout the sheet.

Olympic and Paralympic Games, Atlanta

1996 (9 JULY) *Two phosphor bands. Perf 14½ × 14*

1930	**1255**	26p multicoloured	1·10	1·00 □ □
		a. Horiz strip of 5. Nos. 1930/4	5·00	5·50 □ □
1931	**1256**	26p multicoloured	1·10	1·00 □ □
1932	**1257**	26p multicoloured	1·10	1·00 □ □
1933	**1258**	26p multicoloured	1·10	1·00 □ □
1934	**1259**	26p multicoloured	1·10	1·00 □ □
	Set of 5		4·50	4·50 □ □
	First Day Cover			5·00 □
	Presentation Pack		4·50	□
	PHQ Cards (set of 5)		6·00	11·50 □ □
	Gutter Strip of 10		11·00	□

For these designs with the face value expressed as '1st' see **MS**2554.

1260 Prof. Dorothy Hodgkin (scientist)

1261 Dame Margot Fonteyn (ballerina)

1262 Dame Elisabeth Frink (sculptress)

1263 Dame Daphne du Maurier (novelist)

1264 Dame Marea Hartman (sports administrator)

Europa. Famous Women

1996 (6 AUG.) *One phosphor band (20p) or two phosphor bands (others). Perf 14½*

1935	**1260**	20p dull blue-green, brownish grey and black	60	25 □ □
1936	**1261**	26p dull mauve, brownish grey and black . . .	75	25 □ □

1937	1262	31p bronze, brownish grey and black . . .	1·10	1·10	☐ ☐
1938	1263	37p silver, brownish grey and black	1·25	1·40	☐ ☐
1939	1264	43p gold, brownish grey and black	1·50	1·50	☐ ☐
		Set of 5	4·75	4·50	☐ ☐
		First Day Cover		5·00	☐
		Presentation Pack	4·75		☐
		PHQ Cards (set of 5)	6·00	11·50	☐ ☐
		Set of 5 Gutter Pairs	12·00		☐

Nos. 1936/7 include the 'EUROPA' emblem.

1265 *Muffin the Mule*

1266 *Sooty*

1267 *Stingray*

1268 *The Clangers*

1269 *Dangermouse*

50th Anniversary of Children's Television

1996 (3 Sept.)–97 *One phosphor band* (20p) *or two phosphor bands* (others). *Perf* 14½ × 14

1940	1265	20p multicoloured	55	20	☐ ☐
		a. Perf 15 × 14 (23.9.97)	2·00	2·00	☐ ☐
1941	1266	26p multicoloured	80	20	☐ ☐
1942	1267	31p multicoloured	1·00	1·50	☐ ☐
1943	1268	37p multicoloured	1·40	1·75	☐ ☐
1944	1269	43p multicoloured	1·60	2·00	☐ ☐
		Set of 5	4·75	4·75	☐ ☐
		First Day Cover		4·75	☐
		Presentation Pack	4·75		☐
		PHQ Cards (set of 5)	6·00	11·50	☐ ☐
		Set of 5 Gutter Pairs	10·50		☐

No. 1940a comes from stamp booklets.

1270 Triumph TR3

1271 MG TD

1272 Austin-Healey 100

1273 Jaguar XK120

1274 Morgan Plus 4

Classic Sports Cars

1996 (1 Oct.) *One phosphor band* (20p) *or two phosphor bands* (others). *Perf* 14½

1945	1270	20p multicoloured	55	20	☐ ☐
1946	1271	26p multicoloured	1·10	20	☐ ☐
1947	1272	37p multicoloured	1·40	1·90	☐ ☐
1948	1273	43p multicoloured	1·60	1·90	☐ ☐
1949	1274	63p multicoloured	1·75	2·00	☐ ☐
		Set of 5	5·75	6·00	☐ ☐
		First Day Cover		5·50	☐
		Presentation Pack	6·00		☐
		PHQ Cards (set of 5)	6·00	11·50	☐ ☐
		Set of 5 Gutter Pairs	13·00		☐

1275 The Three Kings

1276 The Annunciation

1277 The Journey to Bethlehem

1278 The Nativity

1279 The Shepherds

Christmas

1996 (28 Oct.) *One phosphor band* (2nd) *or two phosphor bands* (*others*)

1950	**1275**	(2nd) multicoloured	. . .	75	20	□	□
1951	**1276**	(1st) multicoloured	. . .	1·00	35	□	□
1952	**1277**	31p multicoloured	. . .	1·25	1·75	□	□
1953	**1278**	43p multicoloured	. . .	1·25	1·75	□	□
1954	**1279**	63p multicoloured	. . .	1·50	2·00	□	□
		Set of 5	. . . .	5·50	5·50	□	□
		First Day Cover	. . . .		6·00		□
		Presentation Pack	. . . .	5·75			□
		PHQ Cards (set of 5)	. . . . . .	6·00	11·50	□	□
		Set of 5 Gutter Pairs	. . . . . .	13·00			□

Collectors Pack 1996

1996 (28 Oct.) *Comprises Nos.* 1901/4 *and* 1915/54

CP1954a	Collectors Pack	. . . .	55·00		□

Post Office Yearbook

1996 (28 Oct.) *Comprises Nos.* 1901/4 *and* 1915/54 *in hardback book with slip case*

YB1954a	Yearbook	. . . .	60·00		□

1280 Gentiana acaulis (Georg Ehret)

1281 Magnolia grandiflora (Ehret)

1282 *Camellia japonica* (Alfred Chandler)

1283 *Tulipa* (Ehret)

1284 *Fuchsia* 'Princess of Wales' (Augusta Withers)

1285 *Tulipa gesneriana* (Ehret)

1286 *Guzmania splendens* (Charlotte Sowerby)

1287 *Iris latifolia* (Ehret)

1288 *Hippeastrum rutilum* (Pierre-Joseph Redoute)

1289 *Passiflora coerulea* (Ehret)

T **1280/9** were printed together, *se-tenant,* in booklet panes of 10 stamps and 20 half stamp-size labels.

Greeting Stamps. 19th-century Flower Paintings

1997 (6 Jan.) *Two phosphor bands. Perf* 14½ × 14 (*with one elliptical hole on each vertical side*)

1955	**1280**	(1st) multicoloured	. . . .	85	90	□	□
		a. Booklet pane. Nos.					
		1955/64	. . . .	11·25	11·25	□	□
1956	**1281**	(1st) multicoloured	. . . .	85	90	□	□
1957	**1282**	(1st) multicoloured	. . . .	85	90	□	□
1958	**1283**	(1st) multicoloured	. . . .	85	90	□	□
1959	**1284**	(1st) multicoloured	. . . .	85	90	□	□
1960	**1285**	(1st) multicoloured	. . . .	85	90	□	□
1961	**1286**	(1st) multicoloured	. . . .	85	90	□	□
1962	**1287**	(1st) multicoloured	. . . .	85	90	□	□

1963	**1288**	(1st) multicoloured	85	90	☐ ☐
1964	**1289**	(1st) multicoloured	85	90	☐ ☐
		Set of 10	9·00	8·00	☐ ☐
		First Day Cover		10·00	☐
		Presentation Pack	16·00		☐
		PHQ Cards (set of 10)	16·00	28·00	☐ ☐

Nos. 1955/64 were re-issued on 21 January 2003 in *se-tenant* sheets of 20, each accompanied by a label showing flowers or personal photograph. Such sheets are perforated without elliptical holes.

For Nos. 1955, 1958 and 1962 perf 15 × 14 see Nos. 2463/5.

1290 'King Henry VIII'

1291 'Catherine of Aragon'

1292 'Anne Boleyn'

1293 'Jane Seymour'

1294 'Anne of Cleves'

1295 'Catherine Howard'

1296 'Catherine Parr'

T **1290/6** were printed together, *se-tenant*, in horizontal strips of 6 throughout the sheet.

450th Death Anniversary of King Henry VIII

1997 (21 JAN.) *Two phosphor bands. Perf 15 (No. 1965) or 14 × 15 (others)*

1965	**1290**	26p multicoloured	1·00	90	☐ ☐
1966	**1291**	26p multicoloured	1·25	1·00	☐ ☐
		a. Horiz strip of 6. Nos.			
		1966/71	8·00	8·50	☐ ☐
1967	**1292**	26p multicoloured	1·25	1·00	☐ ☐
1968	**1293**	26p multicoloured	1·25	1·00	☐ ☐
1969	**1294**	26p multicoloured	1·25	1·00	☐ ☐
1970	**1295**	26p multicoloured	1·25	1·00	☐ ☐
1971	**1296**	26p multicoloured	1·25	1·00	☐ ☐
		Set of 7	7·75	6·50	☐ ☐
		First Day Cover		9·50	☐
		Presentation Pack	10·00		☐
		PHQ Cards (set of 7)	10·00	18·00	☐ ☐
		Gutter Pair and Gutter Block of 12	17·00		☐

1297 St Columba in Boat

1298 St Columba on Iona

1299 St Augustine with King Ethelbert

1300 St Augustine with Model of Cathedral

Religious Anniversaries

1997 (11 MAR.) *Two phosphor bands. Perf 14½*

1972	**1297**	26p multicoloured	75	35	☐ ☐
1973	**1298**	37p multicoloured	1·10	1·50	☐ ☐
1974	**1299**	43p multicoloured	1·50	1·50	☐ ☐
1975	**1300**	63p multicoloured	2·00	2·10	☐ ☐
		Set of 4	4·75	5·00	☐ ☐
		First Day Cover		5·75	☐
		Presentation Pack	5·25		☐
		PHQ Cards (set of 4)	5·75	11·50	☐ ☐
		Set of 4 Gutter Pairs	11·50		☐

Nos. 1972/3 commemorate the 1400th death anniversary of St Columba and Nos. 1974/5 the 1400th anniversary of the arrival of St Augustine of Canterbury in Kent.

1301   **1302**

Self-adhesive Coil Stamps

1997 (18 MAR.) *Photo Enschedé. One centre phosphor band (2nd) or two phosphor bands (1st). Perf 14 × 15 die-cut (with one elliptical hole on each vertical side)*

1976	**1301**	(2nd) bright blue	2·75	2·50	□	□
1977	**1302**	(1st) bright orange-red .	2·75	2·75	□	□
	Set of 2		4·50	5·25	□	□
	First Day Cover			5·50	□	
	Presentation Pack		6·50		□	

Nos. 1976/7, which were priced at 20p and 26p, were each sold in rolls of 100 with the stamps separate on the backing paper.

Machin stamps printed in gold were issued on 21 April 1997 for the Royal Golden Wedding. These are listed as definitives under Nos. 1664*b* (1st) and Y1683*b* 26p.

1303 *Dracula*

1304 *Frankenstein*

1305 *Dr Jekyll and Mr Hyde*

1306 *The Hound of the Baskervilles*

Minimum Price. The minimum price quoted is 10p. This represents a handling charge rather than a basis for valuing common stamps. Where the actual value of a stamp is less than 10p this may be apparent when set prices are shown, particularly for sets including a number of 10p stamps. It therefore follows that in valuing common stamps the 10p catalogue price should not be reckoned automatically since it covers a variation in real scarcity.

Europa. Tales and Legends. Horror Stories

1997 (13 MAY) *Two phosphor bands. Perf 14 × 15*

1980	**1303**	26p multicoloured	1·00	40	□	□
1981	**1304**	31p multicoloured	1·10	1·50	□	□
1982	**1305**	37p multicoloured	1·30	1·75	□	□
1983	**1306**	43p multicoloured	1·75	2·00	□	□
	Set of 4		4·75	5·50	□	□
	First Day Cover			5·50	□	
	Presentation Pack		5·25		□	
	PHQ Cards (set of 4)		5·75	11·50	□	□
	Set of 4 Gutter Pairs		12·00		□	

Nos. 1980/3 commemorate the birth bicentenary of Mary Shelley (creator of Frankenstein) with the 26p and 31p values incorporating the 'EUROPA' emblem.

1307 Reginald Mitchell and Supermarine Spitfire MkIIA

1308 Roy Chadwick and Avro Lancaster MkI

1309 Ronald Bishop and De Havilland Mosquito B MkXVI

1310 George Carter and Gloster Meteor T Mk7

1311 Sir Sidney Camm and Hawker Hunter FGA Mk9

British Aircraft Designers

1997 (10 JUNE) *One phosphor band (20p) or two phosphor bands (others)*

1984	**1307**	20p multicoloured	75	40	□	□
1985	**1308**	26p multicoloured	1·10	1·25	□	□
1986	**1309**	37p multicoloured	1·40	1·25	□	□
1987	**1310**	43p multicoloured	1·50	1·60	□	□
1988	**1311**	63p multicoloured	2·00	2·00	□	□
	Set of 5		6·00	6·50	□	□
	First Day Cover			6·50	□	
	Presentation Pack		6·50		□	
	PHQ Cards		6·00	13·00	□	□
	Set of 5 Gutter Pairs		15·00		□	

1312 Carriage Horse and Coachman

1313 Lifeguards Horse and Trooper

1314 Household Cavalry Drum Horse and Drummer

1315 Duke of Edinburgh's Horse and Groom

'All The Queen's Horses'. 50th Anniv of the British Horse Society
1997 (8 July) *One phosphor band* (20p) *or two phosphor bands* (*others*). *Perf* 14½

1989	**1312**	20p multicoloured	. . . .	80	45	□ □
1990	**1313**	26p multicoloured	. . . .	1·10	1·50	□ □
1991	**1314**	43p multicoloured	. . . .	1·50	1·50	□ □
1992	**1315**	63p multicoloured	. . . .	2·00	2·00	□ □
		Set of 4	. . . .	5·00	5·25	□ □
		First Day Cover	. . . .		5·75	□
		Presentation Pack	. . . .	5·50		□
		PHQ Cards (set of 4)	. . . . . .	5·75	11·50	□ □
		Set of 4 Gutter Pairs	. . . . . .	12·00		□

CASTLE

Harrison printing (Nos. 1611/14)

CASTLE

Enschedé printing (Nos. 1993/6)

Differences between Harrison and Enschedé printings:
   Harrison – 'C' has top serif and tail of letter points to right.
      'A' has flat top. 'S' has top and bottom serifs.
   Enschedé – 'C' has no top serif and tail of letter points
      upwards. 'A' has pointed top. 'S' has no serifs.

1997 (29 July) *Designs as Nos. 1611/14 with Queen's head in silhouette as T* **1044**, *but re-engraved as above. Perf* 15 × 14 (*with one elliptical hole on each vertical side*).

1993	**880**	£1·50 deep claret and gold†	10·00	6·00	□ □
1994	**881**	£2 indigo and gold†	. . .	12·00	2·25	□ □

1995	**1044**	£3 violet and gold†	. . .	26·00	3·50	□ □
1996	**882**	£5 deep brown and gold†	28·00	10·00	□ □
		Set of 4	. . . .	68·00	18·00	□ □
		Set of 4 Gutter Pairs	. . . . . .	£140		□
		Presentation Pack (P.O Pack No.			
		40)	. . . .	£150		□

† The Queen's head on these stamps is printed in optically variable ink which changes colour from gold to green when viewed from different angles.

1316 Haroldswick, Shetland

1317 Painswick, Gloucestershire

1318 Beddgelert, Gwynedd

1319 Ballyroney, County Down

Sub-Post Offices
1997 (12 Aug.) *One phosphor band* (20p) *or two phosphor bands* (*others*). *Perf* 14½

1997	**1316**	20p multicoloured	. . . .	75	50	□ □
1998	**1317**	26p multicoloured	. . . .	1·00	1·00	□ □
1999	**1318**	43p multicoloured	. . . .	1·50	1·50	□ □
2000	**1319**	63p multicoloured	. . . .	2·25	2·25	□ □
		Set of 4	. . . .	5·50	5·00	□ □
		First Day Cover	. . . .		5·75	□
		Presentation Pack	. . . .	5·00		□
		PHQ Cards (set of 4)	. . . . . .	5·75	11·50	□ □
		Set of 4 Gutter Pairs	. . . . . .	12·00		□

Nos. 1997/2000 also mark the centenary of the National Federation of Sub-Postmasters.

Enid Blyton's *Noddy*

Enid Blyton's *Famous Five*

1320 Noddy

1321 Famous Five

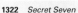
Enid Blyton's *Secret Seven*

1322 Secret Seven

Enid Blyton's *Faraway Tree*

1323 Faraway Tree

Enid Blyton's *Malory Towers*

1324 Malory Towers

Birth Centenary of Enid Blyton (children's author)
1997 (9 SEPT.) *One phosphor band* (20p) *or two phosphor bands* (*others*). *Perf* 14 × 14½

2001	**1320**	20p multicoloured	50	45 □ □
2002	**1321**	26p multicoloured	1·00	1·25 □ □
2003	**1322**	37p multicoloured	1·25	1·25 □ □
2004	**1323**	43p multicoloured	1·50	2·00 □ □
2005	**1324**	63p multicoloured	1·50	2·00 □ □
		Set of 5	5·25	6·00 □ □
		First Day Cover		6·00 □
		Presentation Pack	5·75	□
		PHQ Cards (*set of* 5)	6·00	13·00 □ □
		Set of 5 *Gutter Pairs*	12·00	□

1325 Children and Father Christmas pulling Cracker

1326 Father Christmas with Traditional Cracker

1327 Father Christmas riding Cracker

1328 Father Christmas on Snowball

1329 Father Christmas and Chimney

Christmas. 150th Anniversary of the Christmas Cracker
1997 (27 OCT.) *One phosphor band* (2nd) *or two phosphor bands* (*others*)

2006	**1325**	(2nd) multicoloured	75	20 □ □
2007	**1326**	(1st) multicoloured	90	30 □ □
2008	**1327**	31p multicoloured	1·00	1·50 □ □
2009	**1328**	43p multicoloured	1·25	1·75 □ □
2010	**1329**	63p multicoloured	1·60	2·00 □ □
		Set of 5	5·00	5·50 □ □
		First Day Cover		6·00 □
		Presentation Pack	5·75	□
		PHQ Cards (*set of* 5)	6·00	13·00 □ □
		Set of 5 *Gutter Pairs*	12·00	□

The 1st value was re-issued on 3 October 2000, in sheets of 10 in photogravure, each stamp with a *se-tenant* label, in connection with 'customised' service available from the Philatelic Bureau. On 1 October 2002 in sheet size of 20 in lithography the 1st value was again issued but perforated 14½ × 14. The labels show either Christmas greetings or a personal photograph.

1330 Wedding Photograph, 1947

1331 Queen Elizabeth II and Prince Philip, 1997

Royal Golden Wedding
1997 (13 Nov.) *One phosphor band* (20p) *or two phosphor bands* (*others*). *Perf* 15

2011	**1330**	20p gold, yellow-brown and grey-black . . .	85	45 □ □
2012	**1331**	26p multicoloured	1·10	70 □ □
2013	**1330**	43p gold, bluish green and grey-black . . .	1·90	2·25 □ □
2014	**1331**	63p multicoloured	2·50	3·00 □ □
		Set of 4	5·75	5·75 □ □
		First Day Cover		8·25 □
		Presentation Pack	6·25	□
		Souvenir Book (*contains Nos.* 1664b, 1989/92 *and* 2011/14) .	50·00	□
		PHQ Cards (*set of* 4)	5·75	11·50 □ □
		Set of 4 *Gutter Pairs*	12·00	□

Collectors Pack 1997

1997 (13 Nov.) *Comprises Nos. 1965/75, 1980/92 and 1997/2014*

CP2014a   *Collectors Pack* . . . . 65·00   ☐

Post Office Yearbook

1997 (13 Nov.) *Comprises Nos. 1965/75, 1980/92 and 1997/2014 in hardback book with slip case*

YB2014a   *Yearbook* . . . . 67·00   ☐

20 **ENDANGERED SPECIES**
Common dormouse
Muscardinus avellanarius

1332   Common Doormouse

26 **ENDANGERED SPECIES**
Lady's slipper orchid
Cypripedium calceolus

1333   Lady's Slipper Orchid

31 **ENDANGERED SPECIES**
Song thrush
Turdus philomelos

1334   Song Thrush

37 **ENDANGERED SPECIES**
Shining ram's-horn snail
Segmentina nitida

1335   Shining Ram's-horn Snail

43 **ENDANGERED SPECIES**
Mole cricket
Gryllotalpa gryllotalpa

1336   Mole Cricket

63 **ENDANGERED SPECIES**
Devil's bolete
Boletus satanas

1337   Devil's Bolete

Endangered Species

1998 (20 Jan.) *One side phosphor band* (20p) *or two phosphor bands* (others). *Perf* 14 × 14½

2015	**1332**	20p multicoloured	60	40	☐	☐
2016	**1333**	26p multicoloured	75	40	☐	☐
2017	**1334**	31p multicoloured	1·00	2·00	☐	☐
2018	**1335**	37p multicoloured	1·25	1·25	☐	☐
2019	**1336**	43p multicoloured	1·40	1·75	☐	☐
2020	**1337**	63p multicoloured	1·90	2·25	☐	☐
		Set of 6	6·25	6·50	☐	☐
		First Day Cover		6·25		☐
		Presentation Pack	6·75			☐
		PHQ Cards (*Set of 6*)	6·00	14·00	☐	☐
		Set of 6 Gutter Pairs	15·00			☐

1338   Diana, Princess of Wales (photo by Lord Snowdon)

1339   At British Lung Foundation Function, April 1997 (photo by John Stillwell)

1340   Wearing Tiara, 1991 (photo by Lord Snowdon)

1341   On Visit to Birmingham, October 1995 (photo by Tim Graham)

1342   In Evening Dress, 1987 (photo by Terence Donovan)

T **1338/42** were printed together, *se-tenant,* in horizontal strips of 5 throughout the sheet.

Diana, Princess of Wales Commemoration

1998 (3 Feb.) *Two phosphor bands*

2021	**1338**	26p multicoloured	90	90	☐	☐
		a. *Horiz strip of* 5. *Nos.* 2021/5	4·50	4·50	☐	☐
2022	**1339**	26p multicoloured	90	90	☐	☐
2023	**1340**	26p multicoloured	90	90	☐	☐

2024	**1341**	26p multicoloured	90	90 ☐ ☐
2025	**1342**	26p multicoloured	90	90 ☐ ☐
		Set of 5	4·00	4·00 ☐ ☐
		First Day Cover		5·50 ☐
		Presentation Pack	16·00	☐
		Presentation Pack (*Welsh*) . . .	£150	☐
		Gutter Strip of 10	10·00	☐

1343 Lion of England and Griffin of Edward III

1344 Falcon of Plantagenet and Bull of Clarence

1345 Lion of Mortimer and Yale of Beaufort

1346 Greyhound of Richmond and Dragon of Wales

1347 Unicorn of Scotland and Horse of Hanover

T **1343/7** were printed together, *se-tenant,* in horizontal strips of 5 throughout the sheet.

650th Anniversary of the Order of the Garter. The Queen's Beasts

1998 (24 Feb.) *Two phosphor bands*

2026	**1343**	26p multicoloured	90	90 ☐ ☐
		a. *Horiz strip of* 5. *Nos.*		
		2026/30	4·50	4·50 ☐ ☐
2027	**1344**	26p multicoloured	90	90 ☐ ☐
2028	**1345**	26p multicoloured	90	90 ☐ ☐
2029	**1346**	26p multicoloured	90	90 ☐ ☐
2030	**1347**	26p multicoloured	90	90 ☐ ☐
		Set of 5	4·00	4·00 ☐ ☐
		First Day Cover		5·25 ☐
		Presentation Pack	5·00	☐
		PHQ Cards (*set of* 5)	6·00	13·00 ☐ ☐
		Gutter Block of 10	10·00	☐

The phosphor bands on Nos. 2026/30 are only half the height of the stamps and do not cover the silver parts of the designs.

1348

Booklet Stamps

1998 (10 Mar.) *Design as T* **157** (*issued 1952–54*), *but with face values in decimal currency as T* **1348**. *One side phosphor band* (20p) *or two phosphor bands* (*others*). *Perf* 14 (*with one elliptical hole on each vertical side*)

2031	**1348**	20p light green	70	75 ☐ ☐
2032		26p red-brown	90	95 ☐ ☐
2033		37p light purple	2·75	2·75 ☐ ☐
		Set of 3	4·00	4·00 ☐ ☐

> For further Wilding designs see Nos. 2258/9, **MS**2326, **MS**2367 and 2378/80.

1349 St John's Point Lighthouse, County Down

1350 Smalls Lighthouse, Pembrokeshire

1351 Needles Rock Lighthouse, Isle of Wight, *c* 1900

1352 Bell Rock Lighthouse, Arbroath, mid-19th-century

1353 Eddystone Lighthouse, Plymouth, 1698

Lighthouses

1998 (24 Mar.) *One side phosphor band* (20p) *or two phosphor bands* (*others*). *Perf* 14½ × 14

2034	**1349**	20p multicoloured	50	40	☐	☐
2035	**1350**	26p multicoloured	75	50	☐	☐
2036	**1351**	37p multicoloured	1·10	1·50	☐	☐
2037	**1352**	43p multicoloured	1·50	1·75	☐	☐
2038	**1353**	63p multicoloured	2·10	2·50	☐	☐
		Set of 5	5·50	6·00	☐	☐
		First Day Cover		5·75	☐	
		Presentation Pack	6·00		☐	
		PHQ Cards (set of 5)	6·00	13·00	☐	☐
		Set of 5 Gutter Pairs	13·50		☐	

Nos. 2034/8 commemorate the 300th anniversary of the first Eddystone Lighthouse and the final year of manned light-houses.

Self-adhesive stamps

1998 (6 Apr.) *Photo Enschedé, Questa or Walsall. Designs as T 913/14. One centre phosphor band* (2nd) *or two phosphor bands* (1st). *Perf* 15 × 14 *die-cut* (*with one elliptical hole on each vertical side*)

2039		(2nd) bright blue	30	35	☐	☐
		b. Perf 14½ × 14 die-cut	£150		☐	☐
2040		(1st) bright orange-red	40	45	☐	☐
		b. Perf 14½ × 14 die-cut	£150		☐	☐
		Set of 2	70	80	☐	☐

Nos. 2039/40 were initially priced at 20p and 26p, and were available in coils of 200 (Enschedé), sheets of 100 (Enschedé, Questa or Walsall) or self-adhesive booklets (Questa or Walsall). See also Nos. 2295/8.

1354   Tommy Cooper

1355   Eric Morecambe

1356   Joyce Grenfell

1357   Les Dawson

1358   Peter Cook

Comedians

1998 (23 Apr.) *One phosphor band* (20p) *or two phosphor bands* (*others*). *Perf* 14½ × 14

2041	**1354**	20p multicoloured	50	50	☐	☐
2042	**1355**	26p multicoloured	75	85	☐	☐
2043	**1356**	37p multicoloured	1·25	1·25	☐	☐
2044	**1357**	43p multicoloured	1·50	1·50	☐	☐
2045	**1358**	63p multicoloured	1·75	2·10	☐	☐
		Set of 5	5·25	5·50	☐	☐
		First Day Cover		6·00	☐	
		Presentation Pack	6·00		☐	
		PHQ Cards (set of 5)	6·00	13·00	☐	☐
		Set of 5 Gutter Pairs	13·50		☐	

1359   Hands forming Heart   1360   Adult and Child holding Hands

1361   Hands forming Cradle   1362   Hands taking Pulse

50th Anniversary of National Health Service

1998 (23 June) *One side phosphor band* (20p) *or two phosphor bands* (*others*). *Perf* 14 × 14½

2046	**1359**	20p multicoloured	50	50	☐	☐
2047	**1360**	26p multicoloured	90	90	☐	☐
2048	**1361**	43p multicoloured	1·50	1·50	☐	☐
2049	**1362**	63p multicoloured	2·10	2·10	☐	☐
		Set of 4	4·50	4·50	☐	☐
		First Day Cover		5·75	☐	
		Presentation Pack	5·50		☐	
		PHQ Cards (set of 4)	5·75	11·50	☐	☐
		Set of 4 Gutter Pairs	11·00		☐	

For full information on all future British issues, collectors should write to Royal Mail, Freepost EH3647, 21 South Gyle Crescent, Edinburgh EH12 9PE.

1363 The Hobbit (J. R. R. Tolkien)

1364 The Lion, The Witch and the Wardrobe (C. S. Lewis)

1365 The Phoenix and the Carpet (E. Nesbit)

1366 The Borrowers (Mary Norton)

1367 Through the Looking Glass (Lewis Carroll)

Famous Children's Fantasy Novels

1998 (21 July) *One phosphor band (20p) or two phosphor bands (others)*

2050	**1363**	20p multicoloured	. . . .	50	45	☐	☐
2051	**1364**	26p multicoloured	. . . .	75	55	☐	☐
2052	**1365**	37p multicoloured	. . . .	1·25	1·50	☐	☐
2053	**1366**	43p multicoloured	. . . .	1·50	1·50	☐	☐
2054	**1367**	63p multicoloured	. . . .	2·10	2·00	☐	☐
		Set of 5	. . . .	5·75	5·75	☐	☐
		First Day Cover	. . . .		5·75	☐	
		Presentation Pack	. . . .	6·00		☐	
		PHQ Cards (set of 5)	. . . . . .	6·00	13·00	☐	☐
		Set of 5 Gutter Pairs	. . . . . .	13·00		☐	

Nos. 2050/4 commemorate the birth centenary of C. S. Lewis and the death centenary of Lewis Carroll.

1368 Woman in Yellow Feathered Costume

1369 Woman in Blue Costume and Headdress

1370 Group of Children in White and Gold Robes

1371 Child in 'Tree' Costume

Europa. Festivals. Notting Hill Carnival

1998 (25 Aug.) *One centre phosphor band (20p) or two phosphor bands (others). Perf 14 × 14½*

2055	**1368**	20p multicoloured	. . . .	75	45	☐	☐
2056	**1369**	26p multicoloured	. . . .	95	55	☐	☐
2057	**1370**	43p multicoloured	. . . .	1·50	2·00	☐	☐
2058	**1371**	63p multicoloured	. . . .	2·00	2·75	☐	☐
		Set of 4	. . . .	4·75	4·75	☐	☐
		First Day Cover	. . . .		5·75		☐
		Presentation Pack	. . . .	5·25		☐	
		PHQ Cards (set of 4)	. . . . . .	5·75	11·50	☐	☐
		Set of 4 Gutter Pairs	. . . . . .	12·50		☐	

Nos. 2055/6 include the 'EUROPA' emblem.

1372 Sir Malcolm Campbell's Bluebird, 1925

1373 Sir Henry Segrave's Sunbeam, 1926

1374 John G. Parry Thomas's Babs, 1926

1375 John R. Cobb's Railton Mobil Special, 1947

1376 Donald Campbell's Bluebird CN7, 1964

British Land Speed Record Holders

1998 (29 SEPT.–13 OCT.) *One phosphor band* (20p) *or two phosphor bands* (*others*). *Perf* 15 × 14

2059	1372	20p multicoloured (centre band)	50	25	☐	☐
		a. Perf 14½ × 13½ (side band) (13 Oct.) . . .	1·40	50	☐	☐
2060	1373	26p multicoloured	75	30	☐	☐
2061	1374	30p multicoloured	1·25	1·50	☐	☐
2062	1375	43p multicoloured	1·50	1·60	☐	☐
2063	1376	63p multicoloured	2·00	2·40	☐	☐
		Set of 5	5·50	5·50	☐	☐
		First Day Cover		6·00		☐
		Presentation Pack	6·25		☐	
		PHQ Cards (set of 5)	6·00	13·00	☐	☐
		Set of 5 Gutter Pairs	13·00		☐	

No. 2059*a*, which occurs with the phosphor band at the left or right of the stamp, comes from stamp booklets. There are minor differences of design between No. 2059 and No. 2059*a*, which also omits the copyright symbol and date.

Nos. 2059/63 commemorate the 50th death anniversary of Sir Malcolm Campbell.

1377 Angel with Hands raised in Blessing

1378 Angel praying

1379 Angel playing Flute

1380 Angel playing Lute

1381 Angel praying

Christmas. Angels

1998 (2 NOV.) *One phosphor band* (20p) *or two phosphor bands* (*others*)

2064	1377	20p multicoloured	50	50	☐	☐
2065	1378	26p multicoloured	75	60	☐	☐
2066	1379	30p multicoloured	1·25	1·50	☐	☐
2067	1380	43p multicoloured	1·50	1·60	☐	☐
2068	1381	63p multicoloured	2·00	2·25	☐	☐
		Set of 5	5·75	5·75	☐	☐
		First Day Cover		6·00		☐
		Presentation Pack	6·50		☐	
		PHQ Cards (set of 5)	6·00	13·00	☐	☐
		Set of 5 Gutter Pairs	13·00		☐	

Collectors Pack 1998

1998 (2 NOV.) *Comprises Nos.* 2015/30, 2034/8 *and* 2041/68

CP2068a	Collectors Pack	95·00	☐

Post Office Yearbook

1998 (2 NOV.) *Comprises Nos.* 2015/30, 2034/8 *and* 2041/68 *in hardback book with slip case*

YB2068a	Yearbook	85·00	☐

20

26

1382 Greenwich Meridian and Clock (John Harrison's chronometer)

1383 Industrial Worker and Blast Furnace (James Watt's discovery of steam power)

43

63

1384 Early Photos of Leaves (Henry Fox-Talbot's photographic experiments)

1385 Computer inside Human Head (Alan Turing's work on computers)

Millennium Series. The Inventors' Tale

1999 (12 JAN.–21 SEPT.) *One centre phosphor band* (20p) *or two phosphor bands* (*others*). *Perf* 14 × 14½

2069	1382	20p multicoloured	75	70	☐	☐
2070	1383	26p multicoloured	95	1·00	☐	☐
2071	1384	43p multicoloured	1·50	1·60	☐	☐
2072	1385	63p multicoloured	2·25	2·40	☐	☐
		a. Perf 13½ × 14 (21 Sept.)	3·50	3·50	☐	☐
		Set of 4	5·25	5·25	☐	☐
		First Day Cover		10·00		☐
		Presentation Pack	7·50		☐	
		PHQ Cards (set of 4)	8·50	13·00	☐	☐
		Set of 4 Gutter Pairs	13·00		☐	

No. 2072*a* comes from stamp booklets.

1386 Airliner hugging Globe (International air travel)

1387 Woman on Bicycle (Development of the bicycle)

1388 Victorian Railway Station (Growth of public transport)

1389 Captain Cook and Maori (Captain James Cook's voyages)

Millennium Series. The Travellers' Tale

1999 (2 Feb.) *One centre phosphor band* (20p) *or two phosphor bands* (others). *Perf* 14 × 14½

2073	**1386**	20p multicoloured	75	70 □ □
2074	**1387**	26p multicoloured	95	1·00 □ □
2075	**1388**	43p grey-black, stone and bronze	1·50	1·60 □ □
2076	**1389**	63p multicoloured	2·25	2·40 □ □
	Set of 4		5·25	5·25 □ □
	First Day Cover			8·00 □
	Presentation Pack		7·50	□
	PHQ Cards (set of 4)		8·50	13·00 □ □
	Set of 4 Gutter Pairs		13·00	□

1390

1999 (16 Feb.) (*a*) *Embossed and litho Walsall. Self-adhesive. Die-cut perf* 14 × 15

2077 **1390** (1st) grey (face value) (Queen's head in colourless relief) (phosphor background around head) . . . . . 3·00 2·25 □ □

(b) Recess Enschedé. Perf 14 × 14½

2078 **1390** (1st) grey-black (2 phosphor bands) . . . . 3·00 2·25 □ □

(c) Typo Harrison. Perf 14 × 15

2079 **1390** (1st) black (2 phosphor bands) . . . . 3·00 2·25 □ □

Set of 3 . . . . 8·00 6·00 □ □

Nos. 2077/9 were only issued in £7·54 stamp booklets.

1391 Vaccinating Child (pattern in cow markings) (Jenner's development of smallpox vaccine)

1392 Patient on Trolley (nursing care)

1393 Penicillin Mould (Fleming's discovery of penicillin)

1394 Sculpture of Test-tube Baby (development of in vitro fertilization)

Millennium Series. The Patients' Tale

1999 (2 Mar.) *One centre phosphor band* (20p) *or two phosphor bands* (others). *Perf* 13½ × 14

2080	**1391**	20p multicoloured	75	70 □ □
2081	**1392**	26p multicoloured	95	1·00 □ □
2082	**1393**	43p multicoloured	1·50	1·60 □ □
2083	**1394**	63p multicoloured	2·25	2·40 □ □
	Set of 4		5·25	5·25 □ □
	First Day Cover			8·00 □
	Presentation Pack		7·50	□
	PHQ Cards (set of 4)		8·50	13·00 □ □
	Set of 4 Gutter Pairs		13·00	□

Minimum Price. The minimum price quoted is 10p. This represents a handling charge rather than a basis for valuing common stamps. Where the actual value of a stamp is less than 10p this may be apparent when set prices are shown, particularly for sets including a number of 10p stamps. It therefore follows that in valuing common stamps the 10p catalogue price should not be reckoned automatically since it covers a variation in real scarcity.

1395 Dove and Norman Settler (medieval migration to Scotland)

1396 Pilgrim Fathers and Red Indian (17th-century migration to America)

1397 Sailing Ship and Aspects of Settlement (19th-century migration to Australia)

1398 Hummingbird and Superimposed Stylised Face (20th-century migration to Great Britain)

Millennium Series. The Settlers' Tale

1999 (6 APR.) *One centre phosphor band* (20p) *or two phosphor bands* (*others*). *Perf* 14 × 14½

2084	**1395**	20p multicoloured	75	70	□	□
2085	**1396**	26p multicoloured	95	1·00	□	□
2086	**1397**	43p multicoloured	2·00	1·75	□	□
2087	**1398**	63p multicoloured	3·00	3·00	□	□
		Set of 4	5·75	5·75	□	□
		First Day Cover		8·00		□
		Presentation Pack	7·50		□	
		PHQ Cards (set of 4)	8·50	13·00	□	□
		Set of 4 Gutter Pairs	13·00		□	

1399 Woven Threads (woollen industry)

1400 Salts Mill, Saltaire (worsted cloth industry)

1401 Hull on Slipway (shipbuilding)

1402 Lloyd's Building (City of London finance centre)

Millennium Series. The Workers' Tale

1999 (4 MAY) *One centre phosphor band* (19p) *or two phosphor bands* (*others*). *Perf* 14 × 14½

2088	**1399**	19p multicoloured	75	70	□	□
2089	**1400**	26p multicoloured	95	1·00	□	□
2090	**1401**	44p multicoloured	1·75	1·60	□	□
2091	**1402**	64p multicoloured	2·25	2·40	□	□
		Set of 4	5·25	5·25	□	□
		First Day Cover		8·00		□
		Presentation Pack	7·50		□	
		PHQ Cards (set of 4)	8·50	13·00	□	□
		Set of 4 Gutter Pairs	13·00		□	

1403 Freddie Mercury (lead singer of Queen) ('Popular Music')

1404 Bobby Moore with World Cup, 1966 ('Sport')

1405 Dalek from *Dr Who* (science-fiction series) ('Television')

1406 Charlie Chaplin (film star) ('Cinema')

Millennium Series. The Entertainers' Tale

1999 (1 JUNE) *One centre phosphor band* (19p) *or two phosphor bands* (*others*). *Perf* 14 × 14½

2092	**1403**	19p multicoloured	75	70	□	□
2093	**1404**	26p multicoloured	95	1·00	□	□

2094	1405	44p multicoloured	1·50	1·60	□	□
2095	1406	64p multicoloured	2·25	2·40	□	□
		Set of 4	5·25	5·25	□	□
		First Day Cover		8·00		□
		Presentation Pack	7·50		□	
		PHQ Cards (set of 4)	8·50	13·00	□	□
		Set of 4 Gutter Pairs	13·00		□	

1407 Prince Edward and Miss Sophie Rhys-Jones **1408**
(from photos by John Swannell)

Royal Wedding

1999 (15 JUNE) *Two phosphor bands*

2096	1407	26p multicoloured	85	85	□	□
2097	1408	64p multicoloured	2·50	2·50	□	□
		Set of 2	3·00	3·00	□	□
		First Day Cover		4·75		□
		Presentation Pack	4·00		□	
		PHQ Cards (set of 2)	8·50	6·75	□	□
		Set of 2 Gutter Pairs	7·00		□	

1409 Suffragette behind Prison Window ('Equal Rights for Women') **1410** Water Tap ('Right to Health')

1411 Generations of School Children ('Right to Education') **1412** 'MAGNA CARTA' ('Human Rights')

Millennium Series. The Citizens' Tale

1999 (6 JULY) *One centre phosphor band* (19p) *or two phosphor bands* (others). *Perf* 14 × 14½

2098	1409	19p multicoloured	75	70	□	□
2099	1410	26p multicoloured	95	1·00	□	□

1413 Molecular Structures ('DNA decoding') **1414** Galapagos Finch and Fossilized Skeleton ('Darwin's theory of evolution')

1415 Rotation of Polarized Light by Magnetism (Faraday's work on electricity) **1416** Saturn (development of astronomical telescopes)

Millennium Series. The Scientists' Tale

1999 (3 AUG.–21 SEPT.) *One centre phosphor band* (19p) *or two phosphor bands* (others). *Perf* 13½ × 14 (19p, 64p) *or* 14 × 14½ (26p, 44p)

2102	1413	19p multicoloured	75	70	□	□
2103	1414	26p multicoloured	1·50	1·00	□	□
		b. Perf 14½ × 14 (21 Sept.)	3·00	3·00	□	□
2104	1415	44p multicoloured	1·50	1·60	□	□
		a. Perf 14½ × 14 (21 Sept.)	2·75	2·75	□	□
2105	1416	64p multicoloured	2·25	2·40	□	□
		Set of 4	5·25	5·25	□	□
		First Day Cover		8·00		□
		Presentation Pack	7·50		□	
		PHQ Cards (set of 4)	8·50	13·00	□	□
		Set of 4 Gutter Pairs	13·00		□	

Nos. 2103*b* and 2104*a* come from stamp booklets.

For full information on all future British issues, collectors should write to Royal Mail, Freepost EH3647, 21 South Gyle Crescent, Edinburgh EH12 9PE.

1416a

Solar Eclipse
1999 (11 AUG.) *Sheet* 89 × 121 *mm. Two phosphor bands. Perf* 14 × 14½

MS2106	**1416a**	64p × 4 multicoloured	21·00	21·00	☐	☐
		First Day Cover		22·00		☐

1417 Upland Landscape
(Strip farming)

1418 Horse-drawn
Rotary Seed Drill
(Mechanical farming)

1419 Man peeling Potato
(Food imports)

1420 Aerial View of Combine
Harvester (Satellite
agriculture)

Millennium Series. The Farmers' Tale
1999 (7 SEPT.) *One centre phosphor band* (19p) *or two phosphor bands* (*others*). *Perf* 14 × 14½

2107	**1417**	19p multicoloured	75	70	☐	☐
2108	**1418**	26p multicoloured	95	1·00	☐	☐
2109	**1419**	44p multicoloured	1·50	1·60	☐	☐
2110	**1420**	64p multicoloured	2·25	2·40	☐	☐
		Set of 4	5·25	5·25	☐	☐
		First Day Cover		8·00		☐
		Presentation Pack	7·50		☐	
		PHQ Cards (*set of 4*)	8·50	13·00	☐	☐
		Set of 4 Gutter Pairs	13·00		☐	

No. 2107 includes the 'EUROPA' emblem.

1421 Robert the Bruce
(Battle of Bannockburn,
1314)

1422 Cavalier and Horse
(English Civil War)

1423 War Graves Cemetery,
The Somme (World
Wars)

1424 Soldiers with Boy
(Peace-keeping)

Millennium Series. The Soldiers' Tale
1999 (5 OCT.) *One centre phosphor band* (19p) *or two phosphor bands* (*others*). *Perf* 14 × 14½

2111	**1421**	19p black, stone and silver	75	70	☐	☐
2112	**1422**	26p multicoloured	95	1·00	☐	☐
2113	**1423**	44p grey-black, black and silver	2·00	1·60	☐	☐
2114	**1424**	64p multicoloured	2·50	2·40	☐	☐
		Set of 4	5·75	5·25	☐	☐
		First Day Cover		8·00		☐
		Presentation Pack	7·50		☐	
		PHQ Cards (*set of 4*)	8·50	13·00	☐	☐
		Set of 4 Gutter Pairs	13·00		☐	

For full information on all future British issues, collectors should write to Royal Mail, Freepost EH3647, 21 South Gyle Crescent, Edinburgh EH12 9PE.

1425 'Hark the herald angels sing', and Hymnbook (John Wesley)

1426 King James I and Bible (Authorised Version of Bible)

1431 'World of Literature' (Lisa Milroy)

1432 'New Worlds' (Sir Howard Hodgkin)

Millennium Series. The Artists' Tale

1999 (7 Dec.) *One centre phosphor band* (19p) *or two phosphor bands* (others). *Perf* 14 × 14½

2119	**1429**	19p multicoloured	. . . .	75	70	☐ ☐
2120	**1430**	26p multicoloured	. . . .	95	1·00	☐ ☐
2121	**1431**	44p multicoloured	. . . .	1·50	1·60	☐ ☐
2122	**1432**	64p multicoloured	. . . .	2·25	2·40	☐ ☐
		Set of 4	. . . .	5·25	5·25	☐ ☐
		First Day Cover	. . . .		8·00	☐
		Presentation Pack	. . . . . .	7·50		☐
		PHQ Cards (set of 4)	. . . . . .	8·50	13·00	☐ ☐
		Set of 4 Gutter Pairs	. . . . . .	13·00		☐

1427 St Andrews Cathedral, Fife ('Pilgrimage')

1428 Nativity ('First Christmas')

Millennium Series. The Christians' Tale

1999 (2 Nov.) *One centre phosphor band* (19p) *or two phosphor bands* (others). *Perf* 14 × 14½

2115	**1425**	19p multicoloured	. . . .	75	70	☐ ☐
2116	**1426**	26p multicoloured	. . . .	95	1·00	☐ ☐
2117	**1427**	44p multicoloured	. . . .	1·50	1·60	☐ ☐
2118	**1428**	64p multicoloured	. . . .	2·25	2·40	☐ ☐
		Set of 4	. . . .	5·25	5·25	☐ ☐
		First Day Cover	. . . .		8·00	☐
		Presentation Pack	. . . .	7·50		☐
		PHQ Cards (set of 4)	. . . . . .	8·50	13·00	☐ ☐
		Set of 4 Gutter Pairs	. . . . . .	13·00		☐

Collectors Pack 1999

1999 (7 Dec.) *Comprises Nos.* 2069/76, 2080/105 *and* 2107/22

CP2122a   Collectors Pack   . . . . . .   £130   ☐

Post Office Yearbook

1999 (7 Dec.) *Comprises Nos.* 2069/76, 2080/105 *and* 2107/22 *in hardback book with slip case*

YB2122a   Yearbook   . . . .   £130   ☐

1429 'World of the Stage' (Allen Jones)

1430 'World of Music' (Bridget Riley)

1433a

Millennium Series. 'Millennium Timekeeper'

1999 (14 Dec.) *Sheet* 120 × 89 *mm. Multicoloured. Two phosphor bands. Perf* 14 × 14½

MS2123 **1433***a* 64p Clock face and map
of North America; 64p Clock face
and map of Asia; 64p Clock face
and map of Middle East; 64p Clock

face and map of Europe	24·00	24·00 ☐ ☐	
First Day Cover		20·00	☐
Presentation Pack	30·00		☐
PHQ Cards (set of 5)	14·00	32·00 ☐ ☐	

No. **MS**2123 also exists overprinted 'EARLS COURT, LONDON 22–28 MAY 2000 THE STAMP SHOW 2000' from Exhibition Premium Passes, costing £10, available from 1 March 2000.

1437   Queen Elizabeth II

New Millennium

2000 (6 Jan.) *Photo De La Rue, Questa or Walsall* (No. 2124); *Questa or Walsall* (No. 2124*d*). *Two phosphor bands. Perf* 15 × 14 (*with one elliptical hole on each vertical side*)

2124	**1437** (1st) olive-brown	1·00	1·00 ☐ ☐	
	d. Perf 14	1·00	1·00 ☐ ☐	
	First Day Cover		3·00	☐
	Presentation Pack	6·00		☐
	PHQ Card (23 May)	5·00	16·00 ☐ ☐	

No. 2124 comes from sheets or stamp booklets and No. 2124*d* from booklets only.

1438   Barn Owl (World Owl Trust, Muncaster)

1439   Night Sky (National Space Science Centre, Leicester)

1440   River Goyt and Textile Mills (Torrs Walkway, New Mills)

1441   Cape Gannets (Seabird Centre, North Berwick)

Millennium Projects (1st series). 'Above and Beyond'

2000 (18 Jan.–26 May) *One centre phosphor band* (19p) *or two phosphor bands* (*others*). *Perf* 14 × 14½ (1st, 44p) *or* 13½ × 14 (*others*)

2125	**1438**	19p multicoloured	1·25	70 ☐ ☐
2126	**1439**	26p multicoloured	95	1·00 ☐ ☐
2126*a*		(1st) multicoloured		
		(26 May)	5·25	3·50 ☐ ☐
2127	**1440**	44p multicoloured	1·50	1·75 ☐ ☐
2128	**1441**	64p multicoloured	2·50	2·50 ☐ ☐
		Set of 4 (ex No. 2126a)	5·75	5·75 ☐ ☐
		First Day Cover		8·00 ☐
		Presentation Pack	6·50	☐
		PHQ Cards (set of 4)	8·50	13·00 ☐ ☐
		Set of 4 Gutter Pairs	15·00	☐

No. 2126*a* was only issued in £2·70 and £6·83 stamp booklets.

1442   Millennium Beacon (Beacons across the Land)

1443   Garratt Steam Locomotive No. 143 pulling Train (Rheilffordd Eryri, Welsh Highland Railway)

1444   Lightning (Dynamic Earth Centre, Edinburgh)

1445   Multicoloured Lights (Lighting Croydon's Skyline)

Millennium Projects (2nd series). 'Fire and Light'

2000 (1 Feb.) *One centre phosphor band* (19p) *or two phosphor bands* (*others*). *Perf* 14 × 14½

2129	**1442**	19p multicoloured	75	70 ☐ ☐
2130	**1443**	26p multicoloured	1·25	1·00 ☐ ☐
2131	**1444**	44p multicoloured	1·50	1·50 ☐ ☐
2132	**1445**	64p multicoloured	2·25	2·50 ☐ ☐
		Set of 4	5·50	5·50 ☐ ☐
		First Day Cover		8·00 ☐
		Presentation Pack	6·50	☐
		PHQ Cards (set of 4)	8·50	13·00 ☐ ☐
		Set of 4 Gutter Pairs	15·00	☐

1446   Queen Victoria and Queen Elizabeth II

2000 (15 Feb.) *Design T* **929***, but redrawn with '1st' face value as*
T **1446***. Two phosphor bands. Perf* 14 (*with one elliptical hole*
on each vertical side)
2133 **1446** (1st) brownish black
                  and cream . . . . 1·50   1·25 ☐ ☐
     No. 2133 was only issued in stamp booklets.

1451   Reed Beds, River Braid   1452   South American
        (ECOS, Ballymena)   Leaf-cutter Ants
                                          ('Web of Life' Exhibition,
                                          London Zoo)

1447   Beach Pebbles   1448   Frog's Legs and Water
        (Turning the Tide,   Lilies (National Pondlife
        Durham Coast)   Centre, Merseyside)

1453   Solar Sensors (Earth   1454   Hydroponic Leaves
        Centre, Doncaster)   (Project SUZY, Teesside)

Millennium Projects (4th series). 'Life and Earth'
2000 (4 Apr.) *One centre phosphor band* (2nd) *or two phosphor*
bands (*others*). *Perf* 14 × 14½
2138 **1451** (2nd) multicoloured . . .   75   70 ☐ ☐
2139 **1452** (1st) multicoloured . . .   1·25   1·00 ☐ ☐
2140 **1453** 44p multicoloured . . .   1·50   1·50 ☐ ☐
2141 **1454** 64p multicoloured . . .   2·25   1·50 ☐ ☐
        Set of 4 . . . .   5·50   5·50 ☐ ☐
        First Day Cover . . . . . .   8·00   ☐
        Presentation Pack . . . .   6·50   ☐
        PHQ Cards (*set of 4*) . . . . . 8·50 13·00 ☐ ☐
        Set of 4 Gutter Pairs . . . . . . 15·00   ☐

1449   Cliff Boardwalk   1450   Reflections in Water
        (Parc Arfordirol,   (Portsmouth Harbour
        Llanelli Coast)   Development)

Millennium Projects (3rd series). 'Water and Coast'
2000 (7 Mar.) *One centre phosphor band* (19p) *or two phosphor*
bands (*others*). *Perf* 14 × 14½
2134 **1447** 19p multicoloured   75   70 ☐ ☐
2135 **1448** 26p multicoloured . . . .   1·25   1·00 ☐ ☐
2136 **1449** 44p black, grey and silver   1·50   1·50 ☐ ☐
2137 **1450** 64p multicoloured . . . .   2·25   2·50 ☐ ☐
        Set of 4 . . . .   5·50   5·50 ☐ ☐
        First Day Cover . . . .   8·00   ☐
        Presentation Pack . . . . 6·50   ☐
        PHQ Cards (*set of 4*) . . . . . 8·50 13·00 ☐ ☐
        Set of 4 Gutter Pairs . . . . . . 15·00   ☐

1455   Pottery Glaze   1456   Bankside Galleries
        (Ceramica Museum,   (Tate Modern, London)
        Stoke-on-Trent)

1457 Road Marking (Cycle Network Artworks)

1458 People of Salford (Lowry Centre, Salford)

Millennium Projects (5th series). 'Art and Craft'

2000 (2 MAY) *One centre phosphor band* (2nd) *or two phosphor bands* (*others*). *Perf* 14 × 14½

2142	**1455**	(2nd) multicoloured . . .	75	70	☐	☐
2143	**1456**	(1st) multicoloured . . .	1·25	1·00	☐	☐
2144	**1457**	45p multicoloured . . .	1·50	1·50	☐	☐
2145	**1458**	65p multicoloured . . .	2·25	2·50	☐	☐
	Set of 4		5·50	5·50	☐	☐
	First Day Cover			8·00		☐
	Presentation Pack		7·50		☐	
	PHQ Cards (set of 4)		8·50	13·00	☐	☐
	Set of 4 Gutter Pairs		15·00		☐	

'Stamp Show 2000' International Stamp Exhibition, London. Jeffrey Matthews Colour Palette

2000 (22 MAY) *Sheet,* 124 × 70 mm, *containing stamps as T* **367** *with two labels. Phosphorised paper. Perf* 15 × 14 (*with one elliptical hole on each vertical side*)

MS2146 4p new blue; 5p dull red-brown; 6p yellow-olive; 10p dull orange; 31p dp mauve; 39p brt magenta; 64p turq-green; £1 bluish violet . . . . 18·00 18·00 ☐ ☐

First Day Cover . . . . 18·00 ☐

Exhibition Card (*wallet, sold at £4.99, containing one mint sheet and one cancelled on postcard*) . . . . 65·00 ☐

The £1 value is printed in Iriodin ink which gives a shiny effect to the solid part of the background behind the Queen's head.

1459

'Stamp Show 2000' International Stamp Exhibition, London. 'Her Majesty's Stamps'

2000 (23 MAY) *Sheet* 121 × 89 mm. *Phosphorised paper. Perf* 15 × 14 (*with one elliptical hole on each vertical side of stamps as T* **1437**)

MS2147 **1459** (1st) olive-brown (Type **1437**) × 4; £1 slate-green (as Type **163**) . . . . 21·00 21·00 ☐ ☐

First Day Cover . . . . 22·00 ☐

Presentation Pack . . . . 90·00 ☐

PHQ Cards (set of 2) . . . . 16·00 28·00 ☐ ☐

The £1 value is an adaptation of the 1953 Coronation 1s. 3d. stamp. It is shown on one of the PHQ cards with the other depicting the complete miniature sheet.

See also No. 2380 for *T* **163** from £7·46 stamp booklet.

1460 Children playing (Millennium Greens Project)

1461 Millennium Bridge, Gateshead

1462 Daisies (Mile End Park, London)

1463 African Hut and Thatched Cottage ('On the Meridian Line' Project)

Millennium Projects (6th series). 'People and Places'

2000 (6 JUNE) *One centre phosphor band* (2nd) *or two phosphor bands* (*others*). *Perf* 14 × 14½

2148	**1460**	(2nd) multicoloured . . .	75	70	☐	☐
2149	**1461**	(1st) multicoloured . . .	1·25	1·00	☐	☐
2150	**1462**	45p multicoloured . . .	1·50	1·50	☐	☐
2151	**1463**	65p multicoloured . . .	2·25	2·50	☐	☐
	Set of 4		5·50	5·50	☐	☐
	First Day Cover			8·00		☐
	Presentation Pack		7·50		☐	
	PHQ Cards (set of 4)		8·50	13·00	☐	☐
	Set of 4 Gutter Pairs		15·00		☐	

| 1464 | Raising the Stone (Strangford Stone, Killyleagh) | 1465 | Horse's Hooves (Trans Pennine Trail, Derbyshire) |

| 1470 | Sycamore Seeds (Millennium Seed Bank, Wakehurst Place, Surrey) | 1471 | Forest, Doire Dach ('Forest for Scotland') |

Millennium Projects (8th series). 'Tree and Leaf'

2000 (1 AUG.) *One centre phosphor band* (2nd) *or two phosphor bands* (others). *Perf* 14 × 14½

2156	**1468**	(2nd) multicoloured . . .	75	70	☐ ☐
2157	**1469**	(1st) multicoloured	1·25	1·00	☐ ☐
2158	**1470**	45p multicoloured . . .	1·50	1·60	☐ ☐
2159	**1471**	65p multicoloured . . .	2·50	2·50	☐ ☐
	Set of 4	. . . .	5·50	5·50	☐ ☐
	First Day Cover	. . . .		8·00	☐
	Presentation Pack	. . . .	7·50		☐
	PHQ Cards (set of 4)	. . . . . .	8·50	13·00	☐ ☐
	Set of 4 Gutter Pairs	. . . . . .	15·00		☐

| 1466 | Cyclist (Kingdom of Fife Cycle Ways, Scotland) | 1467 | Bluebell Wood (Groundwork's 'Changing Places' Project) |

Millennium Projects (7th series). 'Stone and Soil'

2000 (4 JULY) *One centre phosphor band* (2nd) *or two phosphor bands* (others). *Perf* 14 × 14½

2152	**1464**	(2nd) brownish black, grey-black and silver	75	70	☐ ☐
2153	**1465**	(1st) multicoloured . . .	1·25	1·00	☐ ☐
2154	**1466**	45p multicoloured . . .	1·50	1·75	☐ ☐
2155	**1467**	65p multicoloured . . .	2·50	2·50	☐ ☐
	Set of 4	. . . .	5·50	5·75	☐ ☐
	First Day Cover	. . . .		8·00	☐
	Presentation Pack	. . . .	7·50		☐
	PHQ Cards (set of 4)	. . . . . .	8·50	13·00	☐ ☐
	Set of 4 Gutter Pairs	. . . . . .	15·00		☐

| 1472 | Queen Elizabeth the Queen Mother |

| 1468 | Tree Roots ('Yews for the Millennium' Project) | 1469 | Sunflower ('Eden' Project, St. Austell) |

1472*a* Royal Family on Queen Mother's 100th Birthday (from photo by J. Swannell)

Queen Elizabeth the Queen Mother's 100th Birthday

2000 (4 Aug.) *Phosphorised paper plus two phosphor bands. Perf 14½*

2160	**1472**	27p multicoloured . . .	2·50	2·75	□	□

MS2161 121 × 89 mm. **1472a** 27p Queen Elizabeth II; 27p Prince William; 27p Queen Elizabeth the Queen Mother; 27p Prince Charles 11·00 11·00 □ □

First Day Cover (**MS**2161)	12·00	□
Presentation Pack (**MS**2161) . .	28·00	□
PHQ Cards (*set of* 5) . . . . . . 11·00	24·00	□ □

No. 2160 was only issued in stamp booklets and in No. **MS**2161.

The complete miniature sheet is shown on one of the PHQ cards with the others depicting individual stamps.

1473 Head of *Gigantiops destructor* (Ant) (Wildscreen at Bristol)

1474 Gathering Water Lilies on Broads (Norfolk and Norwich Project)

1475 X-ray of Hand holding Computer Mouse (Millennium Point, Birmingham)

1476 Tartan Wool Holder (Scottish Cultural Resources Access Network)

Millennium Projects (9th series). 'Mind and Matter'

2000 (5 Sept.) *One centre phosphor band* (2nd) *or two phosphor bands* (*others*). *Perf* 14 × 14½

2162	**1473**	(2nd) multicoloured . . .	75	70	□	□
2163	**1474**	(1st) multicoloured . . .	1·25	1·00	□	□
2164	**1475**	45p multicoloured . . .	1·50	1·75	□	□
2165	**1476**	65p multicoloured . . .	2·25	2·50	□	□
		Set of 4	5·50	5·75	□	□
		First Day Cover		8·00		□
		Presentation Pack	7·50			□
		PHQ Cards (*set of 4*)	8·50	13·00	□	□
		Set of 4 Gutter Pairs	15·00			□

1477 Acrobatic Performers (Millennium Dome)

1478 Football Players (Hampden Park, Glasgow)

1479 Bather (Bath Spa Project)

1480 Hen's Egg under Magnification (Centre for Life, Newcastle)

Millennium Projects (10th series). 'Body and Bone'

2000 (3 Oct.) *One centre phosphor band* (2nd) *or two phosphor bands* (*others*). *Perf* 14 × 14½ (2nd) *or* 13½ × 14 (*others*)

2166	**1477**	(2nd) black, slate-blue and silver	75	70	□	□
2167	**1478**	(1st) multicoloured . . .	1·25	1·00	□	□
2168	**1479**	45p multicoloured . . .	1·50	1·50	□	□
2169	**1480**	65p multicoloured . . .	2·25	2·50	□	□
		Set of 4	5·50	5·75	□	□
		First Day Cover		8·00		□
		Presentation Pack	7·50			□
		PHQ Cards (*set of 4*)	8·50	13·00	□	□
		Set of 4 Gutter Pairs	15·00			□

1481 Virgin and Child Stained Glass Window, St. Edmundsbury Cathedral (Suffolk Cathedral Millennium Project)

1482 Floodlit Church of St. Peter and St. Paul, Overstowey (Church Floodlighting Trust)

1483 12th-cent. Latin Gradual (St. Patrick Centre, Downpatrick)

1484 Chapter House Ceiling, York Minster (York Millennium Mystery Plays)

Millennium Projects (11th series). 'Spirit and Faith'

2000 (7 Nov.) One centre phosphor band (2nd) or two phosphor bands (others). Perf 14 × 14½

2170	**1481**	(2nd) multicoloured	. . .	75	70	□	□
2171	**1482**	(1st) multicoloured	. . .	1·25	1·00	□	□
2172	**1483**	45p multicoloured	. . .	1·50	1·50	□	□
2173	**1484**	65p multicoloured	. . .	2·25	2·50	□	□
	Set of 4	. . . .		5·50	5·50	□	□
	First Day Cover	. . . .			8·00		□
	Presentation Pack	. . . .		7·50		□	
	PHQ Cards (set of 4)	. . . . .		8·50	13·00	□	□
	Set of 4 Gutter Pairs	. . . . .		15·00		□	

Post Office Yearbook

2000 (7 Nov.) Comprises Nos. **MS**2125/6, 2127/32, 2134/45, 2148/59 and **MS**2161/81 in hardback book with slip case

YB2181a   Yearbook   . . . .   £100   □

The last two issues in the Millennium Projects Series were supplied for insertion into the above at a later date.

1485 Church Bells (Ringing in the Millennium)

1486 Eye (Year of the Artist)

1487 Top of Harp (Canolfan Mileniwm, Cardiff)

1488 Figure within Latticework (TS2K Creative Enterprise Centres, London)

Millennium Projects (12th series). 'Sound and Vision'

2000 (5 Dec.) One centre phosphor band (2nd) or two phosphor bands (others). Perf 14 × 14½

2174	**1485**	(2nd) multicoloured	. . .	75	70	□	□
2175	**1486**	(1st) multicoloured	. . .	1·25	1·00	□	□
2176	**1487**	45p multicoloured	. . .	1·50	1·50	□	□
2177	**1488**	65p multicoloured	. . .	2·25	2·50	□	□
	Set of 4	. . . .		5·50	5·50	□	□
	First Day Cover	. . . .			8·00		□
	Presentation Pack	. . . .		7·50		□	
	PHQ Cards (set of 4)	. . . . .		8·50	13·00	□	□
	Set of 4 Gutter Pairs	. . . . .		15·00		□	

Collectors Pack 2000

2000 (5 Dec.) Comprises Nos. **MS**2125/6, 2127/32, 2134/45, 2148/59 and **MS**2161/81

CP2181a   Collectors Pack   . . . .   £120   □

1489 'Flower' ('Nurture Children')

1490 'Tiger' ('Listen to Children')

1491 'Owl' ('Teach Children')

1492 'Butterfly' ('Ensure Children's Freedom')

New Millennium. Rights of the Child. Face Paintings

2001 (16 Jan.) One centre phosphor band (2nd) or two phosphor bands (others). Perf 14 × 14½

2178	**1489**	(2nd) multicoloured	. . .	75	75	□	□
2179	**1490**	(1st) multicoloured	. . .	1·00	1·10	□	□
2180	**1491**	45p multicoloured	. . .	1·60	1·75	□	□
2181	**1492**	65p multicoloured	. . .	2·40	2·50	□	□
	Set of 4	. . . .		5·75	5·75	□	□
	First Day Cover	. . . .			7·50		□
	Presentation Pack	. . . .		7·50		□	
	PHQ Cards (set of 4)	. . . . .		8·50	13·00	□	□
	Set of 4 Gutter Pairs	. . . . .		14·00		□	

1493 'Love'

1494 'THANKS'

1495 'abc' (New Baby)

1496 'WELCOME'

1497 'Cheers'

'Occasions' Greetings Stamps

2001 (6 Feb.) *Two phosphor bands. Perf 14½ × 14*

2182	**1493**	(1st) multicoloured	....	1·10	1·10 ☐ ☐
2183	**1494**	(1st) multicoloured	....	1·10	1·10 ☐ ☐
2184	**1495**	(1st) multicoloured	....	1·10	1·10 ☐ ☐
2185	**1496**	(1st) multicoloured	....	1·10	1·10 ☐ ☐
2186	**1497**	(1st) multicoloured	....	1·10	1·10 ☐ ☐
		Set of 5	....	5·00	5·00 ☐ ☐
		First Day Cover	....		6·50 ☐
		Presentation Pack (13 Feb.)	...	6·50	☐
		PHQ Cards (*set of* 5)	.....	8·50	13·00 ☐ ☐
		Set of 5 *Gutter Pairs*	......	13·00	☐

The silver-grey backgrounds are printed in Iriodin ink which gives a shiny effect.

Nos. 2182/6 were printed in photogravure. They were subsequently re-issued on 1 May, as sheets of 20, printed in lithography instead of photogravure with each stamp accompanied by a half stamp-size label showing either postal symbols or a personal photograph.

1498 Dog and Owner on Bench

1499 Dog in Bath

1500 Boxer at Dog Show

1501 Cat in Handbag

1502 Cat on Gate

1503 Dog in Car

1504 Cat at Window

1505 Dog behind Fence

1506 Cat watching Bird

1507 Cat in Washbasin

T **1498/1507** were printed together in sheetlets of 10 (5 × 2), with the surplus self-adhesive paper around each stamp retained.

Cats and Dogs

2001 (13 Feb.) *Self-adhesive. Two phosphor bands. Die-cut perf 15 × 14*

2187	**1498**	(1st) black, grey and silver	1·25	1·00 ☐ ☐
		a. Sheetlet. Nos. 2187/96	15·00	11·50 ☐ ☐
2188	**1499**	(1st) black, grey and silver	1·25	1·00 ☐ ☐
2189	**1500**	(1st) black, grey and silver	1·25	1·00 ☐ ☐
2190	**1501**	(1st) black, grey and silver	1·25	1·00 ☐ ☐
2191	**1502**	(1st) black, grey and silver	1·25	1·00 ☐ ☐
2192	**1503**	(1st) black, grey and silver	1·25	1·00 ☐ ☐
2193	**1504**	(1st) black, grey and silver	1·25	1·00 ☐ ☐
2194	**1505**	(1st) black, grey and silver	1·25	1·00 ☐ ☐
2195	**1506**	(1st) black, grey and silver	1·25	1·00 ☐ ☐
2196	**1507**	(1st) black, grey and silver	1·25	1·00 ☐ ☐
		Set of 10	....	11·00	9·00 ☐ ☐
		First Day Cover	....		15·00 ☐
		Presentation Pack	....	20·00	☐
		PHQ Cards (*set of* 10)	......	14·00	30·00 ☐ ☐

1508 'RAIN'

1509 'FAIR'

1510 'STORMY'

1511 'VERY DRY'

Nos. 2197/200 show the four quadrants of a barometer dial which are combined on the miniature sheet.

The Weather

2001 (13 Mar.) *One side phosphor band* (19p) *or two phosphor bands* (others). *Perf* 14½

2197	**1508**	19p multicoloured	70	75 □ □
2198	**1509**	27p multicoloured	85	1·00 □ □
2199	**1510**	45p multicoloured	1·50	1·50 □ □
2200	**1511**	65p multicoloured	2·40	2·50 □ □
		Set of 4	5·00	5·50 □ □
		First Day Cover		7·00 □
		Presentation Pack	12·50	□
		Set of 4 Gutter Pairs	14·00	□
MS2201		105 × 105 mm. Nos. 2197/200	13·00	13·00 □ □
		First Day Cover		15·00 □
		PHQ Cards (set of 5)	8·50	16·00 □ □

The reddish violet on both the 27p and the miniature sheet is printed in thermochromic ink which changes from reddish violet to light blue when exposed to heat.

The PHQ cards depict the four values and the miniature sheet.

1512 *Vanguard* Class
Submarine, 1992

1513 *Swiftsure* Class
Submarine, 1973

1514 *Unity* Class Submarine, 1939

1515 'Holland' Type Submarine, 1901

1516 White Ensign

1517 Union Jack

1518 Jolly Roger flown by H.M.S. *Proteus* (submarine)

1519 Flag of Chief of Defence Staff

Centenary of Royal Navy Submarine Service

2001 (10 Apr.–22 Oct.) *One centre phosphor band* (2nd) *or two phosphor bands* (others). (a) *Submarines. PVA gum. Perf* 15 × 14

2202	**1512**	(2nd) multicoloured	70	75 □ □
		a. Perf 15½ × 15 (22 Oct.)	3·75	3·00 □ □
2203	**1513**	(1st) multicoloured	85	90 □ □
		a. Perf 15½ × 15 (22 Oct.)	3·75	3·00 □ □
2204	**1514**	45p multicoloured	1·75	1·60 □ □
		a. Perf 15½ × 15 (22 Oct.)	3·75	3·00 □ □
2205	**1515**	65p multicoloured	2·40	2·50 □ □
		a. Perf 15½ × 15 (22 Oct.)	3·75	3·00 □ □
		Set of 4	5·25	5·25 □ □
		First Day Cover		7·50 □
		Presentation Pack	7·00	□
		PHQ Cards (set of 4)	8·50	14·00 □ □
		Set of 4 Gutter Pairs	13·50	□

(b) *Flags. Sheet* 92 × 97 mm. *PVA gum. Perf* 14½

MS2206	**1516** (1st) multicoloured;	
	1517 (1st) multicoloured; **1518**	
	(1st) multicoloured; **1519** (1st)	
	multicoloured (22 Oct.)	9·00	9·00 □ □
	First Day Cover		11·00 □
	Presentation Pack	12·00	□
	PHQ Cards (set of 5)	5·00	12·00 □ □

(c) *Self-adhesive. Die-cut perf* 15½ × 14 (*No. 2207*)
or 14½ (*others*)

2207	**1513**	(1st) multicoloured (17 Apr.)	40·00	37·00 □ □
2208	**1516**	(1st) multicoloured (22 Oct.)	12·00	12·00 □ □
2209	**1518**	(1st) multicoloured (22 Oct.)	12·00	12·00 □ □

Nos. 2202*a*/5*a* only come from stamp booklets.

The five PHQ cards depict the four designs and the complete miniature sheet.

Nos. 2207/9 only come from two different £1.62 booklets.

Type **1516** was re-issued on 21 June 2005 in sheets of 20, printed in lithography instead of photogravure, with half stamp-size *se-tenant* labels showing signal flags.

Designs as Type **1517** were issued on 27 July 2004 in sheets of 20 printed in lithography instead of photogravure with each vertical row of stamps alternated with half stamp-size labels.

1520 Leyland X2 Open-top, London General B Type, Leyland Titan TD1 and AEC Regent 1	**1521** AEC Regent 1, Daimler COG5, Utility Guy Arab Mk II and AEC Regent III RT Type

1522 AEC Regent III RT Type, Bristol KSW5G Open-top, AEC Routemaster and Bristol Lodekka FSF6G	**1523** Bristol Lodekka FSF6G, Leyland Titan PD3/4, Leyland Atlantean PDR1/1 and Daimler Fleetline CRG6LX-33

1524 Daimler Fleetline CRG6LX-33, MCW Metrobus DR102/43, Leyland Olympian ONLXB/1R and Dennis Trident

T **1520/4** were printed together, *se-tenant*, in horizontal strips of 5 throughout the sheet. The illustrations of the first bus on No. 2210 and the last bus on No. 2214 continue onto the sheet margins.

150th Anniversary of First Double-decker Bus

2001 (15 MAY) *'All-over' phosphor. Perf* 14½ × 14

2210	**1520**	(1st) multicoloured . . .	1·10	1·10 □ □
		a. Horiz strip of 5. Nos. 2210/14	5·50	5·75 □ □
2211	**1521**	(1st) multicoloured . . .	1·10	1·10 □ □
2212	**1522**	(1st) multicoloured . . .	1·10	1·10 □ □
2213	**1523**	(1st) multicoloured . . .	1·10	1·10 □ □
2214	**1524**	(1st) multicoloured . . .	1·10	1·10 □ □
		Set of 5	5·25	5·25 □ □
		First Day Cover		6·50 □
		Presentation Pack	8·00	□
		PHQ Cards (set of 5)	8·50	24·00 □ □
		Gutter Strip of 10	12·00	□
MS2215	120 × 105 mm. Nos. 2210/14		9·75	9·75 □ □
		First Day Cover		15·00 □

In No. **MS**2215 the illustrations of the AEC Regent III RT Type and the Daimler Fleetline CRG6LX-33 appear twice.

1525 Toque Hat by Pip Hackett	**1526** Butterfly Hat by Dai Rees

1527 Top Hat by Stephen Jones	**1528** Spiral Hat by Philip Treacy

Fashion Hats

2001 (19 JUNE) *'All-over' phosphor. Perf* 14½

2216	**1525**	(1st) multicoloured . . .	85	90 □ □
2217	**1526**	(E) multicoloured . . .	1·10	1·25 □ □
2218	**1527**	45p multicoloured . . .	1·60	1·60 □ □
2219	**1528**	65p multicoloured . . .	2·50	2·50 □ □
		Set of 4	5·50	5·50 □ □
		First Day Cover		7·25 □
		Presentation Pack	7·50	□
		PHQ Cards (set of 4)	8·50	14·00 □ □
		Set of 4 Gutter Pairs	13·00	□

1529 Common Frog

1530 Great Diving Beetle

1531 Three-spined Stickleback

1532 Southern Hawker Dragonfly

1535 Mr. Punch

1536 Judy

1537 Beadle

1538 Crocodile

Europa. Pond Life

2001 (10 July) *Two phosphor bands*

2220	**1529**	(1st) multicoloured . . .	1·00	1·00	□	□
2221	**1530**	(E) multicoloured . . .	1·25	1·25	□	□
2222	**1531**	45p multicoloured . . .	1·50	1·50	□	□
2223	**1532**	65p multicoloured . . .	2·00	2·25	□	□
		Set of 4	5·50	5·75	□	□
		First Day Cover		11·00		□
		Presentation Pack	7·50		□	
		PHQ Cards (set of 4)	8·50	14·00	□	□
		Set of 4 Gutter Pairs	15·00		□	

The 1st and E values incorporate the 'EUROPA' emblem.

The bluish silver on all four values is in Iriodin ink and was used as a background for those parts of the design below the water line.

1533 Policeman

1534 Clown

Nos. 2224/9 were printed together, *se-tenant*, in horizontal strips of 6 throughout the sheet.

Punch and Judy Show Puppets

2001 (4 Sept.) *Two phosphor bands.* (*a*) *PVA gum. Perf* 14 × 15

2224	**1533**	(1st) multicoloured . . .	80	75	□	□
		a. Horiz strip of 6.				
		Nos. 2224/9	5·00	5·25	□	□
2225	**1534**	(1st) multicoloured . . .	80	75	□	□
2226	**1535**	(1st) multicoloured . . .	80	75	□	□
2227	**1536**	(1st) multicoloured . . .	80	75	□	□
2228	**1537**	(1st) multicoloured . . .	80	75	□	□
2229	**1538**	(1st) multicoloured . . .	80	75	□	□
		Set of 6	4·50	4·00	□	□
		First Day Cover		7·00		□
		Presentation Pack	7·00		□	
		PHQ Cards (set of 6)	8·50	18·00	□	□
		Gutter Block of 12	13·00		□	

(*b*) *Self-adhesive. Die-cut perf* 14 × 15½

2230	**1535**	(1st) multicoloured . . .	10·00	10·00	□	□
2231	**1536**	(1st) multicoloured . . .	10·00	10·00	□	□

Nos. 2230/1 were only issued in £1.62 stamp booklets.

For full information on all future British issues, collectors should write to Royal Mail, Freepost EH3647, 21 South Gyle Crescent, Edinburgh EH12 9PE.

1539 Carbon 60 Molecule (Chemistry)

1540 Globe (Economic Sciences)

1541 Embossed Dove (Peace)

1542 Crosses (Physiology or Medicine)

1543 Poem 'The Addressing of Cats' by T. S. Eliot in Open Book (Literature)

1544 Hologram of Boron Molecule (Physics)

Centenary of Nobel Prizes

2001 (2 Oct.) *One side phosphor band* (2nd) *or phosphor frame (others). Perf* 14½

2232	**1539**	(2nd) black, silver and grey-black	75	65	□	□
2233	**1540**	(1st) multicoloured . . .	1·00	90	□	□
2234	**1541**	(E) black, silver and bright green	1·00	1·25	□	□
2235	**1542**	40p multicoloured . . .	1·25	1·25	□	□
2236	**1543**	45p multicoloured . . .	1·50	1·75	□	□
2237	**1544**	65p black and silver . .	2·25	2·50	□	□
	Set of 6	. . . .	7·50	7·50	□	□
	First Day Cover	. . . .		9·50		□
	Presentation Pack	. . . .	10·00		□	
	PHQ Cards (*set of* 6)	. . . . . .	10·00	18·00	□	□
	Set of 6 *Gutter Pairs*	. . . . . .	20·00		□	

The grey-black on No. 2232 is printed in thermochromic ink which temporarily changes to pale grey when exposed to heat. The centre of No. 2235 is coated with a eucalyptus scent.

1545 Robins with Snowman

1546 Robins on Bird Table

1547 Robins skating on Bird Bath

1548 Robins with Christmas Pudding

1549 Robins in Paper Chain Nest

Christmas. Robins

2001 (6 Nov.) *Self-adhesive. One centre phosphor band* (2nd) *or two phosphor bands* (others). *Die-cut perf* 14½

2238	**1545**	(2nd) multicoloured . . .	75	70	□	□
2239	**1546**	(1st) multicoloured . . .	1·00	1·00	□	□
2240	**1547**	(E) multicoloured . . .	1·00	1·10	□	□
2241	**1548**	45p multicoloured . . .	1·50	1·50	□	□
2242	**1549**	65p multicoloured . . .	2·00	2·25	□	□
	Set of 5	. . . .	6·00	6·00	□	□
	First Day Cover	. . . .		9·50		□
	Presentation Pack	. . . .	8·00		□	
	PHQ Cards (*set of* 5)	. . . . . .	11·00	16·00	□	□

The 1st value was re-issued on 30 September 2003, in sheets of 20, in lithography instead of photogravure, each stamp *se-tenant* with a Christmas label or a personal photograph. The sheet contained die-cut perforated stamps and labels.

The 2nd and 1st class stamps were issued again on 1 November 2005 in sheets of 20 containing ten 1st class and ten 2nd class stamps, each stamp accompanied by a *se-tenant* label showing a snowman.

Collectors Pack 2001

2001 (6 Nov.) *Comprises Nos.* 2178/2200, 2202/**MS**2206, 2210/14, 2216/29 *and* 2232/42

CP2242a	*Collectors Pack*	. . . .	£120	□

2001 (6 Nov.) *Comprises Nos. 2178/96*, **MS**2201/6, **MS**2215/29 *and 2232/42 in hardback book with slip case*

YB2242a	Yearbook	£110	☐

1550	'How the Whale got his Throat'

1551	'How the Camel got his Hump'

1552	'How the Rhinoceros got his Skin'

1553	'How the Leopard got his Spots'

1554	'The Elephant's Child'

1555	'The Sing-Song of Old Man Kangaroo'

1556	'The Beginning of the Armadillos'

1557	'The Crab that played with the Sea'

1558	'The Cat that walked by Himself'

1559	'The Butterfly that stamped'

T **1550/9** were printed together in sheetlets of 10 (5×2), with the surplus self-adhesive paper around each stamp retained.

Centenary of Publication of Rudyard Kipling's Just So Stories

2002 (15 Jan.) *Self-adhesive. Two phosphor bands. Die-cut perf* 15 × 14

2243	1550	(1st) multicoloured	95	85	☐	☐
		a. Sheetlet. Nos. 2243/52	10·00	10·00	☐	☐
2244	1551	(1st) multicoloured	95	85	☐	☐
2245	1552	(1st) multicoloured	95	85	☐	☐
2246	1553	(1st) multicoloured	95	85	☐	☐
2247	1554	(1st) multicoloured	95	85	☐	☐
2248	1555	(1st) multicoloured	95	85	☐	☐
2249	1556	(1st) multicoloured	95	85	☐	☐
2250	1557	(1st) multicoloured	95	85	☐	☐
2251	1558	(1st) multicoloured	95	85	☐	☐
2252	1559	(1st) multicoloured	95	85	☐	☐
		Set of 10	9·00	8·00	☐	☐
		First Day Cover		11·00		☐
		Presentation Pack	12·00			☐
		PHQ Cards (set of 10)	8·50	28·00	☐	☐

1560	Queen Elizabeth II, 1952 (Dorothy Wilding)

1561	Queen Elizabeth II, 1968 (Cecil Beaton)

1562	Queen Elizabeth II, 1978 (Lord Snowdon)

1563	Queen Elizabeth II, 1984 (Yousef Karsh)

1564	Queen Elizabeth II, 1996 (Tim Graham)

1565

Golden Jubilee. Studio portraits of Queen Elizabeth II by photographers named

2002 (6 FEB.) *One centre phosphor band* (2nd) *or two phosphor bands* (others). *W* **1565**. *Perf* 14½ × 14

2253	**1560**	(2nd) multicoloured	75	55	☐	☐
2254	**1561**	(1st) multicoloured	1·00	80	☐	☐
2255	**1562**	(E) multicoloured	1·25	1·25	☐	☐
2256	**1563**	45p multicoloured	1·50	1·50	☐	☐
2257	**1564**	65p multicoloured	2·25	2·25	☐	☐
		Set of 5	6·50	6·00	☐	☐
		First Day Cover		8·00		☐
		Presentation Pack	7·50		☐	
		PHQ Cards (set of 5)	4·50	14·00	☐	☐
		Set of 5 Gutter Pairs	16·00		☐	

Stamps from sheets had the watermark sideways: those from stamp booklets had the watermark upright.

1566

Booklet Stamps

2002 (6 FEB.) *Designs as* 1952-54 *issue, but with service indicator as T* **1566**. *One centre phosphor band* (2nd) *or two phosphor bands* (1st). *W* **1565**. *Uncoated paper. Perf* 15 × 14 (*with one elliptical hole on each vertical side*)

2258	**1566**	(2nd) carmine-red	1·20	1·00	☐	☐
2259	**154**	(1st) green	1·25	1·25	☐	☐
		Set of 2	2·40	2·25	☐	☐

Nos. 2258/9 were only issued in £7.29 stamp booklets.

See also Nos. 2031/3, **MS**2326, **MS**2367 and 2378/80.

1571 Flowers ('best wishes')

'Occasions' Greetings Stamps

2002 (5 MAR.) 03 *Two phosphor bands.* (*a*) *Litho. PVA gum. Perf* 15 × 14

2260	**1567**	(1st) multicoloured	1·00	1·00	☐	☐
2261	**1568**	(1st) multicoloured	1·00	1·00	☐	☐
2262	**1569**	(1st) multicoloured . . .	1·00	1·00	☐	☐
2263	**1570**	(1st) multicoloured	1·00	1·00	☐	☐
2264	**1571**	(1st) multicoloured	1·00	1·00	☐	☐
		Set of 5	4·75	4·75	☐	☐
		First Day Cover		6·75		☐
		Presentation Pack	6·00		☐	
		PHQ Cards (set of 5)	4·50	14·00	☐	☐
		Set of 5 Gutter Pairs	12·00		☐	

(*b*) *Photo. Self-adhesive. Die-cut perf* 15 × 14

2264a	**1569**	(1st) multicoloured (4.3.03)	4·00	4·00

Nos. 2260/4 were re-issued on 23 April 2002 in sheets of 20 perforated 14½ × 14, either of one design or *se-tenant*, with each stamp accompanied by a half stamp-size label showing either greetings or a personal photograph.

No. 2262 was also issued in sheets of 20 with *se-tenant* labels in connection with the Hong Kong Stamp Expo on 30 January 2004. It was issued again on 21 April 2005 in sheets of 20 perforated 14½ × 14 with *se-tenant* labels for Pacific Explorer 2005 World Stamp Expo.

No. 2264a was only issued in £1·62 stamp booklets in which the surplus self-adhesive paper around each stamp was removed.

1567 Rabbits ('a new baby')

1568 'LOVE'

1572 Studland Bay, Dorset

1573 Luskentyre, South Harris

1569 Aircraft Sky-writing 'hello'

1570 Bear pulling Potted Topiary Tree (Moving Home)

1574 Cliffs, Dover, Kent

1575 Padstow Harbour, Cornwall

1576 Broadstairs, Kent

1577 St. Abb's Head, Scottish Borders

1578 Dunster Beach, Somerset

1579 Newquay Beach, Cornwall

1580 Portrush, County Antrim

1581 Sand-spit, Conwy

T 1572/81 were printed together, *se-tenant*, in blocks of 10 (5 × 2) hroughout the sheet.

British Coastlines

2002 (19 Mar.) *Two phosphor bands. Perf 14½*

2265	1572	27p multicoloured	75	80	□	□
		a. Block of 10.				
		Nos. 2265/74	8·75	8·75	□	□
2266	1573	27p multicoloured	75	80	□	□
2267	1574	27p multicoloured	75	80	□	□
2268	1575	27p multicoloured	75	80	□	□
2269	1576	27p multicoloured	75	80	□	□
2270	1577	27p multicoloured	75	80	□	□
2271	1578	27p multicoloured	75	80	□	□
2272	1579	27p multicoloured	75	80	□	□
2273	1580	27p multicoloured	75	80	□	□
2274	1581	27p multicoloured	75	80	□	□
		Set of 10	7·00	7·25	□	□
		First Day Cover		11·50		□
		Presentation Pack	10·50		□	
		PHQ Cards (set of 10)	9·25	28·00	□	□
		Gutter Block of 20	20·00		□	

1582 Slack Wire Act

1583 Lion Tamer

1584 Trick Tri-cyclists

1585 Krazy Kar

1586 Equestrienne

Europa. Circus

2002 (10 Apr.) *One centre phosphor band* (2nd) *or two phosphor bands* (others). *Perf* 14½

2275	1582	(2nd) multicoloured	50	60	□	□
2276	1583	(1st) multicoloured	75	85	□	□
2277	1584	(E) multicoloured	1·00	1·25	□	□
2278	1585	45p multicoloured	1·75	1·50	□	□
2279	1586	65p multicoloured	2·75	2·25	□	□
		Set of 5	6·00	6·00	□	□
		First Day Cover		8·00	□	□
		Presentation Pack	7·50		□	
		PHQ Cards (set of 5)	4·50	14·00	□	□
		Set of 5 Gutter Pairs	16·00		□	

The 1st and E values incorporate the "EUROPA" emblem.

Due to the funeral of the Queen Mother, the actual issue of Nos. 2275/9 was delayed from 9 April which is the date that appears on first day covers.

1587 Queen Elizabeth the Queen Mother

Queen Elizabeth the Queen Mother Commemoration

2002 (25 APR.) *Vert designs as T 955/8 with changed face values and showing both the Queen's head and frame in black as in T 1587. Two phosphor bands. Perf 14 × 15*

2280	**1587**	(1st) multicoloured	1·00	85	☐	☐
2281	**956**	(E) black and indigo . .	1·25	1·10	☐	☐
2282	**957**	45p multicoloured . .	1·50	1·50	☐	☐
2283	**958**	65p black, stone and sepia	2·00	2·25	☐	☐
	Set of 4		5·50	5·50	☐	☐
	First Day Cover			8·00		☐
	Presentation Pack		7·00		☐	
	Set of 4 Gutter Pairs		14·00		☐	

2nd

1st

1588 Airbus A340-600 (2002) **1589** Concorde (1976)

E

45

1590 Trident (1964) **1591** VC 10 (1964)

65

1592 Comet (1952)

50th Anniversary of Passenger Jet Aviation. Airliners

2002 (2 MAY) *One centre phosphor band (2nd) or two phosphor bands (others). Perf 14½. (a) Photo De La Rue. PVA gum*

2284	**1588**	(2nd) multicoloured	75	55	☐	☐
2285	**1589**	(1st) multicoloured	1·00	80	☐	☐
2286	**1590**	(E) multicoloured	1·25	1·25	☐	☐
2287	**1591**	45p multicoloured	1·50	1·50	☐	☐
2288	**1592**	65p multicoloured	2·00	2·25	☐	☐
	Set of 5		6·00	6·00	☐	☐
	First Day Cover			8·00		☐
	Presentation Pack		7·50		☐	
	Set of 5 Gutter Pairs		16·00		☐	
MS2289	120 × 105 mm. Nos. 2284/8 .		8·25	8·25	☐	☐
	First Day Cover			8·00	☐	
	PHQ Cards (set of 6)		5·25	7·00	☐	☐

(b) *Photo Questa. Self-adhesive*

2290	**1589**	(1st) multicoloured	4·00	4·00	☐	☐

The complete miniature sheet is shown on one of the PHQ cards with the others depicting individual stamps.

No. 2290 was only issued in £1.62 stamp booklets.

1st

WORLD CUP 2002

1593 Crowned Lion with Shield of St. George

1594 Top Left Quarter of English Flag, and Football **1595** Top Right Quarter of English Flag, and Football

1596 Bottom Left Quarter of English Flag, and Football **1597** Bottom Right Quarter of English Flag, and Football

World Cup Football Championship, Japan and Korea

2002 (21 MAY) *Two phosphor bands. Perf* 14½ × 14 (*a*) *PVA gum*

2291	**1593**	(1st) deep turquoise-blue, scarlet-vermilion and silver	. . . . .	2·50	2·50 □ □

MS2292 145 × 74 mm. No. 2291; **1594** (1st) multicoloured; **1595** (1st) multicoloured; **1596** (1st) multicoloured;

1597 (1st) multicoloured	. . . .	5·50	5·75 □ □
First Day Cover (**MS**2292)	. . .	5·75 □
Presentation Pack (**MS**2292)	. .	6·25 □
PHQ Cards (set of 6)	. . . . .	5·25	9·00 □ □
Gutter Pair (No. 2291)	. . . . .	11·00 □

(*b*) *Self-adhesive. Die-cut perf* 15 × 14

2293	**1594**	(1st) multicoloured	. . .	3·00	3·00 □ □
2294	**1595**	(1st) multicoloured	. . . .	3·00	3·00 □ □

The complete miniature sheet is shown on one of the PHQ cards with the others depicting individual stamps from **MS**2292 and No. 2291.

Nos. 2293/4 were only issued in £1.62 stamp booklets.

Stamps as Type **1597** were also issued in sheets of 20, *se-tenant* with half stamp-sized labels, printed in lithography instead of photogravure. The labels show either match scenes or personal photographs.

Self-adhesive Stamps

2002 (5 JUNE–4 JULY) *Self-adhesive. Photo Questa, Walsall or Enschedé (No. 2295) or Walsall (others). Two phosphor bands. Perf* 15 × 14 *die-cut (with one elliptical hole on each vertical side)*

2295	**914**	(1st) gold	. . . .	1·00	1·00 □ □
2296	**1093a**	(E) deep blue (4 July)	. . .	1·25	1·25 □ □
2297	**367a**	42p deep olive-grey (4 July)	. . . .	1·25	1·25 □ □
2298		68p grey-brown (4 July)	.	2·00	2·00 □ □
	Set of 4	. . . .	5·00	5·00 □ □
	PHQ Card (No. 2295)	. . . . .	45	2·00 □ □

Further printings of No. 2295 in sheets of 100 appeared on 4 July 2002 produced by Enschedé and on 18 March 2003 printed by Walsall.

1598 Swimming

1599 Running

1600 Cycling

1601 Long Jumping

1602 Wheelchair Racing

17th Commonwealth Games, Manchester

2002 (16 JULY) *One side phosphor band (2nd) or two phosphor bands (others). Perf* 14½

2299	**1598**	(2nd) multicoloured	. . . .	75	55 □ □
2300	**1599**	(1st) multicoloured	. . . .	1·00	80 □ □
2301	**1600**	(E) multicoloured	. . . .	1·25	1·25 □ □
2302	**1601**	47p multicoloured	. . . .	1·50	1·50 □ □
2303	**1602**	68p multicoloured	. . . .	2·00	2·25 □ □
	Set of 5	. . . .	6·00	6·00 □ □
	First Day Cover	. . . .	8·00 □
	Presentation Pack	. . . .	7·50 □
	PHQ Cards (set of 5)	. . . . .	4·75	15·00 □ □
	Set of 5 Gutter Pairs	. . . . .	14·00 □

1603 Tinkerbell

1604 Wendy, John and Michael Darling in front of Big Ben

1605 Crocodile and Alarm Clock

1606 Captain Hook

1607 Peter Pan

150th Anniversary of Great Ormond Street Children's Hospital.
Peter Pan *by Sir James Barrie*
2002 (20 Aug.) *One centre phosphor band* (2nd) *or two phosphor bands* (*others*). *Perf* 15 × 14

2304	**1603**	(2nd) multicoloured	. . . .	75	55	☐ ☐
2305	**1604**	(1st) multicoloured	. . . .	1·00	80	☐ ☐
2306	**1605**	(E) multicoloured	. . . .	1·25	1·25	☐ ☐
2307	**1606**	47p multicoloured	. . . .	1·50	1·50	☐ ☐
2308	**1607**	68p multicoloured	. . . .	2·00	2·25	☐ ☐
		Set of 5	. . . .	6·00	6·00	☐ ☐
		First Day Cover	. . . .		8·00	☐
		Presentation Pack	. . . .	7·50		☐
		PHQ Cards (*set of* 5)	. . . . . .	4·75	15·00	☐ ☐
		Set of 5 *Gutter Pairs*	. . . . . .	16·00		☐

1608 Millennium Bridge, 2001

1609 Tower Bridge, 1894

1610 Westminster Bridge, 1864

1611 'Blackfriars Bridge, c1800' (William Marlow)

1612 'London Bridge, c1670' (Wenceslaus Hollar)

Bridges of London
2002 (10 Sept.) *One centre phosphor band* (2nd) *or two phosphor bands* (*others*). (*a*) *Litho. PVA gum. Perf* 15 × 14

2309	**1608**	(2nd) multicoloured	. . . .	75	55	☐ ☐
2310	**1609**	(1st) multicoloured	. . . .	1·00	80	☐ ☐
2311	**1610**	(E) multicoloured	. . . .	1·25	1·25	☐ ☐
2312	**1611**	47p multicoloured	. . . .	1·50	1·50	☐ ☐
2313	**1612**	68p multicoloured	. . . .	2·00	2·25	☐ ☐
		Set of 5	. . . .	6·50	6·00	☐ ☐
		First Day Cover	. . . .		9·00	☐
		Presentation Pack	. . . .	8·00		☐
		PHQ Cards (*set of* 5)	. . . . . .	4·00	7·00	☐ ☐
		Set of 5 *Gutter Pairs*	. . . . . .	16·00		☐

(*b*) *Photo. Self-adhesive. Die-cut perf* 14½ × 14

2314	**1609**	(1st) multicoloured	. . . .	6·00	6·00	☐ ☐

No. 2314 was only issued in £1.62 stamp booklets.

1613 Galaxies and Nebula

Astronomy
2002 (24 Sept.) *Sheet* 120 × 89 *mm. Multicoloured. Two phosphor bands. Perf* 14½ × 14

MS2315 **1613** (1st) Planetary nebula in Aquila; (1st) Seyfert 2 galaxy in Pegasus; (1st) Planetary nebula in Norma; (1st) Seyfert 2 galaxy in Circinus . . . . 5·25 5·25 ☐ ☐
First Day Cover . . . . 5·75 ☐
Presentation Pack . . . . 5·50 ☐
PHQ Cards (*set of* 5) . . . . . . 4·75 15·00 ☐ ☐

The five PHQ cards depict the four designs and the complete miniature sheet.

1614 Green Pillar Box, 1857

1615 Horizontal Aperture Box, 1874

1616 Air Mail Box, 1934

1617 Double Aperture Box, 1939

1618 Modern Style Box, 1980

1619 Blue Spruce Star

1620 Holly

1621 Ivy

1622 Mistletoe

1623 Pine Cone

150th Anniversary of the First Pillar Box

2002 (8 Oct.) *One centre phosphor band* (2nd) *or two phosphor bands* (*others*). *Perf* 14 × 14½

2316	**1614**	(2nd)	multicoloured	. . . .	75	55	☐ ☐
2317	**1615**	(1st)	multicoloured	. . . .	1·00	80	☐ ☐
2318	**1616**	(E)	multicoloured	. . . .	1·25	1·25	☐ ☐
2319	**1617**	47p	multicoloured	. . . .	1·50	1·50	☐ ☐
2320	**1618**	68p	multicoloured	. . . .	2·00	2·25	☐ ☐
	Set of 5		. . . .		6·00	6·00	☐ ☐
	First Day Cover		. . . .			8·50	☐
	Presentation Pack		. . . .		7·50		☐
	PHQ Cards (set of 5)		. . . . . .		4·75	16·00	☐ ☐
	Set of 5 Gutter Pairs		. . . . . .		14·00		☐

Christmas

2002 (5 Nov.) *Self-adhesive. One centre phosphor band* (2nd) *or two phosphor bands* (*others*). *Die-cut perf* 14½ × 14

2321	**1619**	(2nd)	multicoloured	. . . .	75	55	☐ ☐
2322	**1620**	(1st)	multicoloured	. . . .	1·00	80	☐ ☐
2323	**1621**	(E)	multicoloured	. . . .	1·25	1·25	☐ ☐
2324	**1622**	47p	multicoloured	. . . .	1·50	1·50	☐ ☐
2325	**1623**	68p	multicoloured	. . . .	2·00	2·25	☐ ☐
	Set of 5		. . . .		6·00	6·00	☐ ☐
	First Day Cover		. . . .			8·50	☐
	Presentation Pack		. . . .		7·50		☐
	PHQ Cards (set of 5)		. . . . . .		4·75	16·00	☐ ☐

Collectors Pack 2002

2002 (5 Nov.) *Comprises Nos. 2243/57, 2260/4, 2265/88, 2291/2, 2299/313 and* **MS**2315/25

CP2325a Collectors Pack . . . . £100 ☐

Post Office Yearbook

2002 (5 Nov.) *Comprises Nos. 2243/57, 2260/4, 2265/88, 2291//2, 2299/313 and* **MS**2315/25 *in hardback book with slip case*

YB2325a Yearbook . . . . 95·00 ☐

50th Anniversary of Wilding Definitives (1st issue)

2002 (5 DEC.) *Sheet, 124 × 70 mm, containing designs as T 154/5 and 157/60 (1952–54 issue), but with values in decimal currency as T 1348 or with service indicator as T 1566, printed on pale cream. One centre phosphor band (2nd) or two phosphor bands (others). W 1565. Perf 15 × 14 (with one elliptical hole on each vertical side)*

MS2326 1p orange-red; 2p ultramarine;
5p red-brown; (2nd) carmine-red;
(1st) green; 33p brown; 37p
magenta; 47p bistre-brown; 50p
green and label showing national

emblems	7·00	7·00	☐	☐
First Day Cover		10·00		☐
Presentation Pack	£100		☐	
PHQ Cards (set of 5)	3·00	12·00	☐	☐

The PHQ cards depict the (2nd), (1st), 33p, 37p and 47p stamps.

See also No. **MS**2367.

1624 Barn Owl landing

1625 Barn Owl with folded Wings and Legs down

1626 Barn Owl with extended Wings and Legs down

1627 Barn Owl in Flight with Wings lowered

1628 Barn Owl in Flight with Wings raised

1629 Kestrel with Wings folded

1630 Kestrel with Wings fully extended upwards

1631 Kestrel with Wings horizontal

1632 Kestrel with Wings partly extended downwards

1633 Kestrel with Wings fully extended downwards

T **1624/33** were printed together, *se-tenant*, in blocks of 10 (5 × 2) throughout the sheet.

Birds of Prey

2003 (14 JAN.) *Phosphor background. Perf 14½*

2327	**1624**	(1st) multicoloured	70	80	☐	☐
		a. Block of 10.				
		Nos. 2327/36	9·00	8·75	☐	☐
2328	**1625**	(1st) multicoloured	70	80	☐	☐
2329	**1626**	(1st) multicoloured	70	80	☐	☐
2330	**1627**	(1st) multicoloured	70	80	☐	☐
2331	**1628**	(1st) multicoloured	70	80	☐	☐
2332	**1629**	(1st) multicoloured	70	80	☐	☐
2333	**1630**	(1st) multicoloured	70	80	☐	☐
2334	**1631**	(1st) multicoloured	70	80	☐	☐
2335	**1632**	(1st) multicoloured	70	80	☐	☐
2336	**1633**	(1st) multicoloured	70	80	☐	☐
		Set of 10	6·25	7·25	☐	☐
		First Day Cover		11·00		☐
		Presentation Pack	12·00		☐	
		PHQ Cards (set of 10)	9·25	28·00	☐	☐
		Gutter Block of 20	24·00		☐	

1634 'Gold star, See me, Playtime'

1635 '1♥U, XXXX, S.W.A.L.K.'

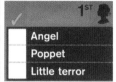

1636 'Angel, Poppet, Little terror'

1637 'Yes, No, Maybe'

1638 'Oops!, Sorry, Will try harder'

1639 'I did it!, You did it!, We did it!'

T **2337/42** were printed together, *se-tenant*, in blocks of 6 (3 × 2) throughout the sheet.

'Occasions' Greetings Stamps

2003 (4 Feb.) *Two phosphor bands. Perf 14½ × 14*

2337	**1634**	(1st) lemon and new blue	70	80	□	□
		a. Block of 6.				
		Nos. 2337/42	5·50	5·50	□	□
2338	**1635**	(1st) red and deep				
		ultramarine	70	80	□	□
2339	**1636**	(1st) purple and bright				
		yellow-green	70	80	□	□
2340	**1637**	(1st) bright yellow-green				
		and red	70	80	□	□
2341	**1638**	(1st) deep ultramarine and				
		lemon	70	80	□	□
2342	**1639**	(1st) new blue and purple	70	80	□	□
	Set of 6		3·75	4·25	□	□
	First Day Cover			8·00		□
	Presentation Pack		7·00			□
	PHQ Cards (set of 6)		5·25	18·00	□	□
	Gutter Block of 12		7·00			□

Nos. 2337/42 were also available in *se-tenant* sheets of 20 containing four examples of Nos. 2338 and 2340 and three of each of the others. The stamps are accompanied by half stamp-size printed labels or a personal photograph.

1640 Completing the Genome Jigsaw

1641 Ape with Moustache and Scientist

1642 DNA Snakes and Ladders

1643 'Animal Scientists'

1644 Genome Crystal Ball

50th Anniversary of Discovery of DNA

2003 (25 Feb.) *One centre phosphor band (2nd) or two phosphor bands (others). Perf 14½*

2343	**1640**	(2nd) multicoloured	1·00	55	□	□
2344	**1641**	(1st) multicoloured	1·00	80	□	□
2345	**1642**	(E) multicoloured	1·25	1·25	□	□
2346	**1643**	47p multicoloured	1·50	1·50	□	□
2347	**1644**	68p multicoloured	2·00	2·25	□	□
	Set of 5		6·50	6·00	□	□
	First Day Cover			9·00		□
	Presentation Pack		8·00			□
	PHQ Cards (set of 5)		4·75	18·00	□	□
	Set of 5 Gutter Pairs		15·00			□

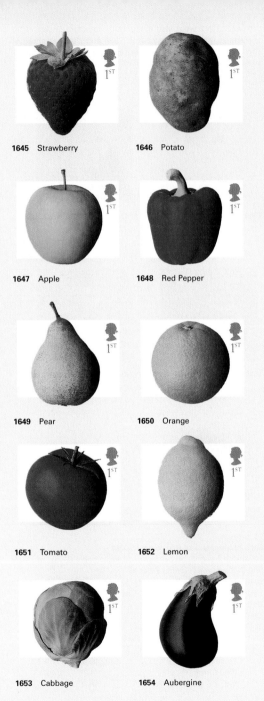

1645 Strawberry

1646 Potato

1647 Apple

1648 Red Pepper

1649 Pear

1650 Orange

1651 Tomato

1652 Lemon

1653 Cabbage

1654 Aubergine

T **1645/54** were printed together in sheets of 10 with the surplus self-adhesive paper around each stamp retained. The stamp pane is accompanied by a similar-sized pane of self-adhesive labels showing ears, eyes, mouths, hats etc which are intended for the adornment of fruit and vegetables depicted. This pane is separated from the stamps by a line of roulettes.

Fruit and Vegetables

2003 (25 MAR.) *Self-adhesive. Two phosphor bands. Perf 14½ × 14 die-cut (without teeth around protruding tops or bottoms of the designs)*

2348	**1645**	(1st) multicoloured		70	80 □	□
		a. *Sheetlet. Nos.* 2348/57 and pane of decorative labels . .		9·00	9·00 □	□
2349	**1646**	(1st) multicoloured		70	80 □	□
2350	**1647**	(1st) multicoloured		70	80 □	□
2351	**1648**	(1st) multicoloured		70	80 □	□
2352	**1649**	(1st) multicoloured		70	80 □	□
2353	**1650**	(1st) multicoloured		70	80 □	□
2354	**1651**	(1st) multicoloured		70	80 □	□
2355	**1652**	(1st) multicoloured		70	80 □	□
2356	**1653**	(1st) multicoloured		70	80 □	□
2357	**1654**	(1st) multicoloured		70	80 □	□
		Set of 10		6·25	7·25 □	□
		First Day Cover			11·00	□
		Presentation Pack		60·00		□
		PHQ Cards (set of 10)		9·25	12·00 □	□

1655

Overseas Booklet Stamps

2003 (27 MAR.)–**2004** *Self-adhesive. Two phosphor bands. Perf 15 × 14 die-cut with one elliptical hole on each vertical side*

2357a		(Worldwide postcard) grey-black, rosine and ultramarine . . .	65	70 □	□
2358	**1655**	(Europe) new blue and rosine	80	85 □	□
2359		(Worldwide) rosine and new blue	1·60	1·70 □	□
		First Day Cover (Nos. 2358/9) .		5·25	□
		Presentation Pack (Nos. 2358/9)	3·00		□
		PHQ Card (No. 2358)	45	2·00 □	□

Nos. 2358/9 were intended to pay postage on mail up to 40 grams to either Europe (52p) or to foreign destinations outside Europe (£1.12). No. 2359a was intended to pay postcard rate to foreign destinations (43p).

Operationally they were only available in separate booklets of 4, initially sold at £2.08, £4.48 and £1.72, with the surplus self-adhesive paper around each stamp removed. Single examples of the stamps were available from philatelic outlets as sets of two or in presentation packs.

For first day cover and presentation pack for No. 2359a see below Nos. Y1667/1803.

1656 Amy Johnson (pilot) and Biplane

1657 Members of 1953 Everest Team

1658 Freya Stark (traveller and writer) and Desert

1659 Ernest Shackleton (Antarctic explorer) and Wreck of *Endurance*

1660 Francis Chichester (yachtsman) and *Gipsy Moth IV*

1661 Robert Falcon Scott (Antarctic explorer) and Norwegian Expedition at the Pole

Extreme Endeavours (British Explorers)

2003 (29 APR.) *One centre phosphor band* (2nd) *or two phosphor bands* (others). (a) *Photo Questa. PVA gum. Perf* 15 × 14½

2360	**1656**	2nd) multicoloured	....	50	50	□ □
2361	**1657**	(1st) multicoloured	....	75	75	□ □
2362	**1658**	(E) multicoloured	....	1·25	1·50	□ □
2363	**1659**	42p multicoloured	....	1·25	1·75	□ □
2364	**1660**	47p multicoloured	....	1·50	2·00	□ □
2365	**1661**	68p multicoloured	....	2·00	2·50	□ □

Set of 6	....	7·00	7·75	□ □
First Day Cover	....		11·00	□
Presentation Pack	....	9·00		□
PHQ Cards (set of 6)	......	3·25	9·50	□ □
Set of 6 Gutter Pairs	......	18·00		□

(b) *Photo De La Rue. Self-adhesive. Die-cut perf* 14½

2366	**1657**	(1st) multicoloured	....	3·00	3·00 □ □

The phosphor bands on Nos. 2361/5 are at the centre and right of each stamp.

No. 2366 was only issued in £1.62 stamp booklets in which the surplus self-adhesive paper around each stamp was removed.

50th Anniversary of Wilding Definitives (2nd issue)

2003 (20 MAY) *Sheet,* 124 × 70 *mm, containing designs as* T **155/8** *and* **160** *(1952–54 issue), but with values in decimal currency as* T **1348** *or with service indicator as* T **1566**, *printed on pale cream. One centre phosphor band* (20p) *or two phosphor bands* (others). W **1565**. P 15 × 14 *(with one elliptical hole on each vertical side).*

MS2367	4p deep lilac; 8p ultramarine; 10p reddish purple; 20p bright green; 28p bronze-green; 34p brown-purple; (E) chestnut; 42p Prussian blue; 68p grey-blue and label showing national emblems	10·50	11·25	□ □
First Day Cover	....		13·00	□
Presentation Pack	....	15·00		□

1662 Guardsmen in Coronation Procession

1663 East End Children reading Coronation Party Poster

1664 Queen Elizabeth II in Coronation Chair with Bishops of Durham and Bath & Wells

1665 Children in Plymouth working on Royal Montage

1666 Queen Elizabeth
II in Coronation
Robes (photograph
by Cecil Beaton)

1667 Children's Race at
East End Street Party

1668 Coronation Coach
passing through
Marble Arch

1669 Children in Fancy
Dress

1670 Coronation Coach
outside Buckingham
Palace

1671 Children eating at
London Street Party

T **1662/71** were printed together, *se-tenant,* in blocks of 10
(5 × 2) throughout sheets of 60

50th Anniversary of Coronation

2003 (2 June) *W* **1565**. *Two phosphor bands. Perf* 14½ × 14

2368	**1662**	(1st) multicoloured	45	50	□	□
		a. Block of 10.				
		Nos. 2368/77	8·75	8·75	□	□
2369	**1663**	(1st) black and gold	45	50	□	□
2370	**1664**	(1st) multicoloured	45	50	□	□
2371	**1665**	(1st) black and gold	45	50	□	□
2372	**1666**	(1st) multicoloured	45	50	□	□
2373	**1667**	(1st) black and gold	45	50	□	□
2374	**1668**	(1st) multicoloured	45	50	□	□
2375	**1669**	(1st) black and gold	45	50	□	□
2376	**1670**	(1st) multicoloured	45	50	□	□
2377	**1671**	(1st) black and gold	45	50	□	□
		Set of 10	4·50	5·00	□	□
		First Day Cover		11·00		□
		Presentation Pack	20·00			□
		PHQ Cards (set of 10)	3·75	8·00		□
		Gutter Block of 20	20·00			□

No. 2372 does not show the Queen's head in gold as do the
other nine designs.

50th Anniversary of Coronation. Booklet Stamps

2003 (2 June) *Designs as T* **160** (*Wilding definitive of 1952*) *and*
163 (*Coronation commemorative of 1953*), *but with values in
decimal currency as T* **1348**. *W* **1565**. *Two phosphor bands.
P* 15 × 14 (*with one elliptical hole on each vertical side for
Nos. 2378/9*)

2378	**160**	47p bistre-brown	5·00	2·50	□	□
2379		68p grey-blue	5·00	2·50	□	□
2380	**163**	£1 deep yellow-green .	50·00	45·00	□	□
		Set of 3	55·00	45·00	□	□

Nos. 2378/80 were only available in £7.46 stamp booklets.
Stamps as Nos. 2378/9, but on pale cream, were also included
in the Wilding miniature sheets, Nos. **MS**2326 or **MS**2367. A £1
design as No. 2380, but on phosphorised paper, was previously
included in the "Stamp Show 2000" miniature sheet, No.
MS2147.

1672 Prince William in
September 2001
(Brendan Beirne)

1673 Prince William in
September 2000
(Tim Graham)

1674 Prince William in
September 2001
(Camera Press)

1675 Prince William in
September 2001
(Tim Graham)

21st Birthday of Prince William of Wales

2003 (17 June) *Phosphor backgrounds. Perf* 14½

2381	**1672**	28p multicoloured	1·00	50	□	□
2382	**1673**	(E) dull mauve, grey-black				
		and light green . . .	1·25	1·50	□	□

2383	**1674**	47p multicoloured	1·75	2·00	☐	☐
2384	**1675**	68p sage-green, black and bright green	2·50	2·00	☐	☐
		Set of 4	6·00	6·00	☐	☐
		First Day Cover		9·00		☐
		Presentation Pack	18·00		☐	
		PHQ Cards (set of 4)	1·50	4·25	☐	☐
		Set of 4 Gutter Pairs	13·00		☐	

1676 Loch Assynt, Sutherland

1677 Ben More, Isle of Mull

1678 Rothiemurchus, Cairngorms

1679 Dalveen Pass, Lowther Hills

1680 Glenfinnan Viaduct, Lochaber

1681 Papa Little, Shetland Islands

A British Journey: Scotland

2003 (15 JULY) *One centre phosphor band* (2nd) *or two phosphor bands* (others). *Perf* 14½. (a) *PVA gum*

2385	**1676**	(2nd) multicoloured	50	35	☐	☐
2386	**1677**	(1st) multicoloured	75	50	☐	☐
2387	**1678**	(E) multicoloured	1·25	1·25	☐	☐

2388	**1679**	42p multicoloured	1·25	1·50	☐	☐
2389	**1680**	47p multicoloured	1·50	2·00	☐	☐
2390	**1681**	68p multicoloured	2·00	2·50	☐	☐
		Set of 6	7·00	7·75	☐	☐
		First Day Cover		10·00		☐
		Presentation Pack	9·50		☐	
		PHQ Cards (set of 6)	2·25	6·25	☐	☐
		Set of 6 Gutter Pairs	16·00		☐	

(b) Self-adhesive. Die-cut perf 14½

2391	**1677**	(1st) multicoloured . . .	3·00	3·00	☐	☐

No. 2391 was only issued in £1.68 stamp booklets in which the surplus self-adhesive paper around each stamp was removed.

1682 'The Station' (Andrew Davidson)

1683 'Black Swan' (Stanley Chew)

1684 'The Cross Keys' (George Mackenney)

1685 'The Mayflower' (Ralph Ellis)

1686 'The Barley Sheaf' (Joy Cooper)

British Pub Signs

2003 (12 AUG.) *Two phosphor bands. Perf* 14 × 14½

2392	**1682**	(1st) multicoloured	75	50	☐	☐
2393	**1683**	(E) multicoloured	2·00	2·00	☐	☐
2394	**1684**	42p multicoloured	1·50	1·50	☐	☐
2395	**1685**	47p multicoloured	1·75	2·00	☐	☐

2396	**1686**	68p multicoloured	2·00	2·25 ☐ ☐
		Set of 5	7·50	7·75 ☐ ☐
		First Day Cover		10·00 ☐
		Presentation Pack	9·00	☐
		PHQ Cards (set of 5)	1·90	5·50 ☐ ☐
		Set of 5 Gutter Pairs	17·00	☐

(b) Photo DLR. Self-adhesive. Die-cut perf $14\frac{1}{2} \times 14$

2403	**1687**	(1st) multicoloured	3·00	3·00 ☐ ☐

The complete miniature sheet is shown on one of the PHQ cards with the others depicting individual stamps.

No. 2403 was only issued in £1.68 stamp booklets in which the surplus self-adhesive paper around each stamp was removed.

1687 Meccano Constructor Biplane, c. 1931

1688 Wells-Brimtoy Clockwork Double-decker Omnibus, c. 1938

1689 Hornby M1 Clockwork Locomotive and Tender, c. 1948

1690 Dinky Toys Ford Zephyr, c. 1956

1691 Mettoy Friction Drive Space Ship Eagle, c. 1960

Classic Transport Toys

2003 (18 Sept.) *Two phosphor bands. (a) Photo Enschedé. PVA gum. Perf $14\frac{1}{2} \times 14$*

2397	**1687**	(1st) multicoloured	75	50 ☐ ☐
2398	**1688**	(E) multicoloured	1·25	1·25 ☐ ☐
2399	**1689**	42p multicoloured	1·50	1·50 ☐ ☐
2400	**1690**	47p multicoloured	1·75	1·75 ☐ ☐
2401	**1691**	68p multicoloured	2·00	2·50 ☐ ☐
		Set of 5	7·00	7·25 ☐ ☐
		First Day Cover		9·50 ☐
		Presentation Pack	9·00	☐
		PHQ Cards (set of 6)	2·75	6·25 ☐ ☐
		Set of 5 Gutter Pairs	16·00	☐
MS2402	115 × 105 mm. Nos. 2397/401		7·00	8·25 ☐ ☐
		First Day Cover		9·50 ☐

1692 Coffin of Denytenamun, Egyptian, c. 900BC

1693 Alexander the Great, Greek, c. 200BC

1694 Sutton Hoo Helmet, Anglo-Saxon, c. AD600

1695 Sculpture of Parvati, South Indian, c. AD1550

1696 Mask of Xiuhtecuhtli, Mixtec-Aztec, c. AD1500

1697 Hoa Hakananai'a, Easter Island, c. AD1000

250th Anniversary of the British Museum

2003 (7 OCT.) *One side phosphor band* (2nd), *two phosphor bands* ((1st), (E), 47p) *or phosphor background at left and band at right* (42p, 68p). *Perf* 14 × 14½

2404	**1692**	(2nd) multicoloured	50	35	□ □
2405	**1693**	(1st) multicoloured	75	50	□ □
2406	**1694**	(E) multicoloured	1·25	1·25	□ □
2407	**1695**	42p multicoloured	1·25	1·50	□ □
2408	**1696**	47p multicoloured	1·50	2·00	□ □
2409	**1697**	68p multicoloured	2·00	2·75	□ □
	Set of 6		7·00	7·75	□ □
	First Day Cover			10·00	□
	Presentation Pack		9·00		□
	PHQ Cards (*set of 6*)		2·75	6·50	□ □
	Set of 6 Gutter Pairs		18·00		□

1698 Ice Spiral

1699 Icicle Star

1700 Wall of Ice Blocks

1701 Ice Ball

1702 Ice Hole

1703 Snow Pyramids

Christmas. Ice Sculptures by Andy Goldsworthy

2003 (4 NOV.) *Self-adhesive. One side phosphor band* (2nd), *'all-over' phosphor* (1st) *or two bands* (others). *Die-cut perf* 14½ × 14

2410	**1698**	(2nd) multicoloured . . .	75	35	□ □
2411	**1699**	(1st) multicoloured . . .	1·25	50	□ □
2412	**1700**	(E) multicoloured	1·50	1·50	□ □
2413	**1701**	53p multicoloured	1·75	1·75	□ □
2414	**1702**	68p multicoloured	2·00	2·00	□ □
2415	**1703**	£1.12 multicoloured . . .	2·00	2·00	□ □
	Set of 6		9·00	9·00	□ □
	First Day Cover			12·50	□
	Presentation Pack		11·00		□
	PHQ Cards (*set of 6*)		4·00	8·00	□ □

The 2nd and 1st class were also issued in separate sheets of 20, each stamp printed in lithography instead of photogravure and accompanied by a half stamp-size *se-tenant* label showing either animals, ice sculptures or a personal photograph.

Collectors Pack 2003

2003 (4 NOV.) *Comprises Nos.* 2327/57, 2360/5, 2368/77, 2381/90, 2392/401 *and* 2404/15

CP2415*a*	*Collectors Pack*	£100	□

Post Office Yearbook

2003 (4 NOV.) *Comprises Nos.* 2327/57, 2360/5, 2368/77, 2381/90, 2392/401 *and* 2404/15

YB2415*a*	*Yearbook*	£100	□

1704 Rugby Scenes

England's Victory in Rugby World Cup Championship, Australia

2003 (19 DEC.) *Sheet* 115 × 85 *mm. Multicoloured. Two phosphor bands. Perf* 14

MS2416	**1704**	(1st) England flags and fans; (1st) England team standing in circle before match; 68p World Cup trophy; 68p Victorious England players after match . .	6·00	8·00	□ □
	First Day Cover			12·00	□
	Presentation Pack		11·00		□

1705 *Dolgoch*, Rheilffordd Talyllyn Railway, Gwynedd

1706 CR Class 439, Bo'ness and Kinneil Railway, West Lothian

1707 GCR Class 8K, Leicestershire

1708 GWR Manor Class Bradley Manor, Severn Valley Railway, Worcestershire

1709 SR West Country class Blackmoor Vale, Bluebell Railway, East Sussex

1710 BR Standard class, Keighley & Worth Valley Railway, Yorkshire

Classic Locomotives

2004 (13 JAN.) *One side phosphor band* (20p) *or two phosphor bands* (others). *Perf* 14½

2417	**1705**	20p multicoloured	65	65	□	□
2418	**1706**	28p multicoloured	90	90	□	□
2419	**1707**	(E) multicoloured	1·20	1·20	□	□
2420	**1708**	42p multicoloured	1·30	1·30	□	□
2421	**1709**	47p multicoloured	1·50	1·50	□	□
2422	**1710**	68p multicoloured	2·20	2·20	□	□

Set of 6	7·75	7·75	□	□
First Day Cover		12·00		□
Presentation Pack	30·00		□	
PHQ Cards (set of 6)	5·75	12·00	□	□
Set of 6 Gutter Pairs	12·00			
MS2423 190 × 67 mm. Nos. 2417/22 .	25·00	25·00	□	□
First Day Cover		10·50		□

1711 Postman

1712 Face

1713 Duck

1714 Baby

1715 Aircraft

T **1711/15** were printed together, *se-tenant*, as horizontal strips of 5 in sheets of 25 (5 × 5).

'Occasions' Greetings Stamps

2004 (3 FEB.) *Two phosphor bands. Perf* 14½ × 14

2424	**1711**	(1st) bright mauve and black	90	90	□	□
		a. Horiz strip of 5. Nos. 2424/8	5·00	5·00	□	□
2425	**1712**	(1st) magenta and black .	90	90	□	□
2426	**1713**	(1st) lemon and black . .	90	90	□	□
2427	**1714**	(1st) pale turquoise-green and black . .	90	90	□	□
2428	**1715**	(1st) bright new blue and black	90	90	□	□

Set of 5	4·50	4·50	□	□
First Day Cover		6·50		□
Presentation Pack	6·25		□	
PHQ Cards (set of 5)	4·75	10·00	□	□
Gutter Block of 10	9·00		□	

Nos. 2424/8 were also issued in sheets of 20 containing the five designs *se-tenant* with half stamp-size printed message labels. Similar sheets containing either Nos. 2424 and 2428 or Nos. 2425/7 came with personal photographs on the labels.

1716 Map showing Middle Earth

1717 Forest of Lothlórien in Spring

1718 Dust-jacket for *The Fellowship of the Ring*

1719 Rivendell

1720 The Hall at Bag End

1721 Orthanc

1722 Doors of Durin

1723 Barad-dûr

1724 Minas Tirith

1725 Fangorn Forest

T **1716/25** were printed together, *se-tenant*, in blocks of 10 (5 × 2) throughout the sheet.

50th Anniversary of Publication of **The Fellowship of the Ring** *and* **The Two Towers** *by J. R. R. Tolkien*

2004 (26 Feb.) *Two phosphor bands. Perf* 14½

2429	**1716**	(1st) multicoloured	. . .	90	90	☐	☐
		a. Block of 10. Nos.					
		2429/38	. . . .	9·00	10·00	☐	☐
2430	**1717**	(1st) multicoloured	. . .	90	90	☐	☐
2431	**1718**	(1st) multicoloured	. . .	90	90	☐	☐
2432	**1719**	(1st) multicoloured	. . .	90	90	☐	☐
2433	**1720**	(1st) multicoloured	. . .	90	90	☐	☐
2434	**1721**	(1st) multicoloured	. . .	90	90	☐	☐
2435	**1722**	(1st) multicoloured	. . .	90	90	☐	☐
2436	**1723**	(1st) multicoloured	. . .	90	90	☐	☐
2437	**1724**	(1st) multicoloured	. . .	90	90	☐	☐
2438	**1725**	(1st) multicoloured	. . .	90	90	☐	☐
		Set of 10	. . . .	9·00	9·00	☐	☐
		First Day Cover	. . . .		10·00		☐
		Presentation Pack	. . . .	25·00		☐	
		PHQ Cards (set of 10)	. . . . . .	9·75	12·00	☐	☐
		Gutter Block of 20	. . . .		12·00		☐

1726 Ely Island, Lower Lough Erne

1727 Giant's Causeway, Antrim Coast

1728 Slemish, Antrim Mountains

1729 Banns Road, Mourne Mountains

1730 Glenelly Valley, Sperrins

1731 Islandmore, Strangford Lough

A British Journey: Northern Ireland

2004 (16 Mar.) *One side phosphor band* (2nd) *or two phosphor bands* (others). *Perf* 14½ (a) *PVA gum*

2439	**1726**	(2nd) multicoloured . . .	65	65	□	□
2440	**1727**	(1st) multicoloured . . .	90	90	□	□
2441	**1728**	(E) multicoloured . . .	1·20	1·20	□	□
2442	**1729**	42p multicoloured . . .	1·30	1·30	□	□
2443	**1730**	47p multicoloured . . .	1·50	1·50	□	□
2444	**1731**	68p multicoloured . . .	2·20	2·20	□	□
		Set of 6	7·75	7·75	□	□
		First Day Cover		12·00		□
		Presentation Pack	12·00		□	
		PHQ Cards (set of 6)	5·75	12·00	□	□
		Set of 6 Gutter Pairs	12·00		□	

(b) *Self-adhesive. Die-cut perf* 14½

2445	**1727**	(1st) multicoloured . . .	2·50	2·50	□	□

No. 2445 was only issued in £1.68 stamp booklets in which the surplus self-adhesive paper around each stamp was removed.

1732 'Lace 1 (trial proof) 1968' (Sir Terry Frost)	**1733** 'Coccinelle' (Sonia Delaunay)

Centenary of the Entente Cordiale. Contemporary Paintings

2004 (6 Apr.) *Two phosphor bands. Perf* 14 × 14½

2446	**1732**	28p grey, black and rosine	1·00	85	□	□
2447	**1733**	57p multicoloured	2·25	2·50	□	□
		Set of 2	3·00	3·00	□	□
		First Day Cover		4·50		□
		Presentation Pack	4·25		□	
		Presentation Pack (UK and French stamps)	15·00		□	
		PHQ Cards (set of 2)	1·90	5·00	□	□
		Set of 2 Gutter Pairs	5·00		□	
		Set of 2 Traffic Light Gutter Blocks of 4	15·00		□	

Stamps in similar designs were issued by France and these are included in the joint Presentation Pack.

1734 'RMS *Queen Mary 2*, 2004' (Edward D. Walker)	**1735** 'SS *Canberra* 1961' (David Cobb)

1736 'RMS *Queen Mary* 1936' (Charles Pears)	**1737** 'RMS *Mauretania*, 1907' (Thomas Henry)

1738 'SS *City of New York*, 1888' (Raphael Monleaon y Torres)	**1739** 'PS *Great Western*, 1838' (Joseph Walter)

Ocean Liners

2004 (13 Apr.) *Two phosphor bands.* (a) *PVA gum. Perf* 14½ × 14

2448	**1734**	(1st) multicoloured . . .	90	90	□	□
2449	**1735**	(E) multicoloured . . .	1·30	1·30	□	□
2450	**1736**	42p multicoloured . . .	1·30	1·30	□	□
2451	**1737**	47p multicoloured . . .	1·50	1·50	□	□
2452	**1738**	57p multicoloured . . .	1·80	1·80	□	□
2453	**1739**	68p multicoloured . . .	2·20	2·20	□	□
		Set of 6	9·00	9·00	□	□
		First Day Cover		10·00		□
		Presentation Pack	11·00		□	
		PHQ Cards (set of 7)	6·75	10·00	□	□
		Set of 6 Gutter Pairs	18·00		□	
MS2454		114 × 104 mm. Nos. 2448/53	18·00	18·00	□	□
		First Day Cover		18·00		□

(b) *Self-adhesive. Die-cut perf* 14½ × 14

2455	**1734**	(1st) multicoloured . . .	2·50	2·50	□	□

Nos. 2448/55 commemorate the introduction to service of the Queen Mary 2.

No. 2455 was only issued in £1.68 stamp booklets in which the surplus self-adhesive paper around each stamp was removed.

The complete miniature sheet is shown on one of the PHQ cards with the others depicting individual stamps.

1740 Dianthus Allwoodii Group

1741 Dahlia 'Garden Princess'

1742 Clematis 'Arabella'

1743 Miltonia 'French Lake'

1744 Lilium 'Lemon Pixie'

1745 Delphinium 'Clifford Sky'

Bicentenary of the Royal Horticultural Society (1st issue)

2004 (25 MAY) *One side phosphor band* (2nd) *or 'all-over' phosphor* (others). *Perf* 14½

2456	**1740**	(2nd) multicoloured	...	70	70	☐	☐
2457	**1741**	(1st) multicoloured	...	90	90	☐	☐
2458	**1742**	(E) multicoloured	...	1·30	1·30	☐	☐
2459	**1743**	42p multicoloured	...	1·40	1·50	☐	☐
2460	**1744**	47p multicoloured	...	1·50	2·00	☐	☐
2461	**1745**	68p multicoloured	...	2·20	3·50	☐	☐
	Set of 6	. . . .		8·00	9·50	☐	☐
	First Day Cover	. . . .			11·00		☐
	Presentation Pack	. . . .			11·00		☐
	PHQ Cards (*set of* 7)	. . . . .		6·75	12·00	☐	☐
	Set of 6 *Gutter Pairs*	. . . . .			16·00		☐
MS2462	115 × 105 mm. Nos. 2456/61			8·00	8·00	☐	☐
	First Day Cover	. . . .			9·50		☐

The complete miniature sheet is shown on one of the PHQ cards with the others depicting individual stamps.

The 1st class stamp was also issued in sheets of 20, printed in lithography instead of photogravure, each stamp accompanied by a *se-tenant* stamp-size label.

Bicentenary of the Royal Horticultural Society (2nd issue). Booklet stamps

2004 (25 MAY) *Designs as Nos.* 1955, 1958 *and* 1962 (1997 *Greeting Stamps 19th-century Flower Paintings*). *Two phosphor bands. Perf* 15 × 14 (*with one elliptical hole on each vertical side*)

2463	**1280**	(1st) multicoloured	...	1·50	1·50	☐	☐
2464	**1283**	(1st) multicoloured	...	50	50	☐	☐
2465	**1287**	(1st) multicoloured	...	1·50	1·50	☐	☐
	Set of 3	. . . .			2·75	2·75	☐ ☐

On Nos. 2463/5 the phosphor bands appear at the left and the centre of each stamp.

Nos. 2463/5 were only available in £7.23 stamp booklets.

1746 Barmouth Bridge

1747 Hyddgen, Plynlimon

1748 Brecon Beacons

1749 Pen-pych, Rhondda Valley

1750 Rhewl, Dee Valley

1751 Marloes Sands

A British Journey: Wales

2004 (15 JUNE) *One centre phosphor band (2nd), 'all-over' phosphor (1st) or two phosphor bands (others). (a) PVA gum. Perf 14½*

2466	**1746**	(2nd) multicoloured ...	70	70 ☐ ☐
2467	**1747**	(1st) multicoloured ...	90	90 ☐ ☐
2468	**1748**	40p multicoloured ...	1·75	1·50 ☐ ☐
2469	**1749**	43p multicoloured ...	2·00	2·00 ☐ ☐
2470	**1750**	47p multicoloured ...	2·50	3·00 ☐ ☐
2471	**1751**	68p multicoloured ...	3·50	4·00 ☐ ☐
		Set of 6	10·00	10·00 ☐ ☐
		First Day Cover		11·00
		Presentation Pack	11·00	☐
		PHQ Cards (set of 6)	5·75	12·00 ☐ ☐
		Set of 6 Gutter Pairs	16·00	☐

(b) Self-adhesive. Die-cut perf 14½

2472	**1747**	(1st) multicoloured ...	2·50	2·50 ☐ ☐

The 1st and 40p values include the 'EUROPA' emblem.

No. 2472 was only issued in £1·68 stamp booklets in which the surplus self-adhesive paper around each stamp was removed.

250th Anniversary of the Royal Society of Arts

2004 (10 AUG.) *Two phosphor bands. Perf 14*

2473	**1752**	(1st) multicoloured ...	95	95 ☐ ☐
2474	**1753**	40p multicoloured ...	1·30	1·30 ☐ ☐
2475	**1754**	43p multicoloured ...	1·40	1·40 ☐ ☐
2476	**1755**	47p multicoloured ...	1·50	1·50 ☐ ☐
2477	**1756**	57p silver, vermilion and black	1·90	1·90 ☐ ☐
2478	**1757**	68p silver, vermilion and black	2·20	2·20 ☐ ☐
		Set of 6	9·25	9·25 ☐ ☐
		First Day Cover		12·00 ☐
		Presentation Pack	11·00	☐
		PHQ Cards (set of 6)	5·75	12·00 ☐ ☐
		Set of 6 Gutter Pairs	18·00	☐

1752 Sir Rowland Hill Award

1753 William Shipley (Founder of Royal Society of Arts)

1754 'RSA' as Typewriter Keys and Shorthand

1755 Chimney Sweep

1756 'Gill Typeface'

1757 'Zero Waste'

1758 Pine Marten

1759 Roe Deer

1760 Badger

1761 Yellow-necked Mouse

1762 Wild Cat

1763 Red Squirrel

1764 Stoat

1765 Natterer's Bat

1766 Mole

1767 Fox

T **1758/67** were printed together, *se-tenant*, in blocks of 10 (5 × 2) throughout the sheet.

Woodland Animals

2004 (16 SEPT.) *Two phosphor bands. P 14½*

2479	**1758**	(1st) multicoloured	. . .	90	90	☐	☐
		a. Block of 10. Nos.					
		2479/88		9·00	10·00	☐	☐
2480	**1759**	(1st) multicoloured	. . .	90	90	☐	☐
2481	**1760**	(1st) multicoloured	. . .	90	90	☐	☐
2482	**1761**	(1st) multicoloured	. . .	90	90	☐	☐
2483	**1762**	(1st) multicoloured	. . .	90	90	☐	☐
2484	**1763**	(1st) multicoloured	. . .	90	90	☐	☐
2485	**1764**	(1st) multicoloured	. . .	90	90	☐	☐
2486	**1765**	(1st) multicoloured	. . .	90	90	☐	☐
2487	**1766**	(1st) multicoloured	. . .	90	90	☐	☐
2488	**1767**	(1st) multicoloured	. . .	90	90	☐	☐
		Set of 10		9·00	9·00	☐	☐
		First Day Cover			12·00		☐
		Presentation Pack		12·00		☐	
		PHQ Cards (set of 10)		9·75	14·00	☐	☐
		Gutter Block of 20		18·00		☐	

1768 Pte. McNamara, 5th Dragoon Guards, Heavy Brigade Charge, Battle of Balaklava

1769 Piper Muir, 42nd Regt of Foot, Amphibious Assault on Kerch

1770 Sgt. Maj. Edwards, Scots Fusilier Guards, Gallant Action, Battle of Inkerman

1771 Sgt. Powell, 1st Regt of Foot Guards, Battles of Alma and Inkerman

1772 Sgt. Maj. Poole, Royal Sappers and Miners, Defensive Line, Battle of Inkerman

1773 Sgt. Glasgow, Royal Artillery, Gun Battery besieged Sevastopol

150th Anniversary of the Crimean War

2004 (12 OCT.) *One centre phosphor band* (2nd) *or two phosphor bands* (others). *Perf* 14

2489	**1768**	(2nd) multicoloured . . .	70	70	□	□
2490	**1769**	(1st) multicoloured . . .	90	90	□	□
2491	**1770**	40p multicoloured . . .	2·00	2·00	□	□
2492	**1771**	57p multicoloured . . .	2·50	2·50	□	□
2493	**1772**	68p multicoloured . . .	2·75	3·00	□	□
2494	**1773**	£1·12 multicoloured . . .	4·50	5·00	□	□
		Set of 6	12·00	12·00	□	□
		First Day Cover		13·50	□	
		Presentation Pack	12·50		□	
		PHQ Cards (set of 6)	5·75	14·00	□	□
		Set of 6 Gutter Pairs	20·00		□	
		Set of 6 Traffic Light Pairs . . .	25·00		□	

Nos. 2489/94 show 'Crimean Heroes' photographs taken in 1856.

1774 Father Christmas on Snowy Roof

1775 Celebrating the Sunrise

1776 On Roof in Gale

1777 With Umbrella in Rain

1778 In Fog on Edge of Roof with Torch

1779 Sheltering from Hailstorm behind Chimney

Christmas

2004 (2 Nov.) *One centre phosphor band* (2nd) *or two phosphor bands* (others). *Perf* 14½ × 14. (a) *Self-adhesive.*

2495	**1774**	(2nd) multicoloured . . .	70	70	□	□
2496	**1775**	(1st) multicoloured . . .	90	90	□	□
2497	**1776**	40p multicoloured . . .	1·30	1·30	□	□
2498	**1777**	57p multicoloured . . .	1·80	1·80	□	□
2499	**1778**	68p multicoloured . . .	2·20	2·20	□	□
2500	**1779**	£1·12 multicoloured . . .	3·75	3·75	□	□
		Set of 6	11·00	12·00	□	□
		First Day Cover		13·50	□	
		Presentation Pack	12·50		□	
		PHQ Cards (set of 7)	6·75	14·00	□	□

(b) PVA gum

MS2501	115 × 105 mm. As Nos. 2495/500	10·50	12·00	□	□
	First Day Cover		13·50	□	

The seven PHQ cards depict the six individual stamps and the miniature sheet.

The 2nd and 1st class stamps were also issued in sheets of 20 printed in lithography instead of photogravure containing ten 1st class and ten 2nd class stamps, each stamp accompanied by a *se-tenant* stamp-size label showing Father Christmas. Separate sheets of either 20 1st or 20 2nd class were available with personal photographs.

Collectors Pack 2004

2004 (2 Nov.) *Comprises Nos.* 2417/22, 2424/44, 2446/53, 2456/61, 2466/71 *and* 2473/2500

CP2500*a* Collectors Pack . . . . 65·00 □

Post Office Yearbook

2004 (2 Nov.) *Comprises Nos.* 2417/22, 2424/44, 2446/53, 2456/61, 2466/71 *and* 2473/2500

YB2500*a* Yearbook . . . . 80·00 □

1780 British Saddleback Pigs

1781 Khaki Campbell Ducks

1782 Suffolk Horses

1783 Dairy Shorthorn Cattle

1784   Border Collie Dog

1785   Light Sussex Chicks

1786   Suffolk Sheep

1787   Bagot Goat

1788   Norfolk Black Turkeys

1789   Embden Geese

T **1780/9** were printed together, *se-tenant*, in blocks of 10 (5 × 2) throughout the sheet.

Farm Animals

2005 (11 JAN.) *Two phosphor bands. Perf* 14½

2502	**1780**	(1st) multicoloured	. . .	65	1·00 □ □
		a. Block of 10. Nos.			
		2502/11	. . . . . .	10·00	12·00 □ □
2503	**1781**	(1st) multicoloured	. . . .	65	1·00 □ □
2504	**1782**	(1st) multicoloured	. . . .	65	1·00 □ □
2505	**1783**	(1st) multicoloured	. . . .	65	1·00 □ □
2506	**1784**	(1st) multicoloured	. . . .	65	1·00 □ □
2507	**1785**	(1st) multicoloured	. . . .	65	1·00 □ □
2508	**1786**	(1st) multicoloured	. . . .	65	1·00 □ □
2509	**1787**	(1st) multicoloured	. . . .	65	1·00 □ □
2510	**1788**	(1st) multicoloured	. . . .	65	1·00 □ □
2511	**1789**	(1st) multicoloured	. . . .	65	1·00 □ □
		Set of 10	. . . .	6·00	9·00 □ □
		First Day Cover	. . . .		10·00 □
		Presentation Pack	. . . .	13·00	□
		PHQ Cards (set of 10)	. . . . .	7·25	14·00 □ □
		Gutter Block of 10	. . . .	16·00	□

Nos. 2502/11 were also issued in sheets of 20, printed in lithography instead of photogravure, containing two of each of the ten designs, arranged in vertical strips of five alternated with printed labels.

1790   Old Harry Rocks, Studland Bay

1791   Wheal Coates, St. Agnes

1792   Start Point, Start Bay

1793   Horton Down, Wiltshire

1794   Chiselcombe, Exmoor

1795   St. James's Stone, Lundy

A British Journey. South West England

2005 (8 FEB.) *One centre phosphor band* (2nd) *or two phosphor bands* (others). *Perf* 14½

2512	**1790**	(2nd) multicoloured	. . . .	50	50 □ □
2513	**1791**	(1st) multicoloured	. . . .	50	75 □ □
2514	**1792**	40p multicoloured	. . . .	1·00	1·75 □ □
2515	**1793**	43p multicoloured	. . . .	1·25	2·00 □ □
2516	**1794**	57p multicoloured	. . . .	1·50	2·50 □ □
2517	**1795**	68p multicoloured	. . .	2·00	3·00 □ □
		Set of 6	. . . .	8·00	10·00 □ □
		First Day Cover	. . . .		7·75 □
		Presentation Pack	. . . .	8·75	□
		PHQ Cards (set of 6)	. . . . . .	4·25	5·75 □ □
		Set of 6 Gutter Pairs	. . . . . .	16·00	□

1796   'Mr Rochester'

1797   'Come to Me'

1798 'In the Comfort of her Bonnet'

1799 'La Ligne des Rats'

1800 'Refectory'

1801 'Inspection'

150th Death Anniversary of Charlotte Brontë. Illustrations of Scenes from Jane Eyre by Paula Rego

2004 (24 Feb.) *One centre phosphor band* (2nd) *or two phosphor bands* (others). *Perf* 14 × 14½

2518	**1796**	(2nd) multicoloured	30	35	□	□
2519	**1797**	(1st) multicoloured	40	45	□	□
2520	**1798**	40p multicoloured	60	65	□	□
2521	**1799**	57p silver, brownish grey and black	85	90	□	□
2522	**1800**	68p multicoloured	1·00	1·10	□	□
2523	**1801**	£1.12 silver, brownish grey and black	1·70	1·80	□	□
	Set of 6	4·75	5·25	□	□
	First Day Cover		6·25		□
	Presentation Pack	5·75		□	
	PHQ Cards (set of 6)	3·00	8·00	□	□
	Set of 6 Gutter Pairs	9·75		□	
	Set of 6 Traffic Light gutter blocks of four	25·00		□	□

MS2524 114 × 105 mm. Nos. 2518/23   4·75   5·25 □ □
First Day Cover . . . .   6·25 □ □

The complete miniature sheet is shown on one of the PHQ cards with the others depicting individual stamps.

1802 Spinning Coin

1803 Rabbit out of Hat Trick

1804 Knotted Scarf Trick

1805 Card Trick

1806 Pyramid under Fez Trick

Centenary of the Magic Circle

2005 (15 Mar.) *Two phosphor bands. Perf* 14½ × 14

2525	**1802**	(1st) multicoloured . . .	40	45	□	□
2526	**1803**	40p multicoloured	60	65	□	□
2527	**1804**	47p multicoloured	95	1·00	□	□
2528	**1805**	68p multicoloured	1·00	1·10	□	□
2529	**1806**	£1.12 multicoloured	1·70	1·80	□	□
	Set of 5	4·50	5·00	□	□
	First Day Cover		5·75		□
	Presentation Pack	5·25		□	
	PHQ Cards (set of 5)	2·25	7·00	□	□
	Set of 5 Gutter Pairs	9·25		□	

Nos. 2525/9 are each printed with instructions for the illusion or trick on the stamp.

No. 2525 can be rubbed with a coin to reveal the 'head' or 'tail' of a coin. The two versions, which appear identical before rubbing, are printed in alternate rows of the sheet, indicated by the letters H and T in the side margins of the sheet.

No. 2525 was also issued in sheets of 20 with *se-tenant* labels showing magic tricks, printed in lithography instead of photogravure.

Nos. 2526 and 2528 each show optical illusions.

The spotted scarf on No. 2527 and the fezzes on No. 2529 are printed in thermochromic inks which fade temporarily when exposed to heat, making the pyramid under the centre fez visible.

50th Anniversary of First Castles Definitives

2005 (22 Mar.) *Sheet* 127 × 73 *mm, containing horiz designs as* T **166/9** (*Castles definitive of 1955-58*) *but with values in decimal currency, printed on pale cream. 'All-over' phosphor. Perf* 11 × 11½.

MS2530 **166** 50p brownish-black; **169** 50p black; **167** £1 dull vermilion; **168** £1 royal blue . . . . . .   4·50   4·75 □ □
First Day Cover . . . .   6·00 □
Presentation Pack . . . .   5·25 □
PHQ Cards (set of 5) . . . . . .   2·20   7·00 □ □

1807 Prince Charles and Mrs Camilla Parker Bowles

Royal Wedding
2005 (9 APR.) *Sheet 85 × 115 mm. Multicoloured. 'All-over' phosphor. Perf 13½ × 14*
MS2531 1807 30p × 2 Prince Charles and Mrs Camilla Parker Bowles laughing; 68p × 2 Prince Charles and Mrs Camilla Parker Bowles smiling into camera .   3·00   3·25 □ □
    First Day Cover ....   4·00   □
    Presentation Pack .... 3·75   □

1808 Hadrian's Wall, England

1809 Uluru-Kata Tjuta National Park, Australia

1810 Stonehenge, England

1811 Wet Tropics of Queensland, Australia

1812 Blenheim Palace, England

1813 Greater Blue Mountains Area, Australia

1814 Heart of Neolithic Orkney, Scotland

1815 Purnululu National Park, Australia

Nos. 2532/3, 2534/5, 2536/7 and 2538/9 were each printed together, *se-tenant*, in horizontal pairs.

World Heritage Sites
2005 (21 APR.) *One side phosphor band* (2nd) *or two phosphor bands* (others). *Perf* 14½

2532	**1808**	(2nd) multicoloured	30	35 □ □
		a. Horiz pair. Nos.		
		2532/3	60	70 □ □
2533	**1809**	(2nd) multicoloured	30	35 □ □
2534	**1810**	(1st) multicoloured	45	50 □ □
		a. Horiz pair. Nos.		
		2534/5	90	1·00 □ □
2535	**1811**	(1st) multicoloured	45	50 □ □
2536	**1812**	47p multicoloured	70	75 □ □
		a. Horiz pair. Nos.		
		2536/7	1·40	1·50 □ □
2537	**1813**	47p multicoloured	70	75 □ □
2538	**1814**	68p multicoloured	1·00	1·10 □ □
		a. Horiz pair. Nos.		
		2538/9	2·00	2·20 □ □
2539	**1815**	68p multicoloured	1·00	1·10 □ □
		Set of 8	4·75	5·25 □ □
		First Day Cover		6·50 □
		Presentation Pack	5·75	□
		PHQ Cards (*set of* 8)	3·50	9·00 □ □
		Set of 8 Gutter Pairs	9·75	□

Stamps in these designs were also issued by Australia.

1816 Ensign of the Scots Guards, 2002

1817 Queen taking the salute as Colonel-in-Chief of the Grenadier Guards, 1983

1818 Trumpeter of the Household Cavalry, 2004

1819 Welsh Guardsman, 1990s

1820 Queen riding side-saddle, 1972

1821 Queen and Duke of Edinburgh in Carriage, 2004

Trooping the Colour

2005 (7 June) *One phosphor band* (2nd), *two phosphor bands* (others). *Perf* 14½

2540	**1816**	(2nd) multicoloured	. . .	30	35 □	□
2541	**1817**	(1st) multicoloured	. . .	45	50 □	□
2542	**1818**	42p multicoloured	. . . .	65	70 □	□
2543	**1819**	60p multicoloured	. . . .	90	95 □	□
2544	**1820**	68p multicoloured	. . . .	1·00	1·10 □	□
2545	**1821**	£1.12 multicoloured	. . . .	1·70	1·80 □	□
		Set of 6		5·00	5·25 □	□
		First Day Cover			6·50	□
		Presentation Pack		5·75		□
		PHQ Cards (set of 6)		2·75	8·00 □	□
		Set of 6 Gutter Pairs		10·50		□
MS2546	115 × 105 mm. Nos. 2540/5 .			5·00	5·25 □	□
		First Day Cover			6·50	□

1822

60th Anniversary of End of the Second World War

2005 (5 July) *Sheet* 115 × 105 *mm containing design as* T **1200** (1995 *Peace and Freedom*) *but with service indicator and No.* 1664b × 5. *Two phosphor bands. Perf* 15 × 14 (*with one elliptical hole on each vert side*) (1664b) *or* 14½ × 14 (*other*)

MS2547 **1822**	(1st) gold × 5; (1st) silver,			
	blue and grey-black	2·75	3·00 □	□
	First Day Cover		3·75	□

1823 Norton F.1, Road Version of Race Winner (1991)

1824 BSA Rocket 3, Early Three Cylinder 'Superbike' (1969)

1825 Vincent Black Shadow, Fastest Standard Motorcycle (1949)

1826 Triumph Speed Twin, Two Cylinder Innovation (1938)

1930 **Brough Superior** bespoke luxury motorcycle

1914 **Royal Enfield** small engined motor bicycle

1827 Brough Superior, Bespoke Luxury Motorcycle (1930)

1828 Royal Enfield, Small Engined Motor Bicycle (1914)

Motorcycles

2005 (19 July) *Two phosphor bands. Perf 14 × 14½*

2548	**1823**	(1st) multicoloured	. . .	45	50 ☐ ☐
2549	**1824**	40p multicoloured	. . . .	60	65 ☐ ☐
2550	**1825**	42p multicoloured	. . . .	65	70 ☐ ☐
2551	**1826**	47p multicoloured	. . . .	70	75 ☐ ☐
2552	**1827**	60p multicoloured	. . . .	90	95 ☐ ☐
2553	**1828**	68p multicoloured	. . . .	1·00	1·10 ☐ ☐
	Set of 6	. . . .		4·25	4·50 ☐ ☐
	First Day Cover	. . . .			5·75 ☐
	Presentation Pack	. . . .		5·00	☐
	PHQ Cards (set of 6)	. . . . . .		2·75	7·50 ☐ ☐
	Set of 6 Gutter Pairs	. . . . . .		8·75	☐

1829

London's Successful Bid for Olympic Games, 2012

2005 (5 Aug.) *Sheet 115 × 105 mm containing designs as T **1255/9**, but with service indicator. Multicoloured. Two phosphor bands. Perf 14½*

MS2554 **1829** (1st) Athlete celebrating × 2; (1st) Throwing the javelin; (1st) Swimming; (1st) Athlete on starting blocks; (1st) Basketball 2·75 3·00 ☐ ☐

First Day Cover	. . . .		3·75 ☐
Presentation Pack		3·50	☐

Stamps from **MS2554** are all inscribed 'London 2012—Host City' and have imprint date '2005'. The design as Type **1259** omits the Olympic rings.

1830 African Woman eating Rice

1831 Indian Woman drinking Tea

1832 Boy eating Sushi

1833 Woman eating Pasta

1834 Woman eating Chips

1835 Teenage Boy eating Apple

Europa. Gastronomy. Changing Tastes in Britain

2005 (23 Aug.) *One side phosphor band (2nd) or two phosphor bands (others). Perf 14½*

2555	**1830**	(2nd) multicoloured	. . .	30	35 ☐ ☐
2556	**1831**	(1st) multicoloured	. . . .	45	50 ☐ ☐
2557	**1832**	42p multicoloured	. . .	65	70 ☐ ☐
2558	**1833**	47p multicoloured	. . .	75	80 ☐ ☐
2559	**1834**	60p multicoloured	. . .	90	95 ☐ ☐
2560	**1835**	68p multicoloured	. . .	1·00	1·10 ☐ ☐
	Set of 6	. . . .		4·00	4·25 ☐ ☐
	First Day Cover	. . . .			5·25 ☐
	Presentation Pack	. . . .		4·75	☐
	PHQ Cards (set of 6)	. . . . . .		2·75	7·00 ☐ ☐
	Set of 6 Gutter Pairs	. . . . . .		8·25	☐

The 1st and 42p values include the 'EUROPA' emblem.

1836 *Inspector Morse*

1837 *Emmerdale*

1838 *Rising Damp*

1839 *The Avengers*

1840 *The South Bank Show*

1841 *Who Wants to be a Millionaire*

50th Anniversary of Independent Television. Classic ITV Programmes

2005 (15 SEPT.) *One side phosphor band* (2nd) *or two phosphor bands* (others). *Perf* 14½ × 14.

2561	**1836**	(2nd) multicoloured	. . . .	30	35 ☐ ☐
2562	**1837**	(1st) multicoloured	. . . .	45	50 ☐ ☐
2563	**1838**	42p multicoloured	. . . .	65	70 ☐ ☐
2564	**1839**	47p multicoloured	. . . .	70	75 ☐ ☐
2565	**1840**	60p multicoloured	. . . .	90	95 ☐ ☐
2566	**1841**	68p multicoloured	. . . .	1·00	1·10 ☐ ☐
		Set of 6	. . . .	4·00	4·25 ☐ ☐
		First Day Cover	. . . .		5·25 ☐
		Presentation Pack	. . . .	4·75	☐
		PHQ Cards (set of 6)	. . . . . .	1·80	6·00 ☐ ☐
		Set of 6 Gutter Pairs	. . . . . .	8·25	☐

The 1st class stamps were also issued in sheets of 20 with each stamp accompanied by a half stamp-size *se-tenant* label.

1842 *Guzmania splendens* (Charlotte Sowerby)

Nos. 2567/72 were printed together, *se-tenant*, in booklet panes of 6 in which the surplus self-adhesive paper around each stamp was removed.

'Smilers' Booklet stamps

2005 (4 OCT.) *Designs as Types* **992**, **1221**, **1286**, **1517** and **1568/9** *but smaller,* 20 × 23 *mm, and inscribed* 1st *as T* **1842**. *Self-adhesive. Two phosphor bands. Die-cut perf* 15 × 14½

2567	**1842**	(1st) multicoloured	. . . .	45	50 ☐ ☐
		a. Booklet pane. Nos. 2567/72	. . . .	2·50	☐
2568	**1569**	(1st) multicoloured	. . . .	45	50 ☐ ☐
2569	**1568**	(1st) multicoloured	. . . .	45	50 ☐ ☐
2570	**1517**	(1st) multicoloured	. . . .	45	50 ☐ ☐
2571	**992**	(1st) multicoloured	. . . .	45	50 ☐ ☐
2572	**1221**	(1st) multicoloured	. . . .	45	50 ☐ ☐
		Set of 6	. . . .	2·50	3·00 ☐ ☐
		First Day Cover	. . . .		3·75 ☐

THE ASHES ENGLAND WINNERS 2005

1843 Cricket Scenes

England's Ashes Victory

2005 (6 OCT.) *Sheet* 115 × 90 *mm. Multicoloured. Two phosphor bands. Perf* 14½ × 14.

MS2573 **1843** (1st) England team with Ashes trophy; (1st) Kevin Pieterson, Michael Vaughan and Andrew Flintoff on opening day of First Test, Lords; 68p Michael Vaughan, Third Test, Old Trafford; 68p Second Test Edgbaston

. . . .	3·00	3·25 ☐ ☐
First Day Cover		4·00 ☐
Presentation Pack	3·75	☐

1844 *Entrepreante* with dismasted British *Belle Isle*

1845 Nelson wounded on Deck of HMS *Victory*

1846 British Cutter *Entrepreante* attempting to rescue Crew of burning French *Achille*

1847 Cutter and HMS *Pickle* (schooner)

1848 British Fleet attacking in Two Columns

1849 Franco/Spanish Fleet putting to Sea from Cadiz

Nos. 2574/5, 2576/7 and 2578/9 were each printed together, *se-tenant*, in horizontal pairs throughout the sheets, each pair forming a composite design.

Bicentenary of the Battle of Trafalgar (1st issue). Scenes from 'Panorama of the Battle of Trafalgar' by William Heath

2005 (18 Oct.) *Two phosphor bands. Perf* 15 × 14½.

2574	**1844**	(1st) multicoloured	45	50	☐	☐
		a. Horiz pair. Nos.				
		2574/5	90	1·00	☐	☐
2575	**1845**	(1st) multicoloured	45	50	☐	☐

2576	**1846**	42p multicoloured	65	70	☐	☐
		a. Horiz pair. Nos.				
		2576/7	1·30	1·40	☐	☐
2577	**1847**	42p multicoloured	65	70	☐	☐
2578	**1848**	68p multicoloured	1·00	1·10	☐	☐
		a. Horiz pair. Nos.				
		2578/9	2·00	2·20	☐	☐
2579	**1849**	68p multicoloured	1·00	1·10	☐	☐
		Set of 6	4·00	4·50	☐	☐
		First Day Cover		5·50		☐
		Presentation Pack	5·00		☐	
		PHQ Cards (set of 7)	3·00	7·50	☐	☐
		Set of 3 Gutter Strips of 4 . . .	8·50		☐	
MS2580	190 × 68 mm. Nos. 2574/9		4·00	4·50	☐	☐

The phosphor bands are at just left of centre and at right of each stamp

The seven PHQ cards depict the six individual stamps and the miniature sheet.

Bicentenary of the Battle of Trafalgar (2nd issue). Booklet stamp.

2005 (18 Oct.) *Design as Type* **1516** (*White Ensign from* 2001 *Submarine Centenary*). *Two phosphor bands. Perf* 14½.

2581	**1516**	(1st) multicoloured . . .	90	90	☐	☐

No. 2581 was only available in £7.26 stamp booklets.

1850 Black Madonna and Child from Haiti

1851 'Madonna and Child' (Marianne Stokes)

1852 'The Virgin Mary with the Infant Christ'

1853 Choctaw Virgin Mother and Child (Fr. John Giuliani)

1854 'Madonna and the Infant Jesus' (from India)

1855 'Come let us adore Him' (Dianne Tchumut)

Christmas. Madonna and Child Paintings

2005 (1 Nov.) *One side phosphor band* (2nd) *or two phosphor bands* (others). *Perf* 14½ × 14.

(a) Self-adhesive

2582	**1850**	(2nd) multicoloured	. . . .	30	35 □ □
2583	**1851**	(1st) multicoloured	. . . .	45	50 □ □
2584	**1852**	42p multicoloured	. . . .	65	70 □ □
2585	**1853**	60p multicoloured	. . . .	90	95 □ □
2586	**1854**	68p multicoloured	. . . .	1·00	1·10 □ □
2587	**1855**	£1.12 multicoloured	. . . .	1·70	1·80 □ □
		Set of 6	. . . .	5·00	5·25 □ □
		First Day Cover	. . . .		6·50 □
		Presentation Pack	. . . .	5·75	□
		PHQ Cards (set of 7)	. . . . . .	3·00	8·50 □ □

(b) PVA gum

MS2588 115 × 102 mm. As Nos.

2582/7	. . . .	5·00	5·25 □ □
First Day Cover	. . . .		6·50 □

The seven PHQ cards depict the six individual stamps and the miniature sheet.

Collectors Pack

2005 (1 Nov.) *Comprises Nos.* 2502/23, 2525/9, **MS**2531/45, 2548/53, 2555/66, 2574/9 and 2582/7
CP2587*a* Collectors Pack . . . . 50·00 □

Post Office Yearbook

2005 (1 Nov.) *Comprises Nos.* 2502/23, 2525/9, **MS**2531/45, 2548/53, 2555/66, 2574/9 and 2582/7
YB2587*a* Yearbook . . . . 60·00 □

Miniature Sheet Collection

2005 (1 Nov.) *Comprises Nos.* **MS**2524, **MS**2530/1, **MS**2546/7, **MS**2554, **MS**2580 and **MS**2588
MS2588*a* Miniature Sheet Collection 33·00 □

REGIONAL ISSUES

PERFORATION AND WATERMARK. All the following Regional stamps are perforated 15 × 14, unless otherwise stated.

For listing of First Day Covers see pages 173/5.

1 England

EN **1**　Three Lions

EN **2**　Crowned Lion
　　　　with Shield of
　　　　St. George

EN **3**　Oak Tree

EN **4**　Tudor Rose

2001 (23 APR.)–**02** *Printed in photogravure by De La Rue or Questa* (*Nos.* EN1/2), *De La Rue* (*others*). *One centre phosphor band* (2nd) *or two phosphor bands* (*others*). *Perf* 15 × 14 (*with one elliptical hole on each vertical side*)

EN1	EN **1**	(2nd) slate-green and silver	60	40	□	□
EN2	EN **2**	(1st) lake-brown and silver	75	60	□	□
EN3	EN **3**	(E) olive-green and silver	1·00	75	□	□
EN4	EN **4**	65p deep reddish lilac and silver	2·50	2·25	□	□
EN5		68p deep reddish lilac and silver	2·00	1·75	□	□

Presentation Pack (*P.O. Pack No.* 54)
(*Nos.* EN1/4) . . . . 7·00　□
PHQ Cards (*set of* 4) (*Nos.* EN1/4)　1·50　10·00 □ □

Nos. EN1/3 were initially sold at 19p, 27p and 36p, the latter representing the basic European airmail rate.

Combined Presentation Packs for England, Northern Ireland, Scotland and Wales

Presentation Pack (*P.O. Pack No.* 59) (*contains* 68p *from England, Northern Ireland, Scotland and Wales* (*Nos.* EN5, NI93, S99, W88)) . . . . . . 8·00　□

Presentation Pack (*P.O. Pack No.* 68) (*contains* 40p *from England, Northern Ireland, Scotland and Wales* (*Nos.* EN9, NI97, S112, W101)) . . . . . 6·25　□

Presentation Pack (*P.O. Pack No.* 69) (*contains* 42p *from England, Northern Ireland, Scotland and Wales* (*Nos.* EN10, NI98, S113, W102)) .　3·25　□

2003 (14 OCT.)–**05.** *As Nos.* EN1/3 *and* EN5 *but with white borders. Printed in photogravure by Walsall or De La Rue (*2nd*),* 40p, 42p*) or De La Rue* (*others*). *One centre phosphor band* (2nd) *or two phosphor bands* (*others*). *Perf* 15×14 (*with one elliptical hole on each vertical side*).

EN6	EN **1**	(2nd) slate-green and silver	65	50	□	□
EN7	EN **2**	(1st) lake-brown and silver	75	70	□	□
EN8	EN **3**	(E) olive-green and silver	1·00	90	□	□
EN9		40p olive-green and silver	1·25	1·25	□	□
EN10		42p olive-green and silver	65	70	□	□
EN11	EN **4**	68p deep reddish lilac and silver	2·00	1·75	□	□

Presentation Pack (*P.O. Pack No.* 63) (*Nos.* EN6/8, EN11) . . .　5·00　□
PHQ Cards (*set of* 4) (*Nos.* EN6/8, EN11) . . . .　1·70　4·00 □ □

Nos. EN6/8 were initially sold at 20p, 28p and 38p, the latter representing the basic European airmail rate.

2 Northern Ireland

N **1**   N **2**   N **3**   N **4**

1958–67 *Wmk* **179**

NI1	N **1**	3d lilac	15	10 □ □
		p. One centre phosphor		
		band	15	15 □ □
NI2		4d blue	15	15 □ □
		p. Two phosphor bands	15	15 □ □
NI3	N **2**	6d purple	20	25 □ □
NI4		9d bronze-green (2		
		phosphor bands) . .	30	70 □ □
NI5	N **3**	1s 3d green	30	70 □ □
NI6		1s 6d blue (2 phosphor		
		bands)	30	70 □ □

1968–69 *One centre phosphor band* (*Nos.* NI8/9) *or two phosphor bands* (*others*). *No wmk*

NI7	N **1**	4d blue	15	15 □ □
NI8		4d sepia	15	15 □ □
NI9		4d vermilion	20	20 □ □
NI10		5d blue	20	20 □ □
NI11	N **3**	1s 6d blue	2·25	2·50 □ □
		Presentation Pack (*comprises*		
		Nos. NI1p, NI4/6, NI8/10) . . .	3·50	□

Decimal Currency

1971–91 *Type* N **4**. *No wmk*

(a) Printed in photogravure with phosphor bands

NI12	2½p magenta (1 centre band) .	70	45 □ □
NI13	3p ultramarine (2 bands) . . .	30	25 □ □
NI14	3p ultramarine (1 centre band)	20	15 □ □
NI15	3½p olive-grey (2 bands)	20	25 □ □
NI16	3½p olive-grey (1 centre band)	20	25 □ □
NI17	4½p grey-blue (2 bands)	30	25 □ □
NI18	5p violet (2 bands)	1·00	1·00 □ □
NI19	5½p violet (2 bands)	20	20 □ □
NI20	5½p violet (1 centre band) . . .	20	25 □ □
NI21	6½p blue (1 centre band)	20	20 □ □
NI22	7p brown (1 centre band) . .	35	25 □ □
NI23	7½p chestnut (2 bands)	1·25	1·25 □ □
NI24	8p rosine (2 bands)	35	35 □ □
NI25	8½p yellow-green (2 bands) . .	35	40 □ □
NI26	9p violet (2 bands)	40	40 □ □
NI27	10p orange-brown (2 bands) .	40	50 □ □
NI28	10p orange-brown (1 centre		
	band)	50	50 □ □
NI29	10½p blue (2 bands)	40	50 □ □
NI30	11p scarlet (2 bands)	50	50 □ □

(b) Printed in photogravure on phosphorised paper

NI31	12p yellowish green	50	50 □ □
NI32	13½p purple-brown	60	70 □ □
NI33	15p ultramarine	60	70 □ □

(c) Printed in lithography. Perf 14 (11½p, 12½p, 14p (*No.* NI38), 15½p, 16p, 18p, (*No.* NI45), 19½p, 20½p, 22p (*No.* NI53), 26p (*No.* NI60), 28p (*No.* NI62)) *or* 15 × 14 (*others*)

NI34	11½p drab (1 side band)	85	85 □ □
NI35	12p bright emerald (1 side band)	70	80 □ □
NI36	12½p light emerald (1 side band)	60	60 □ □
	a. Perf 15 × 14	5·25	5·25 □ □
NI37	12½p pale chestnut (1 side band)	80	50 □ □
NI38	14p grey-blue (phosphorised		
	paper)	75	75 □ □
NI39	14p deep blue (1 centre band)	75	60 □ □
NI40	15p bright blue (1 centre band)	90	60 □ □
NI41	15½p pale violet (phosphorised		
	paper)	80	80 □ □
NI42	16p drab (phosphorised paper)	1·00	1·00 □ □
	a. Perf 15 × 14	8·25	8·50 □ □
NI43	17p grey-blue (phosphorised		
	paper)	90	95 □ □
NI44	17p deep blue (1 centre band)	1·00	80 □ □
NI45	18p deep violet (phosphorised		
	paper)	1·00	1·00 □ □
NI46	18p olive-grey (phosphorised		
	paper)	1·00	90 □ □
NI47	18p bright green (1 centre band)	1·00	95 □ □
	a. Perf 14	2·50	2·50 □ □
NI48	18p bright green (1 side band)	2·25	2·25 □ □
NI49	19p bright orange-red		
	(phosphorised paper) . . .	1·00	1·00 □ □
NI50	19½p olive-grey (phosphorised		
	paper)	1·50	1·75 □ □
NI51	20p brownish black		
	(phosphorised paper) . . .	1·00	80 □ □
NI52	20½p ultramarine (phosphorised		
	paper)	4·50	4·25 □ □
NI53	22p blue (phosphorised paper)	1·10	1·10 □ □
NI54	22p yellow-green (phosphorised		
	paper)	1·10	1·10 □ □
NI55	22p bright orange-red		
	(phosphorised paper) . . .	1·25	90 □ □
NI56	23p bright green (phosphorised		
	paper)	1·25	1·10 □ □
NI57	24p Indian red (phosphorised		
	paper)	1·25	1·25 □ □
NI58	24p chestnut (phosphorised		
	paper)	1·10	90 □ □
NI59	24p chestnut (2 bands)	2·25	2·50 □ □
NI60	26p rosine (phosphorised		
	paper)	1·25	1·25 □ □
	a. Perf 15 × 14	3·00	3·25 □ □
NI61	26p drab (phosphorised paper)	1·75	1·75 □ □
NI62	28p deep violet-blue		
	(phosphorised paper) . . .	1·50	1·50 □ □
	a. Perf 15 × 14	1·25	1·25 □ □

NI63	28p deep bluish grey (phosphorised paper) ...	1·50	1·50 □ □	
NI64Ea	31p bright purple (phosphorised paper) ...	1·90	1·75 □ □	
NI65	32p greenish blue (phosphorised paper) ...	1·75	1·75 □ □	
NI66	34p deep bluish grey (phosphorised paper) ...	1·75	1·75 □ □	
NI67	37p rosine (phosphorised paper)	2·00	2·50 □ □	
NI68	39p bright mauve (phosphorised paper) ...	2·00	2·25 □ □	

Nos. NI48 and NI59 were only issued in stamp booklets.

Presentation Pack (P.O. Pack No. 29) (contains 2½p (NI12), 3p (NI13), 5p (NI18), 7½p (NI23)) .... 3·50 □

Presentation Pack (P.O. Pack No. 61) (contains 3p (NI14), 3½p (NI15), 5½p (NI19), 8p (NI24) *later with* 4½p (NI17) *added*) . 2·25 □

Presentation Pack (P.O. Pack No. 84) (contains 6½p (NI21), 8½p (NI25), 10p (NI27), 11p (NI30)) 2·00 □

Presentation Pack (P.O. Pack No. 129d) (contains 7p (NI22), 9p (NI26), 10½p (NI29), 11½p (NI34), 12p (NI31), 13½p (NI32), 14p (NI38), 15p (NI33), 18p (NI45), 22p (NI53)) .... 9·00 □

Presentation Pack (P.O. Pack No. 4) (contains 10p (NI28), 12½p (NI36), 16p (NI42), 20½p (NI52), 26p (NI60), 28p (NI62)) .... 17·00 □

Presentation Pack (P.O. Pack No. 8) (contains 10p (NI28), 13p (NI37), 16p (NI42a), 17p (NI43), 22p (NI54), 26p (NI60), 28p (NI62), 31p (NI64)) .... 18·00 □

Presentation Pack (P.O. Pack No. 12) (contains 12p (NI35), 13p (NI37), 17p (NI43), 18p (NI46), 22p (NI54), 26p (NI60a), 28p (NI62a), 31p (NI64)) ..... 16·00 □

Combined Presentation Packs for Northern Ireland, Scotland and Wales

Presentation Pack (P.O. Pack No. 17) (contains 14p, 19p, 23p, 32p *from Northern Ireland, Scotland and Wales (Nos.* NI39, NI49, NI56, NI65, S54, S62, S67, S77, W40, W50, W57, W66)) .... 16·00 □

Presentation Pack (P.O. Pack No. 20) (contains 15p, 20p, 24p, 34p *from Northern Ireland, Scotland and Wales (Nos.* NI40, NI51, NI57, NI66, S56, S64, S69, S78, W41, W52, W58, W67)) .... 15·00 □

Presentation Pack (P.O. Pack No. 23) (contains 17p, 22p, 26p, 37p *from Northern Ireland, Scotland and Wales (Nos.* NI44, NI55, NI61, NI67, S58, S66, S73, S79, W45, W56, W62, W68)) .... 15·00 □

Presentation Pack (P.O. Pack No. 26) (contains 18p, 24p, 28p, 39p *from Northern Ireland, Scotland and Wales (Nos.* NI47, NI58, NI63, NI68, S60, S70, S75, S80, W48, W59, W64, W69)) .... 15·00 □

1993 (7 DEC.)–**2000** (*a*) *Printed in lithography by Questa. Perf* 15 × 14 (*with one elliptical hole on each vertical side*)

NI69	N **4** 19p bistre (1 centre band)	90	80 □ □	
NI70	19p bistre (1 side band) ..	1·25	1·75 □ □	
NI71	20p bright green (1 centre band)	1·50	1·50 □ □	
NI72	25p red (2 bands)	75	75 □ □	
NI73	26p red-brown (2 bands)	1·75	1·75 □ □	
NI74	30p deep olive-grey (2 bands)	1·25	1·25 □ □	
NI75	37p bright mauve (2 bands)	2·75	3·00 □	
NI76	41p grey-brown (2 bands)	1·50	1·75 □ □	
NI77	63p light emerald (2 bands)	4·75	5·00 □ □	

(*b*) *Printed in photogravure by Walsall* (19*p*, 20*p*, 26*p* (*No.* NI81*b*), 38*p*, 40*p*, 63*p*, 64*p*, 65*p*), *Harrison or Walsall* (26*p* (*No.* NI81), 37*p*). *Perf* 14 (*No.* NI80) *or* 15 × 14 (*others*) (*both with one elliptical hole on each vertical side*)

NI78	N **4** 19p bistre (1 centre band)	1·25	1·25 □ □	
NI79	20p bright green (1 centre band)	75	70 □ □	
NI80	20p bright green (1 side band)	2·75	3·00 □ □	
NI81	26p chestnut (2 bands) ..	1·25	1·00 □ □	
	b. Perf 14	2·75	2·75 □ □	
NI82	37p bright mauve (2 bands)	2·25	2·25 □ □	
NI83	38p ultramarine (2 bands)	4·25	4·00 □ □	
NI84	40p deep azure (2 bands)	2·00	2·00 □ □	
NI85	63p light emerald (2 bands)	4·75	5·00 □ □	
NI86	64p turquoise-green (2 bands)	6·00	6·00 □ □	
NI87	65p greenish blue (2 bands)	2·75	3·00 □ □	

Nos. NI70, NI80 and NI81*b* were only issued in stamp booklets. No. NI70 exists with the phosphor band at the left or right of the stamp.

Presentation Pack (*P.O. Pack No.*
47) (*contains* 19p, 26p, 38p,
64p (*Nos.* NI78, NI81, NI83
NI86)) . . . .   10·00   □

Presentation Pack (*P.O. Pack No.*
52) (*contains* 1st, 40p, 65p)
(*Nos.* NI84, NI87, NI88*b*) . .   10·00   □

Combined Presentation Packs for Northern Ireland, Scotland and Wales

Presentation Pack (*P.O. Pack No.*
31) (*contains* 19p, 25p, 30p,
41p *from Northern Ireland,
Scotland and Wales* (*Nos.*
NI69, NI72, NI74, NI76, S81,
S84, S86, S88, W70, W73,
W75, W77)) . . . .   15·00   □

Presentation Pack (*P.O. Pack No.*
36) (*contains* 20p, 26p, 37p,
63p *from Northern Ireland,
Scotland and Wales* (*Nos.*
NI71, NI73, NI75, NI77, S83,
S85, S87, S89, W72, W74
W76, W78)) . . . .   24·00   □

Presentation Pack (*P.O. Pack No.*
42) (*contains* 20p (1 *centre
band*), 26p, 37p, 63p *from
Northern Ireland, Scotland
and Wales* (*Nos.* NI79,
NI81/2, NI85, S90/3, W79/82)) 24·00   □

N 5

2000 (15 Feb.–25 Apr.) *Type* N **4** *redrawn with* '1st' *face value as Type* N **5**. *Two phosphor bands. Perf* 14 (*with one elliptical hole on each vertical side*)

NI88 N **5** (1st) bright orange-red . .   2·75   2·75   □ □
             b. Perf 15 ×14 (25 Apr.)   9·00   7·00   □ □

No. NI88 was only issued in stamp booklets. No. NI88*b* was issued in sheets on 25 April.

N **6**   Basalt Columns,
          Giant's Causeway

N **7**   Aerial View
          of Patchwork
          Fields

N **8**   Linen Pattern   N **9**   Vase Pattern
                                             from Belleck

2001 (6 Mar.)–02 *Printed in lithography by De La Rue* (68p), *De La Rue or Walsall* (E), *Walsall or Enschedé* (2nd) *or Walsall* (*others*). *One centre phosphor band* (2nd) *or two phosphor bands* (*others*). *Perf* 15 × 14 (*with one elliptical hole on each vertical side*)

NI89 N **6** (2nd) black, new blue,
               bright magenta and
               greenish yellow . . .   50   35 □ □
NI90 N **7** (1st) black, new blue and
               greenish yellow . . .   1·00   1·00 □ □
NI91 N **8** (E) black, new blue and
               pale orange . . . . .   1·25   1·25 □ □
NI92 N **9** 65p black, bright magenta
               and greenish yellow   2·75   2·75 □ □
NI93   68p black, bright magenta
               and greenish yellow   2·75   2·75 □ □
Presentation Pack (*P.O. Pack
No.* 53) (*Nos.* NI89/92) . . . . .   7·00   □
PHQ Cards (*set of 4*) (*Nos.*
NI89/92) . . . .   1·50   10·00 □ □

Nos. NI89, NI90 and NI91 were initially sold at 19p, 27p and 36p, the latter representing the basic European airmail rate.

For combined presentation packs for all four Regions, see under England.

2003 (14 Oct.)–05. *As Nos.* NI89/91 *and* NI93 *but with white borders. Printed in lithography by Walsall* (NI98) *or De La Rue* (*others*). *One centre phosphor band* (2nd) *or two phosphor bands* (*others*). *Perf* 15 × 14 (*with one elliptical hole on each vertical side*).

NI94 N **6** (2nd) black, new blue, bright
               magenta and greenish
               yellow   50   35 □ □
NI95 N **7** (1st) black, new blue and
               greenish yellow . . .   60   50 □ □
NI96 N **8** (E) black and new blue .   75   65 □ □
NI97   40p black and new blue .   1·25   1·25 □ □
NI98   42p black, new blue and
               orange-yellow   65   70 □ □
               a. Black, new blue and
               greenish yellow . . .   65   70 □ □
NI99 N **9** 68p black, bright magenta
               and greenish yellow   2·75   2·75 □ □
Presentation Pack (*P.O. Pack No.*
66) (*Nos.* NI94/6, NI99) . . . .   6·00   □
PHQ Cards (*set of 4*) (*Nos.*
NI94/6, NI99) . . . .   1·50   10·00 □ □

Nos. NI94/6 were initially sold at 20p, 28p and 38p, the latter representing the basic European airmail rate.

No. NI98 (Walsall printing) appears bluish grey and No. NI98a (De La Rue printing) appears olive-grey.

3 Scotland

S **1**   S **2**   S **3**   S **4**

1958–67 *Wmk* **179**

S1	S **1**	3d lilac	15	15	□	□
		p. Two phosphor bands	13·00	2·75	□	□
		pa. One side band . . .	20	25	□	□
		pb. One centre band . .	15	15	□	□
S2		4d blue	15	15	□	□
		p. Two phosphor bands	15	15	□	□
S3	S **2**	6d purple	20	15	□	□
		p. Two phosphor bands	20	20	□	□
S4		9d bronze-green (2 phosphor bands) . .	35	40	□	□
S5	S **3**	1s 3d green	40	40	□	□
		p. Two phosphor bands	40	40	□	□
S6		1s 6d blue (2 phosphor bands)	45	50	□	□

No. S1*pa* exists with the phosphor band at the left or right of the stamp.

1967–70 *One centre phosphor band* (Nos. S7, S9/10) *or two phosphor bands* (others). No wmk

S7	S **1**	3d lilac	10	15	□	□
S8		4d blue	10	15	□	□
S9		4d sepia	10	10	□	□
S10		4d vermilion	10	10	□	□
S11		5d blue	20	10	□	□
S12	S **2**	9d bronze-green	5·50	5·50	□	□
S13	S **3**	1s 6d blue	1·75	1·50	□	□
		Presentation Pack (containing Nos. S3, S5p, S7, S9/13) . . .	8·00		□	

Decimal Currency

1971–93 *Type* S **4**. *No wmk*

(a) *Printed in photogravure by Harrison and Sons with phosphor bands. Perf* 15 × 14

S14	2½p magenta (1 centre band) .	25	20	□	□
S15	3p ultramarine (2 bands) . . .	35	15	□	□
S16	3p ultramarine (1 centre band)	15	15	□	□
S17	3½p olive-grey (2 bands)	20	25	□	□
S18	3½p olive-grey (1 centre band)	20	25	□	□
S19	4½p grey-blue (2 bands)	30	25	□	□
S20	5p violet (2 bands)	1·00	1·25	□	□
S21	5½p violet (2 bands)	20	20	□	□
S22	5½p violet (1 centre band) . . .	20	25	□	□
S23	6½p blue (1 centre band)	20	20	□	□
S24	7p brown (1 centre band) . .	30	30	□	□
S25	7½p chestnut (2 bands)	1·25	1·25	□	□
S26	8p rosine (2 bands)	45	40	□	□

S27	8½p yellow-green (2 bands) . .	40	40 □ □
S28	9p violet (2 bands)	40	40 □ □
S29	10p orange-brown (2 bands) .	45	50 □ □
S30	10p orange-brown (1 centre band)	40	50 □ □
S31	10½p blue (2 bands)	45	50 □ □
S32	11p scarlet (2 bands)	50	50 □ □

(b) *Printed in photogravure by Harrison and Sons on phosphorised paper. Perf* 15 × 14

S33	12p yellowish green	50	50 □ □
S34	13½p purple-brown	70	80 □ □
S35	15p ultramarine	60	70 □ □

(c) *Printed in lithography by John Waddington. One side phosphor band (11½p, 12p, 12½p, 13p) or phosphorised paper (others). Perf* 14

S36	11½p drab	80	80 □ □
S37	12p bright emerald	2·00	2·00 □ □
S38	12½p light emerald	60	70 □ □
S39	13p pale chestnut	75	75 □ □
S40	14p grey-blue	75	75 □ □
S41	15½p pale violet	80	80 □ □
S42	16p drab	80	85 □ □
S43Ea	17p grey-blue	1·25	1·00 □ □
S44	18p deep violet	80	80 □ □
S45	19½p olive-grey	1·75	1·75 □ □
S46	20½p ultramarine	3·50	3·50 □ □
S47	22p blue	1·00	1·00 □ □
S48	22p yellow-green	4·25	4·25 □ □
S49	26p rosine	1·25	1·25 □ □
S50	28p deep violet-blue	1·25	1·25 □ □
S51	31p bright purple	2·50	2·50 □ □

(d) *Printed in lithography by Questa. Perf* 15 × 14

S52	12p bright emerald (1 side band)	2·00	2·25 □ □
S53	13p pale chestnut (1 side band)	70	75 □ □
S54	14p deep blue (1 centre band)	60	70 □ □
S55	14p deep blue (1 side band) . .	80	90 □ □
S56	15p bright blue (1 centre band)	70	70 □ □
S57	17p grey-blue (phosphorised paper)	4·00	4·00 □ □
S58	17p deep blue (1 centre band)	1·00	1·10 □ □
S59	18p olive-grey (phosphorised paper)	1·10	85 □ □
S60	18p bright green (1 centre band)	1·25	90 □ □
	a. Perf 14	1·00	1·00 □ □
S61	18p bright green (1 side band)	2·75	3·00 □ □
S62	19p bright orange-red (phosphorised paper) . . .	70	70 □ □
S63	19p bright orange-red (2 bands)	2·25	2·00 □ □
S64	20p brownish black (phosphorised paper) . . .	95	95 □ □
S65	22p yellow-green (phosphorised paper)	1·25	1·50 □ □
S66	22p bright orange-red (phosphorised paper) . . .	1·25	90 □ □

S67	23p bright green (phosphorised paper)	1·25	1·10 □ □
S68	23p bright green (2 bands) . .	14·00	14·00 □ □
S69	24p Indian red (phosphorised paper)	1·25	1·25 □ □
S70	24p chestnut (phosphorised paper)	1·40	1·25 □ □
	a. Perf 14	3·00	3·25 □ □
S71	24p chestnut (2 bands)	2·75	3·00 □ □
S72	26p rosine (phosphorised paper)	3·75	4·00 □ □
S73	26p drab (phosphorised paper)	1·25	1·25 □ □
S74	28p deep violet-blue (phosphorised paper) . . .	1·25	1·25 □ □
S75	28p deep bluish grey (phosphorised paper) . . .	1·25	1·50 □ □
	a. Perf 14	6·50	6·75 □ □
S76	31p bright purple (phosphorised paper)	2·25	2·25 □ □
S77	32p greenish blue (phosphorised paper) . . .	1·75	2·00 □ □
S78	34p deep bluish grey (phosphorised paper) . . .	1·75	1·75 □ □
S79	37p rosine (phosphorised paper)	2·00	2·25 □ □
S80	39p bright mauve (phosphorised paper)	2·00	2·25 □ □
	a. Perf 14	4·50	4·75 □ □

Nos. S55, S61, S63, S68 and S71 were only issued in stamp booklets.

Presentation Pack (*P.O. Pack No. 27*) (*contains* 2½p (S14), 3p (S15), 5p (S20), 7½p (S25)) . .   3·50 □

Presentation Pack (*P.O. Pack No. 62*) (*contains* 3p (S16), 3½p (S17), 5½p (S21), 8p (S26), *later with* 4½p (S19) *added*) .   2·50 □

Presentation Pack (*P.O. Pack No. 85*) (*contains* 6½p (S23), 8½p (S27), 10p (S29), 11p (S32)) .   2·00 □

Presentation Pack (*P.O. Pack No. 129b*) (*contains* 7p (S24), 9p (S28), 10½p (S31), 11½p (S36), 12p (S33), 13½p (S34), 14p (S40), 15p (S35), 18p (S44), 22p (S47)) . . . .   9·00 □

Presentation Pack (*P.O. Pack No. 2*) (*contains* 10p (S30), 12½p (S38), 16p (S42), 20½p (S46), 26p (S49), 28p (S50)) . . . . .   17·00 □

Presentation Pack (*P.O. Pack No. 6*) (*contains* 10p (S30), 13p (S39), 16p (S42), 17p (S43), 22p (S48), 26p (S49), 28p (S50), 31p (S51)) . . . .   17·00 □

Presentation Pack (P.O. Pack No.
10) (contains 12p (S52), 13p
(S53), 17p (S57), 18p (S59),
22p (S65), 26p (S72), 28p (S74),
31p (S76)) . . . . 16·00 □

For combined packs containing values from all three Regions see under Northern Ireland.

1993 (7 Dec.)–**98** (a) Printed in lithography by Questa. Perf 15 × 14 (with one elliptical hole on each vertical side)

S81	S **4**	19p bistre (1 centre band)	80	70 □	□
S82		19p bistre (1 side band) .	3·00	3·25 □	□
S83		20p bright green (1 centre band)	1·50	1·50 □	□
S84		25p red (2 bands)	1·10	1·00 □	□
S85		26p red-brown (2 bands)	1·75	2·00 □	□
S86		30p deep olive-grey (2 bands)	1·25	1·25 □	□
S87		37p bright mauve (2 bands)	2·75	3·00 □	□
S88		41p grey-brown (2 bands)	1·75	2·00 □	□
S89		63p light emerald (2 bands)	4·00	4·25 □	□

(b) Printed in photogravure by Walsall (20p, 26p (No. S91a), 63p), Harrison or Walsall (26p (No. S91), 37p). Perf 14 (No. S90a) or 15 × 14 (others) (both with one elliptical hole on each vertical side)

S90	S **4**	20p bright green (1 centre band)	1·00	60 □	□
S90a		20p bright green (1 side band)	2·75	2·75 □	□
S91		26p chestnut (2 bands) .	1·00	1·00 □	□
		a. Perf 14	2·75	2·75 □	□
S92		37p bright mauve (2 bands)	1·50	1·50 □	□
S93		63p light emerald (2 bands)	4·00	4·00 □	□

Nos. S82, S90a and S91a were only issued in stamp booklets. For combined presentation packs for all three Regions, see under Northern Ireland.

S **5** Scottish Flag

S **6** Scottish Lion

S **7** Thistle

S **8** Tartan

1999 (8 June)–**2002** Printed in photogravure by De La Rue (68p), De La Rue, Questa or Walsall (2nd, 1st) or Walsall (others). One centre phosphor band (2nd) or two phosphor bands (others). Perf 15 × 14 (with one elliptical hole on each vertical side)

S94	S **5**	(2nd) new blue, blue and silver	30	35 □	□
S95	S **6**	(1st) greenish yellow, deep rose-red, rose-red and silver	40	45 □	□
S96	S **7**	(E) bright lilac, deep lilac and silver	1·75	1·75 □	□
S97	S **8**	64p greenish yellow, bright magenta, new blue, grey-black and silver	9·00	7·75 □	□
S98		65p greenish yellow, bright magenta, new blue, grey-black and silver	3·00	3·25 □	□
S99		68p greenish yellow, bright magenta, new blue, grey-black and silver	3·25	3·25 □	□

Presentation Pack (P.O. Pack
No. 45) (contains 2nd, 1st, E,
64p) (Nos. S94/7)) . . . . . . 10·00 □
Presentation Pack (P.O. Pack
No. 50) (contains 65p) (No. S98)) 6·50 □
Presentation Pack (P.O. Pack
No. 55) (contains 2nd, 1st, E,
65p) (Nos. S94/6, S98) . . . . 6·00 □
PHQ Cards (Nos. S94/7) . . . . 1·50 10·00 □ □

Nos. S94, S95 and S96 were initially sold at 19p, 26p and 30p, the latter representing the basic European airmail rate.

For combined presentation packs for all four Regions, see under England.

S **9**

2000 (15 Feb.) Type S **4** redrawn with '1st' face value as Type S **9**. Two phosphor bands. Perf 14 (with one elliptical hole on each vertical side)

S108 S **9** (1st) bright orange-red . . 3·00 3·25 □ □

No. S108 was only issued in stamp booklets.

2003 (14 Oct.)–**05**. *As Nos. S94/6 and S99 but with white borders. Printed in photogravure by Walsall or De La Rue (42p) or De La Rue (others). One centre phosphor band (2nd) or two phosphor bands (others). Perf 15 × 14 (with one elliptical hole on each vertical side).*

S109	S 5	(2nd) new blue, blue and silver	30	35	☐	☐
S110	S 6	(1st) rose-red, greenish yellow, deep rose-red and silver	45	50	☐	☐
S111	S 7	(E) bright lilac, deep lilac and silver	60	65	☐	☐
S112		40p bright lilac, deep lilac and silver	1·25	1·25	☐	☐
S113		42p bright lilac, deep lilac and silver	65	70	☐	☐
S114	S 8	68p bright magenta, greenish yellow, new blue, grey-black and silver	1·10	1·20	☐	☐
		Presentation Pack (P.O. Pack No. 64) (Nos. S109/11, S114) . . .	2·75		☐	
		PHQ Cards (set of 4) (Nos. S109/11, S114)	1·70	4·00	☐	☐

Nos. S109/11 were initially sold at 20p, 28p and 38p, the latter representing the basic European airmail rate.

Opening of New Scottish Parliament Building

2004 (5 Oct.) *Sheet 123 × 70 mm. Printed in photogravure by De La Rue. One centre phosphor band (2nd) or two phosphor bands (others). Perf 15 × 14 (with one elliptical hole on each vertical side).*

MSS120	Nos. S109, S110 × 2 and S112 × 2	5·00	5·00	☐	☐
	First Day Cover		7·25	☐	

For full information on all future British issues, collectors should write to Royal Mail, Freepost EH3647, 21 South Gyle Crescent, Edinburgh EH12 9PE.

4 Wales

W 1   W 2   W 3

1958–67 *Wmk* **179**

W1	W 1	3d lilac	15	15	☐	☐
		p. One centre phosphor band	20	15	☐	☐
W2		4d blue	20	15	☐	☐
		p. Two phosphor bands	20	15	☐	☐
W3	W 2	6d purple	35	30	☐	☐
W4		9d bronze-green (2 phosphor bands) . .	40	35	☐	☐
W5	W 3	1s 3d green	40	40	☐	☐
W6		1s 6d blue (2 phosphor bands)	40	40	☐	☐

1967–69 *One centre phosphor band (Nos. W7, W9/10) or two phosphor bands (others). No wmk.*

W7	W 1	3d lilac	10	15	☐	☐
W8		4d blue	10	15	☐	☐
W9		4d sepia	15	15	☐	☐
W10		4d vermilion	15	15	☐	☐
W11		5d blue	15	15	☐	☐
W12	W 3	1s 6d blue	3·50	3·50	☐	☐
		Presentation Pack (comprises Nos. W4, W6/7, W9/11)	4·00		☐	

W 4 With 'p'   W 5 Without 'p'

Decimal Currency

1971–92 *Type* W **4**. *No wmk.*

(a) Printed in photogravure with phosphor bands

W13	2½p magenta (1 centre band) .	20	20	☐	☐
W14	3p ultramarine (2 bands) . . .	25	20	☐	☐
W15	3p ultramarine (1 centre band)	25	25	☐	☐
W16	3½p olive-grey (2 bands)	20	30	☐	☐
W17	3½p olive-grey (1 centre band)	20	30	☐	☐
W18	4½p grey-blue (2 bands)	30	30	☐	☐
W19	5p violet (2 bands)	1·25	1·25	☐	☐
W20	5½p violet (2 bands)	25	30	☐	☐
W21	5½p violet (1 centre band) . . .	25	30	☐	☐
W22	6½p blue (1 centre band)	20	20	☐	☐
W23	7p brown (1 centre band) . .	25	25	☐	☐
W24	7½p chestnut (2 bands)	1·75	1·75	☐	☐

W25	8p rosine (2 bands)	30	35 □	□
W26	8½p yellow-green (2 bands) . .	30	35 □	□
W27	9p violet (2 bands)	40	40 □	□
W28	10p orange-brown (2 bands) .	40	40 □	□
W29	10p orange-brown (1 centre band)	40	40 □	□
W30	10½p blue (2 bands)	45	45 □	□
W31	11p scarlet (2 bands)	45	45 □	□

(b) Printed in photogravure on phosphorised paper

W32	12p yellow-green	50	50 □	□
W33	13½p purple-brown	60	70 □	□
W34	15p ultramarine	60	70 □	□

(c) Printed in lithography. Perf 14 (11½p, 12½p, 14p (No. W39), 15½p. 16p, 18p (No. W46), 19½p, 20½p, 22p (No. W54), 26p (No. W61), 28p (No. W63) or 15 × 14 (others)

W35	11½p drab (1 side band)	90	80 □	□
W36	12p bright emerald (1 side band)	2·00	2·00 □	□
W37	12½p light emerald (1 side band)	70	70 □	□
	a. Perf 15 × 14	4·75	4·25 □	□
W38	13p pale chestnut (1 side band)	60	60 □	□
W39	14p grey-blue (phosphorised paper)	70	70 □	□
W40	14p deep blue (1 centre band)	75	75 □	□
W41	15p bright blue (1 centre band)	80	75 □	□
W42	15½p pale violet (phosphorised paper)	75	75 □	□
W43	16p drab (phosphorised paper)	1·75	1·75 □	□
	a. Perf 15 × 14	1·75	1·75 □	□
W44	17p grey-blue (phosphorised paper)	70	80 □	□
W45	17p deep blue (1 centre band)	90	80 □	□
W46	18p deep violet (phosphorised paper)	1·00	95 □	□
W47	18p olive-grey (phosphorised paper)	95	90 □	□
W48	18p bright green (1 centre band)	75	75 □	□
	b. Perf 14	5·25	5·25 □	□
W49	18p bright green (1 side band)	2·00	2·00 □	□
W50	19p bright orange-red (phosphorised paper) . . .	1·00	80 □	□
W51	19½p olive-grey (phosphorised paper)	1·75	2·00 □	□
W52	20p brownish black (phosphorised paper)	90	90 □	□
W53	20½p ultramarine (phosphorised paper)	3·50	3·50 □	□
W54	22p blue (phosphorised paper)	1·10	1·10 □	□
W55	22p yellow-green (phosphorised paper)	95	1·10 □	□
W56	22p bright orange-red (phosphorised paper) . . .	1·00	1·10 □	□
W57	23p bright green (phosphorised paper)	1·00	1·10 □	□
W58	24p Indian red (phosphorised paper)	1·25	1·25 □	□
W59	24p chestnut (phosphorised paper)	75	75 □	□
	b. Perf 14	4·75	5·25 □	□
W60	24p chestnut (2 bands)	1·25	1·50 □	□
W61	26p rosine (phosphorised paper)	1·10	1·10 □	□
	a. Perf 15 × 14	5·75	6·00 □	□
W62	26p drap (phosphorised paper)	1·75	1·75 □	□
W63	28p deep violet-blue (phosphorised paper)	1·50	1·50 □	□
	a. Perf 15 × 14	1·50	1·50 □	□
W64	28p deep bluish grey (phosphorised paper) . . .	1·50	1·50 □	□
W65	31p bright purple (phosphorised paper)	1·75	1·75 □	□
W66	32p greenish blue (phosphorised paper)	1·75	1·75 □	□
W67	34p deep bluish grey (phosphorised paper) . . .	1·75	1·75 □	□
W68	37p rosine (phosphorised paper)	2·25	2·25 □	□
W69	39p bright mauve (phosphorised paper)	2·25	2·25 □	□

Nos. W49 and W60 were only issued in stamp booklets. The former exists with the phosphor band at the left or right of the stamp.

Presentation Pack (P.O. Pack No. 28) (contains 2½p (W13), 3p (W14), 5p (W19), 7½p (W24)) .	3·50	□
Presentation Pack (P.O. Pack No. 63) (contains 3p (W15), 3½p (W16), 5½p (W20), 8p (W25), *later with* 4½p (W18) *added*) .	2·50	□
Presentation Pack (P.O. Pack No. 86) (contains 6½p (W22), 8½p (W26), 10p (W28), 11p (W31))	2·00	□
Presentation Pack (P.O. Pack No. 129c) (contains 7p (W23), 9p (W27), 10½p (W30), 11½p (W35), 12p (W32), 13½p (W33), 14p (W39), 15p (W34), 18p (W46), 22p (W54)) .	9·00	□
Presentation Pack (P.O. Pack No. 3) (contains 10p (W29), 12½p (W37), 16p (W43), 20½p (W53), 26p (W61), 28p (W63))	17·00	□
Presentation Pack (P.O. Pack No. 7) (contains 10p (W29), 13p (W38), 16p (W43a), 17p (W44), 22p (W55), 26p (W61), 28p (W63), 31p (W65))	17·00	□
Presentation Pack (P.O. Pack No. 11) (contains 12p (W36), 13p (W38), 17p (W44), 18p (W47), 22p (W55), 26p (W61a), 28p (W63a), 31p (W65))	16·00	□

For combined packs containing values from all three Regions see under Northern Ireland.

1993 (7 Dec.)–**96** *Printed in lithography by Questa. Perf* 15 × 14 (*with one elliptical hole on each vertical side*)

W70	W **4**	19p bistre (1 centre band)	80	70 □ □
W71		19p bistre (1 side band) .	3·75	4·00 □ □
W72		20p bright green (1 centre band)	1·75	2·00 □ □
W73		25p red (2 bands)	1·25	1·00 □ □
W74		26p red-brown (2 bands)	2·00	2·25 □ □
W75		30p deep olive-grey (2 bands)	1·25	1·25 □ □
W76		37p bright mauve (2 bands)	2·75	3·00 □ □
W77		41p grey-brown (2 bands)	2·00	2·00 □ □
W78		63p light emerald (2 bands)	4·50	4·75 □ □

No. W71 was only issued in stamp booklets.

For combined presentation packs for all three Regions see under Northern Ireland.

1997 (1 July)–**98** *Printed in photogravure by Walsall* (20*p*, 26*p* (*No.* W80*a*), 63*p*), *Harrison or Walsall* (26*p* (*No.* W80), 37*p*) *Perf* 14 (*No.* W79*a*) *or* 15 × 14 (*both with one elliptical hole on each vertical side*)

W79	W **5**	20p bright green (1 centre band)	80	80 □ □
W79*a*		20p bright green (1 side band)	2·25	2·00 □ □
W80		26p chestnut (2 bands) .	1·00	1·00 □ □
		a. Perf 14	2·75	2·75 □ □
W81		37p bright mauve (2 bands)	2·75	2·75 □ □
W82		63p light emerald (2 bands)	4·00	4·50 □ □

Presentation Pack (*P.O. Pack No.* 39) (*Nos.* W79 *and* W80/2) . . 15·00 □

Nos. W79*a* and W80*a* were only issued in stamp booklets.

W **6**   Leek

W **7**   Welsh Dragon

W **8**   Daffodil

W **9**   Prince of Wales Feathers

1999 (8 June)–**2002** *Printed in photogravure by De La Rue* (68*p*), *Walsall or De La Rue* (1st), (2nd), (*No.*W83) *or Walsall* (*others*). *One phosphor band* (2nd) *or two phosphor bands* (*others*). *Perf* 14 (*No.* W83*a*) *or* 15 × 14 (*others*) (*both with one elliptical hole on each vertical side*)

W83	W **6**	(2nd) orange-brown, yellow-orange and black (1 centre band) . . .	60	50 □ □
W83*a*		(2nd) orange-brown, yellow-orange and black (1 side band)	3·75	4·00 □ □
W84	W **7**	(1st) blue-green, greenish yellow, silver and black	1·00	60 □ □
W85	W **8**	(E) greenish blue, deep greenish blue and grey-black	1·50	1·50 □ □
W86	W **9**	64p violet, gold, silver and black	7·00	7·75 □ □
W87		65p violet, gold, silver and black	3·00	3·25 □ □
W88		68p violet, gold, silver and black	2·75	2·75 □ □

Presentation Pack (*P.O. Pack No.* 46) (*contains* 2nd, 1st, E, 64p) (*Nos.* W83, W84/6)) . . . . . . 14·00 □

Presentation Pack (*P.O. Pack No.* 51) (*contains* 65p) (No. W87)) 3·00 □

Presentation Pack (*P.O. Pack No.* 56) (*contains* 2nd, 1st, E, 65p) (*Nos.* W83, W84/5, W87)) . . . 8·00 □

PHQ Cards (*Nos.* W83, W84/6) . 1·50 10·00 □ □

Nos. W83, W84 and W85 were initially sold at 19p, 26p and 30p, the latter representing the basic European airmail rate.

No. W83*a* was only issued in stamp booklets.

For combined presentation packs for all four Regions, see under England.

W **10**

2000 (15 Feb.) *Type* W **4** *redrawn with* '1af/st' *face value as Type* W **10**. *Two phosphor bands. Perf* 14 (*with one elliptical hole on each vertical side*)

W97   W **10**   (1st) bright orange-red .   3·00   2·75 □ □

No. W97 was only issued in stamp booklets.

2003 (14 OCT.)–**05.** *As Nos.* W83, W84/5 *and* W88, *but with white borders. Printed in photogravure by Walsall or De La Rue* (42p) *or De La Rue* (*others*). *One centre phosphor band* (2nd) *or two phosphor bands* (*others*). *Perf* 15×14 (*with one elliptical hole on each vertical side*).

W98	W **6**	(2nd) orange-brown, deep orange-brown and black	30	35 ☐ ☐
W99	W **7**	(1st) blue-green, greenish yellow, silver and black	45	50 ☐ ☐
W100	W **8**	(E) greenish blue, deep greenish blue and grey-black	60	65 ☐ ☐
W101		40p greenish blue, deep greenish blue and grey-black	1·25	1·25 ☐ ☐
W102		42p greenish blue, deep greenish blue and grey-black	65	70 ☐ ☐
W103	W **9**	68p violet, gold, silver and black	1·10	1·20 ☐ ☐
		Presentation Pack (*P.O. Pack No.* 65) (*Nos.* W98/100, W103) . .	2·75	☐
		PHQ Cards (*set of* 4) (*Nos.* W98/100, W103)	1·70	4·00 ☐ ☐

Nos. W98/100 were initially sold at 20p, 28p and 38p, the latter representing the basic European airmail rate.

ISLE OF MAN

Regional Issues

1   **2**   **3**

1958–67 *Wmk* **179**. *Perf* 15 × 14

1	**1**	2½d red	50	1·25 ☐ ☐
2	**2**	3d lilac	50	20 ☐ ☐
		p. One centre phosphor band	20	50 ☐ ☐
3		4d blue	1·50	1·50 ☐ ☐
		p. Two phosphor bands . .	20	30 ☐ ☐

1968–69 *One centre phosphor band* (*Nos.* 5/6) *or two phosphor bands* (*others*). *No wmk*

4	**2**	4d blue	25	30 ☐ ☐
5		4d sepia	25	40 ☐ ☐
6		4d vermilion	45	75 ☐ ☐
7		5d blue	45	75 ☐ ☐

Decimal Currency

1971 (7 JULY) *One centre phosphor band* (2½p) *or two phosphor bands* (*others*). *No wmk*

8	**3**	2½p magenta	20	15 ☐ ☐
9		3p ultramarine	20	15 ☐ ☐
10		5p violet	40	60 ☐ ☐
11		7½p chestnut	40	75 ☐ ☐
		Presentation Pack	2·75	☐

For comprehensive listings of the Independent Administration issues of the Isle of Man, see Stanley Gibbons *Collect Channel Islands and Isle of Man Stamps*.

CHANNEL ISLANDS
1 General Issue

C **1**   Gathering Vraic   C **2**   Islanders gathering Vraic

Third Anniversary of Liberation

1948 (10 MAY) *Wmk Type* **127**. *Perf* 15 × 14

C1	C **1**	1d red	25	30 ☐ ☐
C2	C **2**	2½d blue	25	30 ☐ ☐
		First Day Cover		35·00 ☐

2 Guernsey

(a) War Occupation Issues

Stamps issued under British authority during the German Occupation.

1   **2**   **3**

1941–44 *Rouletted.* (a) *White paper. No wmk*

1f	1	½d green	. . . .	3·00	2·00	□	□
2		1d red	. . . .	2·25	1·25	□	□
3a		2½d blue	. . . .	6·00	5·00	□	□

(b) *Bluish French bank-note paper. Wmk loops*

4	1	½d green	. . . .	27·00	21·00	□	□
5		1d red	. . . .	14·00	21·00	□	□

(b) Regional Issues

1958–67 *Wmk* **179**. *Perf* 15 × 14

6	2	2½d red	. . . .	35	40	□	□
7	3	3d lilac	. . . .	30	30	□	□
		p. One centre phosphor band		15	20	□	□
8		4d blue	. . . .	25	30	□	□
		p. Two phosphor bands . .		15	20	□	□

1968–69 *One centre phosphor band (Nos. 10/11) or two phosphor bands* (others). *No wmk*

9	3	4d blue	. . . .	10	20	□	□
10		4d sepia	. . . .	10	15	□	□
11		4d vermilion	. . . .	20	25	□	□
12		5d blue	. . . .	20	30	□	□

For comprehensive listings of the Independent Postal Administration issues of Guernsey, see Stanley Gibbons *Collect Channel Islands and Isle of Man Stamps.*

3 Jersey

(a) War Occupation Issues

Stamps issued under British authority during the German Occupation.

1   **2**   Old Jersey Farm   **3**   Portelet Bay

4   Corbière Lighthouse   **5**   Elizabeth Castle

6   Mont Orgueil Castle   **7**   Gathering Vraic (seaweed)

1941–42 *White paper. No wmk Perf* 11

1	1	½d green	. . . .	5·25	3·75	□	□
2		1d red	. . . .	6·25	3·50	□	□

1943 *No wmk Perf* 13½

3	2	½d green	. . . .	9·75	10·00	□	□
4	3	1d red	. . . .	2·25	50	□	□
5	4	1½d brown	. . . .	7·00	5·75	□	□
6	5	2d orange	. . . .	6·50	2·00	□	□
7a	6	2½d blue		1·00	1·75	□	□
8	7	3d violet	. . . .	1·25	2·75	□	□
		Set of 6		26·00	21·00	□	□

(b) Regional Issues

1958–67 *Wmk* **179**. *Perf* 15 × 14

9	8	2½d red	. . . .	30	45	□	□
10	9	3d lilac	. . . .	30	25	□	□
		p. One centre phosphor band		15	15	□	□
11		4d blue	. . . .	25	30	□	□
		p. Two phosphor bands . .		15	25	□	□

1968–69 *One centre phosphor band (4d values) or two phosphor bands* (5d). *No wmk*

12	9	4d sepia	. . . .	15	25	□	□
13		4d vermilion	. . . .	15	25	□	□
14		5d blue	. . . .	15	50	□	□

For comprehensive listings of the Independent Postal Adminstration issues of Jersey, see Stanley Gibbons *Collect Channel Islands and Isle of Man Stamps.*

REGIONAL FIRST DAY COVERS

PRICES for First Day Covers listed below are for stamps, as indicated, used on illustrated envelopes and postmarked with operational cancellations (before 1964) or with special First Day of Issue cancellations (1964 onwards). First Day postmarks of 8 June 1964 and 7 February 1966 were of the machine cancellation 'envelope' type.

£sd Issues

18 Aug. 1958	Guernsey 3d (No. 7)	20·00	☐
	Isle of Man 3d (No. 2)	32·00	☐
	Jersey 3d (No. 10)	20·00	☐
	Northern Ireland 3d (No. NI1)	30·00	☐
	Scotland 3d (No. S1)	17·00	☐
	Wales 3d (No. W1)	12·00	☐
29 Sept. 1958	Northern Ireland 6d, 1s 3d (Nos. NI3, NI5)	35·00	☐
	Scotland 6d, 1s 3d (Nos. S3, S5)	25·00	☐
	Wales 6d, 1s 3d (Nos. W3, W5)	25·00	☐
8 June 1964	Guernsey 2½d (No. 6)	30·00	☐
	Isle of Man 2½d (No. 1)	45·00	☐
	Jersey 2½d (No. 9)	30·00	☐
7 Feb. 1966	Guernsey 4d (No. 8)	8·00	☐
	Isle of Man 4d (No. 3)	15·00	☐
	Jersey 4d (No. 11)	10·00	☐
	Northern Ireland 4d (No. NI2)	7·00	☐
	Scotland 4d (No. S2)	7·00	☐
	Wales 4d (No. W2)	7·00	☐
1 March 1967	Northern Ireland 9d, 1s 6d (Nos. NI4, NI6)	4·00	☐
	Scotland 9d, 1s 6d (Nos. S4, S6)	6·00	☐
	Wales 9d, 1s 6d (Nos. W4, W6)	4·00	☐
4 Sept. 1968	Guernsey 4d, 5d (Nos. 10, 12)	3·00	☐
	Isle of Man 4d, 5d (Nos. 5, 7)	4·00	☐
	Jersey 4d, 5d (Nos. 12, 14)	3·00	☐
	Northern Ireland 4d, 5d (Nos. NI8, NI10)	3·00	☐
	Scotland 4d, 5d (Nos. S9, S11)	3·00	☐
	Wales 4d, 5d (Nos. W9, W11)	3·00	☐

Decimal Issues

7 July 1971	Isle of Man 2½p, 3p, 5p, 7½p (Nos. 8/11)	3·00	☐
	Northern Ireland 2½p, 3p, 5p, 7½p (Nos. NI12/13, NI18, NI23)	3·50	☐
	Scotland 2½p, 3p, 5p, 7½p (Nos. S14/15, S20, S25)	3·00	☐
	Wales 2½p, 3p, 5p, 7½p (Nos. W13/14, W19, W24)	3·00	☐
23 Jan. 1974	Northern Ireland 3p, 3½p, 5½p, 8p (Nos. NI14/15, NI19, NI24)	2·40	☐
	Scotland 3p, 3½p, 5½p, 8p (Nos. S16/17, S21, S26)	2·50	☐
	Wales 3p, 3½p, 5½p, 8p (Nos. W15/16, W20, W25)	2·50	☐
6 Nov. 1974	Northern Ireland 4½p (No. NI17)	1·50	☐
	Scotland 4½p (No. S19)	1·50	☐
	Wales 4½p (No. W18)	1·50	☐
14 Jan. 1976	Northern Ireland 6½p, 8½p (Nos. NI21, NI25)	1·50	☐
	Scotland 6½p, 8½p (Nos. S23, S27)	1·50	☐
	Wales 6½p, 8½p (Nos. W22, W26)	1·50	☐
20 Oct. 1976	Northern Ireland 10p, 11p (Nos. NI27, NI30)	1·75	☐
	Scotland 10p, 11p (Nos. S29, S32)	1·50	☐
	Wales 10p, 11p (Nos. W28, W31)	1·50	☐
18 Jan. 1978	Northern Ireland 7p, 9p, 10½p (Nos. NI22, NI26, NI29)	1·75	☐
	Scotland 7p, 9p, 10½p (Nos. S24, S28, S31)	1·75	☐
	Wales 7p, 9p, 10½p (Nos. W23, W27, W30)	1·75	☐
23 July 1980	Northern Ireland 12p, 13½p, 15p (Nos. NI31/3)	3·00	☐
	Scotland 12p, 13½p, 15p (Nos. S33/5)	2·75	☐
	Wales 12p, 13½p, 15p (Nos. W32/4)	3·00	☐
8 April 1981	Northern Ireland 11½p, 14p, 18p, 22p (Nos. NI34, NI38, NI45, NI53)	2·50	☐
	Scotland 11½p, 14p, 18p, 22p (Nos. S36, S40, S44, S47)	2·50	☐
	Wales 11½p, 14p, 18p, 22p (Nos. W35, W39, W46, W54)	2·50	☐
24 Feb. 1982	Northern Ireland 12½p, 15½p, 19½p, 26p (Nos. NI36, NI41, NI50, NI60)	4·00	☐
	Scotland 12½p, 15½p, 19½p, 26p (Nos. S38, S41, S45, S49)	3·50	☐
	Wales 12½p, 15½p, 19½p, 26p (Nos. W37, W42, W51, W61)	3·50	☐
27 April 1983	Northern Ireland 16p, 20½p, 28p (Nos. NI42, NI52, NI62)	4·00	☐
	Scotland 16p, 20½p, 28p (Nos. S42, S46, S50)	4·00	☐
	Wales 16p, 20½p, 28p (Nos. W43, W53, W63)	3·50	☐
23 Oct. 1984	Northern Ireland 13p, 17p, 22p, 31p (Nos. NI37, NI43, NI54, NI64)	4·75	☐
	Scotland 13p, 17p, 22p, 31p (Nos. S39, S43, S48, S51)	4·00	☐
	Wales 13p, 17p, 22p, 31p (Nos. W38, W44, W55, W65)	4·25	☐

7 Jan. 1986	*Northern Ireland* 12*p* (*No.* NI35)	2·00	☐
	Scotland 12*p* (*No.* S37)	2·00	☐
	Wales 12*p* (*No.* W36)	2·00	☐
6 Jan. 1987	*Northern Ireland* 18*p* (*No.* NI46)	2·00	☐
	Scotland 18*p* (*No.* S59)	1·80	☐
	Wales 18*p* (*No.* W47)	2·00	☐
8 Nov. 1988	*Northern Ireland* 14*p*, 19*p*, 23*p*, 32*p* (*Nos.* NI39, NI49, NI56, NI65)	4·25	☐
	Scotland 14*p*, 19*p*, 23*p*, 32*p* (*Nos.* S54, S62, S67, S77) . . .	4·25	☐
	Wales 14*p*, 19*p*, 23*p*, 32*p* (*Nos.* W40, W50, W57, W66)	4·50	☐
28 Nov. 1989	*Northern Ireland* 15*p*, 20*p*, 24*p*, 34*p* (*Nos.* NI40, NI51, NI57, NI66)	5·00	☐
	Scotland 15*p*, 20*p*, 24*p*, 34*p* (*Nos.* S56, S64, S69, S78) . . .	5·00	☐
	Wales 15*p*, 20*p*, 24*p*, 34*p* (*Nos.* W41, W52, W58, W67)	5·00	☐
4 Dec. 1990	*Northern Ireland* 17*p*, 22*p*, 26*p*, 37*p* (*Nos.* NI44, NI55, NI61, NI67)	5·00	☐
	Scotland 17*p*, 22*p*, 26*p*, 37*p* (*Nos.* S58, S66, S73, S79) . . .	5·00	☐
	Wales 17*p*, 22*p*, 26*p*, 37*p* (*Nos.* W45, W56, W62, W68)	5·00	☐
3 Dec. 1991	*Northern Ireland* 18*p*, 24*p*, 28*p*, 39*p* (*Nos.* NI47, NI58, NI63, NI68)	5·50	☐
	Scotland 18*p*, 24*p*, 28*p*, 39*p* (*Nos.* S60, S70, S75, S80) . . .	5·50	☐
	Wales 18*p*, 24*p*, 28*p*, 39*p* (*Nos.* W48, W59, W64, W69)	5·50	☐
7 Dec 1993	*Northern Ireland* 19*p*, 25*p*, 30*p*, 41*p* (*Nos.* NI69, NI72, NI74, NI76)	6·00	☐
	Scotland 19*p*, 25*p*, 30*p*, 41*p* (*Nos.* S81, S84, S86, S88) . . .	6·00	☐
	Wales 19*p*, 25*p*, 30*p*, 41*p* (*Nos.* W70, W73, W75, W77)	6·00	☐
23 July 1996	*Northern Ireland* 20*p* (1 *centre band*), 26*p*, 37*p*, 63*p* (*Nos.* NI71, NI73, NI75, NI77)	8·75	☐
	Scotland 20*p* (1 *centre band*), 26*p*, 37*p*, 63*p* (*Nos.* S83, S85, S87, S89)	8·75	☐
	Wales 20*p*, 26*p*, 37*p*, 63*p* (*Nos.* W72, W74, W76, W78)	7·00	☐
1 July 1997	*Wales* 20*p* (1 *centre band*), 26*p*, 37*p*, 63*p* (*Nos.* W79 and W80/2)	6·00	☐
8 June 1999	*Northern Ireland* 38*p*, 64*p* (*Nos.* NI83, NI86)	4·00	☐
	Scotland 2nd, 1st, E, 64*p* (*Nos* S94/7)	6·00	☐
	Wales 2nd, 1st, E, 64*p* (*Nos.* W83, W84/6)	6·00	☐
25 Apr 2000	*Northern Ireland* 1st, 40*p*, 65*p* (*Nos.* NI84, NI87, NI88*b*)	7·00	☐
	Scotland 65*p* (*No.* S98)	3·00	☐
	Wales 65*p* (*No.* W87)	3·00	☐
6 Mar 2001	*Northern Ireland* 2nd, 1st, E, 65*p* (*Nos.* NI89/92)	4·50	☐
23 Apr 2001	*England* 2nd, 1st, E, 65*p* (*Nos.* EN1/4)	3·25	☐
4 July 2002	*England* 68*p* (*No.* EN5)	1·75	☐
	Northern Ireland 68*p* (*No.* NI93)	2·50	☐
	Scotland 68*p* (*No.* S99)	1·75	☐
	Wales 68*p* (*No.* W88)	1·75	☐
14 Oct 2003	*England* 2nd, 1st, E, 68*p* (*Nos.* EN6/8, EN11)	3·25	☐
	Northern Ireland 2nd, 1st, E, 68*p* (*Nos.* NI94/6, NI99)	3·25	☐
	Scotland 2nd, 1st, E, 68*p* (*Nos.* S109/11, S114)	3·25	☐
	Wales 2nd, 1st, E, 68*p* (*Nos.* W98/100, W103)	3·25	☐
11 May 2004	*England* 40*p* (*No.* EN9)	2·75	☐
	Northern Ireland 40*p* (*No.* NI97)	2·75	☐
	Scotland 40*p* (*No.* S112)	2·75	☐
	Wales 40*p* (*No.* W101)	2·75	☐
5 Apr 2005	*England* 42*p* (*No.* EN11)	1·40	☐
	Northern Ireland 42*p* (*No.* NI98)	1·40	☐
	Scotland 42*p* (*No.* S113)	1·40	☐
	Wales 42*p* (*No.* W102)	1·40	☐

POSTAGE DUE STAMPS

PERFORATION. All postage due stamps to No. D101 are perf 14 × 15.

D 1   D 2

1914–22 *Wmk Type* **100** *(Royal Cypher* ('Simple')) *sideways*

D1	D 1	½d green		50	25 □ □
D2		1d red		50	25 □ □
D3		1½d brown		48·00	20·00 □ □
D4		2d black		50	25 □ □
D5		3d violet		5·00	75 □ □
D6		4d green		18·00	5·00 □ □
D7		5d brown		7·00	3·50 □ □
D8		1s blue		40·00	4·75 □ □
		Set of 8		£110	32·00 □ □

1924–31 *Wmk Type* **111** *(Block* G v R) *sideways*

D10	D 1	½d green		1·25	75 □ □
D11		1d red		60	25 □ □
D12		1½d brown		47·00	22·00 □ □
D13		2d black		1·00	25 □ □
D14		3d violet		1·50	25 □ □
D15		4d green		15·00	4·25 □ □
D16		5d brown		65·00	45·00 □ □
D17		1s blue		8·50	75 □ □
D18	D 2	2s 6d purple/*yellow*		85·00	1·75 □ □
		Set of 9		£200	60·00 □ □

1936–37 *Wmk Type* **125** (E 8 R) *sideways*

D19	D 1	½d green		12·00	10·50 □ □
D20		1d red		2·00	1·75 □ □
D21		2d black		12·00	12·00 □ □
D22		3d violet		2·00	2·00 □ □
D23		4d green		40·00	34·00 □ □
D24a		5d brown		28·00	28·00 □ □
D25		1s blue		11·00	8·50 □ □
D26	D 2	2s 6d purple/*yellow*		£320	12·00 □ □
		Set of 8		£390	90·00 □ □

1937–38 *Wmk Type* **127** (G vi R) *sideways*

D27	D 1	½d green		13·00	8·75 □ □
D28		1d red		3·00	50 □ □
D29		2d black		2·75	30 □ □
D30		3d violet		10·50	30 □ □
D31		4d green		£110	10·00 □ □
D32		5d brown		16·50	75 □ □
D33		1s blue		78·00	75 □ □
D34	D 2	2s 6d purple/*yellow*		85·00	1·25 □ □
		Set of 8		£260	18·00 □ □

1951–52 *Colours changed and new value* (1½d) *Wmk Type* **127** (G vi R) *sideways*

D35	D 1	½d orange		3·50	3·50 □ □
D36		1d blue		1·50	75 □ □
D37		1½d green		2·00	2·00 □ □
D38		4d blue		50·00	22·00 □ □
D39		1s brown		28·00	5·25 □ □
		Set of 5		75·00	28·00 □ □

1954–55 *Wmk Type* **153** *(Mult Tudor Crown and* E 2 R) *sideways*

D40	D 1	½d orange		4·75	5·25 □ □
D41		2d black		22·00	18·00 □ □
D42		3d violet		62·00	52·00 □ □
D43		4d blue		26·00	26·00 □ □
D44		5d brown		20·00	15·50 □ □
D45	D 2	2s 6d purple/*yellow*		£135	5·75 □ □
		Set of 6		£225	£100 □ □

1955–57 *Wmk Type* **165** *(Mult St Edward's Crown and* E 2 R) *sideways*

D46	D 1	½d orange		2·75	3·25 □ □
D47		1d blue		5·00	1·50 □ □
D48		1½d green		8·50	7·00 □ □
D49		2d black		45·00	3·50 □ □
D50		3d violet		6·00	1·50 □ □
D51		4d blue		25·00	6·00 □ □
D52		5d brown		26·00	20·00 □ □
D53		1s brown		65·00	2·25 □ □
D54	D 2	2s 6d purple/*yellow*		£200	8·25 □ □
D55		5s red/*yellow*		£150	32·00 □ □
		Set of 10		£425	65·00 □ □

1959–63 *Wmk Type* **179** *(Mult St Edward's Crown) sideways*

D56	D 1	½d orange		15	1·25 □ □
D57		1d blue		15	50 □ □
D58		1½d green		2·50	2·50 □ □
D59		2d black		1·10	50 □ □
D60		3d violet		30	30 □ □
D61		4d blue		30	30 □ □
D62		5d brown		45	60 □ □
D63		6d purple		50	30 □ □
D64		1s brown		90	30 □ □
D65	D 2	2s 6d purple/*yellow*		3·00	50 □ □
D66		5s red/*yellow*		8·25	1·00 □ □
D67		10s blue/*yellow*		11·50	5·75 □ □
D68		£1 black/*yellow*		45·00	8·25 □ □
		Set of 13		68·00	20·00 □ □

1968–69 *Design size* 22½ × 19 *mm. No wmk*

D69	D 1	2d black		75	1·00 □ □
D70		3d violet		1·00	1·00 □ □
D71		4d blue		1·00	1·00 □ □
D72		5d orange-brown		8·00	11·00 □ □
D73		6d purple		2·25	1·75 □ □
D74		1s brown		4·00	2·50 □ □
		Set of 6		16·50	20·00 □ □

1968–69 *Design size* 21½ × 17½ *mm. No wmk*

D75	D 1	4d blue		7·00	6·75 □ □
D76		8d red		50	1·00 □ □

D 3

D 4

Decimal Currency

1970–77 *No wmk*

D77	D 3	½p turquoise-blue . . .	15	2·50	☐	☐
D78		1p reddish purple . . .	15	15	☐	☐
D79		2p myrtle-green	20	15	☐	☐
D80		3p ultramarine	20	15	☐	☐
D81		4p yellow-brown	25	15	☐	☐
D82		5p violet	25	15	☐	☐
D83		7p red-brown	35	1·00	☐	☐
D84	D 4	10p red	30	30	☐	☐
D85		11p green	50	1·00	☐	☐
D86		20p brown	60	25	☐	☐
D87		50p ultramarine	2·00	1·25	☐	☐
D88		£1 black	4·00	1·00	☐	☐
D89		£5 orange-yellow and black	36·00	1·50	☐	☐
		Set of 13	40·00	7·75	☐	☐

Presentation Pack (P.O. Pack No. 36) (Nos. D77/82, D84, D86/8) . . . . 20·00 ☐

Presentation Pack (P.O. Pack No. 93) (Nos. D77/88) . . . . . . 10·00 ☐

D 5 **D 6** **D 7**

1982 *No wmk*

D90	D 5	1p lake	10	30	☐	☐
D91		2p bright blue	30	30	☐	☐
D92		3p deep mauve	15	30	☐	☐
D93		4p deep blue	15	25	☐	☐
D94		5p sepia	20	25	☐	☐
D95	D 6	10p light brown	30	40	☐	☐
D96		20p olive-green	50	60	☐	☐
D97		25p deep greenish blue .	80	90	☐	☐
D98		50p grey-black	1·75	1·75	☐	☐
D99		£1 red	3·25	1·25	☐	☐
D100		£2 turquoise-blue . . .	7·00	4·25	☐	☐
D101		£5 dull orange	14·00	2·25	☐	☐
		Set of 12	24·00	10·00	☐	☐
		Set of 12 Gutter Pairs	48·00		☐	
		Presentation Pack	48·00		☐	

1994 (15 FEB.) *Perf* 15 × 14 (*with one elliptical hole on each vertical side*)

D102	D 7	1p red, yellow and black	10	75	☐	☐
D103		2p magenta, purple and black	10	75	☐	☐
D104		5p yellow, red-brown and black	15	50	☐	☐
D105		10p yellow, emerald and black	30	75	☐	☐
D106		20p blue-green, violet and black	75	1·50	☐	☐
D107		25p cerise, rosine and black	1·50	2·00	☐	☐
D108		£1 violet, magenta and black	7·00	10·00	☐	☐
D109		£1.20 greenish blue, blue-green and black	8·00	12·00	☐	☐
D110		£5 greenish black, blue-green and black	30·00	20·00	☐	☐
		Set of 9	45·00	45·00	☐	☐
		First Day Cover		22·00		☐
		Presentation Pack	50·00		☐	

ROYAL MAIL POSTAGE LABELS

These imperforate labels were issued as an experiment by the Post Office. Special microprocessor-controlled machines were installed at post offices in Cambridge, London, Shirley (Southampton) and Windsor to provide an after-hours sales service to the public. The machines printed and dispensed the labels according to the coins inserted and the buttons operated by the customer. Values were initially available in $\frac{1}{2}$p steps to 16p and in addition, the labels were sold at philatelic counters in two packs containing either 3 values ($3\frac{1}{2}$, $12\frac{1}{2}$, 16p) or 32 values ($\frac{1}{2}$p to 16p).

From 28 August 1984 the machines were adjusted to provide values up to 17p. After 31 December 1984 labels including $\frac{1}{2}$p values were withdrawn. The machines were taken out of service on 30 April 1985.

Machine postage-paid impression in red on phosphorised paper with grey-green background design. No watermark. imperforate.

1984 (1 MAY–28 AUG.)

Set of 32 ($\frac{1}{2}$p to 16p)	15·00	22·00 □ □
Set of 3 ($3\frac{1}{2}$p, $12\frac{1}{2}$p, 16p)	2·50	3·00 □ □
Set of 3 on First Day Cover		
(1 May)		6·50 □
Set of 2 ($16\frac{1}{2}$p, 17p) (28 August)	4·00	3·00 □ □

OFFICIAL STAMPS

Various stamps of Queen Victoria and King Edward VII overprinted in Black.

I.R.

OFFICIAL
(O 1)

I. R.

OFFICIAL
(O 2)

O.W.

OFFICIAL
(O 3)

ARMY

OFFICIAL
(O 4)

ARMY

OFFICIAL
(O 5)

**GOVᵀ
PARCELS**
(O 7)

**BOARD
OF
EDUCATION**
(O 8)

R.H.

OFFICIAL
(O 9)

ADMIRALTY

OFFICIAL
(O 10)

1 Inland Revenue

Overprinted with Types O 1 or O 2 (5s, 10s, £1)

1882–1901 *Queen Victoria*

O 1	52	$\frac{1}{2}$d green	60·00	20·00 □ □
O 5		$\frac{1}{2}$d blue	60·00	22·00 □ □
O13	71	$\frac{1}{2}$d vermilion	8·00	3·00 □ □
O17		$\frac{1}{2}$d green	10·00	6·00 □ □
O 3	57	1d lilac (Die II)	4·00	2·00 □ □
O 6	64	$2\frac{1}{2}$d lilac	£300	£100 □ □
O14	74	$2\frac{1}{2}$d purple on blue . . .	£100	10·00 □ □
O 4	43	6d grey (Plate 18)	£325	80·00 □ □
O18	79	6d purple on red	£300	80·00 □ □
O 7	65	1s green	£3500	£900 □ □
O15	82	1s green	£450	£175 □ □
O19		1s green and red	£2000	£550 □ □
O 9	59	5s red	£3000	£1000 □ □
O10	60	10s blue	£4250	£1250 □ □
O11	61	£1 brown (Wmk Crowns)	£32000	£16000 □ □
O12		£1 brown (Wmk Orbs) . .	£48000	£22000 □ □
O16		£1 green	£6500	£1500 □ □

1902–04 *King Edward VII*

O20	83	$\frac{1}{2}$d blue-green	22·00	3·00 □ □
O21		1d red	15·00	2·00 □ □
O22	86	$2\frac{1}{2}$d blue	£650	£175 □ □
O23	83	6d purple	.£120000	£70000 □ □
O24	93	1s green and red	£1900	£450 □ □
O25	95	5s red	£9000	£5000 □ □
O26	96	10s blue	£45000	£22000 □ □
O27	97	£1 green	£35000	£16000 □ □

2 Office of Works

Overprinted with Type O 3

1896–1902 *Queen Victoria*

O31	71	$\frac{1}{2}$d vermilion	£200	£100 □ □
O32		$\frac{1}{2}$d green	£300	£150 □ □
O33	57	1d lilac (Die II)	£350	£100 □ □
O34	78	5d dull purple and blue .	£1800	£600 □ □
O35	81	10d dull purple and red . .	£2800	£850 □ □

1902–03 *King Edward VII*

O36	83	$\frac{1}{2}$d blue-green	£500	£150 □ □
O37		1d red	£500	£150 □ □
O38	85	2d green and red	£1300	£350 □ □
O39	86	$2\frac{1}{2}$d blue	£1600	£500 □ □
O40	92	10d purple and red	£20000	£4750 □ □

3 Army

Overprinted with Types O 4 ($\frac{1}{2}d$, 1d) or O 5 (2$\frac{1}{2}d$, 6d)

1896–1901 *Queen Victoria*

O41	71	$\frac{1}{2}$d vermilion	3·50	1·50	☐	☐
O42		$\frac{1}{2}$d green	4·00	7·00	☐	☐
O43	57	1d lilac (Die II)	3·50	2·50	☐	☐
O44	74	2$\frac{1}{2}$d purple on blue	30·00	20·00	☐	☐
O45	79	6d purple on red	75·00	40·00	☐	☐

Overprinted with Type O 4

1902 *King Edward VII*

O48	83	$\frac{1}{2}$d blue-green	5·00	2·00	☐	☐
O49		1d red	5·00	2·00	☐	☐
O50		6d purple	£150	70·00	☐	☐

4 Government Parcels

Overprinted with Type O 7

1883–1900 *Queen Victoria*

O69	57	1d lilac (Die II)	70·00	15·00	☐	☐
O61	62	1$\frac{1}{2}$d lilac	£300	60·00	☐	☐
O65	72	1$\frac{1}{2}$d purple and green . . .	70·00	7·00	☐	☐
O70	73	2d green and red	£140	20·00	☐	☐
O71	77	4$\frac{1}{2}$d green and red	£225	£175	☐	☐
O62	63	6d green	£1500	£600	☐	☐
O66	79	6d purple on red	£140	25·00	☐	☐
O63	64	9d green	£1250	£500	☐	☐
O67	80	9d purple and blue	£200	35·00	☐	☐
O64	44	1s brown (Plate 13)	£700	£175	☐	☐
O64c		1s brown (Plate 14)	£1500	£250	☐	☐
O68	82	1s green	£350	£140	☐	☐
O72		1s green and red	£350	£125	☐	☐

1902 *King Edward VII*

O74	83	1d red	30·00	12·00	☐	☐
O75	85	2d green and red	£225	30·00	☐	☐
O76	83	6d purple	£225	30·00	☐	☐
O77	91	9d purple and blue	£450	£100	☐	☐
O78	93	1s green and red	£750	£175	☐	☐

5 Board of Education

Overprinted with Type O 8

1902 *Queen Victoria*

O81	78	5d dull purple and blue .	£1500	£400	☐	☐
O82	82	1s green and red	£4500	£2500	☐	☐

1902–04 *King Edward VII*

O83	83	$\frac{1}{2}$d blue-green	£150	35·00	☐	☐
O84		1d red	£150	35·00	☐	☐
O85	86	2$\frac{1}{2}$d blue	£2500	£200	☐	☐
O86	89	5d purple and blue	£12000	£3500	☐	☐
O87	93	1s green and red	£65000		☐	

6 Royal Household

Overprinted with Type O 9

1902 *King Edward VII*

O91	83	$\frac{1}{2}$d blue-green	£300	£180	☐	☐
O92		1d red	£250	£150	☐	☐

7 Admiralty

Overprinted with Type O 10

1903 *King Edward Vii*

O101	83	$\frac{1}{2}$d blue-green	25·00	12·00	☐	☐
O102		1d red	15·00	6·00	☐	☐
O103	84	1$\frac{1}{2}$d purple and green . . .	£185	£110	☐	☐
O104	85	2d green and red	£250	£125	☐	☐
O105	86	2$\frac{1}{2}$d blue	£300	£110	☐	☐
O106	87	3d purple on yellow . . .	£275	£120	☐	☐

PHILATELIC, NUMISMATIC AND PHILATELIC MEDALLIC COVERS

On 2 June 1993 Royal Mail and the Royal Mint prepared a commemorative cover to celebrate the 40th anniversary of the Coronation of Her Majesty The Queen. The cover bore the Royal Mint's Coronation Anniversary Crown and the £10 'Britannia' stamp, issued on 2 March 1993 (No. 1658).

On 1 March 1994 a similar cover was produced for the 25th Anniversary of the Investiture of HRH The Prince of Wales. The cover bore the set of five stamps issued on that date (Nos. 1810/14), showing paintings by Prince Charles, and a commemorative medal struck by the Royal Mint.

So began a series of Philatelic Numismatic Covers (PNC) and Philatelic Medallic Covers (PMC) produced by Royal Mail and the Royal Mint.

This listing comprises only those jointly produced covers sold by the Philatelic Bureau. Privately sponsored covers incorporating coins or medals are outside its scope.

No.	Date	Issue	Stamps	Coin/Medal	Price
RMC1	2.6.93	Coronation 40th Anniv	1658	£5 Coin	28·00
RMC2	1.3.94	Prince of Wales Investiture 25th Anniv	1810/14	Medal	22·00
RMC3	27.7.94	Bank of England 300th Anniv	1666×4 +label	£2 Coin	20·00
RMC4	20.5.95	R. J. Mitchell Birth Cent	1666×4+label	Medal	20·00
RMC5	15.8.95	End of Second World War 50th Anniv	1873, 1875	£2 Coin	20·00
RMC6	29.10.95	William Wyon Birth Bicent	Y1707	Medal	20·00
RMC7	21.4.96	Queen's 70th Birthday	1666×4+label	£5 Coin	24·00
RMC8	14.5.96	European Football Championship	1925/9	£2 Coin	20·00
RMC9	1.10./3.11.96	Classic Sports Cars	1945/9	Medal	20·00
RMC10	28.1.97	King Henry VIII 450th Death Anniv	1965/71	£1 Coin	20·00
RMC11	30.6.97	Transfer of Hong Kong to Chinese Rule	1666×4+label	Hong Kong $5 Coin	20·00
RMC12	23.8.97	British Aircraft Designers	1984/8	£2 Coin	20·00
RMC13	20.11.97	Royal Golden Wedding	2011/14	£5 Coin	24·00
RMC14	24.2.98	Order of the Garter 650th Anniv	2026/30	£1 Coin	20·00
RMC15	5.7.98	NHS 50th Anniv	2046/9	50p Coin	20·00
RMC16	25.8.98	Notting Hill Carnival	2055/8	50p Coin	20·00
RMC17	14.11.98	HRH Prince of Wales 50th Birthday	1666×4+label	£5 Coin	24·00
RMC18	12.5.99	Berlin Airlift 50th Anniv	1666×4+label	Medal	20·00
RMC19	1.7.99	New Scottish Parliament Building	S94/7	£1 Coin	20·00
RMC20	1.10.99	Rugby World Cup, Wales	1664a×4+label	£2 Coin	20·00
RMC21	31.12.99	Millennium	MS2123	£5 Coin	34·00
RMC22	4.4.00	National Botanic Garden of Wales	2124×4+label	£1 Coin	20·00

RMC23	14.8.00	150 *Years of Public Libraries*	2116, 2121, 2100	50p Coin	20·00
RMC24	4.8.00	*Queen Mother's* 100th *Birthday*	**MS**2161	£5 Coin	24·00
RMC25	1.1.01	Archers *Radio Programme* 50th *Anniv*	2107/8, 2110	Medal	20·00
RMC26	24.5.01	*RN Submarine Service Cent*	2202/5	Medal	20·00
RMC27	20.6.01	*Queen Victoria Death Cent*	2133+label	£5 Coin	24·00
RMC28	2.10.01	*Northern Ireland*	NI89/92	£1 Coin	20·00
RMC29	1.6.02	*Golden Jubilee*	2253/7	£5 Coin	24·00
RMC30	31.5.02	*World Cup Football, Japan & Korea*	5×1st from **MS**2292	£1 Coin	20·00
RMC31	16.7.02	17th *Commonwealth Games, Manchester*	2299/303	4×£2 Coins	30·00
RMC32	11.12.02	*Queen Mother Commemoration*	2280/3	£5 Coin	24·00
RMC33	25.2.03	*Discovery of DNA 50th Anniv*	2343/7	£2 Coin	21·00
RMC34	2.6.03	*Coronation 50th Anniv*	2368/77	£5 Coin	24·00
RMC35	27.8.03	*Extreme Endeavours*	2360/5	£1 Coin	20·00
RMC36	7.10.03	*British Museum 250th Anniv*	2404/9	Medal	20·00
RMC37	13.1.04	*Classic Locomotives*	2417/22	£2 Coin	21·00
RMC38	6.4.04	*Entente Cordiale Cent*	2446/7 + France 50c, 75c	£5 Coin	25·00
RMC39	13.4.04	*Ocean Liners*	2448/53	Medal	22·00
RMC40	25.5.04	*RHS Bicentenary*	2456/61	Medal	21·00
RMC41	30.11.04	*Scotland Definitive*	S109/10, S112/13	£1 Coin	20·00
RMC42	24.2.05	*Charlotte Brontë 150th Death Anniv*	2518/23	50p Coin	20·00
RMC43	1.3.05	*Wales Definitive*	W98/9, W101/2	£1 Coin	20·00
RMC44	21.4.05	*World Heritage Sites*	2532/5+Australia 2×50c. & 2×$1	50p Coin + Australia 50c.	24·00
RMC45	5.7.05	*End of the War 60th Anniv*	**MS**2547	Medal and £2 Coin	24·00
RMC46	18.10.05	*Battle of Trafalgar Bicent*	2574/9	2×£5 Coins	37·00

COLLECT BRITISH STAMPS

Priority order form
Four easy ways to order

Phone:
020 7836 8444
Overseas: +44 (0)20 7836 8444

Fax:
020 7557 4499
Overseas: +44 (0)20 7557 4499

Email:
stampsales@stanleygibbons.co.uk

Post:
Stamp Mail Order Department
Stanley Gibbons Ltd, 399 Strand
London, WC2R 0LX, England

Customer details

Account Number _____

Name _____

Address _____

_____ Postcode _____

Country _____ Email _____

Tel no _____ Fax no _____

Payment details

Registered Postage & Packing   £3.60

I enclose my cheque/postal order for £.............
in full payment. Please make cheques/postal
orders payable to Stanley Gibbons Ltd. Cheques
must be in £ sterling and drawn on a UK bank

Please debit my credit card for £............. in
full payment. I have completed the Credit
Card section below.

Card Number

☐☐☐☐ ☐☐☐☐ ☐☐☐☐ ☐☐☐☐

Start Date (Switch & Amex)   Expiry Date   Issue No (switch)

☐☐☐☐   ☐☐☐☐   ☐☐

Signature _____   Date _____

COLLECT
BRITISH STAMPS

Condition	SG No.	Description	Price
		SUB TOTAL	£
		Postage & Packing	£3.60
		Grand Total	£

Please complete payment, name and address details overleaf